Controversies on Campus

Debating the Issues Confronting American Universities in the 21st Century

Joy Blanchard, Editor

Foreword by Scott L. Thomas

D0488159

PRAEGER™

An Imprint of ABC-CLIO, LLC
Santa Barbara, California • Denver, Colorado

Copyright © 2018 by ABC-CLIO, LLC

All rights reserved. No part of this publication may be reproduced, stored in a retrieval system, or transmitted, in any form or by any means, electronic, mechanical, photocopying, recording, or otherwise, except for the inclusion of brief quotations in a review, without prior permission in writing from the publisher.

Library of Congress Cataloging-in-Publication Data

Names: Blanchard, Joy, editor.
Title: Controversies on campus : debating the issues confronting American
    universities in the 21st century / Joy Blanchard, editor ; foreword by Scott L. Thomas.
Description: Santa Barbara, California : Praeger, An Imprint of ABC-CLIO, 2018. |
    Includes bibliographical references and index.
Identifiers: LCCN 2017039204 | ISBN 9781440852190 (set : alk. paper) |
    ISBN 9781440852206 (ebook)
Subjects: LCSH: Education, Higher—Aims and objectives—United States. |
    Universities and colleges—United States—Administration. | Educational
    change—United States.
Classification: LCC LA227.4 .C68 2018 | DDC 378.73—dc23
LC record available at https://lccn.loc.gov/2017039204

ISBN: 978-1-4408-5219-0 (print)
        978-1-4408-5220-6 (ebook)

22 21 20 19 18   1 2 3 4 5

This book is also available as an eBook.

Praeger
An Imprint of ABC-CLIO, LLC

ABC-CLIO, LLC
130 Cremona Drive, P.O. Box 1911
Santa Barbara, California 93116-1911
www.abc-clio.com

This book is printed on acid-free paper ∞

Manufactured in the United States of America

Contents

Foreword

This important volume addresses a wide range of contemporary higher-education issues in America, nicely capturing an array of pressures unique to our times while also highlighting a set of core higher-education issues that have endured since at least World War II. The warrant for the chapters comprising this volume can be found in the nation-building investments made in the United States immediately after World War II. Those efforts were designed to encourage both economic and military development through science and socioeconomic mobility by providing meaningful educational opportunities to a wider cross section of the American public. The rise of the modern research university is rooted in an array of federal policy decisions born in the Great Depression and World War II eras. Important policy artifacts of this period would include President Roosevelt's commissioning of Vannevar Bush whose 1945 report, "Science—The Endless Frontier," marked the beginning of federal science policy. George Zook's 1947 report, "Higher Education for American Democracy," is surely another signal moment in American policy that encouraged much broader participation and shaped the stage for today's university system in the United States. Although one might quickly point to concrete legislation in the Serviceman's Readjustment Act of 1944 as an inflection point for the growth of the modern university, it would be a significant omission to overlook the monumental impact of these presidential commissions. The National Science Foundation was born of Bush's 1945 report, and today's public focus on access and opportunity is a direct outgrowth of the Truman Commission report overseen by Zook. The diversification of participation across the remainder of the 20th century provides a foundation for many of the authors contributing to this volume.

The diversification of participation in higher education has been pronounced over the past 50 years in particular. From a demographer's lens, this diversification was quite predictable. From a policy maker's lens, higher education's role in leveraging this diversity presented one of the 20th century's greatest opportunities. Indeed, higher education contributed powerfully to the nation-building stance of the United States in the second half of the 20th century. From the lens of campus planners and leaders, finding productive ways to incorporate a broader spectrum of the diversity of the American population ensured steady growth in enrollments and campus expansion, particularly in the post–civil rights era, enabling one of the world's most robust systems of postsecondary education. The first section of this volume takes up questions rooted in this diversification and expansion, addressing topics related to access, admissions, retention, and immigration.

As might be expected, realizing the promise of diversity in education has proven challenging across this period. But through all this emerged a system that has proven to be financially and politically unsustainable—or, rather, one that we are unwilling to sustain to ensure a level of quality that the college experience promised for those of privilege who attended across this expansion. One response to this challenge of sustainability is the shift in the national conversation from higher education as an essential public good to one of a private good. This privatization of higher education invites the application of market rules to guide investments and expected returns and powerfully alters expectations about the public role of higher education. In this context, the final section in the volume considers important questions of the economy and finance of higher education, enduring questions that have been the focus of generations of higher-education scholars.

These two sections serve as valuable bookends for treatments of topics related to campus violence, guns, athletics, free speech, substance abuse, and other topics defining the culture of the contemporary college and university campus. Other chapters offer insight to the changed nature of considerations about curriculum and ongoing technological advances that enable a wholesale reconceptualization of the delivery of the substantive context defining that curriculum. In the whole, the volume offers an insightful illustration of the complexity of many of the most important and durable issues of our time.

Scott L. Thomas
Burlington, Vermont
July 25, 2017

PART 1

Contemporary Opportunities and Challenges around Diversifying American Universities

Understanding the Controversy around Race-Based Affirmative Action in American Higher Education

Dwayne Kwaysee Wright and Liliana M. Garces

As a policy and practice that attempts to address persistent racial inequities in education, race-based affirmative action in higher education (i.e., the consideration of race as a factor in admissions) has been a politically polarizing and academically controversial issue. In fact, some observers have noted that public debates around affirmative action have been more dividing in America than debates over abortion, the death penalty, or even marriage equality (Schuck 2002). This chapter provides an overview, in the higher education context, of this issue, its history, and the underlying perspectives that inform the controversy: color blindness, race neutrality, and color consciousness. The color-blind perspective supposes that race should never matter and it is never necessary to increase racial equity; the race-neutral perspective notes that the consideration of race is not necessary if other characteristics can be used to produce as much, if not more, diversity; and the color-consciousness perspective argues that the use of race is necessary if we are to address racial inequity.

We outline these perspectives below and argue that color consciousness is the approach most supported by the available evidence.

Definitions: What Is Affirmative Action?

The degree to which people are either in favor of or against affirmative action largely depends on how the policy is defined (Sterba 2009). Because most of the court cases surrounding affirmative action policies have focused on "race-conscious admissions policies to institutions of higher education," affirmative action and race-conscious admissions have become virtually synonyms and used interchangeably. Such thinking in our public discourse, however, ignores numerous institutional policies and procedures that fall under the broad umbrella of affirmative action. Such policies include legacy admissions, athletic scholarships, gender-conscious admissions, and admissions policies that take into consideration sexual orientation or gender expression/identity (Bondarenko 2013; Guisado 2013; Lamb 1992; Nicolas 2014).

Although defining affirmative action as race-based admissions can be somewhat reductionist, it is a useful entry point for understanding this debate. Thus, in this chapter, we define affirmative action practices and policies as those that include the use of race as one factor (among others) in a holistic review process for admission to postsecondary institutions. This focus on race is not to ignore the various markers of social identity that shape students' experiences, such as gender, sexual orientation, a disability, and socioeconomic status. The use of race in college admissions, however, triggers the most stringent test of judicial review by the courts under the Equal Protection Clause of the Fourteenth Amendment ("strict scrutiny"). Thus, any admissions policy that considers race and is allowed by the courts would most likely mean that any similar policy would also be upheld if it used another nonracial social characteristic.

The Historical and Legal Context of Affirmative Action

The history of race-based affirmative action policies can start at several places. Dr. Philip Rubio (2009), for example, dates his historical discussion back to 1619, claiming that "critical to the affirmative action debate today is the legacy of historical differential between black and white work, . . . compensation for that work, and the black challenge to what legal scholar Cheryl Harris calls 'whiteness as property'" (2). Here, we trace the history of affirmative action principally through court cases that challenged the use of the practice over the years under the Equal Protection Clause of the Fourteenth Amendment to the U.S. Constitution. The Fourteenth Amendment was passed after the Civil War to ensure the equal treatment of the newly freed slaves and provides, in relevant part, that "[n]o state shall . . . deny to any person within its jurisdiction the equal protection of the laws" (U.S. Constitution, Fourteenth Amendment).

At least two of the perspectives presented in this chapter, the color-conscious and the color-blind views, represent opposing interpretations of the language of the Fourteenth Amendment. Under the color-blind perspective, the Equal Protection Clause mandated the complete prohibition of the government's use of race going forward. Equal, according to this view, means treat everyone the same. From the color-conscious perspective, the Equal Protection Clause mandated the antisubordination of the minority by the majority. Equal, according to this view, means that we treat everyone according to the historical disadvantages imposed by a denial of opportunity in America that occurred (and still does occur) due to race and ethnicity (Ladson-Billings 2006). (In this article, we adopt the latter interpretation of the term "equal" and also refer to it as "equity.") Legal developments, starting with the seminal case "ending" state-sanctioned segregation in secondary schools, *Brown v. Board of Education* (1954), illustrate these different interpretations of the Equal Protection Clause.

From *Brown v. Board of Education* (1954) to *Regents of the University of California v. Bakke* (1978)

In *Brown v. Board of Education of Topeka*, Black students sought admission to public schools in their community. They had been denied admission to schools attended by White children under laws requiring or permitting segregation based on race. The Black students alleged that such segregation deprived them of the equal protection of the law under the Fourteenth Amendment. The U.S. Supreme Court in a unanimous decision agreed with the students and overruled the "separate but equal" doctrine. In *Brown*, by mandating that schools desegregate, the Court in 1954 embraced a race-conscious philosophy in that it sought not just to impose equality going forward but to give Black students opportunities that they had been denied until that point.

In the higher education context, the first major modern-day U.S. Supreme Court case involving affirmative action was *Regents of the University of California v. Bakke* (1978). Allan Bakke (a White male) had been denied admission to the medical school at the University of California at Davis for two consecutive years. At the time, the medical school's "special admissions program" allowed disadvantaged members of certain minoritized races to be considered exclusively for 16 of the 100 places in each year's class. Members of all races could qualify under the school's general admissions program for the other 84 places in the class. Bakke had been denied admission to the school under the general admissions program even though applicants with lower entrance examination scores had been admitted under the special admissions program.

The U.S. Supreme Court in a split (4–1–4) decision in *Bakke* would come to define the fork in the road at which the Court moved toward its modern understanding of the use of race in higher education admissions today. Justice Lewis F. Powell's opinion, which expressed three main principles, has become known as the controlling opinion in *Bakke*. First, for purposes of the Equal Protection Clause, he believed that racial/ethnic distinctions *of all sorts*—without regard to whether they are intended to help or hurt its intended beneficiaries—were inherently "suspect" and thus called for "the most exacting judicial examination" (i.e., strict scrutiny).[1] This test requires institutions to demonstrate a "compelling interest" and means that are "narrowly tailored" to obtain that interest.

Second, Justice Powell established that the special admissions program in *Bakke* could not be justified: (a) to assure within the student body a specified percentage of a particular racial group because that would be "*discrimination for its own sake,*" (b) to counter the effects of "societal discrimination" because that was too broad for the government to address, or (c) to increase the number of physicians who would practice in communities currently underserved, because (in Powell's opinion) there was no evidence that the special admissions program was either needed or geared to promote such a goal. Finally, what he permitted instead was the "diversity rationale." That is, making race one of several factors in the admissions process to promote the "educational benefits of diversity." As an example of a constitutionally permissible admissions program, Justice Powell referred to Harvard University's admissions program, which, according to Powell, did not set rigid quotas for minorities but instead involved the individualized consideration of each student.

Helpfully, *Bakke* is a good example of the difference between two of the different perspectives outlined in this chapter. In *Bakke*, Justice Powell famously announced his view that "the guarantee of equal protection cannot mean one thing when applied to one individual and something else when applied to a person of another color. If both are not accorded the same protection, then it is not equal" (Bakke 1978, 289–290). Justice Powell's statement articulates the view of the color-blind perspective. To this view, Justice Harry Blackmun answered in his concurrence/dissent in *Bakke* that "in order to get beyond racism, we must first take account of race . . . [a]nd in order to treat some persons equally, we must treat them differently" (Bakke 1978, 407). This statement articulates the color-conscious perspective. These two opposing statements would come to crystallize the controversial debate that would rage in the courts and in higher education for the four decades after *Bakke*. They represent two very different views of what "equal" means in America and how racial equity is achieved in higher education.

The Michigan Cases: *Grutter v. Bollinger* and *Gratz v. Bollinger*

A quarter of a century after *Bakke*, the U.S. Supreme Court would again rule on the use of race in college admissions in a pair of cases called *Grutter v. Bollinger* (2003) and *Gratz v. Bollinger* (2003). In *Gratz*, the University of Michigan's undergraduate admissions policy was based on a point system that automatically granted 20 points to applicants from underrepresented minoritized groups. The Court found that this policy made race the determinative admission factor for virtually every "minimally qualified" underrepresented minoritized applicant. The court declared that such a policy was "not narrowly tailored" to achieve University of Michigan's asserted "compelling interest" in diversity and ruled it unconstitutional.

In contrast, when the Court in *Grutter* examined the University of Michigan Law School's admissions program, it found the law school's plan focused on "academic ability and a 'flexible' assessment of applicants' talents, experiences, and potential to contribute to the learning of those around them" (315). The Court declared that this plan did not define diversity solely in terms of race and ethnicity but considered these as "plus" factors affecting overall diversity. For these reasons, in *Grutter* (in contrast to *Gratz*), the Court held that the law school's admissions plan was "narrowly tailored" to further the school's compelling interest in obtaining the "educational benefits that flow from diversity." Since then, institutions have been able to use race as one factor (among many other factors) in a holistic review of each individual student. In other words, race cannot be a determinative factor.

Recent Trends and Developments

More recent issues concerning race-conscious admissions in higher education involve the *Fisher v. University of Texas* case, new court cases that bring new plaintiffs, and statewide laws that prohibit the consideration of race in admissions.

Enter Abigail Fisher

The *Fisher* case has been before the U.S. Supreme Court twice. It started when Abigail Fisher applied for admission to the university's 2008 entering class and was rejected. That year, 42 White applicants and 5 applicants of color with lower academic (GPA and SAT) scores gained admission ahead of Fisher (Cashin 2014). Nevertheless, Fisher challenged her rejection in court and argued that her race was the determining factor in her not gaining admission and, therefore, that the university's consideration of race in admissions violated the Equal Protection Clause of the Fourteenth Amendment.

In *Fisher I* (2013), the U.S. Supreme Court held that the trial court and court of appeals seemed to defer to the university's judgment that it "needed" the use of race and no other alternatives were sufficient, rather than to make that determination itself, which is what the legal test required. In its rationale, the Court in *Fisher I* rejected the color-blind perspective (at least as it was presented in that case) but also refused to fully embrace the color-conscious perspective without reservation. What it did establish was a type of presumption for race neutrality that could be overcome if a university adequately showed that other "race-neutral" means did not produce the level of diversity necessary. What *Fisher I* addressed, therefore, was whether, in the court's judgment, the preference for race-neutral approaches had been overcome.

After applying the "correct" standard of strict scrutiny as instructed by the U.S. Supreme Court in the first case, the court of appeals again held in favor of the University of Texas at Austin. Abigail Fisher appealed the decision again, and the Court agreed to hear the case a second time. In this second round (*Fisher v. University of Texas II* 2016), the U.S. Supreme Court, in a 4–3 vote, held that UT Austin's race-conscious admission program met the "strict scrutiny" test and that the university had indeed adequately overcome the preference for race-neutral means, thus allowing it to use a race-conscious admissions practice. The majority opinion was written by Justice Anthony Kennedy (who had dissented in *Grutter*) and joined by Justices Ruth Bader Ginsburg, Stephen Breyer, and Sonia Sotomayor. The Court also stated that the university had an ongoing obligation to use available data "to assess whether changing demographics have undermined the need for a race-conscious policy, and to identify the effects, both positive and negative, of the affirmative-action measures it deems necessary" (19).

Thus, the current stance of the U.S. Supreme Court is that race neutrality is preferred, but if a university can show that such methods are inadequate or not administratively workable, it can use race-conscious methods in a limited way. Higher education institutions must present evidence that "available" and "workable" race-neutral alternatives do not achieve the goals sought with race-conscious methods.

New Cases, New Rationales

Between *Fisher I* and *II*, in November 2014, an organization called the Students for Fair Admissions (SFA) filed dual lawsuits against Harvard University and University of North Carolina at Chapel Hill alleging that both schools were using race in their admissions processes in an unconstitutional way. SFA is a group brought together by Edward Blum, founder of the Project on Fair Representation, a conservative organization dedicated to the elimination of all affirmative action–like policies in America.

These cases are unique for a few reasons. First, the Harvard University case is a challenge to a private (not public) university's admissions policies. Although a public school must follow the regulations under the Fourteenth Amendment, any school (public or private) that accepts federal money must also follow the regulations of Title VI of the 1964 Civil Rights Act. The U.S. Supreme Court has never definitively said whether the rules that apply to the Fourteenth Amendment are the same as those that apply to Title VI. The cases are also unique because the plaintiffs recruited for this case include not just White students but Asian Americans. Proponents of the color-blind perspective, such as Edward Blum and SFA, have begun to use Asian American students to advance what they see as a key weakness of the color-conscious perspective. That is, they see it as not only unfairly favoring Black students over White students but also harming Asian American students. By alleging that race-conscious admissions discriminate against Asian American students, groups like the SFA say they are challenging the typical Black–White binary in which the controversy of affirmative action is typically viewed.

Research is still emerging (and is needed) on this issue. However, the breadth of research produced thus far shows that Asian American, African American, Latino, and White students all benefit from race-conscious admissions and that their interests in supporting the policy align (Chu 2016; Lee 2015; Park and Liu 2014). But, even with this research, the SFA continue to recruit Asian American students, most recently at the University of Texas at Austin, to challenge race-conscious admissions policies (Flanagan and Xie 2017; Gersen, 2017).

These cases are still pending in the courts and will be reviewed in light of *Fisher II*. Time will tell whether these cases present an opportunity to reaffirm the legality of the use of race-conscious programs in higher education or an opportunity for its opponents to attack these programs in a new way. For now, it should be of interest to all involved that *Fisher II* did not end the controversy or public/legal debate around race-conscious admissions.

Current State Bans on Affirmative Action

Over the past decade, those who support a color-blind perspective have attacked affirmative action in the policy arena. Eight states currently ban race-based affirmative action at all public universities. California, Washington, Michigan, Nebraska, Arizona, and Oklahoma all passed bans through voter referenda. In Florida, then governor Jeb Bush issued an executive order creating a ban, and in New Hampshire the legislature passed a bill banning the consideration of race. In addition, the University of Georgia voluntarily dropped consideration of race after several lower court challenges and made the change permanent.

After bans on affirmative action were implemented in California, Florida, Texas, and Washington, selective undergraduate universities experienced a decline in the enrollment of underrepresented students of color (Backes 2012; Hinrichs 2012; Tienda et al. 2003). Studies also documented declines in racial and ethnic student body diversity in the professional fields of law and medicine (Garces and Mickey-Pabello 2015; Karabel 1998; Kidder 2013). Garces (2012, 2013) has also documented a decline in the representation of students of color across and within specific graduate fields of study, outside the professions of law and medicine. The negative consequences associated with bans on race-conscious admissions do not seem to discourage proponents of the color-blind perspective and (in some cases) race neutrality from supporting and advancing them.

In 2014, in a case called *Schuette v. Coalition to Defend Affirmative Action* (2014), proponents of the color-conscious perspective challenged the ban in Michigan as unconstitutional. The Court, however, upheld the constitutionality of the ban. Since *Schuette,* no other states have enacted bans on affirmative action. But with the election of Donald Trump to the White House in 2016 more states may try to prohibit the consideration of race in college admissions through extrajudicial means.

Proposed Responses/Reforms

Here, we return to philosophical perspectives of racial equity that underlie the controversy over race-based affirmative action in postsecondary institutions: color blindness, race neutrality, and color consciousness.

No Place for Race: Color Blindness

The color-blind perspective advocates for the elimination of the use of race in almost all areas of decision making in higher education. Those who embrace this philosophy usually believe that the best way to achieve racial equity in America is to, as Chief Justice Roberts stated in *Parents Involved in Community Schools v. Seattle School District No. 1* (2006), "stop discriminating on the basis of race." Supporters of this view (for example, Schuck 2006) believe that the problem with race relations in America is that we are giving too much power to an artificially created construct by continuing to acknowledge it, and the best way to get "beyond racism" is to craft policies and procedures that do not take race into account for anyone or for any reason. From this perspective, the act of racial classification is in and of itself racial discrimination. Supporters of the color-blind perspective maintain that racial categories do not matter and therefore should not be considered when making decisions about such issues as school admissions.

Adopting this strategy would mean that institutions of higher education would conduct admissions decisions while attempting to ignore race. For example, this would mean that a color-blind institution would not ask students to indicate race on an admissions application and would censor explicitly racial personal statements. Seeing no difference between the White supremacist ideology that produced Jim Crow laws in America and the anti-subordination ideology that gave birth to initial affirmative action policies, these scholars see the problem with race as race itself. In the view of those who would just take race out of the picture, using race (even indirectly) to solve the direct effects of racism is like using "the disease as the cure," to quote the title of a 1979 law review article by recently deceased Justice Antonin Scalia.

Proponents of color blindness point to three major reasons for supporting their argument. First, they argue that in states in which the consideration of race has been banned by ballot initiatives or other measures, the diversity of the student body has not changed (Potter 2016; Sander 1997). As noted, however, other research refutes these claims, demonstrating that bans on affirmative action have led to declines in racial diversity and further stratified higher education with students of color attending less selective institutions than their peers (e.g., Kurlaender, Friedmann, and Chang 2015).

Second, when it comes to elite schools, proponents of color blindness point to a concept known as "mismatch theory" (Sander and Taylor 2012), which claims that race-conscious admissions harm students of color because, based on standardized test scores, they are "overmatched" in an environment that is too competitive for the student's individual needs. In this way, mismatch theory attacks not just raced-based admissions but the idea of "holistic" review altogether because it rests on the premise that test scores in the end should be the determinative factor in college admissions. Opponents of the color-blind approach point to a substantial amount of social science research demonstrating that mismatch effects are either "tiny or nonexistent" or that they suggest the reverse of mismatch. That is, that students of color tend to do better when they attend more selective institutions (e.g., Kidder and Lempert 2015).

Finally, proponents of color blindness think that they have the future of the law on their side. This argument boils down to the fact that if the goal is to make race not matter tomorrow, why not start by just not allowing it to matter today. To support this perspective, proponents of the color-blind approach point to language in the *Grutter* decision, where the Court stated that it: "expect[ed] that 25 years from now, the use of racial preferences will no longer be necessary to further the interest approved today" (343). Although technically not a legally binding part of the ruling, they argue that based on this language any race-conscious admission program in place now has an expiration date of (at most) 2028. On this point, proponents of color blindness ask, if we truly want to be color blind in the future why not start by being color blind right now?

Legal scholars have pointed out how a color-blind perspective is in reality a racial preference for Whiteness (Carbado and Harris 2008), how not taking race into account ignores a crucial part of the identity of minoritized students and in fact discriminates against these students (Boddie 2016), and why being color blind in higher education does nothing but exacerbate racial inequities (e.g., Garces 2016). Additionally, some education scholars have further challenged color blindness as turning a "blind eye" to the role of race and racism in education (Yosso et al. 2004), indicating a move backward toward a time in which people of color did not have either legal or operational access to higher education (Harper, Patton, and Wooden 2009).

Race by Any Means but Race: "Race-Neutral Ways" to Diversity

The race-neutral perspective advocates for racial equity, but it argues for it through means that are void of the explicit use of race. Adopting this strategy would mean that institutions of higher education would conduct admissions decisions without giving explicit consideration to race and instead consider methods that serve as a proxy to obtain the amount of diversity needed to get the educational benefits of diversity. Some have proposed using socioeconomic status instead of race (Kahlenberg and Potter 2014, others have proposed using geography and wealth instead of race (Cashin 2014), or utilizing plans that allow a certain "top percentage" of state high schools the option of automatic admission into prestigious state schools, such as the plan that was at the heart of *Fisher*. The key is that all students qualify for these "admissions assists" regardless of race.

The race-neutral perspective can be described as an "umbrella" perspective. It contains those who support race neutrality because they really want color blindness and see this as a more nuanced way to accomplish their goals. It also holds within its ranks those who would otherwise support color consciousness but see this as an acceptable (less controversial) compromise that can produce approximately the same levels of diversity. This perspective, however, differs from the "color-blind" camp in a few ways. First, while those who support color blindness believe race has no part in the college admissions process, those who support race-neutral alternatives still believe race is important but have conceded that they should not use race explicitly (even in a limited way) to get their desired result. Additionally, those who support race-neutral alternatives support the idea that a certain level of ethnic or racial diversity is necessary to the learning process and to have a proper college environment. In contrast, those who favor color blindness would argue that this should not be a consideration at all.

One major benefit to the use of the race-neutral alternatives strategy is that it has solid legal footing. Race is considered a "suspect classification" and, whenever it is used as a criterion by the state or local government to confer burdens or benefits, it triggers the test of strict scrutiny. However, if race is not explicitly used as a factor, but some other "nonsuspect" classification is, the test of strict scrutiny is not triggered. Therefore, if you could get the same quantity and quality of diversity without using race in the admission process, it would be legally and economically the more efficient approach. Furthermore, the courts do favor the use of race-neutral alternatives (if it can be available and workable) over the explicit use of race. In *Fisher I* and *II*, the Court stated that race can only be used after an institution *considered* all workable race-neutral alternatives. It would seem appropriate that if workable race-neutral alternatives produced as much or more diversity as a race conscious admissions policy, then a court would approve of such a policy. In fact, such a race-neutral policy, may not be subject to legal threat.

However, research provides convincing evidence that race-neutral alternatives to admissions in higher education are both less effective and less efficient in producing racially diverse cohorts (e.g., Andrews and Swinton 2014). In fact, studies have shown that race-neutral alternatives do not in fact produce the same quality and quantity of racial and ethnic diversity as does the consideration of race in the admissions program (Kidder 2016; Long 2015). Socioeconomic status–based affirmative action policies do not yield nearly as much racial diversity as do race-based policies (Reardon et al. 2015). When the introduction of socioeconomic status as a criterion did work, it was a combination of race and class considerations that produced the most diversity (Carnevale, Rose, and Strohl 2014).

Also, the challenges of employing race neutrality, particularly for institutions still concerned with diversifying higher education, are numerous and have been documented as well (Garces and Cogburn 2015, 2016; Jones 2014). This leads to the conclusion that while some race-neutral alternatives may be more "comfortable" for the public to digest, they are not necessarily workable or effective when compared to race-conscious admissions.

With Eyes Open: The Color-Conscious Approach

Finally, the color-consciousness perspective advocates for equity through the temporary use of race-conscious admissions to address the historical and ongoing racial educational disparities that exist. As the cases *Bakke, Grutter,* and *Fisher I* and *II* demonstrated, institutions of higher education have long defended affirmative action policies from the perspective of the color-conscious approach. The way race would be considered would depend on the institution's context but involve a holistic admissions process that considers race as one of many factors. An institution adopting this approach, for example, would consider the race/ethnicity of a minoritized student who is underrepresented on their campus the same way they would consider as a "plus factor" the fact that a student plays piano or speaks several languages.

A voluminous amount of scholarship from various interdisciplinary fields supports the claim that race still shapes experiences in America (Collins 2002; Darling-Hammond 2015; Dowd and Bensimon 2015; Harpalani 2012; West 1993). None of the opposing views outlined here would say race does not matter at all in shaping educational opportunities. To those who follow the color-blind tradition, to eradicate the evil of race mattering, we must discontinue its use for any reason. From the race-neutral position, race matters but we are best morally and legally served using nonrace proxies to address the disadvantages that might occur because of race. It is the color-conscious position that seeks to "speak openly and candidly on the subject of race . . . with eyes open to the unfortunate effects of centuries of racial discrimination," as Justice Sonia Sotomayor wrote in her dissent in *Schuette* (2014, 46). Race matters and therefore we must use race to correct some systematic and institutional inequalities still evident in American society.

It is important to note that almost no one who subscribes to the color-conscious approach to college admissions argues that race should be the only criterion. Instead, they argue that it should be one of many. Although the principles laid out in *Bakke* and *Grutter* may not be most popular among the proponents of the color-conscious approach, they are typically accepted. Those who advocate from the color-conscious perspective are particularly interested in schools whose minoritized student population is at such a low percentage of the overall student population that the likelihood is very high that those minoritized students feel isolated (which undermines their learning) and majority students are unable to interact with minoritized students in such a way as to incur the "educational benefits of diversity" as mentioned in *Grutter*.

Many who support the continued use of race-based affirmative action point to the unequal situation of racial groups within our society as evidence that some type of equalizing factor is still needed. It is true that African Americans and Latinos are attending college and receiving more degrees than before (Nettles and Perna 1997). However, African Americans and Latinos continue to be underrepresented among both undergraduates and bachelor's degree recipients relative to their representation in the traditional college-age population (Perna 2000). Meanwhile, the need to obtain a college degree has arguably never been greater. Individuals with higher levels of education earn more and are more likely than others to be employed today.

Research shows that our present postsecondary system in America mimics the racial inequality it inherits from the K-12 education system, and then it magnifies and projects that inequality into the labor market and society at large (Carnevale and Strohl 2013). Black and Latino unemployment, poverty, and homelessness in America is higher than that of White Americans. Part of the problem, therefore, is the ongoing lack of access to higher education for minorities in this country. At the same time, past explicit racism has given way to a new implicit form of oppression and segregation for both Latinos and African Americans (Bonilla-Silva 2010).

As such, proponents of the color-conscious approach first and foremost believe that education can be (and is) a key to solving America's racial inequity puzzle (Kao and Thompson 2003). They believe that an increase in diversity has a positive effect in increasing educational outcomes (e.g., Chang 1999; Jayakumar 2008) and that the best way to capture, nurture, and maintain diversity on a college campus is through the use of race-conscious admissions (e.g., Jayakumar and Garces 2015). Philosophically they contend that the use of race is necessary to achieve equity because it was through the use of race that the "opportunity gap" in education in America was created.

The color-conscious approach does not come without its own drawbacks. First it is contingent on the premise that education does in fact play a substantial role in combating racial inequity in America, an argument that can be and has been contested (Marsh 2011). Some have criticized the theory behind affirmative action policies in general. Fryer and Loury (2005) challenge the notion that any affirmative action policy always helped its intended beneficiaries.

Others have criticized raced-based affirmative action as misplaced and misguided in operation if not in theory. Such theorists claim that the problem is that affirmative action does not go far enough. For example, Brown and Bell (2008) criticize race-conscious admissions schemes as failing to benefit students they termed "descendants" (U.S.-born descendants of the "original" slaves) and instead favoring Black–White biracial students and first-generation Black immigrants. They cite this as a problem, as they believe that some U.S. institutions are using affirmative action not to make up for past discrimination but to "pad" their diversity numbers with those from minoritized social groups that would have been admitted without affirmative action policies anyway. Guinier (2004) made a similar, yet distinct, criticism of modern-day race-conscious policies in an op-ed when she stated: "Driven by a preoccupation with ranking and sorting individuals rather than serving fundamentally democratic goals, admissions decisions recreate a 'geography of unequal opportunity' in which suburban students succeed and rural and urban students are left behind" (1).

Others critique the rationale on which current affirmative action policies are permitted. The "diversity rationale" for affirmative action seeks not *equity* to remedy past outcomes, but diversity for the benefit of all students whether they have been "oppressed" or not. In fact, the diversity rationale for affirmative action in general and race-conscious admissions in particular that resulted from Justice Powell's opinion in *Bakke* (and was reinforced in

Grutter) have been widely criticized in both legal and social science literature as of late (see, e.g., Berrey 2015; James 2014). Much of this critique brings attention to the fact that a focus on diversity hinders the type of institutional transformation and acknowledgment of racism that needs to take place to achieve racial equity.

Conclusion

Because social science research continues to show that race shapes decisions and actions in both intentional and unconscious ways (e.g., Richeson and Nussbaum 2004), it is important for institutions to adopt a color-conscious approach in their educational policies. It is not only the approach most supported by the available evidence, but it is the only approach presented in this chapter that properly takes into consideration the effects of history on minoritized individuals in America. The perspective of color blindness requires setting aside this history and ignoring the empirical evidence about the ways race continues to shape students' experiences and opportunities. Currently, the U.S. Supreme Court has provided one way forward by embracing race neutrality as the preferred solution and allowing race-conscious practices if a university shows that a race-neutral approach is not workable. Research demonstrates that such an approach cannot adequately address racial equity. It remains to be seen whether institutions will continue to adopt and defend a color-conscious approach in the face of ongoing challenges to race-conscious policies in admissions.

Note

1. There are three levels of judicial scrutiny by which state action is judged in accordance with equal protection: strict scrutiny, intermediate scrutiny, and rational basis review. Strict scrutiny is the hardest test to overcome.

References

Andrews, Rodney J., and Omari H. Swinton. 2014. The persistent myths of "acting white" and race neutral alternatives to affirmative action in admissions. *The Review of Black Political Economy 41*, no. 3: 357–371.

Backes, Ben. 2012. Do affirmative action bans lower minority college enrollment and attainment? Evidence from statewide bans. *Journal of Human Resources 47*, no. 2: 435–455.

Berrey, Ellen. 2015. *The enigma of diversity: The language of race and the limits of racial justice.* Chicago: University of Chicago Press.

Boddie, Elise C. 2016. The indignities of color blindness. *UCLA Law Review Discourse 64*: 64–88.

Bondarenko, Alexander. 2013. Between a rock and a hard place: Why rational basis scrutiny for LGBT classifications is incompatible with opposition to LGBT affirmative action. *Brooklyn Law Review 79*: 1703–1743.

Bonilla-Silva, Eduardo. 2010. *Racism without racists: Color-blind racism and the persistence of racial inequality in the United States.* Lanham, MD: Rowman & Littlefield.

Brown, Kevin, and Jeannine Bell. 2008. Demise of the talented tenth: Affirmative action and the increasing underrepresentation of ascendant blacks at selective higher educational institutions. *Ohio State Law Journal 69*: 1229–1283.

Carbado, Devon W., and Cheryl I. Harris. 2008. The new racial preferences. *California Law Review 96*, no. 5: 1139–1214.

Carnevale, Anthony P., Stephen J. Rose, and Jeff Strohl. 2014. "Achieving racial and economic diversity with race-blind admissions policy. In *The future of affirmative action: New paths to higher education diversity after Fisher v. University of Texas,*" edited by Richard D. Kahlenberg, 2004, 187–202. New York: Century Foundation Press.

Carnevale, Anthony P., and Jeff Strohl. 2013. *Separate and unequal: How higher education reinforces the intergenerational reproduction of white racial privilege.* Washington, DC: Georgetown Public Policy Institute.

Cashin, Sheryll. 2014. *Place, not race: A new vision of opportunity in America.* Boston: Beacon Press.

Chang, Mitchell. 1999. Does racial diversity matter? The educational impact of a racially diverse undergraduate population. *Journal of College Student Development 40*, no. 4: 377–395.

Chu, Chan Hee. 2016. When proportionality equals diversity: Asian Americans and affirmative action. *Asian American Law Journal 23*: 99–144.

Collins, Patricia Hill. 2002. *Black feminist thought: Knowledge, consciousness, and the politics of empowerment.* New York: Routledge.

Darling-Hammond, Linda. 2015. *The flat world and education: How America's commitment to equity will determine our future.* New York: Teachers College Press.

Dowd, Alicia C., and Estela Mara Bensimon. 2015. *Engaging the "race question": Accountability and equity in US higher education.* New York: Teachers College Press.

Fisher v. University of Texas I, 133 S. Ct. 2411 (June 24, 2013).

Fisher v. University of Texas II, 136 S. Ct. 2198 (June 23, 2016).

Flanagan, William, and Michael E. Xie. 2017. Harvard admissions lawsuit plaintiff recruits students for similar case at UT. *The Harvard Crimson*, March 24, 2017. Accessed April 9, 2017. http://www.thecrimson.com/article/2017/3/7/admissions-lawsuit-website-recruits-strudents/

Fryer, Roland G., and Glenn C. Loury. 2005. Affirmative action and its mythology. *The Journal of Economic Perspectives 19*, no. 3: 147–162.

Garces, Liliana M. 2012. Racial diversity, legitimacy, and the citizenry: The impact of affirmative action bans on graduate school enrollment. *Review of Higher Education 36*, no. 1: 93–132.

Garces, Liliana M. 2013. Understanding the impact of affirmative action bans in different graduate fields of study. *American Educational Research Journal 50*, no. 2: 251–284.

Garces, Liliana M. 2016. Lessons from social science for Kennedy's doctrinal inquiry in *Fisher v. University of Texas II. UCLA Law Review Discourse 64*: 18–39.

Garces, Liliana M., and Courtney D. Cogburn. 2015. Beyond declines in student body diversity: How campus-level administrators understand a prohibition on race-conscious postsecondary admissions policies. *American Educational Research Journal 52*: 828–860.

Garces, Liliana M., and Courtney D. Cogburn. 2016. Navigating legal barriers while promoting racial diversity in higher education. In *School integration matters: Research-based strategies to advance equity*, edited by Erica Frankenberg, Liliana M. Garces, and Megan Hopkins, 189. New York: Teachers College Press.

Garces, Liliana M., and David Mickey-Pabello, 2015. Racial diversity in the medical profession: The impact of affirmative action bans on underrepresented student of color matriculation in medical schools. *The Journal of Higher Education 86*: 264–294.

Gersen, Jeannie Suk. "The Uncomfortable Truth About Affirmative Action and Asian-Americans." *The New Yorker*, August 10, 2017. Accessed August 19, 2017. http://www.newyorker.com/news/news-desk/the-uncomfortable -truth-about-affirmative-action-and-asian-americans.

Gratz v. Bollinger, 539 U.S. 244 (June 23, 2003).

Grutter v. Bollinger, 539 U.S. 306 (June 23, 2003).

Guinier, Lani. 2004. Our preference for the privileged. *The Boston Globe*, July 9, 2004. Accessed April 3, 2017. http://www.law.harvard.edu/faculty /guinier/publications/preference.pdf

Guisado, Angelo. 2013. Reversal of fortune: The inapposite standards applied to remedial race, gender, and orientation-based classifications. *Nebraska Law Review 92*: 1–45.

Harpalani, Vinay. 2012. Diversity within racial groups and the constitutionality of race-conscious admissions. *The University of Pennsylvania Journal of Constitutional Law 15*: 463–537.

Harper, Shaun R., Lori D. Patton, and Ontario S. Wooden. 2009. Access and equity for African American students in higher education: A critical race historical analysis of policy efforts. *The Journal of Higher Education 80*, no. 4: 389–414.

Hinrichs, Peter. 2012. The effects of affirmative action bans on college enrollment, educational attainment, and the demographic composition of universities. *Review of Economics and Statistics 94*, no. 3: 712–722.

James, Osamudia. 2014. White like me: The negative impact of the diversity rationale on white identity formation. *New York University Law Review 89*, no. 2: 425–512.

Jayakumar, Uma. 2008. Can higher education meet the needs of an increasingly diverse and global society? Campus diversity and cross-cultural workforce competencies. *Harvard Educational Review 78*, no. 4: 615–651.

Jayakumar, Uma M., and Liliana M. Garces. 2015. *Affirmative action and racial equity: Considering the Fisher case to forge the path ahead.* New York: Routledge.

Jones, Sosanya Marie. 2014. Diversity leadership under race-neutral policies in higher education. *Equality, Diversity and Inclusion: An International Journal 33*, no. 8: 708–720.

Kahlenberg, Richard, and Halley Potter. 2014. Class-based affirmative action works. *The New York Times*, April 27, 2014. Accessed February 8, 2017. http://www.nytimes.com/roomfordebate/2014/04/27/should-affirmative -action-be-based-on-income/class-based-affirmative-action-works

Kao, Grace, and Jennifer S. Thompson. 2003. Racial and ethnic stratification in educational achievement and attainment. *Annual Review of Sociology 29*, no. 1: 417–442.

Karabel, Jerome. 1998. No alternative: The effects of color-blind admissions in California. In *Chilling admissions: The affirmative action crisis and the search for alternatives*, edited by Gary Orfield and Edward Miller, 33–50. Cambridge, MA: Harvard Education Publishing Group.

Kidder, William C. 2013. Misshaping the river: Proposition 209 and lessons for the Fisher case. *Journal of College and University Law 39*: 53–125.

Kidder, William C. 2016. How workable are class-based and race-neutral alternatives at leading American universities? *UCLA Law Review Discourse 64*: 100. Accessed April 1, 2017. http://www.uclalawreview.org/work able-class-based-race-neutral-alternatives-leading-american-univer sities/

Kidder, William C., and Richard Lempert. 2015. The mismatch myth in U.S. higher education. In *Affirmative action and racial equity: Considering the Fisher case to forge the path ahead*, edited by Uma Jayakumar, and Liliana Garces, with Frank Fernandez, 105–129. New York: Routledge.

Kurlaender, Michal, Elizabeth Friedmann, and Tongshan Chang. 2015. Access and diversity at the University of California in the post-affirmative action era. In *Affirmative action and racial equity: Considering the Fisher case to forge the path ahead*, edited by Uma Jayakumar, and Liliana Garces, with Frank Fernandez, 80–101. New York: Routledge.

Ladson-Billings, Gloria. 2006. From the achievement gap to the education debt: Understanding achievement in US schools. *Educational Researcher 35*, no. 7: 3–12.

Lamb, John D. 1992. The real affirmative action babies: Legacy preference at Harvard and Yale. *The Columbia Journal of Law & Social Problems 26*: 491–521.

Lee, Stacy J. 2015. *Unraveling the "model minority" stereotype: Listening to Asian American youth.* New York: Teachers College Press.

Long, Mark C. 2015. Is there a "workable" race-neutral alternative to affirmative action in college admissions? *Journal of Policy Analysis and Management 34*, no. 1: 162–183.

Marsh, John. 2011. *Class dismissed: Why we cannot teach or learn our way out of inequality.* New York: NYU Press.

Nettles, M. T., and L. W. Perna. 1997. *The African American education data book: Higher and adult education* (vol. 1). Fairfax, VA: Frederick D. Patterson Research Institute.

Nicolas, Peter. 2014. Gayffirmative action: The constitutionality of sexual orientation–based affirmative action policies. *Washington University Law Review* 92: 733–792.

Park, Julie J., and Amy Liu. 2014. Interest convergence or divergence? A critical race analysis of Asian Americans, meritocracy, and critical mass in the affirmative action debate. *The Journal of Higher Education, 85,* no. 1: 36–64.

Perna, Laura Walter. 2000. Differences in the decision to attend college among African Americans, Hispanics, and Whites. *Journal of Higher Education* 71: 117–141.

Potter, Halley. 2016. What can we learn from states that ban affirmative action? June 26, 2014. The Century Foundation, Accessed February 8, 2017. https://tcf.org/content/commentary/what-can-we-learn-from-states-that -ban-affirmative-action/

Reardon, Sean F., Rachel Baker, Matt Kasman, Daniel Klasik, and Joseph B. Townsend. 2015. Can socioeconomic status substitute for race in affir-mative action college admission policies? Evidence from a Simulation Model. *Educational Testing Service* 18: 234–245.

Regents of the University of *California v. Bakke,* 438 U.S. 265 (June 28, 1978).

Richeson, Jennifer A., and Richard J. Nussbaum. 2004. The impact of multicul-turalism versus color-blindness on racial bias. *Journal of Experimental Social Psychology* 40, no. 3: 417–423.

Rubio, Philip F. 2009. *A history of affirmative action, 1619–2000.* Oxford, MS: University Press of Mississippi.

Sander, Richard H. 1997. Experimenting with class-based affirmative action. *Journal of legal education* 47, no. 4: 472–503.

Sander, Richard, and Stuart Taylor. 2012. *Mismatch: How affirmative action hurts students it's intended to help, and why universities won't admit it.* New York: Basic Books.

Scalia, Antonin. 1979. The Disease as cure: In order to get beyond racism, we must first take account of race. *Washington University Law Quarterly 1979*: 147–157.

Schuck, Peter H. 2002. Affirmative action: Past, present, and future. *Yale Law & Policy Review* 20: 1–96.

Schuck, Peter H. 2006. *Diversity in America: Keeping government at a safe distance.* Boston: Harvard University Press.

Schuette v. Coalition to Defend Affirmative Action, 134 S.Ct. 1623 (April 22, 2014).

Sterba, James P. 2009. *Affirmative action for the future.* Ithaca, NY: Cornell University Press.

Tienda, Marta, Kevin T. Leicht, Teresa Sullivan, Michael Maltese, and Kim Lloyd. 2003. Closing the gap? Admissions and enrollments at the Texas public flagships before and after affirmative action (Working Paper Series, No. 2003-01). Princeton, NJ: Office of Population Research Princeton University.

West, Cornel. 1993. *Race matters*. New York: Vintage.

Yosso, Tara J., Laurence Parker, Daniel G. Solorzano, and Marvin Lynn. 2004. From Jim Crow to affirmative action and back again: A critical race discussion of racialized rationales and access to higher education. *Review of Research in Education 28*, no. 1: 1–25.

CHAPTER TWO

Access Granted? Challenges, Controversies, and Opportunities around College Access in American Higher Education

Ashley B. Clayton and Darris R. Means

Higher education has seen growth in the number of both institutions and students enrolling; additionally, colleges and universities have become more diverse with changing demographics of students (Jones 2013). In the 2014–2015 academic year, there were 4,627 degree-granting postsecondary institutions in the United States; this number has grown from 4,216 in 2004–2005 and 3,688 in 1994–1995 (Snyder, de Brey, and Dillow 2016). Undergraduate fall enrollment at degree-granting institutions increased 17 percent from 14.8 million to 17.3 million between 2004 and 2014. More recently, between 2010 and 2014, undergraduate enrollment declined slightly each year but is projected to increase from 17.3 million to 19.8 million by 2025 (Snyder, de Brey, and Dillow 2016). Although college enrollment has increased overall, the overarching issue of college access is not without some unique challenges and controversies.

Overview of the Current College Access Problem

Overall postsecondary enrollment rates are on the rise; however, inequities in enrollment based on race and ethnicity, income, and other demographic characteristics persist (Ma, Pender, and Welch 2016; Perna and Kurban 2013). Three main student populations who are still underserved in higher education are students of color, low-income students, and first-generation students (Bragg 2013). In 2014, the college enrollment rate of White 18–24 year olds was 42 percent compared to 33 percent and 35 percent for Black and Hispanic populations, respectively (Snyder, de Brey, and Dillow 2016). These enrollment gaps in race/ethnicity have narrowed over time, but there still remains a large enrollment gap based on family income (Ma, Pender, and Welch 2016). Low-income students have experienced a 7 percentage point enrollment increase from 2005 to 2015 but still enroll in college at much lower rates compared to their more affluent peers (Ma, Pender, and Welch 2016). Students who have no history of college in their families are less likely to apply and enroll in college compared to non-first-generation college students (Choy 2011; Toutkoushian, Stollberg, and Slaton 2018; Ward, Siegel, and Davenport 2012). In addition to these historically underrepresented populations, recent conversations around access have also focused on undocumented students, student veterans, and students with disabilities.

Some may argue that the access challenge of educational attainment has been solved, as there has been a shift in policy conversations to focus on increasing college graduation (Adelman 2007; Ma, Pender, and Welch 2016; Miller et al. 2014; Scott-Clayton and Sacerdote 2016). In the past decade, numerous initiatives, such as Complete College America (2017), have focused on closing educational attainment gaps for traditionally underserved student populations. By directing more attention to degree attainment, conversations about access have started to diminish, sending a message that there is less of an access issue. Some may argue that with an increase in enrollment of underrepresented populations, affirmative action, need-based scholarship programs, and other initiatives, the college access gap has been nearly closed (Engle and Tinto 2008; Miller et al. 2014). Additionally, some people would agree that access is not enough but it is important that students be retained and ultimately earn a degree.

Another controversy around college access is in regard to whose responsibility it is to address the issue. Some may argue that the role of college access falls on the individual student and their family. Others may argue that secondary education should focus on outcomes beyond high school graduation, but college enrollment of high school graduates is not currently built into the K-12 accountability system (McDonough 2005). Institutions of higher education are naturally main players in the college access conversation; however, colleges have to find the balance between three competing enrollment management objectives: college access, selectivity, and revenue (Cheslock and Kroc 2012). The college access objective can plausibly be less of a priority if an institution is more focused on admitting students with strong academic credentials or can contribute large amounts of tuition and fees. Although it is not clear if college access is more of a secondary or postsecondary problem to solve, both the federal government and nonprofit organizations have stepped in with initiatives to address college access. The federal government has provided grant funding for several precollege programs, such as TRIO programs, Gaining Early Awareness and Readiness for Undergraduate Programs (GEAR UP), and the College Access Challenge Grant Program (U.S. Department of Education 2017b). Additionally, nonprofit organizations, such as the National College Advising Corps, have developed initiatives to increase college preparation and enrollment.

College access for many underrepresented groups has improved and overall college enrollment is on the rise. With the increased focus on college retention and completion, it is imperative not to forget college access. This chapter will give an overview of the many controversies and questions surrounding college access in the United States, including whose responsibility it is to increase (or improve) access, which populations still need access, and what institutions and other organizations are doing to support access.

Theoretical Foundations of College Access and Choice

In order to better understand college access, it is important to examine how students make choices about going to college. Numerous studies have examined students' college choice process and identified factors most influential in the process. There have been three major literature reviews on the topic of college access and choice: Hossler, Braxton, and Coopersmith (1989), Paulsen (1990), and most recently Perna (2006). All three of these reviews have consistently highlighted the importance of both economic and sociological theories in guiding research on college access and choice.

In the most current review of the literature, Perna (2006) identified four categories of predictors that determine college enrollment and choice: financial resources, academic preparation and achievement, support from significant others, and knowledge and information about college and financial aid (Perna and Kurban 2013). After synthesizing past research on college access and choice, Perna (2006) developed a conceptual model of college choice that explains how many factors influence a student's decision to attend college. Specifically, the model explains that enrollment decisions are nested within four contextual layers: (1) student and family context; (2) school and community context; (3) higher education context; and (4) the social, economic, and policy context (Perna 2006). Although the student and family are at the innermost layer, the comprehensive model explains that many other factors influence college enrollment decisions. Each layer of the model also raises questions and controversies around who is responsible for college access.

Student and Family Context

The economic theory of human capital is at the core of Perna's conceptual model (2006), which assumes that students' college choice behaviors are based on a comparison of the expected benefits to the expected costs (Becker 1993). Paulsen (2001) explains that human capital theory suggests that a student's decision to invest in a college education will be worthwhile if the expected benefits (e.g., employment, future salary) outweigh the costs (e.g., foregone earnings, tuition, fees). Perna's model (2006) also proposes that students make postsecondary decisions based on their supply of resources (family income and financial aid) and demand for education (academic preparation and academic achievement). For example, low-income students are particularly sensitive to tuition prices and other college costs (Heller 1997, 2013), and might not have a sufficient supply of resources to enroll in college.

The innermost layer of the model, the student and family context, is also known as the habitus. An individual's habitus is an internalized system of thoughts, beliefs, and perceptions that are shaped by one's immediate environment and inevitably influence college aspirations (Bourdieu and Passeron 1977; McDonough 1997; Perna 2006). In the context of college choice, social capital refers to an individual's access to social networks that provide information and assistance to attend college (Coleman 1988; Deil-Amen and Turley 2007; Perna 2006). Students from more affluent and educated backgrounds will have more access to social networks that will further facilitate optimal college-going decisions.

Some might argue that families are ultimately responsible for the postsecondary outcomes of their children. It is plausible that those who view education as a private good that provides students with a competitive advantage and other personal benefits (Labaree 1997) might propose that it is not the responsibility of higher education institutions or the federal government to supply resources and funding. The counterargument is that higher education is a public good and that society as a whole benefits from more individuals going to college (Baum, Ma, Payea 2013; Pusser 2006).

School and Community Context

Layer two of Perna's model (2006), school and community context, is based on McDonough's concept (1997) of "organizational habitus," which acknowledges ways that schools and communities help or hinder the college choice process. School personnel, such as school counselors and teachers, can be influential in providing resources and helping students with college applications (Hossler, Braxton, and Coopersmith 1989; McDonough 2005; Stanton-Salazar 1997). Conversely, some research suggests that the school environments may inhibit college access for low-income and minority students (Stanton-Salazar 1997).

Schools and communities can vary greatly depending on geographic location, resources, and other economic factors. One example of variation is in college counseling resources at the school level (Perna et al. 2008). Private schools often have a designated staff member whose primary responsibility is assisting students with college applications and selection, but far fewer public high schools have this additional resource. College counseling often falls on the shoulders of school counselors who lack both formal training and time to assist students (McDonough 2005). Additionally, college counseling is more readily accessible for students in advanced college preparatory tracks (McDonough 2005; Venezia and Kirst 2005) and of higher socioeconomic status (Linnehan, Weer, and Stonely 2011).

Higher Education Context

The third layer of the model, the higher education context, explains postsecondary institutions' roles in college access and choice (Perna 2006). Different types of colleges indirectly and directly market to specific student populations. Some students may have a limited viewpoint on college options and may only be aware of institutions within a close proximity to their home (Means et al. 2016) or have highly publicized athletic teams (Pope and Pope 2014; Toma and Cross 1998). However, higher education institutions also recruit specific student populations through more intentional marketing strategies (Perna 2006). Students from certain demographic backgrounds might also be drawn to some institutions more than others based on their personal identity and preferences (Nora 2004). For example, due to both marketing efforts and the role of personal preferences, low-income students have higher rates of enrollment in community colleges and for-profit institutions (Baum, Ma, and Payea 2013; Heller 2013).

Institutions of higher education also decide which students they allow to enroll based on their admissions standards. Deciding which students to admit is a complex enrollment management problem. Colleges "wish to enroll underrepresented and economically disadvantaged students, well-prepared students with high test scores and grades, and students who can contribute large amounts of tuition and fees—all at the same time" (Cheslock and Kroc 2012, 221). Although access, academic quality, and revenue are all logical goals, it is nearly impossible to advance all three enrollment objectives simultaneously (Cheslock and Kroc 2012; Humphrey 2006; Schulz 2008). One college might prioritize revenue generation over access for low-income students, especially if that college is heavily tuition-driven. Another might prioritize improving their academic profile over offering spots to students who attended underresourced high schools without test preparation, Advanced Placement, or International Baccalaureate programs. With competing enrollment objectives, some colleges have less incentive to prioritize access.

Social, Economic, and Policy Context

The outermost layer of Perna's model (2006) recognizes the role of the larger social, economic, and policy landscape in college choice. The social context includes demographic characteristics of the population, such as bachelor's degree attainment and poverty levels. The economic context includes labor market characteristics, such as unemployment rates and availability of jobs. Last, the broader public policy context, such as state- and federally funded financial aid programs and K-12 policies, also has an influence on college choice behaviors (Perna and Kurban 2013).

One recent policy shift that has received much attention is the development of state-funded merit-based financial aid programs (Heller 2003). In 1993, Georgia introduced a merit-based scholarship program, Helping Outstanding Pupils Educationally (HOPE), which the state funded with lottery revenues. Taking advantage of an exogenous policy shift, studies found a significant positive effect of the HOPE scholarship program on postsecondary enrollment in Georgia. An early study found that after the implementation of HOPE, postsecondary enrollment rates in Georgia among 18- to 19-year-olds increased from about 30 percent to 37.8 percent (Dynarski 2000). Another more recent study had similar findings, reporting that the HOPE program increased enrollment in Georgia by 5.9 percent, adding 2,889 freshmen per year to Georgia colleges (Cornwell, Mustard, and Sridhar 2006). As a result of Georgia's successful merit-based scholarship program, there has been a growth in state-sponsored merit-aid programs across the country (Hu, Trengove, and Zhang 2012). However, as more states focus on providing financial aid based on merit, there is a concern that need-based aid could get crowded out and have negative consequences for low-income and minority student enrollment (Griffith 2011; Hearn, Jones, and Kurban 2013; Heller 2003). As merit-based programs have outpaced need-based programs, these programs often favor higher income students and White students (Dynarski 2002, 2004; Heller 2003; Ness and Tucker, 2008).

Addressing College Access for Underserved Student Populations

Despite improvements in college enrollment rates (Davis 2010; Jones 2013), research continues to show that pathways to higher education remain inequitable for students, with stratification by race and ethnicity, social class, family history of college, immigration status, ability, and other dimensions of social identity (Bergerson 2009; Bowen, Chingos, and McPherson 2009; Bragg 2013; Engle and Tinto 2008; Perez 2009; Perna and Kurban 2013). College access discussions often focus on low-income students, first-generation college students, and students of color. Although low-income and first-generation students are more likely to be students of color (Engle and Tinto 2008), it is important to acknowledge these identities do not necessarily overlap (Davis 2010). For example, a student of color could be from a high-income family with a long family history of college or a White student could be a first-generation college student from a working-class family. In this section, we examine two sets of challenges to college access prevalent in these populations: (a) those related to how we frame college access and its barriers, and (b) those related to the model minority myth.

College Access and Capital

Theorists and scholars have often used cultural and social capital to frame the challenges and barriers low-income students, first-generation college students, and students of color face in education (e.g., Bourdieu 1986; Bryan et al. 2011; Strayhorn 2010). Cultural capital can be generally described as "an accumulation of cultural knowledge, skills and abilities possessed and inherited by privileged groups in society" (Yosso 2005, 76), while social capital is related to one's connections and networks, which provide access to actual or potential resources, conferring advantage and promoting social mobility (Bourdieu 1986). From a cultural and social capital perspective, research has documented how low-income students, first-generation college students, and students of color often lack knowledge about preparing for higher education, a type of cultural capital, and networks of college-educated family and friends, a type of social capital, that can be used to access higher education. Given the lack of cultural and social capital in underserved populations, policy makers, researchers, and educators may wonder if they should focus on providing these students access to additional social and cultural capital.

However, Yosso (2005) critiqued how educators used cultural and social capital to focus on the deficits of marginalized student populations, while using White middle-class standards to assert "some communities are culturally wealthy while others are culturally poor" (76). Yosso noted that such "deficit thinking takes the position that minority students and families are at fault for poor academic performance because: (a) students enter school without the normative cultural knowledge and skills; and (b) parents neither value nor support their child's education" (2005, 75). Thus, theories of cultural and social capital fail to recognize the assets and resources that marginalized student populations may use to navigate their pathway to higher education, such as encouragement from family to pursue higher education and students' resistance in the face of challenges (Harper 2010; Means and Pyne 2016; Pyne and Means 2013; Yosso 2005). In addition, emphasizing individual and familial barriers and challenges may lead educators and policy makers to neglect the broader, structural barriers that contribute to inequitable college enrollment. In particular, they may overlook the historical and current realities related to racism, classism, other forms of oppression, and the intersection of these forms of oppression that leads to educational inequity for low-income students, first-generation college students, and students of color (Pyne and Means 2013; Quaye, Griffin, and Museus 2015; Yosso 2005).

Yosso (2005) proposed an alternative to traditional notions of cultural and social capital to understand how students, specifically students of color, navigate educational settings. Building upon work from other scholars (e.g., Daniel Solórzano and Octavio Villalpando), Yosso proposed the notion of community cultural wealth to acknowledge the "knowledge, skills, abilities and contacts possessed and utilized by Communities of Color to survive and resist macro and micro-forms of oppression" (2005, 77). Yosso also drew on Critical Race Theory to acknowledge systemic, structural, and institutional barriers related to race and racism that may lead to inequity in education. Yosso's model (2005) identifies six forms of capital: aspirational capital ("the ability to maintain hopes and dreams for the future, even in the face of real and perceived barriers"), familial capital (the expansion of the boundaries of family to include extended family and friends, as well as the commitment to the well-being of family), linguistic capital (the recognition and value of "multiple language and communication skills"), social capital (a network of people that provide emotional support), navigational capital ("skills of maneuvering through social institutions"), and resistant capital (the ability to exercise agency to challenge inequality or oppressive messages) (77–80). Researchers using this model to explore college access inequity have found that these forms of capital support the college-going for low-income students, first-generation college students, and students of color (Jayakumar, Vue, and Allen 2013; Means, Hudson, and Tish 2016).

The Model Minority Myth

In the United States, Asian American and Pacific Islander individuals have the highest college enrollment and attainment rates of all racial groups (Lumina Foundation 2016; Snyder, de Brey, Dillow 2016). According to the Lumina Foundation (2016), approximately 60 percent of Asian American and Pacific Islander adults have attained a postsecondary degree. Because of these assumed high levels of achievement, Asian American and Pacific Islander students are often not viewed as underserved, which perpetuates the model minority myth in academic settings (Museus and Kiang 2009).

According to Museus and Kiang (2009), "The model minority stereotype is the notion that Asian Americans achieve universal and unparalleled academic and occupational success" (6).

Researchers have demonstrated that the model minority myth or stereotype masks differences in attainment by ethnicity and socioeconomic status (Museus and Kiang 2009; Museus and Vue 2013). Although Asian Indian, Pakistani, Chinese, Filipino, Korean, and Japanese individuals have a high college attainment rate, Vietnamese, Cambodian, Laotian, and Hmong individuals have a significantly lower college attainment rate (Museus and Kiang 2009). In addition, the model minority myth does not account for socioeconomic differences among Asian American and Pacific Islander students, which leads to disparities for college access (Museus and Vue 2013). For instance, Museus and Vue (2013) found that "SES disparities exist, with higher SES AAPIs (Asian Americans and Pacific Islanders) developing expectations for, applying to, and matriculating in college at higher rates than their lower SES peers" (68). Regardless of the model minority stereotype, researchers have demonstrated that Asian American students experience racial hostility and marginalization (Museus and Park 2015), which shapes pathways to and through higher education.

College Access Programs and Initiatives

Numerous programs and initiatives have been developed and implemented to increase college access for underrepresented student populations. Some initiatives are over 50 years old while others are much newer. In this section, we highlight some relevant examples of college access interventions and their impact.

Precollege Programs

Numerous programs in the United States are available to assist high school students in preparing for college, ranging from large federally funded programs, such as TRIO and GEAR UP, to smaller institutional and state-funded programs (Corwin, Colyar, and Tierney 2005; Swail and Perna 2002). The overarching goals of precollege programs typically focus on improving students' academic preparation and providing support, encouragement, and information that, collectively, increase the likelihood of college enrollment (Cabrera et al. 2006; Corwin, Colyar, and Tierney 2005; Perna 2015; Swail and Perna, 2002). Many programs target students from low-income, first-generation, and other underserved populations.

Some of the largest precollege programs in the nation are federally funded and serve disadvantaged populations. For instance, the U.S. Department of

Education created Upward Bound, Talent Search, and Student Support Services in the 1960s as the original "TRIO." There are now eight TRIO programs "targeted to serve and assist low-income individuals, first-generation college students, and individuals with disabilities to progress through the academic pipeline from middle school to postbaccalaureate programs" (U.S. Department of Education 2017a). In a large-scale randomized control trial of Upward Bound conducted by Mathematica Policy Research (MPR), there were no statistically significant differences in postsecondary enrollment between students in the Upward Bound program and students in the control group (Seftor, Mamum, and Schirm 2009). However, Cahalan and Goodwin (2014) conducted a follow-up analysis and found that students in the Upward Bound program were more likely to enroll in college and complete a college degree.

Information and Personal Assistance

Some studies have found that providing information and assistance during the postsecondary application process can have positive effects. One study focused on the role of personal assistance in helping low- to moderate-income families complete the Free Application for Federal Student Aid (FAFSA) (Bettinger et al. 2012). Low-income individuals receiving tax preparation assistance at H&R Block were randomly assigned to one of three groups: FAFSA information only, information and personal assistance filling out the FAFSA, or a control group. Students in the combined treatment group (information and personal assistance) were not only more likely to complete the FAFSA, but were also 8.1 percentage points more likely to enroll and 8 percentage points more likely to persist in postsecondary education for two years (Bettinger et al. 2012).

A relatively new set of initiatives aimed at encouraging students to apply for college are statewide college application campaigns (American Council on Education 2017). In fall 2005, North Carolina became the first state to pilot this type of initiative in one high school. During North Carolina's annual College Application Week, sites across the state provide application assistance to high school seniors, and dozens of colleges and universities waive their application fees (College Foundation of North Carolina 2017). In 2007 this grew into a statewide program, and since then North Carolina has seen an increase in applications and enrollments among low-income students (Umbach and Clayton 2014). By 2015, all 50 states had adopted similar programs as part of the American College Application Campaign. Each state designs and operates its campaign independently, but they typically schedule them during the school day in the fall of senior year. These campaigns last between a week and a month, and high school seniors receive assistance with applying to college (American Council on Education 2017).

College Advising

Recently, several college advising models have been developed to provide high school students with assistance in the college enrollment process. One of the largest initiatives of this type is the College Advising Corps: a non-profit organization that places recent college graduates in underserved high schools to serve as full-time college advisers (College Advising Corps 2017a). The program has two main goals: "First, it provides necessary information and support for students who may find it difficult to navigate the complex college admission process. Second, the advisers conduct outreach to under-classmen in an effort to improve the school-wide college-going culture" (Horng et al. 2013, 56). Starting in 2005 with 14 advisers from the University of Virginia serving 16 rural Virginia high schools, the program has now expanded to 14 states with over 500 advisers (College Advising Corps 2017a). The program has conducted a randomized control trial study of its Texas program, and preliminary results suggest that students in high schools with the college adviser are more likely to apply to four-year colleges and enroll in postsecondary education (College Advising Corps 2017b).

A similar advising program is the College Coach Program in Chicago Public Schools. Coaches are not randomly assigned to high schools, although they were "distributed fairly evenly across high schools in terms of socioeconomic composition, racial composition, and academic achievement" (Stephan and Rosenbaum 2013, 204). A study found that, compared to schools without a college coach, students in coached schools completed more applications and enrolled in college at higher rates. Specifically, schools with coaches increased the percentage of students who applied to three or more colleges by 4.7 percentage points, FAFSA completion by 2.6 percentage points, and college enrollment by 1.7 percentage points (Stephan and Rosenbaum 2013).

Some college advising interventions have been successful in examining the causal effects on college access. One pilot study successfully randomized college counseling services to high-achieving, low-income high school students (Avery 2010). Results from this study found that students who received the college counseling treatment submitted more college applications overall and were more likely to enroll in institutions that Barron's ranked as "Most Competitive" (Avery 2010). A more recent study examined the effects of the college advising program, Bottom Line, by capitalizing on a cutoff score that determined admission into the program (Castleman and Goodman 2014). The results from this study found that the Bottom Line advising program "effectively shifts students' enrollment away from two-year or discouraged four-year colleges and toward four-year colleges that the organization believes will be more successful at graduating those students" (Castleman and

Goodman 2014, 10). Specifically, students who received college counseling were 41 percentage points more likely to enroll in one of the colleges that Bottom Line encourages students to attend after high school compared to control group students (Castleman and Goodman 2014).

The Role of Higher Education Institutions in Supporting College Access

Colleges and universities themselves are a critical component of college access and can serve as a mechanism for supporting a student's exposure to higher education by the information they provide, their marketing and recruitment efforts in a community, and their proximity to a high school or community (Perna 2006). As mentioned before, the juxtaposition of institutional type and social identities may influence a student's college choice decisions (Nora 2004). There are three types of institutions that enroll a significant number of low-income students, first-generation college students, and students of color: community colleges, for-profit institutions, and minority-serving institutions (MSIs).

Community Colleges

American community colleges provide technical-based education, transferable general education coursework, dual enrollment opportunities for high school students, and developmental education (Pierce 2017; Pope 2006). Community colleges play a critical role in providing access to low-income students, first-generation college students, and students of color (Bragg 2001; Mullin 2012; Pope 2006). In fact, community colleges "provide access to nearly half of all minority undergraduate students and more than 40% of undergraduate students living in poverty" (Mullin 2012, 4).

Although community colleges play a significant role in providing college access to many underserved student populations (Bragg 2001; Mullin 2012; Pope 2006), researchers have documented low transfer rates from community colleges to bachelor-awarding institutions. For instance, Monaghan and Attewell (2015) found in their study that "only 42 percent of BA-intending students who enter community college and say they hope to transfer actually do transfer to a 4-year institution" (81). The authors found that the number of credit hours completed at a community college could increase the probability of transferring to a bachelor-awarding institution, but the "BA attainment rate for those who transfer after earning a few credits is not statistically significantly different from that of students who completed 60 or more credits at their initial college" (Monaghan and Attewell 2015, 82). However, Monaghan and Attewell (2015) found that "on average transfers are just as likely to graduate with a BA as equivalent students who started at a 4-year college" (85). Thus, educational leaders and policy makers must continue to develop and implement strategies and policies that best support the pathways to BA attainment for students who begin at a community college. Although there are challenges related to transfer rates and these challenges need to continue to be addressed, community colleges provide a critical point of access to higher education for students of color and low-income students unlike many of their 4-year institutional counterparts (Bragg 2001).

For-Profit Institutions

For-profit institutions have been providing educational access for hundreds of years (Beaver 2009; Wittnebel 2012). There are close to 3,400 for-profit institutions participating in the federal financial aid program (Lederman 2015). For-profit four-year institutions and two-year institutions recently saw a 16 percent and 22 percent decrease in student enrollment, respectively (Lederman 2015). Although for-profit institutions enroll significant proportions of the low-income students and students of color in higher education (Beaver 2009; Deming, Goldin, and Katz 2013; Oseguera and Malagon 2011), these institutions have been the center of educational controversy and criticism (Beaver 2009; Wittnebel 2012).

For-profit institutions have been criticized because of students' low degree attainment rates and concerns related to the financial benefits of attending these institutions (Beaver 2012; Deming, Goldin, and Katz 2013). For-profit institutions have lower bachelor's degree completion rates than do non-selective four-year institutions (Deming, Goldin, and Katz 2013). Additionally, students who enroll at a for-profit institution "are more likely to be unemployed and have lower earnings once they leave school than those in community colleges and other nonselective institutions" (Deming, Goldin, and Katz 2013, 141). In addition, students at for-profit institutions have higher student loan default rates (Beaver 2012; Deming, Goldin, and Katz 2013).

With these challenges, educators, policy makers, and the general public may question the value of for-profit institutions. However, given the number of for-profit institutions (over 3,400), it is important to recognize that for-profit institutions are not all the same (Lederman 2015). Deming, Goldin, and Katz (2013) recognized several benefits of for-profit institutions. First, for-profit institutions tend to be more responsive to the labor market (Deming, Goldin, and Katz 2013). Second, "Students might turn to for-profit colleges because local community colleges are over-crowded or otherwise unable to meet their needs" (Deming, Goldin, and Katz 2013, 147). Finally, students at for-profit institutions are less likely to enroll in remedial courses than students at community colleges; remedial course have been questioned regarding their academic effectiveness and for hindering one's progression to graduation (Complete College America 2011; Deming, Goldin, and Katz 2013).

Minority-Serving Institutions

MSIs have a rich and critical history of supporting the educational access and graduation of students of color (Baez, Gasman, and Turner 2008; Harmon 2012). MSIs also serve a significant population of low-income students (Center for MSIs, "A Brief History of MSI" n.d.). Currently, "MSIs enroll over 20 percent of all college students in the United States" (Gasman and Conrad 2013, 1). Although historically Black colleges and universities (HBCUs), tribal colleges and universities (TCUs), Hispanic-serving institutions (HSIs), and Asian American and Native American Pacific Islander–serving institutions are often the focus when discussing MSIs (Baez, Gasman, and Turner 2008; Center for MSIs, "A Brief History of MSI" n.d.; Harmon 2012), MSIs also include other institutions that receive federal funding: Alaska Native–serving institutions, Native American–serving nontribal institutions, Native Hawaiian–serving institutions, and predominantly Black institutions (Center for MSIs, "What Are MSIs" n.d.).

Researchers have discussed how MSIs have lower retention rates than the national average and often have limited financial resources due to inequitable state funding (Baez, Gasman, and Turner 2008; Gasman and Conrad 2013). For example, Jacobs (2015) reported on how HBCUs have dealt with inequitable government funding and a decrease in student enrollment, which contributes to some people's concerns about the long-term survival of these institutions. However, it is important to recognize how inequitable state funding, the lack of attention to MSIs, and the elevation of historically White institutions may be tied to larger systemic issues that have denied, excluded, and marginalized people of color throughout history. In addition, MSIs tend to contribute to students' sense of well-being and have a high success rate with graduating racial minority students in science, technology, engineering, math, and education (Gasman and Conrad 2013). While each MSI has their own rich history, Baez, Gasman, and Turner (2008) argued that the leadership of MSIs should collaborate with each other to "form coalitions that can press state and federal governments for more funding" and expose "a cultural/political phenomenon to all" (4).

Conclusion

College access in the United States is a complex, challenging, and sometimes controversial topic. Although there has been a steady rise in overall enrollment and the enrollment of some underserved populations, gaps remain. As policy conversations continue to shift toward college completion, it is important that access not be forgotten. The progress our nation has made in the realm of college access could be threatened if we redirect too many resources and too much attention from college access to college completion.

It is important that we continue to examine how enrollment is stratified by income, race, socioeconomic status, and other demographic characteristics. It is also critical that we continue to examine which policies and interventions have positive impacts on college access, and for which populations. College access is the foundation and without it, college completion is not an option.

References

Adelman, Clifford. 2007. "Do We Really Have a College Access Problem?" *Change: The Magazine of Higher Learning* 39(4): 48–51.

American Council on Education. 2017. "American College Application Campaign." Accessed May 1, 2017. http://www.acenet.edu/news-room/Pages /American-College-Application-Campaign.aspx

Avery, Christopher. 2010. "The Effects of College Counseling on High-Achieving, Low-Income Students." No. w16359. National Bureau of Economic Research Publications. Accessed May 1, 2017. http://www.nber.org/papers /w16359

Baez, Benjamin, Marybeth Gasman, and Caroline Sotello Viernes Turner. 2008. "On Minority-Serving Institutions." In *Understanding Minority-Serving Institutions*, edited by Benjamin Beez, Marybeth Gasman, and Caroline Sotello Viernes Turner, 3–17. Albany, NY: State University of New York Press.

Baum, Sandy, Jennifer Ma, and Kathleen Payea. 2013. *Education Pays, 2013: The Benefits of Higher Education for Individuals and Society. Trends in Higher Education Series*. New York: College Board Advocacy & Policy Center.

Beaver, William. 2009. "For-Profit Higher Education: A Social and Historical Analysis." *Sociological Viewpoints* 25:53–73.

Beaver, William. 2012. "Fraud in For-Profit Higher Education." *Society* 49(3): 274–278.

Becker, Gary. 1993. *Human Capital: A Theoretical and Empirical Approach with Special References to Education*. Chicago: University of Chicago Press.

Bergerson, Amy A. 2009. "Special Issue: College Choice and Access to College: Moving Policy, Research, and Practice to the 21st Century." *ASHE Higher Education Report* 35(4): 1–141.

Bettinger, Eric P., Bridget Terry Long, Philip Oreopoulos, and Lisa Sanbonmatsu. 2012. "The Role of Application Assistance and Information in College Decisions: Results from the H&R Block FAFSA Experiment." *The Quarterly Journal of Economics* 127(3): 1205–1242.

Bourdieu, Pierre. 1986. "The Forms of Capital." In *Handbook of Theory and Research for the Sociology of Education*, edited by John G. Richardson, 15–29. Westport, CT: Greenwood.

Bourdieu, Pierre, and Jean-Claude Passeron. 1977. *Reproduction in Society, Education and Culture*. Beverly Hills, CA: Sage Publications.

Bowen, William G., Matthew M. Chingos, and Michael S. McPherson. 2009. *Crossing the Finish Line: Completing College at America's Public Universities*. Princeton, NJ: Princeton University Press.

Bragg, Debra D. 2001. "Community College Access, Mission, and Outcomes: Considering Intriguing Intersections and Challenges." *Peabody Journal of Education* 76(1): 93–116.

Bragg, Debra D. 2013. "Pathways to College for Underserved and Nontraditional Students." In *The State of College Access and Completion: Improving College Success for Students from Underrepresented Groups*, edited by Laura W. Perna and Anthony Jones, 34–56. London: Routledge.

Bryan, Julia, Cheryl Moore-Thomas, Norma L. Day-Vines, and Cheryl Holcomb-McCoy. 2011. "School Counselors as Social Capital: The Effects of High School College Counseling on College Application Rates." *Journal of Counseling & Development* 89(2): 190–199.

Cabrera, Alberto F., Regina Deil-Amen, Radhika Prabhu, Patrick T. Terenzini, Chul Lee, and Robert E. Franklin Jr. 2006. "Increasing the College Preparedness of At-Risk Students." *Journal of Latinos and Education* 5(2): 79–97.

Cahalan, Margaret, and David Goodwin. 2014. *Setting the Record Straight: Strong Positive Impacts Found from the National Evaluation of Upward Bound. Re-Analysis Documents Significant Positive Impacts Masked by Errors in Flawed Contractor Reports*. Washington, DC: Pell Institute for the Study of Opportunity in Higher Education. Accessed May 1, 2017. http://www.pellinstitute.org/publications-Setting_the_Record_Straight_June_2014.shtml

Castleman, Benjamin, and Joshua Goodman. 2014. "Intensive College Counseling and the College Enrollment Choices of Low Income Students." Accessed May 1, 2017. http://curry.virginia.edu/uploads/resourceLibrary/30_College_Counseling_and_Enrollment_Choices.pdf

Center for Minority Serving Institutions (MSIs). n.d. "A Brief History of MSI." Accessed May 1, 2017. http://www2.gse.upenn.edu/cmsi/content/brief-history-msi

Center for Minority Serving Institutions (MSIs). n.d. "What Are MSIs?" Accessed May 1, 2017. http://www2.gse.upenn.edu/cmsi/content/what-are-msis

Cheslock, J. J., and Rick Kroc. 2012. "Managing College Enrollments." In *The Handbook for Institutional Researchers*, edited by Richard D. Howard, Gerald W. McLaughlin, and William E. Knight, 221–236. San Francisco, CA: Jossey-Bass.

Choy, Susan. 2011. "Students Whose Parents Did Not Go to College: Postsecondary Access, Persistence, and Attainment. Findings from the Condition of Education, 2001." *The Condition of Education, 2001*. Accessed May 1, 2017. https://nces.ed.gov/pubs2001/2001072_Essay.pdf

Coleman, James S. 1988. "Social Capital in the Creation of Human Capital." *American Journal of Sociology* 94:S95–S120.

College Advising Corps. 2017a. "Mission and History." Accessed May 1, 2017. http://advisingcorps.org/our-work/mission-history/

College Advising Corps. 2017b. "Our Results." Accessed May 1, 2017. http://advisingcorps.org/our-impact/our-results/

College Foundation of North Carolina. 2017. "North Carolina College Application Week." Accessed May 1, 2017. https://www1.cfnc.org/College_Application_Week/College_Application_Week.aspx

Complete College America. "About Complete College America." 2017. Accessed May 1, 2017. http://completecollege.org/about-cca/

Complete College America. "Time Is the Enemy." 2011. Accessed May 1, 2017. http://completecollege.org/docs/Time_Is_the_Enemy.pdf

Cornwell, Christopher, David B. Mustard, and Deepa J. Sridhar. 2006. "The Enrollment Effects of Merit-Based Financial Aid: Evidence from Georgia's HOPE program." *Journal of Labor Economics* 24(4): 761–786.

Corwin, Zoe B., Julia E. Colyar, and William G. Tierney. 2005. "Introduction. Engaging Research and Practice: Extracurricular and Curricular Influences on College Access." In *Preparing for College: Nine Elements of Effective Outreach*, edited by William Tierney, Zoe Corwin, and Julia E. Colyar, 1–9. Albany: State University of New York Press.

Davis, Jeff. 2010. *The First-Generation Student Experience: Implications for Campus Practice, and Strategies for Improving Persistence and Success.* Sterling, VA: Stylus.

Deil-Amen, Regina, and Ruth Lopez Turley. 2007. "A Review of the Transition to College Literature in Sociology." *Teachers College Record* 109(10): 2324–2366.

Deming, David, Claudia Goldin, and Lawrence Katz. 2013. "For-Profit Colleges." *The Future of Children* 23(1): 137–163.

Dynarski, Susan. 2000. "Hope for Whom? Financial Aid for the Middle Class and Its Impact on College Attendance." *National Tax Journal* 53(3): 629–661.

Dynarski, Susan. 2002. "Race, Income, and the Impact of Merit Aid." *Who Should We Help? The Negative Social Consequences of Merit Scholarships.* Paper presented at Harvard University entitled "State Merit Aid Programs: College Access and Equity." Accessed May 1, 2017. https://eric.ed.gov/?id=ED468845

Dynarski, Susan. 2004. "The New Merit Aid." In *College Choices: The Economics of Where to Go, When to Go, and How to Pay for It*, edited by Carolina M. Hoxby, 63–100. Chicago: University of Chicago Press.

Engle, Jennifer, and Vincent Tinto. 2008. *Moving Beyond Access: College Success for Low-Income, First-Generation Students.* Washington, DC: Pell Institute for the Study of Opportunity in Higher Education. Accessed May 1, 2017. http://www.pellinstitute.org/publications-Moving_Beyond_Access_2008.shtml

Gasman, Marybeth, and Clifton F. Conrad. 2013. "Minority Serving Institutions: Educating All Students." Penn Center for Minority Serving Institutions. Philadelphia: University of Pennsylvania.

Griffith, Amanda L. 2011. "Keeping Up with the Joneses: Institutional Changes Following the Adoption of a Merit Aid Policy." *Economics of Education Review* 30(5): 1022–1033.

Harmon, Noel. 2012. *The Role of Minority-Serving Institutions in National College Completion Goals.* Washington, DC: Institute for Higher Education Policy.

Harper, Shaun R. 2010. "An Anti-Deficit Achievement Framework for Research on Students of Color in STEM." *New Directions for Institutional Research* 148:63–74.

Hearn, James C., Anthony P. Jones, and Elizabeth R. Kurban. 2013. "Access, Persistence, and Completion in the State Context." In *The State of College Access and Completion: Improving College Success for Students from Underrepresented Groups*, edited by Laura W. Perna and Anthony Jones, 166–189. London: Routledge.

Heller, Donald E. 1997. "Student Price Response in Higher Education: An Update to Leslie and Brinkman." *The Journal of Higher Education* 68(6): 624–659.

Heller, Donald E. 2003. "The Policy Shift in State Financial Aid Programs." In *Higher Education: Handbook of Theory and Research*, edited by Michael B. Paulsen, 221–261. New York: Springer.

Heller, Donald E. 2013. "The Role of Finances in Postsecondary Access and Success." In *The State of College Access and Completion: Improving College Success for Students from Underrepresented Groups*, edited by Laura W. Perna and Anthony Jones, 96–114. London: Routledge.

Horng, Eileen L., Brent J. Evans, Jesse D. Foster, Hoori S. Kalamkarian, Nicole F. Hurd, and Eric P. Bettinger. 2013. "Lessons Learned from a Data-Driven College Access Program: The National College Advising Corps." *New Directions for Youth Development* 140:55–75.

Hossler, Don, John Braxton, and Georgia Coopersmith. 1989. "Understanding Student College Choice." In *Higher Education: Handbook of Theory and Research 5*, edited by J. C. Smart, 231–288. New York: Agathon.

Hu, Shouping, Matthew Trengove, and Liang Zhang. 2012. "Toward a Greater Understanding of the Effects of State Merit Aid Programs: Examining Existing Evidence and Exploring Future Research Direction." In *Higher Education: Handbook of Theory and Research 27*, edited by J.C. Smart, 291–334. Netherlands: Springer.

Humphrey, Keith B. 2006. "At the Crossroads of Access and Financial Stability: The Push and Pull on the Enrollment Manager." *College and University* 82(1): 11–16.

Jacobs, Robert. 2015. "There's an Unprecedented Crisis Facing America's Historically Black Colleges." *Business Insider.* Accessed May 1, 2017. http://www.businessinsider.com/hbcus-may-be-more-in-danger-of-closing-than-other-schools-2015-3

Jayakumar, Uma, Rican Vue, and Walter Allen. 2013. "Pathways to College for Young Black Scholars: A Community Cultural Wealth Perspective." *Harvard Educational Review* 83(4): 551–579.

Jones, Anthony P. 2013. "Introduction: Improving Postsecondary Access, Persistence, and Completion in the United States: Setting the Stage." In *The State of College Access and Completion: Improving College Success for Students from Underrepresented Groups,* edited by Laura W. Perna and Anthony Jones, 1–9. London: Routledge.

Labaree, David F. 1997. "Public Goods, Private Goods: The American Struggle over Educational Goals." *American Educational Research Journal* 34(1): 39–81.

Lederman, Doug. 2015. "The Shrinking Sector." *Inside Higher Ed.* Accessed May 1, 2017. https://www.insidehighered.com/news/2015/07/24/number -profit-colleges-declines-enrollments-wither

Linnehan, Frank, Christy H. Weer, and Paul Stonely. 2011. "High School Guidance Counselor Recommendations: The Role of Student Race, Socioeconomic Status, and Academic Performance." *Journal of Applied Social Psychology* 41(3): 536–558.

Lumina Foundation. 2016. "A Stronger Nation." Accessed May 1, 2017. http:// strongernation.luminafoundation.org/report/2016/

Ma, Jennifer, Matea Pender, and Meredith Welch. 2016. "Education Pays 2016." *The College Board.* Accessed May 1, 2017. https://trends.collegeboard .org/sites/default/files/education-pays-2016-full-report.pdf

McDonough, Patricia M. 1997. *Choosing Colleges: How Social Class and Schools Structure Opportunity.* Albany, NY: State University of New York Press.

McDonough, Patricia M. 2005. "Counseling Matters: Knowledge, Assistance, and Organizational Commitment in College Preparation." In *Preparing for College: Nine Elements of Effective Outreach,* edited by William G. Tierney, Julia E. Colyar, and Zoë B. Corwin, 69–87. Albany, NY: State University of New York Press.

Means, Darris R., Ashley B. Clayton, Johnathan G. Conzelmann, Patti Baynes, and Paul D. Umbach. 2016. "Bounded Aspirations: Rural, African American High School Students and College Access." *The Review of Higher Education* 39(4): 543–569.

Means, Darris R., Tara D. Hudson, and Elizabeth Tish. 2016. "A Snapshot of College Access and Inequity: Photovoice and the Pathways to Higher Education for Underserved Youth." Paper presentation, Association for the Study of Higher Education, Columbus, Ohio, November 12.

Means, Darris R., and Kimberly B. Pyne. 2016. "After Access: Underrepresented Students' Postmatriculation Perceptions of College Access Capital." *Journal of College Student Retention: Research, Theory & Practice* 17(4): 390–412.

Miller, Abby, Katherine Valle, Jennifer Engle, and Michelle Cooper. 2014. "Access to Attainment: An Access Agenda for 21st Century College Students." *Institute for Higher Education Policy.* Accessed May 1, 2017. http://www

.ihep.org/sites/default/files/uploads/docs/pubs/ihep_access-attainment _report_layout_rd5_web.pdf

Monaghan, David B., and Paul Attewell. 2015. "The Community College Route to the Bachelor's Degree." *Educational Evaluation and Policy Analysis* 37(1): 70–91.

Mullin, Christopher M. 2012. "Why Access Matters: The Community College Student Body." *AACC Policy Brief.* Accessed May 1, 2017. http://www .aacc.nche.edu/Publications/Briefs/Pages/pb02062012.aspx

Museus, Samuel D., and Peter N. Kiang. 2009. "Deconstructing the Model Minority Myth and How It Contributes to the Invisible Minority Reality in Higher Education Research." *New Directions for Institutional Research* 142:5–15.

Museus, Samuel D., and Julie J. Park. 2015. "The Continuing Significance of Racism in the Lives of Asian American College Students." *Journal of College Student Development* 56(6): 551–569.

Museus, Samuel D., and Rican Vue. 2013. "Socioeconomic Status and Asian American and Pacific Islander Students' Transition to College: A Structural Equation Modeling Analysis." *The Review of Higher Education* 37(1): 45–76.

Ness, Erik C., and Richard Tucker. 2008. "Eligibility Effects on College Access: Under-represented Student Perceptions of Tennessee's Merit Aid Program." *Research in Higher Education* 49(7): 569–588.

Nora, Amaury. 2004. "The Role of Habitus and Cultural Capital in Choosing a College, Transitioning from High School to Higher Education, and Persisting in College among Minority and Nonminority Students." *Journal of Hispanic Higher Education* 3(2): 180–208.

Oseguera, Leticia, and Maria C. Malagon. 2011. "For-profit Colleges and Universities and the Latina/o Students Who Enroll in Them." *Journal of Hispanic Higher Education* 10(1): 66–91.

Paulsen, Michael B. 1990. *College Choice: Understanding Student Enrollment Behavior. ASHE-ERIC Higher Education Report No. 6.* ASHE-ERIC Higher Education Reports, The George Washington University, One Dupont Circle, Suite 630, Dept. RC, Washington, D.C. 20036-1183.

Paulsen, Michael B. 2001. "The Economics of Human Capital and Investment in Higher Education." In *The Finance of Higher Education: Theory, Research, Policy, and Practice*, edited by Michael B. Paulsen and John C. Smart, 55–94. New York: Agathon Press.

Perez, William. 2009. *We Are Americans: Undocumented Students Pursuing the American Dream.* Sterling, VA: Stylus.

Perna, Laura W. 2006. "Studying College Access and Choice: A Proposed Conceptual Model." In *Handbook of Theory and Research*, edited by Michael B. Paulsen, 99–157. New York: Springer.

Perna, Laura W. 2015. "Improving College Access and Completion for Low-Income and First-Generation Students: The Role of College Access and Success Programs." Accessed May 1, 2017. http://repository.upenn.edu /gse_pubs/301

Perna, Laura W., and Elizabeth R. Kurban. 2013. "Improving College Access and Choice." In *The State of College Access and Completion: Improving College Success for Students from Underrepresented Groups*, edited by Laura W. Perna and Anthony Jones, 10–33. London: Routledge.

Perna, Laura W., Heather T. Rowan-Kenyon, Scott Loring Thomas, Angela Bell, Robert Anderson, and Chunyan Li. 2008. "The Role of College Counseling in Shaping College Opportunity: Variations across High Schools." *The Review of Higher Education* 31(2): 131–159.

Pierce, Dennis. 2017. "The Rise of Dual Enrollment." *Community College Journal* 87(5): 16-24.

Pope, Myron L. 2006. "Meeting the Challenges to African American Men at Community Colleges." In *African American Men in College*, edited by Michael J. Cuyjet, 210–236. San Francisco: Jossey-Bass.

Pope, Devin G., and Jaren C. Pope. 2014. "Understanding College Application Decisions: Why College Sports Success Matters." *Journal of Sports Economics* 15(2): 107–131.

Pusser, Brian. 2006. "Reconsidering Higher Education and the Public Good." In *Governance and the Public Good*, edited by William G. Tierney, 11–28. Albany, NY: State University of New York Press.

Pyne, Kimberly B., and Darris R. Means. 2013. "Underrepresented and In/visible: A Hispanic First-Generation Student's Narratives of College." *Journal of Diversity in Higher Education* 6(3): 186–198.

Quaye, Stephen John, Kimberly A. Griffin, and Samuel D. Museus. 2015. "Engaging Students of Color." In *Student Engagement in Higher Education: Theoretical Perspectives and Practical Approaches for Diverse Populations*, edited by Shaun R. Harper and Stephen John Quaye, 15–36. New York: Routledge.

Schulz, Scott Andrew. 2008. "Mastering the Art of Balance: An Analysis of How Private Master's Institutions Pursue Institutional Quality, Access, and Financial Stability through Their Enrollment Practices." *Enrollment Management Journal* 2(1): 65–100.

Scott-Clayton, Judith, and Bruce Sacerdote. 2016. "Access to Higher Education: Introduction to the Special Issue." *Economics of Education Review* 51:1–3.

Seftor, Neil S., Arif Mamun, and Allen Schirm. 2009. "The Impacts of Regular Upward Bound on Postsecondary Outcomes 7–9 Years after Scheduled High School Graduation." Mathematica Policy Research Report. Washington, DC: U.S. Department of Education, Policy and Program Studies Service. Accessed May 1, 2017. https://www.mathematica-mpr.com/our -publications-and-findings/publications/the-impacts-of-regular -upward-bound-on-postsecondary-outcomes-79-years-after-scheduled -high-school-graduation

Snyder, Thomas D., Cristobal de Brey, and Sally A. Dillow. 2016. "Digest of Education Statistics 2015, NCES 2016-014." National Center for Education Statistics. Accessed May 1, 2017. https://nces.ed.gov/pubs2016/2016014.pdf

Stanton-Salazar, Ricardo. 1997. "A Social Capital Framework for Understanding the Socialization of Racial Minority Children and Youths." *Harvard Educational Review* 67(1): 1–41.

Stephan, Jennifer L., and James E. Rosenbaum. 2013. "Can High Schools Reduce College Enrollment Gaps with a New Counseling Model?" *Educational Evaluation and Policy Analysis* 35(2): 200–219.

Strayhorn, Terrell L. 2010. "When Race and Gender Collide: Social and Cultural Capital's Influence on the Academic Achievement of African American and Latino Males." *The Review of Higher Education* 33(3): 307–332.

Swail, Watson Scott, and Laura W. Perna. 2002. "Pre-college Outreach Programs." In *Increasing Access to College: Extending Possibilities for All Students*, edited by W. G. Tierney and L. S. Hagedorn, 15–34. Albany: State University of New York Press.

Toma, J. Douglas, and Michael E. Cross. 1998. "Intercollegiate Athletics and Student College Choice: Exploring the Impact of Championship Seasons on Undergraduate Applications." *Research in Higher Education* 39(6): 633–661.

Toutkoushian, Robert K., Robert S. Stollberg, and Kelly A. Slaton. 2018 "Talking 'Bout My Generation." *Teachers College Record* 120(4).

Umbach, Paul D., and Ashley B. Clayton. 2014. "Making It Free and Easy: Exploring the Effects of North Carolina College Application Week on College Access." Paper presented at the Annual Conference of the Association for the Study of Higher Education. Accessed May 1, 2017. http://paul-umbach.com/research/

U.S. Department of Education. 2017a. "Federal TRIO Programs—Home Page." Accessed May 1, 2017. https://www2.ed.gov/about/offices/list/ope/trio/index.html

U.S. Department of Education. 2017b. "Student Service Home Page." Accessed May 1, 2017. https://www2.ed.gov/about/offices/list/ope/student-service.html#programs

Venezia, Andrea, and Michael W. Kirst. 2005. "Inequitable Opportunities: How Current Education Systems and Policies Undermine the Chances for Student Persistence and Success in College." *Educational Policy* 19(2): 283–307.

Ward, Lee, Michael J. Siegel, and Zebulun Davenport. 2012. *First-generation college students: Understanding and improving the experience from recruitment to commencement.* San Francisco: John Wiley & Sons.

Wittnebel, Leo. 2012. "Predator or Proprietor? Challengers to the Liberal Education Throne." *The Journal of Continuing Higher Education* 60(2): 58–65.

Yosso, Tara J. 2005. "Whose Culture Has Capital? A Critical Race Theory Discussion of Community Cultural Wealth." *Race Ethnicity and Education* 8(1): 69–91.

CHAPTER THREE

Challenges in Retention and Access

Charlie Andrews and Rebekah Schulze

Overview

As colleges and universities in the United States respond to societal pressures and legislative mandates to increase the number of individuals who earn college degrees, these institutions have placed a greater emphasis on tracking and promoting the academic success of their students. The effort to track student success has been particularly important in an era marked by expanded access to college. Although greater access is definitely a step toward achieving the goal of a more educated society, it is simply not enough. There have been several research studies and numerous reports on the state of higher education in this country highlighting that almost half of all students who enroll in U.S. colleges and universities have failed to earn a college degree within six years (Freeman, Hall, and Bresciani 2007; Stratton, O'Toole, and Wetzel 2008). Those numbers are even more discouraging for students of color, first-generation college students, and students from lower socioeconomic backgrounds, as all of those factors have been correlated with even lower retention and graduation rates (Otero, Rivas, and Rivera 2007; Tinto 2008). As such, the traditional "sink or swim" approach (which relied heavily on the hope that students entered college with all of the skills and academic preparation needed to be successful) has been replaced by one that utilizes a litany of resources, outreach efforts, and programs designed to facilitate and support students' retention and graduation. According to Steven Aragon (2009), efforts aimed at increasing student learning have created a "challenge for educators to become more competent in the knowledge, skills, abilities, and attitudes that can lead to greater retention" (9).

In addition to the moral and societal reasons for institutions of higher education supporting student persistence, Vincent Tinto urged educators in the early 1990s to increase the number of students who earn college degrees in order to remain competitive in the global knowledge economy (1993). Since then, both state and federal legislators have reinforced that notion by demanding an increase in the percentage of citizens with two-year and four-year degrees. To achieve that goal, there has been an increasing emphasis on creating greater access to higher education using the rationale that if more students are encouraged to attend (coupled with a willingness to admit them) then more individuals will earn college degrees. Of course, the push to admit more students has also raised the question of whether today's college students have the academic preparation needed to be successful in college. That is especially true within the context of measuring and tracking retention rates since institutions are being held accountable for cultivating the success of the students who they admit. More recent work by Tinto has reinforced this concern by highlighting the fact that although access to higher education has increased, the percentage of degree completion has remained relatively constant and has actually decreased for certain populations of students (2008).

Retention for All Students

For all of these reasons and more, the challenges related to tracking and improving student retention cannot be examined without considering the ways that increased access influences those efforts. Along those lines, a "one size fits all" approach to retention simply does not work. As past research has pointed out, more than half of the variance in institutional retention rates is directly related to attributes of the students rather than to institutional factors (Freeman, Hall, and Bresciani 2007). Today's students are diverse, not only in the traditional racial/ethnic/demographic sense but also with regard to their academic backgrounds and myriad personal experiences and stories that have a direct impact on their ability and willingness to persist in the complex landscape they encounter in college. Once again, within the context of greater access, colleges and universities need to develop new approaches and strategies to facilitate the academic progress of students with varying levels of competence in both content knowledge and skills needed to be successful in college. Some of the leading authorities on why college students drop out prior to earning a college degree agree that many students are academically unprepared for the rigors of the academic environments they encounter in college (Daley 2010; Stratton, O'Toole, and Wetzel 2008; Tinto 1993).

According to the decades of research on student success and retention, one strategy that may help institutions fulfill their duty to supporting the success of all students is to focus on ensuring academic success early on. There have been several empirical studies noting that a student's "grade performance at the end of the first term has been shown to be the most important factor in college persistence and eventual degree attainment" (Johnson, 2006, 927). As a result, retention has become about more than just referring students to tutoring services and hoping those will fill the gaps to get them through the prescribed courses and curriculum. As discussed later in the chapter, effective retention efforts must also rely on proactive and intentional advising systems that guide students to take appropriate courses (especially early on) and pursue majors that coincide with their interests and abilities. If institutions truly want to have a positive influence on retention, it is important that they do more to set students up for success by ensuring that they enroll in courses that align with their academic preparation and by providing them with additional resources and support.

Recent Trends and Developments

Addressing Retention without Limiting Access

Given the growing emphasis on retention and graduation, colleges need to examine the myriad factors that are impacting their successes in these areas. An easy solution for most, the "low hanging fruit" as it were, for many institutions has simply been to raise admissions standards. The thought process clearly being that admitting higher caliber students will inevitably improve retention and graduation rates. Unfortunately, when institutions adopt this policy, there are direct negative impacts on access. With the increased pressure on providing greater access to all students, which helps improve social mobility and ensures that more traditionally underrepresented populations and students from less privileged/lower socioeconomic backgrounds view college as a viable option and earn college degrees, there have emerged obvious conflicts with institutions' overall retention goals. In other words, there now exists a struggle between addressing access while also responding to the pressure to improve retention and graduation rates. Although many factors affect retention and graduation rates, the complexity and importance of access must be understood and examined in order to make progress on improving retention and graduation rates.

The concept of access to higher education is one that is consistently on the minds of college administrators. With the rising cost of education, and the continued concerns of inequitable access, institutions continue to look for ways to offer fair and equitable ways for students to obtain college degrees. As demographics continue to shift, institutions must determine what they value and how they measure educational outcomes. In other words, how do they value what they measure, and how do they measure what they value? On the macro level, higher education is still holding to definitions and standards put forth decades ago, leaving many institutions feeling frustrated and stuck. The new era of performance-based funding (addressed later in the chapter), which on the surface is designed to increase retention and graduation, might actually be negatively impacting issues related to providing greater access. Until there is a true educational cultural shift across all institutions, the access needle will not move in any significant or meaningful way. As institutions attempt to respond to calls for greater retention and look even deeper at societal values, they need to be conscious of the policies and decisions that have a significant impact on college access. Thus, higher education, as a whole, needs to be very careful not to undo years of efforts to level the playing field.

The Attainment Gap

Efforts and initiatives related to access aim to ensure equal and fair educational opportunities for all students, regardless of personal characteristics such as race, ethnicity, religion, gender, sexual orientation, socioeconomic status, and disability, among others. Institutions have a responsibility to adopt policies that help eliminate historical gaps and remove any barriers that may unfairly advantage one group over another. Getting a college degree has become even more important in today's world. A job that once required only a high school diploma now requires a bachelor's degree. What once required a bachelor's degree now requires a master's degree, and so on. It has been estimated that by 2018, over 62 percent of the jobs available in the United States will require at least some college credential, such as an associate's degree or higher. More than half of those will require at least a bachelor's degree (Moore, Bridgeland, and Dilulio 2010). To achieve some sort of social mobility and attain a level of economic success—even a modest one—it is becoming increasingly important to attain a college degree. Not all students who are of traditional college age attend institutions at an equal rate. When looking at the current graduation rates being projected, there will not be enough students to fill these jobs by 2025. At that time, it is projected that there will not be enough qualified people to fill open positions in the job market – perhaps as many as 23 million people less qualified for these positions than there are today (Lumina Foundation 2009).

What is perhaps more concerning is that although our country's demographics continue to diversify, our college population does not. Higher education today continues to be stratified by race and social class. Minorities are enrolling in college at an alarmingly lower rate than their White counterparts, and, when they do enroll, it is into the country's less selective institutions. Nineteen percent of White students enrolled in elite institutions, as compared to 9 percent of Blacks, and 16 percent of Latinos (Snyder, de Brey, and Willow 2015). In addition to where they attend, those students from underrepresented populations who do attend college are struggling to persist and graduate. As such, there is a significant attainment gap among students. According to the Lumina Foundation over 30 percent of White adults had four years of college, as compared to 18 percent for African Americans, and 12 percent for Latinos (2009). Income levels are also a factor since socioeconomic status also plays a role with access and college attainment levels. Families whose income levels are under $25,000 face even more barriers attending and graduating from college, having a less than 6 percent chance of finishing (Pell Institute for the Study of Opportunity in Higher Education 2004). Although our demographics have indeed changed over the years, the composition of our college attendees and graduates has failed to keep pace (see Table 3.1).

As colleges and universities work to solve the retention puzzle, they must also consider strategies for narrowing the gap created by the lower retention and completion rates of traditionally underrepresented groups. That does not mean, however, that the answer to improving retention is (or should be) to limit access to those students who are less likely to succeed. Accordingly, several educational scholars have chimed in to remind colleges and universities that they have a responsibility to provide greater access to these traditionally underrepresented groups while also working diligently to remove the barriers that have decreased the percentage of low-income and minority students who complete a four-year degree (Otero, Rivas, and Rivera 2007; Tinto 2008). As Williford and Wadley (2008) noted, the goal of educators should be to enable students to be successful. That applies to all students, from all backgrounds and abilities.

There needs to be an institutional cultural shift at the elite colleges and universities. Institutions need to get away from the idea that only *some*

Table 3.1   Enrollment and Four-Year Graduation Rates by Race and Ethnicity

	Asian	Black	Hispanic	White
Public Nonprofit Four Year	7% (41.6%)	14% (18.6%)	13% (24.8%)	58% (37.9%)
Private Nonprofit Four Year	5% (63.9%)	11% (29.7%)	**9% (47.2%)**	58% (56.3%)
For-Profit Four Year	3% (34.8%)	**25% (9.6%)**	15% (20.9%)	37% (26.4%)

Graduation rates in parentheses.

Source: NCES, IPEDs, 2014, and Fall 2008 Cohort.

campuses are Hispanic-serving institutions, or minority-serving. *All* institutions need to be prepared to support the diversifying groups of students who are enrolling and, at every level—the faculty, staff, and administration—they need to accurately reflect the demographics of the student body. In addition, the programming, curriculum, and institutional missions need to mirror the diverse student body they serve. Until this happens, higher education will continue to be racially and ethnically stratified. Right now, first-generation, low-income, and racially diverse students are not attending elite institutions at a rate that accurately reflects the population. Regardless of institution, they are also not graduating at the same rates as their more advantaged peers. Higher education administrators and scholars have a responsibility to figure out why and address it.

The Problem

Why is this happening? Although there is widespread agreement of the need to increase access to education to increase greater social equity, there lacks consensus about the main barriers for first-generation and minority students (Forster 2006; Kahlenberg 2006). Some argue it is primarily financial, while others say the main issue is lack of academic preparedness. It would be hard to argue that students from low socioeconomic households are not, on the whole, less academically prepared than their wealthier peers. They do not have access to the same social, financial, and cultural capital of their peers; they attend schools that are typically lower performing; they do not have the same resources as their peers for additional support such as tutoring, college counseling, SAT/ACT exam preparation courses, and extracurricular activities, all of which help with college entrance. They also typically graduate high school with lower GPAs and standardized test scores. With all of that in mind, it is also important to note that academic barriers and financial ones are intertwined. One depends on the other and both have contributed to the challenges that many of the historically underserved students have faced while trying not only to make it to college but also to graduate with a degree.

Although first-generation, low-income, and minority students might be able to attend college financially, assuming they are academically prepared, this does not address the disparity of *where* they are attending. As noted in the table above, higher education institutions in the United States are still highly socially and racially stratified, with the majority of low-income and minority students attending public universities. Much more research needs to be done to see why this is still happening, as many of those elite institutions have removed financial barriers for students from low socioeconomic families. Many institutions are creating affordability programs—in effect, removing the financial barriers that in the past have kept students from lower socioeconomic backgrounds from attending. These types of programs began with elite institutions such as Stanford and Harvard, where administrators made a commitment to enable students from families making less than a certain annual income level to attend for free. Other schools have followed, making the commitment that any student who qualifies for financial aid will graduate debt free. Additionally, institutions across the country have created partnerships with local schools and community colleges, through dual enrollment and transfer articulation agreements. In doing so, they helped to increase their enrollments, as well the diversity of their applicants. Many facets of higher education, however, still remain largely undiversified, and the gap will continue to widen if the issue is not addressed and measures are not taken to intentionally eradicate the discrepancies.

Performance-Based Funding

Of course, there have been efforts and programs put in place over the years to attempt to address these inequities. Programs such as the federal TRIO programs (Upward Bound, Talent Search, and Student Support Service) and various other bridge and access programs, both federal and local, have been created to help better prepare and support underserved populations and decrease the barriers keeping them from attending and succeeding in higher education. These programs, however, have traditionally focused on college preparation and readiness. More recently, the emphasis has shifted from not just getting these underserved populations into college, but in retaining and graduating them at higher rates.

This shift occurred most notably with the emergence of performance-based funding metrics that have increased accountability measures within state institutions in an effort to hold institutions accountable for addressing attainment gaps and improving the success rates of all students. Rapidly fading are the days when institutions were given money simply for bodies in seats—per FTE (full-time enrolled) counts. When this was this case, the focus was more on increasing the number of students who enrolled when the doors opened for business each fall semester. Retaining them for any length of time, let alone graduating them, was less of a concern as long as there were new students to take the place of those who might have left. In today's climate of performance-based funding models (which have made their way to several states and are expected to be adopted in many more), the focus, however, has entirely shifted toward one that emphasizes retention and completion rates. When state governments change the game and declare that funding levels will be based on success metrics such as retention and graduation rates, colleges and universities respond by prioritizing efforts that have the most potential to improve those metrics. As that culture shift has occurred, it has become clear that colleges and universities have been pressured into utilizing retention and graduation rates as evidence of their effectiveness (Schugurensky 1999; Watson 2010). This recent trend has pushed the retention and completion agenda to the forefront and has further complicated issues related to access.

Other Considerations

Although many institutions are trying to stay true to their missions and serve all populations, there are a number of other factors that can derail those efforts. In many cases, those factors relate directly to legislative initiatives that make it increasingly difficult to successfully support students in an equitable fashion. In addition to the performance-based funding models that are being adopted in states all across the country, which almost tempt institutions to limit access in order to improve metrics and vie for more funding, many states have also passed laws making student success and retention efforts increasingly difficult.

Another key consideration relates to the increased pressure that college and universities are facing to produce more graduates in the STEM fields, especially at research universities where those disciplines directly link to preeminence. As such, preparing high school and college students for careers in STEM is at the forefront of the United States' educational concerns (Sadler et al. 2012). That pressure to increase the number of STEM degrees is also driven by the fact that the United States has fallen behind other nations and now has one of the lowest rates of graduating students from the STEM disciplines (Thompson and Bolin 2011). Data from the past several years has confirmed that trend by demonstrating how enrollment in these programs has steadily increased but graduation rates have not. This creates another challenge for those concerned with improving overall retention and graduation rates, because students, especially those from low-income and minority backgrounds, are much more successful in completing degrees outside of the STEM disciplines.

Another area of concern is the rise in students' mental health issues and how these can impact retention and graduation. Annually, 50 percent of college students experience overwhelming anxiety, 30 percent experience symptoms of depression that make it difficult for them to function, 6.6 percent consider suicide, and 1.1 percent report actually making a suicide attempt (American College Health Association 2010). Drum et al. found that 55 percent of students have experienced some form of suicidal ideation in their lifetime (2009). Although there are many programs to help students financially, this does not ensure academic success, as "undiscovered, unaddressed, and unmet mental and behavioral health problems among college students can interfere with academic success as surely as a lack of computers, competent staff, or textbooks" (Suicide Prevention Center 2008, 27). Mental health issues continue to impact students on college campuses, and not addressing these issues will certainly have a negative impact on these students' abilities to persist and graduate.

All of these issues have a direct impact on retention efforts mounted by colleges and universities. Improving retention is a complex and difficult problem, to which there is no easy solution. Each campus needs to determine what its major obstacles are and address them all as directly as possible.

Proposed Responses/Reforms

Given the current landscape within higher education, colleges and universities have been expending a great deal of their energies and resources on finding new ways to support student success. The factors described in the last section have complicated these efforts as institutions also work to address issues related to access and responding to the diverse needs of today's students. The process of identifying and admitting students who are "college ready" can no longer rely on traditional measures such as standardized test scores and grade point averages. As such, it has become the responsibility and duty of colleges and universities to recognize, address, and reconcile the challenges created by the lack of academic preparation, financial concerns, and nonacademic factors that threaten their students' success. Increased accountability measures and pressure to produce higher retention and graduation rates in order to maintain funding have also raised the stakes. That threat of reduced funding has administrators strategizing how to utilize existing resources to develop or enhance initiatives that will produce measurable outcomes related to both student persistence and completion rates. This section of the chapter presents a few of the most common and most recent responses to the questions and challenges related to improving retention in an era of increased access.

Intrusive/Proactive Advising

One of the most prominent strategies for addressing and improving retention is the use of targeted academic advising to track and monitor student's academic behavior. Often referred to as intrusive or proactive advising, this approach to facilitating student success often involves identifying students who will benefit from particular interventions based on their struggles with completing certain courses or their inability to stay on track and make progress toward their intended degree. In some cases, intrusive advising efforts also center on outreach to students who might need a nudge or reminder regarding enrollment status (e.g., when they have not registered for future terms or they are not enrolled in enough credits to be considered full-time). More recently, institutions have also begun to utilize predictive analytics to identify student behaviors that are most correlated with attrition and to identify students who are most likely to struggle. As mentioned previously, colleges and universities have also recognized the importance of early success and, as a result, are using targeted advising to ensure that students take the right courses at the right time and that they consider the sequencing of courses to avoid toxic combinations. Finally, the use of early alert systems, which rely heavily on faculty sharing timely information about students who are struggling in their courses (due to failing/subpar assignments or lack of attendance), is another means of using proactive advising to help promote early success and intervening before students end up with failing grades or find themselves on academic probation.

Despite the long history of student services and student support programs, most institutions have only recently started to pay more attention to the actual progress that their students are making toward earning their degrees. For decades, students were left to their own devices to take the correct courses, pass those courses, and hopefully find themselves with enough credits to graduate. At most colleges and universities (except for perhaps the small liberal arts colleges), it was not uncommon nor even alarming for students to take five or six years to earn their bachelor's degree. Often, that path to graduation involved taking and retaking the same courses multiple times and ending up with credits in courses that were not even required. With the increased emphasis on improving retention and the realization that more students enter college with gaps in their academic preparation, colleges and universities are now employing the use of intrusive advising techniques to monitor students' academic progress. For instance, if a student majoring in engineering is struggling to pass his or her math courses or a business major registers for nothing but psychology or political science courses, those students' academic advisers are now more likely to make immediate and frequent contact with them. The subsequent conversations should not only help the students understand the importance of passing critical courses (and all courses for that matter) but might also include a discussion about considering a change of major.

Another element of intrusive or proactive advising relates to students' enrollment patterns. Advisers can take the lead in identifying students as they reach important moments in their academic careers and intervene during those typical "stopping out points." This might be when a student has registered for courses that will put them offtrack for on-time graduation, changed majors, or missed the registration deadline. If advisers can better track enrollment patterns they might be able to catch financial or personal problems early on and help keep students on the path to graduation. By keeping track of students as they progress, institutions can require that they speak with an academic adviser at key points in their programs as well as inform the development of policies that restrict students from making changes to their academic programs that could delay their graduation.

Institutions that have begun to institute more proactive advising strategies have also relied on the use of predictive analytics to identify students who need targeted advising outreach. That can include an analysis of students who have been successful in rigorous or limited access programs to identify those factors that are most predictive of that success. For example, data may indicate that students who earned a minimum grade in certain prerequisite courses were more likely to graduate or, on the flip side, that students who failed a particular course were more likely to drop out or change majors. The use of this type of institutional data can help inform decisions about which students would most benefit from an advising intervention. Predictive analytics are being widely used by companies who specialize in product development and customer service, so it stands to reason that higher education institutions take advantage of data to help address their retention problems. In addition to in-house analyses, there are also a number of companies (e.g., EAB, Civitas Learning, Oracle Analytics) that have developed platforms utilizing students' academic and behavioral data to assist institutions with predicting which students may struggle. Identifying those students early on and providing them with additional support and attention before they struggle is at the core of the proactive approach to delivering academic advising services.

Studies have shown that students who enjoy early academic success are more likely to persist and succeed academically. That is why there has been an increased focus on supporting new students as they navigate the transitions they face during their first year. With that in mind, intrusive academic advising can be utilized to support first-year students and assist them with the process of establishing a foundation on which to build. According to retention scholars like Vincent Tinto and many others, the first year is the most critical in determining whether students will persist (Stovall 2000). An article that appeared in *About Campus* reinforced the notion that institutions must pay particular attention to and channel significant resources toward the first year if they want to improve student retention (Siegel 2011). From an advising perspective, that should include helping students make smart choices that will contribute to their likelihood for success and maintain their confidence about managing the rigors of college-level work.

Finally, an additional advising strategy involves the use of an early alert system to track student progress. The key to this strategy is that it identifies students who are struggling academically as early in the semester as possible. When looking at students in their first semester of college, getting a sense that they are potentially struggling before the first set of grades are even posted goes a long way in helping students enjoy early success. This would also benefit the more underprepared students, thus addressing some of the access concerns presented in this chapter. The greatest challenge to this early alert strategy is that it relies on buy-in and participation from the faculty in order to make it work. When that faculty support can be garnered, institutions can have great success and have a positive impact on their retention strategies by having advisers reach out to students who might be failing exams, not turning in work, or not attending classes. In many cases, these early alert outreach efforts can provide students with the just-in-time nudge or wake-up call that can help them turn their semester around and avoid the potential detrimental effects on retention. The research on retention has shown that students who start the second year in good academic standing are significantly more likely to persist and graduate than those who begin year two on probation.

High-Impact Practices/Increased Student Engagement

Another emerging approach aimed at addressing the retention problem builds upon earlier research on the academic benefits of facilitating students' connection to and engagement with the institutional community and culture. As administrators and researchers began to delve deeper into that notion of student engagement, and as they coupled that with the recognition that students face significant challenges during their transition to college (or to a new institution if they transfer from one to another), they began to examine the types of activities, services, and programs that had the greatest impact on students to identify those that were most likely to predict student success. As Alexander Astin and other pioneers of the college student development movement found, getting students involved on campus can have lasting positive effects on their academic success. More recent research, however, has highlighted the fact that involvement and getting students engaged extends beyond exposure to and participation in cocurricular activities. In fact, there are several other factors that contribute to a student's level of engagement and that can be linked to increased student persistence and retention (Kilgo, et al. 2015). Some of those factors include an overall connection to campus that can be achieved through participation in research, access to resources, cultural activities, and the opportunity to foster relationships with faculty and other mentors (Cole and Espinoza 2008).

As more data were gathered to show how getting students more connected leads to higher levels of academic success, the Association of American Colleges and Universities (AAC&U) identified a number of "high-impact practices" (HIPs) that have been shown to promote greater student engagement, enhance student learning, and foster higher levels of student persistence and retention. In addition to the work that AAC&U has done to verify those claims, other researchers have also found direct links between students' participation in HIPs and their levels of engagement and retention (Brownell and Swaner 2010; Kuh 2008). These HIPs can include academic courses as well as more social or experiential programs, and they help inform and influence

the type of teaching and cocurricular opportunities that have proven to promote deeper learning among students from all backgrounds. That is particularly important because, as mentioned previously, part of the challenge of
addressing retention relates to issues of access and student preparation. As a
result, many institutions have begun to focus on encouraging students to
participate in HIPs as a strategy for increased student learning as well as a
means for addressing the achievement gaps that exist across their student
populations. In fact, the data from the research studies referenced above
have shown that HIPs not only correlate with the success of all students, but
that the benefits for students from traditionally underserved populations
(who are also often commuter students) are disproportionately higher than
those of their peers from more advantaged backgrounds.

More specifically, the HIPs that AAC&U identified as significant for
achieving higher levels of student engagement and learning were: first-year
seminars and experiences, common intellectual experiences, academic
learning communities, writing-intensive courses, collaborative assignments
and projects, undergraduate research, diversity/global learning (including
study abroad experiences), service or community-based learning, intern-
ships, and capstone courses and projects. Although many institutions have
offered several of these options for many years, the connection between student participation and higher rates of student retention and engagement has
only become evident more recently. That is why these HIPs have become a
central part of the conversation surrounding retention and why they are
often a featured point of discussion at any professional conference that
addresses strategies for student success. For those institutions who were
already offering several HIPs on their campuses, the research has helped
solidify their existence and validate the decision to allocate resources to support them. For other institutions, the race is on to develop or adopt as many
HIPs as possible as they attempt to implement proven methods for improving
retention and graduation rates. The benefits to student learning and engagement (which are both linked to retention) that HIPs can potentially provide
are also a key reason that many colleges and universities have made participation in one or more HIPs a mandatory part of their students' collegiate
experience.

According to the National Survey of Student Engagement (NSSE), the
main reason that HIPs are so effective for promoting student success is that
they involve activities, courses, and programs that require meaningful interactions and connections between students and faculty (2007). NSSE's list of
HIPs is a smaller one but it does not include any that are not also included on
the list that was developed by AAC&U. According to their Web site, NSSE
publishes their findings on how student engagement correlates with student
retention and graduation rates. Also, for institutions whose students participate in completing their annual survey, they provide data on how HIPs

impact their students as well as comparison data related to peer groups that each institution helps them identify. As institutions scramble to keep up with their peers, it is also interesting to note that the NSSE data have shown that student participation in HIPs varies more greatly among students within an institution than it does across comparable institutions.

One important note regarding the benefits of HIPs is that they can definitely provide significant support for institutional efforts to help students achieve the early success that was highlighted in previous sections of the chapter. Requiring students to participate in first-year seminars and experiences is perhaps the most obvious way that HIPs support students' successful transition and help them connect quickly to their institutions. Well before researchers began studying the impact of HIPs, there were several studies showing that students who participate in first-year seminar courses are retained at higher rates than those who do not. In addition to first-year seminars, there are several other HIPs that can be promoted as a means for solidifying student engagement during their first year. One example of a common intellectual experience that has been widely used with first-year students at colleges and universities across the United States is the use of a common reading program. By reading the same book and having intentional opportunities to engage with the topic, first-year students get immediately engaged with an academic activity that also allows them to relate and connect to students with whom they may not otherwise interact. Common HIPs that can support the learning and engagement of first-year students include intensive writing experiences and courses, giving them the opportunity to participate in learning communities and incorporating service-learning activities. Although HIPs can and should be utilized throughout students' entire collegiate experiences, introducing students to them early on will foster their early success and encourage them to take advantage of additional HIPs in future years as they work toward graduation.

Curricular/Course Redesign

There have been numerous initiatives and interventions that have made their way into college retention plans over the years, but these have almost exclusively focused on student support services and programs designed to assist students outside of the classroom. One of the flaws with that approach is that those support services typically require that students opt in or show up in order to take advantage of the extra assistance. Even the best tutoring program or student counseling center can only be effective if students are willing to make the time and effort to take advantage of them. As the pressure to improve retention rates has increased and institutions have been faced with the challenge of supporting less academically prepared students, they have begun to turn their attention to identifying barriers within the classroom. That shift makes sense given that reforms made within the class-room and within the courses or curriculum that students are required to complete have the potential to impact the greatest number of students. That is not meant to imply that existing support services and cocurricular pro-grams are ineffective or even that they wouldn't benefit from additional resources, but even the most used of those services still only touches a frac-tion of the total student population. As such, the classroom (which online students experience virtually) is perhaps the only resource on campus that every student has interacted with and relied on as a tool for earning a college degree.

Another reason for focusing on the actual courses and instruction as a strategy for assisting with retention efforts relates to the fact that students' precollege academic preparation poses a potential barrier to those efforts. Several research studies have reported that students' perceptions about their academic deficiencies and their reported difficulties with completing college-level work often lead to the decision to leave college (Freeman, Hall, and Bresciani 2007; Johnson 2006). Along those same lines, Johnson noted that college student attrition is strongly associated with poor college grades and below-average academic performance (2006). More recent research has also highlighted the fact that students' lack of self-knowledge regarding their aca-demic abilities contributed to their lack of success and potential decision to depart (Daley 2010). The ways that this combination of factors (students who are academically unprepared, poor college grades/performance, and lack of self-knowledge regarding academic abilities) contributes to student attrition supports the notion that course redesign initiatives should be explored, espe-cially in the courses in which students traditionally struggle most. In other words, institutions are now examining how they can use different pedago-gies and teaching modalities to foster the academic needs and aspirations of today's college students.

So, then, why haven't past retention efforts focused more on course rede-sign and reforming students' classroom experiences? The most obvious answer is probably that change isn't easy. Higher education institutions have struggled with change for as long as they have existed and the faculty, in particular, have a long history of tradition to uphold. Those faculty members must also be open to the notion that what they are doing might be ineffective for strides to be made toward redesigning courses or engaging them in poten-tially uncomfortable conversations about pedagogical reform. The difficulty of these conversations has perhaps also contributed to the delay in focusing on this approach to addressing the retention problem. However, given the current state of increased accountability and heightened interest in finding new ways to increase retention and graduation rates, administrators have become more and more willing to ask faculty to take an introspective look at their crucial role in supporting and fostering student success. This shift has also been supported by the leading scholars on college student retention. Tinto, for instance, has noted that the classroom has been the aspect of college campuses that has been given the least attention during all of the efforts directed at improving retention. As he noted:

> The classroom is the building block upon which student retention is built and the pivot around which institutional action for student retention must be organized. *But while institutions have invested for years in retention programs, they have yet to significantly reshape the college classroom and student experiences within the classroom.* If we hope to make significant gains in retention and graduation, institutions must focus on the classroom experience and student success in the classroom and align classrooms to one another in ways that provide students a coherent pathway that propels them to program completion. (Tinto 2012, 124–125)

As institutions begin to embark on these course redesign efforts, they have set their sights first on the key gateway courses that many students are required to take and that have traditionally led to the most frequent cases of student failure. Focusing on these gateway courses, which have large student enrollment and low success rates, also aligns with the retention literature that has emphasized the importance of the first year. As such, gateway redesign projects have begun to emerge at colleges and universities across the country. The Gardner Institute is leading that movement and has devoted resources, research, funding, and entire educational conferences to their "Gateways to Completion" initiative. Although these efforts are still evolving, there have already been a number of institutions that have signed on to work with the Gardner Institute team to reform the way they teach gateway courses and to increase the level of their students' learning. In some cases, like in Michigan and Georgia, state institutions have joined forces and resources to tackle their course redesign efforts. Part of that effort involves utilizing institutional data to examine where redesign (i.e., in which courses) may have the potential to impact the greatest number of students. Florida International University (FIU), for instance, utilized institutional data to identify 17 gateway courses that had high enrollment, high failure rates, or both. Those 17 courses were also selected because of their utility in predicting students who were most at-risk of leaving the institution. After identifying and selecting those critical gateway courses, FIU's faculty development professionals worked closely with faculty to encourage and empower them to identify ways of using creative pedagogies and revising curriculum in an effort to improve both student learning and passing rates. Although their work is ongoing, they have already begun to see results. For example, their work with the faculty who teach and administer the college algebra course has resulted in improved instructional practices, more collaborative planning among instructors, and an almost 40 percent increase in the number of students who pass the course. From a retention perspective, that has been especially important given the number of students who have typically left FIU after failing their college algebra course. Over three years, the institution saw a dramatic decrease in the number of students who dropped out after failing college algebra (from 279 students in 2010 to 93 students in 2013).

Retention efforts must include an intentional decision to focus on instruction. That does not mean that faculty need to water down their content or lower their expectations but rather work with their colleagues and students to implement the type of proven instructional strategies that help make content more accessible and ultimately increase student learning. That type of reform has been shown to benefit all students but is even more critical for supporting students from traditionally underserved populations and those who are battling to overcome challenges related to their academic preparation. It has also been shown to be particularly useful at campuses with significant commuter student populations (like FIU) and for those institutions with students who have competing demands for their time (work, family responsibilities, etc.). For these students, Tinto has pointed out that the classroom may be one of the only (if not the only) places where these students have the opportunity to meet and develop relationships with their peers and faculty members. Robert Reason echoed his sentiment, stating that "the classroom may be the only context regularly inhabited by every student," particularly on campuses with many commuter students (2009, 678). All of this points to the need for putting the classroom at the center of the strategic discussions about improving student retention, especially within the context of higher education institutions that aim to provide greater access to all types of students.

Summary

Greater accountability measures and the use of metrics that track student persistence and graduation are becoming a more common tool for evaluating effectiveness at U.S. colleges and universities. Consequently, those institutions must address the needs of their diversifying student populations as they respond to the complex issues surrounding college student retention. That response will require that they pay particular attention to the barriers that not only threaten student success but also cause or contribute to the existing attainment gaps for traditionally underrepresented students. Although minority enrollment at colleges and universities has increased, graduation rates have not. As demographics continue to change, higher education has a responsibility to improve the support mechanisms that lead to higher retention and graduation rates without abandoning its commitment to provide greater access. Those efforts must also take into account the impediments that students' academic preparation, financial constraints, motivation, grit, and access to resources can have on their ability to persist.

With regard to how retention relates to and intersects with access, it should suffice to say that colleges and universities cannot (or at least should not) simply admit students that are more qualified or "college ready." The pressures and impacts of performance-based funding models can surely tempt institutions to consider new admission standards, but that approach would obviously conflict with higher education's goal of providing greater access. Once again, it is not enough to simply admit more students from diverse backgrounds and then hope that they will succeed. Institutions need to consider the individual attributes and needs of their students and then allocate resources to support those students' progress toward graduation. Issues of retention and finding ways to support students from all backgrounds are complicated further by factors such as mental health concerns, the rising cost of college attendance, and an increased emphasis on producing STEM degrees.

Institutions have already begun to implement a number of initiatives aimed at improving their retention and graduation rates. Although borrowing ideas is certainly common within higher education, colleges and universities need to identify and implement those strategies that will work best for their students. There are some strategies, however, that every institution may be able to build from and adapt to fit their specific needs. For example, ensuring that students experience success early on in their academic journey has proven to cultivate long-term academic success for all students. Implementing strategies related to intrusive or proactive advising, increased student engagement through participation in high-impact practices, and curricular or course redesign can also help institutions achieve the type of results they seek with regard to their retention goals. Although there is no singular strategy for solving the retention dilemma, it is clear that the conversations surrounding the issue are here to stay. Colleges and universities need to accept that fact and then use it to drive their efforts to foster and support student success.

References

American Association of Colleges and Universities. 2008. "High-Impact Educational Practices." Accessed March 15, 2017. http://www.aacu.org/leap/hips

American Association of Colleges and Universities. 2017. "Campus Models and Case Studies." Accessed March 15, 2017. https://www.aacu.org/campus-model/3325

American College Health Association, 2010. "Reference Group Executive Summary. Spring 2010." Accessed March 30, 2011. http://www.achancha.org/docs/ACHA-NCHAII

Aragon, Steven. 2000. "Beyond Access: Methods and Models for Increasing Retention and Learning among Minority Students." *New Directions for Community Colleges* 112:1–12.

Brownell, Jayne E., and Lynn E. Swaner. 2010. *Five High-Impact Practices: Research on Learning Outcomes, Completion and Quality.* Washington, DC: Association of American Colleges and Universities.

Cole, Darnell, and Araceli Espinoza. 2008. "Examining the Academic Success of Latino Students in Science, Technology, Engineering and Mathematics (STEM) Majors." *Journal of College Student Development* 49(4): 285–300.

Daley, Frank. 2010. "Why College Students Drop Out and What We Do About It." *College Quarterly* 13(3): 1–5.

Drum, David J., Chris Brownson, Adryon B. Denmark, Shanna E. Smith. 2009. "New Data on the Nature of Suicidal Crises in College Students: Shifting the Paradigm." *Professional Psychology: Research and Practice* 40(3): 213–222.

Forster, Greg. 2006. "The Embarrassing Good News on College Access." *The Chronicle of Higher Education* 52(27): B50–B51.

Freeman, Jerrid P., Eric E. Hall, and Marilee J. Bresciani. 2007. "What Leads Students to Have Thoughts, Talk to Someone about, and Take Steps to Leave Their Institution?" *College Student Journal* 41(4): 755–770.

Johnson, Iryna Y. 2006. "Analysis of Stopout Behavior at a Public Research University: The Multi-Spell Discrete-Time Approach." *Research in Higher Education* 47(8): 905–932.

Kahlenberg. Richard. 2006. "Socioeconomic School Integration." *NCL Review* 85:1545–1594.

Kilgo, Cindy A., Jessica K. Ezell Sheets, and Ernest T. Pascarella. 2015. "The Link Between High-Impact Practices and Student Learning: Some Longitudinal Evidence." *Higher Education* 69(4): 509–525.

Kuh, George D. 2008. *High-Impact Educational Practices: What They Are, Who Has Access to Them, and Why They Matter.* Washington, DC: Association of American Colleges and Universities.

Lumina Foundation for Education. 2009. "A Stronger Nation through Higher Education: How and Why Americans Must Meet a 'Big Goal' for College Attainment." Special Report. Accessed March 29, 2017. http://www.luminafoundation.org/publications/A_stronger_nation_through_higher_education-htt.pdf

Moore, Laura A., John M. Bridgeland, and John J. Dilulio. 2010. "Closing the College Completion Gap: A Guidebook for the Faith Community." The Bill and Melinda Gates Foundation. Accessed March 28. http://www.civicenterprises.net/MediaLibrary/Docs/closing_the_completion_gap.pdf

National Survey of Student Engagement. 2007. "High-Impact Practices." Accessed March 15, 2017. http://nsse.indiana.edu/html/high_impact_practices.cfm

Otero, Rafael, Olivia Rivas, and Roberto Rivera. 2007. "Predicting Persistence of Hispanic Students in Their 1st Year of College." *Journal of Hispanic Higher Education* 6:163–173.

Pell Institute for the Study of Opportunity in Higher Education. 2004. "Raising the Graduation Rates of Low-Income College Students." Accessed March 29, 2017. http://www.pellinstitute.org/graduates/Pell_Web.pdf

Reason, Robert D. 2009. "An Examination of Persistence Research through the Lens of a Comprehensive Conceptual Framework." *Journal of College Student Development* 50(6): 659–682.

Sadler, Philip M., Gerhard Sonnert, Zahra Hazari, and Robert Tai. 2012. "Stability and Volatility of STEM Career Interest in High School: A Gender Study." *Science Education* 96(3): 411–427.

Schugurensky, Daniel. 1999. "Higher Education Restructuring in the Era of Globalization." *Comparative Education: The Dialectic of the Global and the Local* 1999:283–304.

Siegel, Michael J. 2011. "Reimagining the Retention Problem: Moving Our Thinking from End-Product to By-Product." *About Campus* 15:8–18.

Stovall, Martina. 2000. "Using Success Courses for Promoting Persistence and Completion." *New Directions for Community Colleges* 112:44–54.

Stratton, Leslie S., Dennis M. O'Toole, and James N. Wetzel. 2008. "A Multinomial Logit Model of College Stopout and Dropout Behavior." *Economics of Education Review* 27(3): 319–331.

Suicide Prevention Center. 2008. *Suicide Risk and Prevention for Lesbian, Gay, Bisexual, and Transgender Youth*. Newton, MA: Education Development Center.

Thompson, Ruthanne, and Greta Bolin. 2011. "Indicators of Success in STEM Majors: A Cohort Study." *Journal of College Admission* 212:18–24.

Tinto, Vincent. 1993. *Leaving College: Rethinking the Causes and Cures of Student Attrition* (2nd ed.). Chicago, IL: University of Chicago Press.

Tinto, Vincent. 2008. "When Access Is Not Enough." The Carnegie Foundation for the Advancement of Teaching, August.

Tinto, Vincent. 2012. *Completing College: Rethinking Institutional Action*. Chicago, IL: University of Chicago Press.

Watson, Lisa. 2010. "Retention and Graduation Rates as Performance Indicators in 2-year and 4-year Postsecondary Institutions." Unpublished doctoral dissertation. University of New Orleans.

Williford, A. Michael, and Joni Y. Wadley. 2008. "How Institutional Research Can Create and Synthesize Retention and Attrition Information." *Association for Institutional Research* 108:1–24.

CHAPTER FOUR

Undocumented Students: Welcome or Not?

Glenda Droogsma Musoba

Undocumented students have aspirations for college degrees and the American dream but have a legal status that puts their education and future in jeopardy. These students, most of who came to the United States as very young children, face barriers related to college admission, financing their education, and maintaining legal status under the current Deferred Action for Childhood Arrivals (DACA) policies. Even when DACA gives undocumented students legal status while they are students, it does not address their long-term situation. Comprehensive immigration reform that deals with undocumented students and their families has been politically challenging, and a patchwork of state and federal policies continues to leave these students in limbo.

Young adults who live in the United States without the benefits of legal residency often have the same dreams and goals as their neighbors and friends. They often want to go to college or join the workforce and achieve the American dream. Yet being undocumented carries a stigma in our society and legal constraints on their educational opportunities. Most came into this country at a young age but until they acquire DACA status, they live in fear that their parents or family could be deported to their parents' home country. Most just wish for a regular life.

Karen's parents wanted a better life for her and her siblings so they decided to go to the United States to find work when Karen was two years old. Karen's dad got a job milking cows for a large farm, and her mother cleaned hotel rooms. When Karen was 12, they bought a house, and Karen moved on to middle school. That's also when her parents decided Karen was old enough to know that they had overstayed the tourist visa they had used to enter the country 10 years earlier. Karen now understood why they never went to see grandpa and grandma—it was too risky to cross the border when undocumented. Although being undocumented was very worrisome to her parents, life had seemed normal for Karen. That is until she turned 16 and all her friends were getting their driver's licenses and she could not. She made up some story about not feeling ready, but through tears told her best friend the real reason. She had always been a proud Texan, but now she was not sure she belonged. She also could not get a summer job before her senior year of high school so she babysat for her aunt to make a few dollars. That is when the worry became a daily issue. How was she going to get admitted to college? How much would it cost? Could she get any financial aid? She was an A student, but was all the studying worth it if she could not go to college anyway?

Karen is typical of many undocumented high school and college students. The vast majority came to the United States when they were too young to be a part of the decision. Their parents come for the economic opportunity and freedom in America to give their children a better life. The children go to school and grow up in the United States. Some have never been to their parents' country of citizenship, may not speak the language, and in all meaningful ways see themselves as Americans.

Generally, the term undocumented refers to individuals who do not currently have legal status to be in the United States—either they came illegally or they came legally but overstayed their time limit. Some people refer to these individuals as illegal immigrants, but the term undocumented is preferred. For those who came as children, the decision was not their own. There are students who came to the United States who are undocumented, and there are students who were born in the United States and therefore have citizenship, but their parents are undocumented. There are often families where the youngest children are citizens and the older siblings and parents are undocumented. Although citizen students of undocumented parents have an easier time than undocumented students, they still face many challenges. For example, until relatively recently, Florida used parents' residential status to determine in-state tuition eligibility; therefore citizen students who grew up in Florida were charged the out-of-state rate. This is less common now, but citizen students still have parents who are afraid both to provide income documentation and to have other interactions with the government, making their students ineligible for financial aid. These fears are not unfounded, particularly with the political rhetoric and anti-immigrant protests.

In addition, there are categories such as temporary protected status for individuals from unsafe countries or permanent residents who are not citizens (green card holders). Traditionally these students are not considered undocumented. They may not have all the benefits of citizenship, but they are legal and therefore do not have the same fears and challenges. Yet, President Trump included permanent residents in his first executive order banning immigrants from seven countries he identified as national security risks: Iraq, Syria, Sudan, Iran, Somalia, Libya, and Yemen (Keneally 2017).

Overview

The first significant federal action on undocumented children was the 1982 *Plyler v. Doe* decision by the U.S. Supreme Court, which determined states could not deny K-12 students a free public education on account of their immigration status. Although this decision offered general guidance, it did not apply to college students. Under the William J. Clinton administration, Congress passed the Illegal Immigration Reform and Immigrant Responsibility Act of 1996, which among other policies denied undocumented immigrants access to federally funded programs including federal student financial aid for college.

Undocumented students are often called DREAMers in honor of proposed legislation called the Development, Relief, and Education for Alien Minors Act. In 2010 the U.S. House of Representatives passed the DREAM Act, but it failed to overcome a Senate filibuster and failed to become law. Although the bill has been proposed since, it has never been voted on or passed. The DREAM Act would provide a path to citizenship for childhood arrivals who enroll in college or go to the military and meet other conditions. Many advocates for the undocumented still believe this is the best hope for undocumented young adults, but it is not comprehensive immigration reform because it says nothing about their family members.

In 2012, President Obama signed the DACA executive order, which allows college students who came to the United States early in life to apply for deferred status while in college. This allows them to legally work and obtain a driver's license, and it exempts them from deportation. DACA requires that participants (a) are at least 15 years of age but not over 30, (b) came to the United States before their 16th birthday, (c) have continuously resided in the United States since 2007, (d) were physically present in the United States on June 15, 2012, and when making the DACA application, (e) have no other lawful status, (f) are in high school, recently graduated or earned a GED, or are honorably discharged from the U.S. military, and (g) do not have a significant criminal record or pose a threat to national security or public safety. DACA is not legal status, it is a judgment that they are not criminally in the United States and will not be deported. Because DACA is an executive order rather than legislation, it can be overturned by a future president.

In 2014, Obama signed the Deferred Action for Parents of Americans and Lawful Permanent Residents (DAPA) executive order, which would have expanded access to deferred status to more people, but a federal district court judge in Texas blocked the implementation. In a tie four–four decision, the U.S. Supreme Court upheld the lower court's ruling, and therefore DAPA was not implemented. One student commenting on the decision spoke of her fear of her parents' deportation, "You work really hard to get ahead in life, but does any of it matter when you can lose what matters most to you in a moment's notice?" (Rogers 2016).

Recent Trends and Developments

A patchwork of state policies makes college or university access confusing and unfair. Individual state legislatures have taken action welcoming or hostile to undocumented students. At one time or another Arizona, Colorado, Georgia, and Indiana passed legislation restricting undocumented students from receiving in-state tuition, and South Carolina and Alabama banned undocumented students from attending public higher education institutions at any price. In contrast, as of 2016, 18 states had in-state tuition policies for undocumented students who meet certain conditions such as they graduated from high school in the state and have lived in the state for a certain length of time (ULead Network 2016).

This hodgepodge of state policies and DACA executive order offer only a short-term solution to college-age students, as it only defers their undocumented status until graduation. DACA and state policies do not have a path to citizenship or another permanent legal status.

Approximately 65,000 undocumented students graduate from high school every year in the United States. This is from a group of students with a disproportionately low high school graduation rate, therefore the college-going rate for undocumented 18-year-olds is low. Undocumented high school graduates face three key issues for access and success: admission, tuition rate, and financial aid eligibility. Will they be admitted if they live in a state that is "hostile" to undocumented students? Further, things that are simple for documented students are a barrier for the undocumented, even in "friendly" states. For example, most online applications will not advance without the student filling in every cell including the social security number. As undocumented students do not have social security numbers, they must get special assistance to bypass this failsafe feature of the application. This was not designed to be a barrier, but it is.

Once admitted, what price will they be charged? Are they lucky enough to live in a state with in-state tuition policies for undocumented students that grew up there? If they are charged out-of-state tuition prices, it is often too expensive particularly if their parents are working class. Third, are they eligible for any state or institutional financial aid? The FAFSA (Free Application for Federal Student Aid) is often a wake-up call for undocumented students. Their inability to complete the FAFSA or be eligible for federal need-based aid makes college seem unaffordable. In Texas, for instance, undocumented students are eligible for the state's financial aid, but states like this are the exception.

Eligibility for institutional financial aid is usually up to the institution, so in some instances undocumented students are eligible. Private institutions have even more control of their institutional aid and this has particularly been an avenue to higher education for high-achieving undocumented students (Flores 2016). Yet, average and low-achieving undocumented students are not offered private college merit scholarships, making private college tuition out of reach.

DACA and in-state tuition policies have had a positive impact. For instance, the introduction of an in-state tuition policy is correlated with a 14 percent increase in high school graduations among undocumented students in the state (Latino Policy Institute 2011). Similarly, Flores (2010) concluded undocumented Hispanic students in states with in-state tuition policies are 1.54 times more likely to go to college than similar students in states without in-state tuition policies. A similar study in a group of Texas schools showed a 27 percent increase in college enrollment after Texas implemented its in-state tuition policy (Dickson and Pender 2013).

With the election of Donald Trump to the presidency, there is great uncertainty about the future of undocumented residents. Trump vilified undocumented immigrants in his election campaign, promised to immediately overturn Obama's DACA executive order, and said he would deport all undocumented people. Those who fear Trump's words fear DACA records could be used as a list of people to deport. Since taking office, Trump has softened his rhetoric and told ABC News "I do have a big heart . . . Where you have great people that are here that have done a good job, they should be far less worried" (Colvin 2017). White House insiders are divided and suggest Trump is working toward a more long-term solution, but no action has been taken as of this writing.

Approximately 750,000 undocumented students who were childhood arrivals earned deferred status under DACA. Yet gaining access to higher education is only the first step. Undocumented students face all the hurdles of citizen students plus hurdles unique to their undocumented status. In addition to the admission, tuition, and financial aid eligibility issues discussed above, undocumented students face challenges in their career choice, emotional stress, feelings of inclusion/exclusion, language barriers, first-generational status, ability/inability to participate in certain programs, and identity development challenges (Gildersleeve, Rumann, and Mondragón 2010). Academic programs that require fingerprinting or identity checks are perceived as threatening. Similarly, applying for a parking permit or renting textbooks usually means providing a driver's license number, yet before DACA this was not possible for undocumented students.

Undocumented students realize that some careers are not accessible (Ortiz and Hinojosa 2010). For instance, a college major that requires a background check will expose their undocumented status even if they are under DACA. Most public schools require background checks for student teachers and teachers. The same is true for some medical professions. Even if they find a career that interests them, they have no assurance of employment at graduation because DACA ends with graduation. Regardless of qualifications, undocumented students may not be able to work after graduation without breaking the law (Ortiz and Hinojosa 2010). They may feel they need to pursue a career where they could be self-employed or a high-demand field where they are more likely to get legal status.

Students' legal status is relatively fixed (citizen, permanent resident, undocumented, etc.), yet the way students make meaning of their legal status is evolving. Referred to as their legal consciousness, undocumented students use social cues about their sense of inclusion and feeling of belonging in civic society. Their legal status makes them feel excluded, but their daily experiences in K-12 school, churches, and jobs can give them a feeling of inclusion or expand their feelings of exclusion (Flores 2016).

Some individuals advocate for campuses to become sanctuary spaces where campus police forces are instructed to not ask about immigration status. This stopgap measure provides limited security for undocumented students on the campus but does not solve the larger problem. Declaring sanctuary cities or campuses is a political statement of support for undocumented individuals and provides safer spaces but is not a long-term solution.

Proposed Responses

What should be done for these students and future college students who are undocumented? The options to resolve this issue run the political spectrum from extremely conservative to very liberal.

Option I. Deport All Undocumented Individuals

For: Some conservative advocates recommend the deportation of all 11 million undocumented individuals in the United States. When President Trump was campaigning for election, he advocated this position, and among those attending his rallies, it was well received. Those advocating deportation maintain that the first act of these individuals in the United States was to commit a crime by coming in or staying in the United States illegally, and, therefore, they should be returned to their home country regardless of how long they have lived here, worked, and paid taxes. Most hard liners include children in their deportation, maintaining that families should stay together. They believe it is unfair to those individuals who are trying to immigrate legally to let these "violators" stay in front of them. They also speculate that the amnesty that was part of the Immigration Reform and Control Act of 1986 under Reagan has provided an incentive for more illegal immigration with the hope for another amnesty policy (Reichert 2013).

Against: Deportation is not the most popular opinion in the United States (Pew Hispanic Center 2015). Most citizens believe undocumented long-term residents should be given a path to legal status. Deportation would cost between $400 and $600 billion to find, process, and transport the estimated 11 million undocumented immigrants, would shrink the economy by lost workers and consumers, and would cripple certain industries (Collins and Gitis 2015). This expense alone makes it unfeasible.

Yet those opposed to blanket deportation point out the positive actions of undocumented individuals. Most are hardworking, established families who are just trying to make a better life in the United States and achieve the American dream. Many who advocate deportation have misconceptions about undocumented individuals. Undocumented individuals do pay income, sales, and property taxes and pay into social security even though they will not be eligible to receive it at retirement. Not paying taxes is one of the quicker ways to be discovered, and the IRS allows anyone to get a taxpayer identification number even if he or she is not a citizen. Undocumented individuals use government services at a lower rate than citizens; therefore, they are not a burden on our systems. They are ineligible for Medicaid and state children's health programs, and they are generally less likely to use medical services (Goldman, Smith, and Sood 2006). They are less likely to use police services. For example, sanctuary cities—cities that forbid city officials or police from inquiring into immigration status—have similar crime rates as peer cities (Collingwood, Gonzalez-O'Brien and El-Khatib 2016) and lower robbery and homicide rates in neighborhoods with high concentrations of immigrants (Lyons, Vélez, and Santoro 2013). The narrative about the violent undocumented immigrant is false in that undocumented individuals commit crimes at a lower rate than their citizen peers. Undocumented children are a cost in our public schools, but those costs are generally less than their families pay in state income and property taxes, and they contribute to the economy in work and purchasing goods and services (Gans 2007).

Option II. Comprehensive Immigration Reform with a Path to Citizenship for Undocumented Individuals

For: At the other extreme is the belief that undocumented immigrants are here to stay and have demonstrated good citizenship since arriving. Advocates argue that undocumented individuals' contributions far outweigh the one illegal choice. Advocates argue it is unfair to children raised and educated in the United States to send them to a country they do not know. They also consider it a waste of our state investment in their education. Comprehensive immigration reform would apply to college students and their families. The majority of Americans believe that undocumented individuals living in the United States need a path to citizenship (Pew Hispanic Center 2015). Those advocating for a path to citizenship point out that undocumented workers generally work low-skilled jobs that Americans are not interested in doing (Paral 2009). The United States has a long history of immigrants, legal and not, working their way up from unskilled labor, and contemporary immigrants are no exception.

Against: Some argue that undocumented immigrants depress the wages of American workers. Although this connection may be present, it is modest (Paral 2009). The loss of American manufacturing jobs is not the result of undocumented immigrants but rather factories moving overseas, global competition, and automation (humans being replaced by robots in factory lines).

Offering any form of amnesty is seen by some as a "moral hazard" that breaks down the integrity of our rule of law. Those opposed to a path to citizenship often have views that align with those advocating deportation, but there are others who advocate for a guest worker program similar to that practiced in some European countries. A guest worker program would provide legal status without the full privileges of citizenship. There is also a belief that any form of amnesty or path to citizenship rewards criminal behavior and will encourage further illegal immigration.

Both sides agree that comprehensive immigration reform is necessary, but there is much debate about what features would be in that legislation. A comprehensive immigration bill that provided a path to citizenship would benefit undocumented college students, but outlining the nuances of such legislation is beyond our scope here.

Option III. Development, Relief, and Education of Alien Minors Act (DREAM Act)

For: Many advocates for undocumented youths promote the adoption of a DREAM Act. Although there are varying iterations, generally if passed a DREAM Act would provide a path to citizenship for undocumented children who pursue a college degree or two years of military service. Provisions include that applicants (a) must have entered the United States at age 15 or younger, (b) must have been in the United States for five consecutive years, (c) must have a U.S. high school diploma, and (d) must be of good moral character as demonstrated by the lack of a criminal record. The DREAM Act only applies to young people who entered the United States under their parents' control (before age 16); therefore, it does nothing for their parents or other adults over age 35 who are undocumented. The DREAM Act was initially a bipartisan bill proposed by both a Democrat and a Republican legislator, and its appeal is that the children did not make the choice to become undocumented so they should be held innocent of their parents' actions. Further, because undocumented children have gone to school in the United States, these young people often think of themselves as Americans. Generally speaking, the states have invested years in their education and should benefit from their movement into the workforce as taxpayers. A DREAM Act would reward achieving students and inspire undocumented youths to stay in high school and pursue a college education. A DREAM Act has never passed.

Against: Those who oppose the DREAM Act have generally wanted to deal with immigration reform comprehensively rather than just with the most sympathetic group (i.e., children). Further there is a belief that rewarding the children of undocumented immigrants rewards the parents' criminal actions indirectly. Undocumented parents often came to give their children a better life, so the DREAM Act would reward their criminal behavior (Mehlman 2011). Finally, there is a fear that more undocumented individuals will come to the United States if there is a path to citizenship for their children.

Opponents also argue that withholding a benefit undocumented children were not entitled to in the first place is not the same as punishing children for the sins of their parents. Not offering citizenship when they had no expectation of receiving it is not punishment. Further they argue that as undocumented children come of age, they too become culpable for their own illegal actions to remain in the United States (Mehlman 2011). For example, working without legal status would be an illegal act, which makes them culpable, yet their choices are very limited.

Option IV. Continue DACA or pass the Bridge Act

For: As a stopgap measure until comprehensive immigration reform is passed, some advocate for the continuation of DACA with ongoing enrollments as more young people graduate from high school. DACA has been shown to increase high school graduation rates and college-going rates among undocumented youth. In one study, DACA increases the hourly wage of recipients by 42 percent, and 49 percent of survey respondents said their new employment better fit their education (Wong et al. 2016). Moving into the legal job market means higher wages resulting in higher tax revenue and economic growth for the community. In their study, 87 percent of survey respondents were working, 54 percent had purchased their own car, and 12 percent had purchased their first home. These purchases mean sales tax revenue, title fees, and property taxes that are paid by DACA recipients.

A full 90 percent of DACA recipients obtained driver's licenses or state identification cards for the first time through DACA eligibility. This allows DACA recipients to drive to work and school and obtain credit cards or bank accounts. It also reduces the number of drivers forced to drive without a license.

DACA is policy because of presidential action and a future president could issue a different executive order; therefore Senators Lindsey Graham (R-S.C.) and Dick Durbin (D-Ill.) proposed the Bridge Act. The Bridge Act has provisions very similar to DACA, but because it would be legislation rather than an executive order, it would take congressional action to change the Bridge Act. The Bridge Act if passed would be law until Congress passed some form of comprehensive immigration reform. The Bridge Act would not provide a path to citizenship, similar to DACA; it would allow those eligible to remain in the United States and work legally.

Against: Alternatively DACA creates an expectation of future deferred action or amnesty, which many conservatives oppose. Further, DACA provides benefits for those who came here illegally, which some say rewards criminal behavior.

DACA also does not permanently solve the immigration status problem for young people, it just defers the problem until they graduate from college. DACA does not deal with their long-term immigration status. DACA students continually hope for immigration reform before they graduate out of DACA. But as students approach graduation, their fears about their future grow. Students report feeling psychologically exhausted and at times a sense of hopelessness (Kantamneni et al. 2016). Students also report they carry the responsibility to succeed because of their parents' sacrifice. As one student in Kantamneni and colleague's study said, "Seeing my mom struggle so much for us to have what we have is one of the biggest things that pushed me to go to college" (2016, 327).

References

Collingwood, Loren, Benjamin Gonzalez-O'Brien, and Stephen El-Khatib. 2016. *The politics of refuge: Sanctuary cities, crime, and undocumented immigration.* Riverside, CA: Authors. Accessed December 27, 2016. http://www.collin gwoodresearch.com/uploads/8/3/6/0/8360930/shelter_nopols_blind.pdf

Collins, Laura, and Ben Gitis. 2015. *The budgetary and economic costs of addressing unauthorized immigration: Alternative strategies.* Washington, DC: American Action Forum. Accessed December 27, 2016. http://americanaction forum.aaf.rededge.com/uploads/files/research/The_Budgetary _and_Economic_Costs_of_Addressing_Unauthorized_Immigration.pdf

Colvin, Jill. 2017. "Trump mulling fate of young immigrants protected by DACA." *The Associated Press* as published in *The Mercury News*, January 29. Accessed January 13, 2017. http://www.mercurynews.com/2017/01/29 /trump-and-gop-search-for-solution-for-dreamers/

Dickson, Lisa, and Matea Pender. 2013. "Do in-state tuition benefits affect the enrollment of non-citizens? Evidence from universities in Texas." *Economics of Education Review* 37:126–137. doi:10.1016/j.econedurev.2013.08.006

Flores, Andrea. 2016. "Forms of exclusion: Undocumented students navigating financial aid and inclusion in the United States." *American Ethnologist* 44:540–554.

Flores, Stella. M. 2010. "State dream acts: The effect of in-state resident tuition policies and undocumented Latino students." *The Review of Higher Education* 33:239–283. doi:10.1353/rhe.0.0134

Gans, Judith. 2007. *The economic impacts of immigrants in Arizona.* Tucson, AZ: Udall Center for Studies in Public Policy. Accessed January 13, 2017. http://www.fosterglobal.com/policy_papers/EconomicImpactOfImmi grantsInArizona.pdf

Gildersleeve, Ryan Evely, Corey Rumann, and Rodolfo Mondragón. 2010. "Serving undocumented students: Current law and policy." *New Directions for Student Services* 131:5–18. doi:10.1002/ss.364

Goldman, Dana P., James P. Smith, and Neeraj Sood. 2006. "Immigrants and the cost of medical care." *Health Affairs* 25:1700–1711. Accessed December 28, 2016. http://www.rand.org/pubs/external_publications/EP20061105.html

Kantamneni, Neeta, Nichole Shada, Morgan R. Conley, Mary A. Hellwege, Jessica M. Tate, and Sherry C. Wang. 2016. "Academic and career development of undocumented college students: The American dream?" *The Career Development Quarterly* 64:318–332. doi:10.1002/cdq.12068

Keneally, Meghan. 2017. "How the Trump administration is justifying the list of countries banned from travel to the U.S." *ABC News,* January 31. Accessed February 2, 2017. http://abcnews.go.com/Politics/trump-administration -justifying-list-countries-banned-travel-us/story?id=45143197

Latino Policy Institute. 2011. *The effects of in-state tuition for non-citizens: A systematic review of the evidence.* Providence, RI: Roger Williams University. Accessed December 27, 2016. http://www.rwu.edu/sites/default/files/lpi-report.pdf

Lyons, Christopher J., Maria B. Vélez, and Wayne A. Santoro. 2013. "Neighborhood immigration, violence, and city-level immigrant political opportunities." *American Sociological Review* 78:604–632.

Mehlman, Ira. 2011. *Five moral arguments against the DREAM Act.* Townhall.com. Accessed January 23, 2017. http://townhall.com/columnists/iramehlman /2011/07/01/five_moral_arguments_against_the_dream_act

Ortiz, Anna M., and Alejandro Hinojosa. 2010. "Tenuous options: The career development process for undocumented students." In *Understanding and supporting undocumented students,* edited by Jerry Price, 53–65. Hoboken, NJ: Wiley.

Paral, Rob, and Assoc. 2009. *The unemployment and immigration disconnect: Untying the knot Part 1 of 3.* Washington, DC: Immigration Policy Center. Accessed January 21, 2017. https://www.americanimmigrationcouncil.org /sites/default/files/research/Untying_the_Knot_Series_051909.pdf

Pew Hispanic Center. 2015. *Unauthorized immigrants: Who they are and what the public thinks.* Accessed January 21, 2017. http://www.pewresearch.org/key -data-points/immigration

Reichert, Tal. 2013. "What are some Republican arguments against the DREAM Act?" *Quora*, November 14. Accessed February 1, 2017. https://www.quora .com/What-are-some-Republican-arguments-against-the-DREAM-Act

Rogers, Tim. 2016. *Supreme Court tie is a 'huge blow' to immigrant rights*. Fusion .net. Accessed January 15, 2017. http://fusion.net/story/318212/supreme -court-ruling-dapa-daca-immigration/

ULead Network 2016. *National map of undocumented student policies*. Accessed January 21, 2017. http://uleadnet.org/issue/map

Wong, Tom K., Greusa Martinez Rosas, Adrian Reyna, Ignacia Rodriguez, Patrick O'Shea, Tom Jawetz, and Philip E. Wolgin. 2016. *New Study of DACA Beneficiaries Shows Positive Economic and Educational Outcomes*. Washington, DC: Center for American Progress. Accessed January 12, 2017. https://www .americanprogress.org/issues/immigration/news/2016/10/18/146290/new -study-of-daca-beneficiaries-shows-positive-economic-and-educational -outcomes/

CHAPTER FIVE

Diversity on Campus and the Chief Diversity Officer: Purpose and Preparation

Roland W. Mitchell, Chaunda A. Mitchell, Jerry W. Whitmore Jr., and Kenneth Fasching Varner

Introduction

This chapter explores the manner in which universities have sought to develop institutional structures to provide culturally responsive service for the increasingly diverse student population arriving on 21st-century U.S. college campuses. The primary institutional position for meeting these needs that we have focused our inquiry on is the chief diversity officer (CDO). Throughout the chapter we discuss the introduction and evolution of the CDO position with a particular focus on the proper professional and academic preparation for individuals that occupy the position.

Overview

The Brown decision wedded the ethos of the American Creed with America's historical mistreatment of African Americans . . . Specifically, it unites three of America's cultural deities—education, law and science—and enlists them in the cause of remedying the problem of racial segregation (Samuels 2004, 11–12).

The comment above is taken from Albert Samuels's *Is Separate Unequal? Black Colleges and the Challenge to Desegregation.* The quote is particularly powerful because it highlights America's reliance on education, science, and law to provide locations, practices, and answers to some of the nation's most pressing issues. According to Samuels, regardless of the challenge—civil unrest, global competition, or health disparities—for the United States, key answers can be found in education, law, and science. Samuels (2004) goes on to refer to them collectively where *Brown v. Board of Education of Topeka, Kansas,* the unanimous 1954 Supreme Court ruling that struck down state-sanctioned segregation in public schools and other public facilities, is concerned, "as weapons in the crusade to destroy the doctrine of separate but equal" (12).

For the purposes of this chapter, of Samuels's three cultural deities we will focus primarily on education with a specific concentration on higher education. Similar to Samuels's analysis of racial justice and the cultural significance of *Brown,* we will move his social justice informed inquiry along by recognizing that 60 years after *Brown,* U.S. higher education has made moderate progress in admitting a more racially and culturally diverse student population but has consistently struggled at increasing the number of faculty and staff of color (Fasching-Varner et al. 2014). Further, this unbalanced approach to integration has hindered U.S. higher education's ability to provide culturally responsive service once diverse populations arrive on campus (Mitchell, Wood, Witherspoon, 2010; Nguyen, Mitchell, and Mitchell 2016).

Through this chapter we will seek to surface specific structural positions of influence within higher education settings for addressing the vestiges of race-based oppression. And of these structural locations of institutional influence we will focus specifically on the establishment of chief diversity officers (CDO) on U.S. college campuses. Through our exploration of the work of the executive-level administrator charged with addressing diversity on college campuses we will consider (a) institutional structures that hinder/aid the work of diversity, (b) the professional knowledge base needed to conduct the often arduous tasks associated with the position, and (c) the evolving climate that causes the need for the position to be fluid and educationally responsive. To this end, we will open with a brief discussion of the history of Black educational self-determination as the means of connecting the position and the subsequent need for it beyond the three decades that it has formally existed on college campuses.

Recent Trends and Developments

Preeducation as a Panacea in Turbulent Times

How disparate and historically contentious communities can live together for the betterment of all has notably been framed by philosopher W. E. B. Du Bois (1903) as "the problem of the twentieth century . . . the color-line" (13). We argue this challenge has moved beyond Du Bois's 19th-century prediction to plague the 21st century, given that this chapter is being penned during arguably the nation's highest level of political discord since the civil rights movement of the 1960s. Significant domestic and international demographic shifts, changes in global employment patterns, and an increased polarization of political beliefs have challenged the nation to examine its core values and ask difficult questions about our relationship to each other and the world. A key indicator of this being a pivotal moment can be found in the nation's reaction to eight years of governance by the first African American president—a former political organizer with a platform rife with social justice overtures such as legislation in support of gay rights, health care reform focused on the working class, and policies geared toward more equitable relations between police and communities of color. However, this seeming shift toward a more progressive United States was radically altered by the immediate next president being a multibillionaire with an ultraconservative campaign message that promised tighter borders, support of "stop-and-frisk" policies in communities of color, and deregulation (and in some cases the actual disbandment) of key governmental agencies like the Environmental Protection Agency and the Department of Education.

Beyond political gamesmanship or party affiliation, it is difficult to debate the fact that the nation is rapidly moving into increasingly contested social and political territory. Historically in these moments education has been a primary location for establishing national norms to address society-wide challenges. Keep in mind 140 years before the U.S. Constitution was penned, British colonists invested in higher education through the founding of Harvard in 1636, making higher education (notwithstanding agriculture) the nation's first and longest lasting industry (Thelin 2004). An additional historic illustration of education being a key location for addressing social needs can be found in the passage of the Morrill Acts of 1862 and 1890 that endowed the establishment of land grant colleges to focus on the teaching of practical agricultural, science, military science, and engineering as a means to catapult a burgeoning nation to global prominence during the Industrial Revolution (Thelin 2004). During this same era, the W. E. B. Du Bois and Booker T. Washington debate, concerning the most appropriate curriculum and approach to schooling for approximately four million newly emancipated African Americans entering social, political, and professional life, further illustrated education being implemented to address massive social change (Anderson 1988). In the following section we will move beyond our opening broad focus on education as a panacea for social upheaval to consider the ways that contemporary struggles for educational equity on college campuses that have typically focused on student diversity created a lacuna at the executive-level to be filled by the CDO.

The Contested Emergence of Black Institutional Influence on Majority White Campuses

Icons of the U.S. civil rights movement like Arkansas's "Little Rock Nine" (the nine African American students, who integrated Little Rock Central High in 1957, and James Meredith, who became the first African American student at the University of Mississippi in 1962, are chronicled in history for the often life-threatening circumstances that they endured in the name of educational equity. Given the intendedly provocative nature of the collection of ideas in this text, we find it noteworthy that history has focused significantly more attention on the students that championed these causes than the faculty and staff of color who supported their courageous efforts. Could it be the case that those who opposed integration could much more easily be persuaded to support the opening of historically White campuses to students of color than to consider opening them to faculty, staff, and administrators of color? Simply put, although the actions of segregationists like Alabama's George Wallace, famously remembered for blocking school house doors, are socially repugnant to the majority of U.S. citizens, that does not necessarily mean that mainstream America supported the idea of having African Americans—individuals who have been historically presented as intellectually inferior—leading the institutions where they would be sending their children.

Consequently, beyond pervasive recognition of individual students breaking the educational color line, far less recognition of historically marginalized groups in leadership positions on majority White campuses has occurred. We challenge readers to name the first Black president of a historically White university or the first Black faculty member on a White campus with a similar level of notoriety as racial boundary crossing Black students like the University of Alabama's Autherine Lucy or Louisiana State University's A. P. Tureaud Jr., both of whom were the first to integrate their respective campuses at the undergraduate level.

At the dawn of the 21st century, groundbreaking legal battles over university affirmative action policies, such as *Grutter v. Bollinger*[1] and *Fisher v. University of Texas*,[2] still focus on students. Contrastingly, tracking diversity-related efforts by faculty, staff, and administrators of color is important because where students are transient, faculty and administration on the other hand, are in a much more reciprocal and sustained position to the university. This more balanced relationship results from the faculty's control of the curriculum and staff's influence on university policy, physical infrastructure, and financial resources. From this perspective, despite lofty vision statements and market sensitive aspirational goals, the political economy of what a university values can be found in the curriculum and physical space on campus.

The emergence of roughly 600 Black studies departments and cultural centers on majority campuses starting with the University of San Francisco in 1968 represented the beginning of historically marginalized constituents renegotiating their relationship with historically White institutions in a manner that directly impacts curriculum, policy, and academic infrastructure. Further, the half century of tension within Black studies as a discipline and its relationship to institutions founded with inherently patriarchal White supremacists grounding illustrates a historically uneasy relationship between Black studies and academia. According to David Brunsma, interim assistant director of Black Studies at the University of Missouri, "The central mission of the Black Studies Program is to prepare students to critically understand the experiences of people of African descent in the United States, Africa and the Diaspora" (Beeson 2009, 30). However, the grassroots, emancipatory, and interdisciplinary nature of African and Africana diasporic and ethnic studies programs in general essentially challenges an inherent intellectual oppression that centers European ways of knowing/being to the extent that the wisdom and knowledge of non-European cultures is delegitimized in formal academic settings (Ani 1994; Shahjahan 2005). Ethnic studies has as a core principle an ongoing concern that an uncritical engagement with majority White postsecondary institutions may lead to a "domestication" or "disciplining" of ethnic studies programs. Consequently, the establishment of ethnic studies programs, centers, and the faculty and staff that support them set the stage for the emergence of the CDO; an executive-level administrator charged with navigating the racially contested terrain between students, staff, faculty, and external constituents on college campuses (Williams 2013; Williams and Wade-Golden 2008, 2013).

It is our contention that in a similar "cart before the horse" manner to the emergence of a more diverse student population on majority White campuses before developing the needed academic infrastructure, by not addressing several key issues prior to developing the position, the CDO is often placed in a nebulously defined and often embattled position. Lacking clarity and forethought about the function and role of the position, some constituents claim the CDO is intended to eradicate the vestiges of racial strife on campus generally; others call for the position to address disparities in faculty and staff demographics specifically; still others simply arguing the position ensures that the campus is shielded from making decisions that reflect poorly when viewed by communities of color. Situated somewhere between being the "Chief Campus Revolutionary" and the "Cover Your Administration" (CYA) officer, key issues that hinder/facilitate the success of the CDO position are considered in the following section.

Proposed Response/Reforms

Institutional Structures, Purpose, and Role of the CDO

It's my job to make sure that White executive-level administrators at Acme State University do not get in front of Black folks and say and do things that they will regret. (William Hamby, personal communication 2008)

The statement above was made during a visit by a CDO to a Race and Gender in Higher Education course taught by the primary author. The comments highlight one of the greatest challenges of the CDO position. Specifically, the charge that the CDO must guard the university against negative public perceptions concerning myriad social injustices, juxtaposed against the very material fact that from student admissions to faculty and staff leadership opportunities race, class, gender, sexuality, and ability-based systemic disparities continue to radically structure U.S. higher education (Bonner et al. 2015). The CDO has the often arduous task of managing this public perception and equity-seeking minefield as the newest position added to the executive-level organizational chart on many college campuses. Moreover, the emergence of the CDO in theory and in practice provides benefits and challenges for the candidate selected to lead diversity efforts on a college campus. One only has to look at the increasing number of executive-level searches conducted for CDO positions, which highlights that many institutions recognize the value of having a CDO on their campus. Beyond the search for the successful candidate, both the university and the new CDO are tasked with understanding the very real and complex challenges that impact the everyday experiences of faculty, staff, and students of color and other diverse, historically marginalized members of the campus community. Collectively, exhaustive research and our own personal experience highlight the complexity of the politics and related bureaucracy of navigating a large complex system such as higher education that by design is inherently racist, sexist, and, homophobic (Dancy 2010; Edwards 2014; Mitchell 2008; Wooten and Mitchell 2015). As difficult as this task is for the CDO it is equally trying to encapsulate the many benefits and challenges in this chapter. We shall, however, seek to present some of the most pressing benefits and challenges for consideration and reflection.

The presence of a CDO provides an immediate benefit to the university. One can liken this benefit to university "street credibility" (or "street cred") as those universities who possess a CDO among their administrative ranks are seen as progressive, forward-thinking institutions while those institutions who do not have CDOs are often viewed as behind the times or lagging behind in their commitment to diversity, equity, and inclusion. Thus, the presence of a CDO solidifies the university's real or perceived commitment to diversity at the highest level of the administrative structure. CDO positions are often found on the organizational chart of an institution housed in Academic Affairs, Office of the President, or the Office of the Chancellor with either a direct or dotted line reporting to the provost or president. The mere positioning of the CDO close to the power brokers of the institution and a seat at the university's administrative decision-making table should signify a direct and immediate impact to the systems, customs, and traditions that have traditionally marginalized those members of the campus community who have been viewed as other, different, and on the margins. Although this immediate impact may be true in some cases, what is also a reality is that CDOs can become nothing more than the embodiment of a university's symbolic gesture to appease diverse groups or give a ceremonial nod to the idea of diversity in principle but not in practice. A CDO with a seat at the administrative table but possessing limited financial resources, limited staff or functional areas in the administrative portfolio, and limited administrative authority to implement the action items deemed important serves as nothing more than a diversity figurehead. This diversity figurehead is reduced to being present at programs where a diversity figure is needed, attending meetings for discussion but no action, and ultimately searching for credibility from administrators, faculty, and staff based on social interactions and relationship building rather than institutional structure and legitimate positional power afforded to other senior administrative positions on campus.

Even for the savviest CDO there is a constant challenge of situating themselves between being the "Chief Revolutionary Officer" and the CYA officer. This unique positionality of serving in the role as the "insider" who has the ear of the university's executive leadership to provide council, strategy, and deliverables on complex issues does not come without challenges. How can the "insider" balance competing interests of dismantling a system that was not created for diverse groups while protecting the university and its administration from the scrutiny of failing to provide a welcoming environment, access, and equity for these same groups? Additionally, how can this "insider" be an ally for diverse groups without putting their own professional tenure at the university on the line as many of the changes required are systemic, transformational changes that will not only alter but shake up the status quo? The answers to these questions are not static thus creating a constant balancing act for CDOs in determining their position. Is the CDO the person who will lead the protest march against the institution thereby becoming the chief revolutionary officer who is adored and revered by the various affinity groups, fighting injustice while simultaneously chancing the perception of not operating in the best interest of the university? Or will the CDO act as the CYA officer, placating the constituent base with unrealized promises and just enough movement on diversity issues to prevent unrest while members of campus affinity groups remain underresourced, underserved, and underrecruited in the faculty, staff, and student ranks.

If viewing the role of a CDO from a practical perspective, it can be argued that the CDO is an employee of the university and thereby by virtue of employment status serves the best interest of the institution. The challenge is determining whose best interest the CDO should serve: the university's, whose administration may or may not want to implement the full scope of diversity efforts needed to enact the type of systemic change for transforming the campus; or, contrastingly, the diverse campus constituent groups' who have waited for the CDO as the next "messiah" who will come and "save" these groups from their current condition. A firm stance by a CDO in either direction can have long-lasting reverberations for future collaborations, professional employment, and cultural and institutional capital with other university administrators and constituent groups. The most successful CDOs navigate the aforementioned competing interests with an understanding that at different times in their tenure they will find themselves operating in both camps, chief revolutionary officer and cover your administration officer. The ultimate challenge is having those that the CDO serves and is charged with working with understand that it is their duty to both stand with affinity groups and ensure the university is viewed in a positive light while maintaining an authenticity for both interests. This seems to be an impossible task even for the most accomplished professional.

Given the tall order of expectations by the university and disparate constituent groups that we have just outlined, in the next section we will consider the professional knowledge base needed to be a CDO. As we engage in this discussion, we want to point out to the reader that because the position is among the newest on many college campuses, CDOs come from varying professional and intellectual backgrounds with very limited empirical research to ground their practice. The seminal texts in the field are Damon A. Williams and Katrina C. Wade-Golden's (March 2013), *The Chief Diversity Officer: Strategy, Structure and Change Management,* and Williams's (May 2013) companion text, *Strategic Diversity Leadership: Activating Change and Transformation in Higher Education.* Similar to many administrative and practitioner-driven fields, it could very well be the case that the individuals that have the vital insights needed to produce research pertinent to the work of CDOs are so busy doing the work that they have little if any time to write about it. However, as institutions continue to attempt to shape the position and consider individuals' best suited to be CDOs, this professional knowledge base is critical.

The Professional Knowledge Base Needed to Conduct the Often Arduous Tasks Associated with the Position

Very few CDOs have specialized educational credentials or foundational professional experiences that directly inform their roles and responsibilities. Over the course of time, individuals from a variety of professional backgrounds and educational credentials (e.g., law, psychology, higher education administration, business, engineering, humanities, medicine) have occupied the role of the CDO. (Worthington, Stanley, and Lewis 2014)

According to the Glossary of Career Education Programs, the CDO "works to create an inclusive environment for employees or students through recruitment efforts, training sessions, and activity planning." In these regards, CDOs are charged with everything from establishing programs and initiatives to address racial battle fatigue[3] among faculty and staff (Fasching-Varner et al. 2014) to initiating minority-student retention programs, coordinating for Title IX, supporting town and gown diversity initiatives, increasing minority participation in STEM/STEAM-related activities, educating the campus about social justice–related issues, and developing and monitoring equitable employment practices (Harvey 2014). In light of the broad scope of responsibilities that may potentially fall under the purview of the CDO, we ask: if this interdisciplinarily trained administrative jack-of-all-trades, endowed with the negotiating skills of a Cold War diplomat and the inspirational insight of Maya Angelou actually existed, what preparation did they receive to gain the needed competencies?

We recognize that our description is equal parts hyperbolic and facetious and in some regard feeds into the pervasive narrative within many marginalized communities that to receive equal opportunities those on the margins must be 110 percent more qualified than those in the majority. However, we believe this absence of clarity about the proper background for the position magnifies the importance of inquiry into the needed professional knowledge base, characteristics, and dispositions, and key prior work experiences a CDO should possess. Absent clarity on these competencies with no road map to follow, the same simplistic and ill-informed understandings about race, sexuality, ethnicity, class, gender, and ability that institutions are seeking to remedy through the establishment of the CDO position tacitly influence the CDO selection process as well as the development of the scope and range of the CDO's responsibilities. Moreover in academia, a place that for better or worse values intellectual pedigree, professional certification, and documented scholarly expertise, this poorly defined criteria is closely related to why the position is often denied a similar level of direct institutional influence and oversight that other executive-level university administrators are afforded.

As previously stated, given that the position is still in its infancy, absent a substantial literature base to build upon, our more than two decades of professional experiences in diversity-related work (i.e., administrators in diversity offices, CDO search committee members, faculty who teach higher education diversity related courses) and preliminary research findings that range from 2005 to the present provide meaningful illustrations of a couple of fairly common characteristics that often frame the dialogue across constituent groups concerning the selection of a CDO. First, there is a pervasive belief that the CDO should in the broadest sense be a member of a historically marginalized group and in many cases more specifically a racial minority. Next, we have observed a sometimes circuitous debate about whether the person should be a tenured academic who has risen up the ranks of the university administration in a traditional manner or a nontenured individual with a more administratively focused professional portfolio. We will address both of these positions at the conclusion of this section. However, we will start by providing general information about the position.

The U.S. Bureau of Labor Statistics states that the median salary for CDOs in 2016 was $175,110, with applicants for the positions needing a master's degree in human resource management or one of the social sciences and anywhere from 5 to 10 years of experience. Further, many of the more than 1,800 CDO positions are housed at institutions that require applicants to hold a doctorate in one of these fields. Our research of the educational preparation of current CDOs found that in addition to the referenced degrees in human resource management or the social sciences several current influential CDOs have degrees that range from psychology and counseling to higher education, media studies, student affairs administration, philosophy, ethnic studies, business, women and gender studies, and law. According to Witt/Kieffer, a top higher education executive-level search firm, over 75 percent of CDOs have terminal degrees (PhD, EdD, or JD). Further in, Witt/Kieffer's 2011 report titled, *Chief Diversity Officers Assume Larger Role*, several sitting CDOs shared that "academic credentials are highly desirable as they help establish bona fides on campus, particularly with faculty colleagues" (2).

Race and Racial Thinking as a Straight Jacket for CDOs

It is our belief that these fairly nondescript requirements understate the profound challenge the position is intended to address. This framing is particularly troubling considering that the position is charged with engaging systemic oppressions that, as previously stated, have continually dogged U.S. society (McKenna and Pratt, 2015) and higher education (Alger 2013; Anderson 1988; Antonio et al. 2004), specifically, since its inception. Absent clarity about the proper qualifications this vacuum about needed CDO qualities and dispositions is often filled with the essentialists' notion[4] (Fuss 2013) that a key competency for being successful in the position is that a CDO be a member of a historically marginalized group. More specifically, in many cases this group membership is read as a racial minority and even more precisely an African American. Now let us be clear, the dearth of people of color and particularly Yellow, Black, Brown, and indigenous administrators on White campuses leads us to recognize the significance of carving out spaces for executive-level professionals of color. Also, lived experience of racism, sexism, or homophobia, for example, no doubt provides meaningful perspectives and understandings about an institution. However, leading a search for such a complex position under the auspices of an explicit and undertheorized notion that racial identity is a competency that somehow magically endows members of minority communities is problematic in a context that values objective and well-reasoned intellectual expertise (Mitchell and Rosiek 2005). Moreover the danger of this flawed racial reasoning is that it undergirds a parallel rationale for excluding individuals from these same historically marginalized groups from higher level leadership positions like provost, president, and chancellor. In short, these actions establish the CDO position as an office unto itself charged with providing service to the campus "undesirables," for which the CDO in a 21st-century rendition of Rudyard Kipling's "White Man's Burden," oversees the university's lesser children.

This notion of the CDO being the reserved slot for Black, gay, Brown, or female bodies feeds directly into pervasive stereotypes that these historically marginalized groups are less skilled at reasoning, at best inherently instinctual in nature, and thereby ultimately unfit for expanded leadership opportunities in highly structured organizations. It is not our point in this particular chapter to debunk the objective versus subjective, reason versus emotion, or the divide over valuing the mind over the body in Western academia. Ethnic studies, postcolonial, and feminists scholars have already powerfully demonstrated the manner in which the transcendental divide between these binary constructions is not only artificial but most often porous and arbitrarily shifts to benefit the status quo (Shahjahan 2005; Sharoff 2011; Tuck 2009, 2011; Wane 2002). However, through this recognition of the role of race and racism in the CDO selection process we do want to highlight that when surreptitiously under the sway of the pervasive fetishization of reason and framing of racial identity as a static and somehow essential competency for a CDO, ill-informed administrators on majority White campuses are left with caricatures of civil rights era charismatic faith leaders as a model for the CDO.

Our depiction of civil rights era leadership is in no way intended to denigrate the indelible mark on the 20th century of the civil rights era leadership's record of direct and multifaceted resistance to oppression. However, its decontextualized use in this manner contributes to a CDOs embodied race, ethnicity, or gender-based classification serving as an epistemic straitjacket that limits their influence and scope of responsibility to a narrow range of what the majority deems to be "minority affairs." Proof of the negative impact of this racially essentialist and professionally narrowing behavior by those currently in the field can be found in the conclusion of the previously referenced Witt/Kieffer report (2011), in which they found that several CDOs desire to create larger portfolios that are steeped in leadership broadly defined not just diversity leadership. Absent these opportunities Witt/Kieffer found many current CDOs plan to leave their positions in the next three to five years.

To Tenure or Not

The tenure and promotion process represents the antithesis of racial essentialism and simplistic notions of identity politics for employment and advancement opportunities in university settings. Despite the fact that there are significant racial and gender disparities among the ranks of the U.S. faculty that have continuously persisted (Vaccaro and Camba-Kelsay 2016), the undergirding principal for the tenure and promotion process affords an individual the space for the development of a documented record of their scholarly expertise in a coherently defined area of study, at least in theory. Concurrently, a rigorous review of these materials by an institutional, national, and in some cases international collective of disciplinary experts is intended to not only ensure the quality of the scholarship but, if positively assessed, affords a fairly high-level of job security. The combination of this proven expertise and enhanced job security is intended to increase the likelihood that an educators' pursuit of objective knowledge will not be negatively influenced by the various forms of bias that have historically plagued human institutions and communities.

At first glance one may determine that if CDOs are charged with addressing arguably the most deeply entrenched form of institutional biases in college settings then tenure, or some level of enhanced job security, should be required. Additionally, in a much more hierarchical manner, while location on the administrative structure, executive level pay, and a prominent platform for voicing concerns are important, the primary mission/academic core of the university is historically tied to the curriculum—which is controlled by tenured faculty. Not being a member of this group significantly limits a CDO's ability to meaningfully address the key and often contentious issues that are the very impetus for creating the position. Contrastingly, while there are a handful of tenured CDOs nationally, tenure is not an option for the bulk of individuals in the field and is rarely outlined as a qualification in position descriptions. Against this reality, we have observed numerous CDOs who took their positions absent the security afforded to tenured professors, ramping up their professional activity to include enhanced scholarly activity as it relates to research, teaching, and service in the pursuit of tenure. Keep in mind this increased scholarly activity is taking place against the backdrop that nationally tenure-track positions are rapidly declining (Griffey 2016).

By linking tenure for CDOs to our early assertion that it was more palatable for some constituents to see postsecondary institutions diversified at the student level than at the faculty or administrative levels, we can see how from this entrenched segregationist perspective granting the position charged with tending to the affairs of historically underrepresented populations tenure is extremely perplexing. Moreover, following this racist line of reasoning, a tenured CDO is threatening because they have an increased, and in some regard untethered, ability to challenge the systemic vestiges of Jim Crow, patriarchy, homophobia, etc., in higher education by virtue of them possessing the proverbial "golden key"—increased job security associated with tenure. Consequently, for CDOs tenure provides a potentially unparalleled level of influence in the interests of historically marginalized groups on college campuses in that they are endowed with the range and influence of an executive-level administrator and the job security and ability to seek unbiased and when needed inimical truth of a tenured faculty member.

When applied to issues of curriculum, employment practices, and approaches to recruitment and retention, a tenured CDO has significant leverage. However, we also recognize that there are soundly reasoned rationales for why the position may not need to be occupied exclusively by those with tenure. In a general sense, from chief financial officers to executive-level communication and information officers, there are several administrators with similar scope and rank who are untenured. Next, and more substantively, exclusively seeking out individuals with tenure to occupy the CDO position negates a significant group of talented and potentially innovative educators. Given that the profession is still in its nascent phase of development, a large and diverse pool is an asset. Also, the very nature of the tenure and promotion process risks the type of previously stated domestication into academia at the institutional and disciplinary levels that have historically caused marginalized communities to be highly suspect of the unbalanced power relations between themselves and the academy, the scholarly communities at the center of the academy, and members of their indigenous community who gain status in the academy.

A fairly common colloquial version of this phenomenon can be found in the notion of someone being a "sell out" to the beliefs and practices of their indigenous community as a result of being socialized within a more powerful majority community. The lasting effect of the forces of oppression on historically disenfranchised communities causes them to constantly have to balance between their indigenous beliefs and norms and those of the majority (Hill-Collins 1991), as previously referenced in our discussion of the perception of a CDO from a traditionally marginalized group as the chief revolutionary officer or the cover your administration officer.

It may very well be the case that access to the insights and understandings associated with existing in this in-between space at the nexus of the institution and marginalized communities is actually a much more useful predictor of professional competence than racial identity. And although membership in a marginalized group may increase the likelihood of enduring encounters with majority populations that lead to these insights, we want to emphasize again that they are not the product of some biologically predetermined essentialist endowments. In the end, tenure is an intensive type of norming of thought, professional service, and action. Regardless of race, ethnicity, gender, sexuality, or class membership, the tenure process socializes an individual into a particular orientation to their discipline, the academy, and their specific institution. Given that each of these categories has been historically impacted by systemic oppression, as opposed to denying the existence of these tensions, we think it is important for search committees and those responsible for occupying and further developing the CDO position to familiarize themselves with these tensions. Given that areas like ethnic, queer, and gender studies take these tensions as a primary area of inquiry, it may be the case that some familiarity with these and related disciplines is a key competency for an aspiring CDO. The position is clearly evolving and in the concluding section of this chapter we consider the scope and nature of this evolution.

The Evolving Climate: Fluid and Educationally Responsive

Let's be clear, revolutions don't start in the President's office. (Earl Garner, personal Communication, 2016)

The comment above was shared during a meeting hosted in a university president's office by a senior-staff member addressing a panel of educators, community youth organizers, faith leaders, and police officials in the aftermath of one of the recent police shootings of men of color. The meeting was convened to build more positive relationships between educators, law enforcement, and communities of color as the city waited for the Department of Justice findings and braced for the potential for civil unrest. Despite the fact that the modern multiversity often functions as a city unto itself, the reverberations of this and other calamitous events during this period radically impacted the university. There was a possibility that out-of-state student enrollment would be impacted because parents expressed concerns about sending their children to what was perceived to be a racially contested city. In a national climate where declining state support for financing public higher education is a reality, any environmental factors that negatively impact enrollment are of significant importance. Further, students and local community members participated in on-campus protests and consciousness raising rallies that radically altered the contours of the typical town-and-gown divide between universities and local constituents.

For the purposes of this chapter we find the senior staff member's comments particularly poignant because they highlight the contested location of operating in the seat of university sanctioned power—the president's office—recognizing that the nature of his position is one of moderate and incremental change at best, as opposed to the bold transformational aspirations that often spark protest movements. However, the fact that the meeting is occurring between policy makers and constituents of color who often have competing agendas is significant. Simply put, there is a keen, and we believe to be insightful, recognition by this example of both the limits and the possibilities afforded from the position of an executive-level university administrator—a formal part of the university apparatus who is actively reaching out to a disenfranchised and embattled community. From our perspective the message is sent that the administration is explicitly aware of the challenges that disenfranchised communities on and off campus face and are actively seeking input for solutions.

The importance of these engagements informed by culturally critical and action-oriented sensibilities by executive-level administrators cannot be understated. A telling illustration of the consequences of not seeking meaningful input and building relationships with a diverse range of constituents in a university setting can be found in the 2015 ousting of the president and chancellor of the University of Missouri system, Tim Wolfe and R. Bowen Lofton, respectively. The push for Wolfe and Bowen to resign was fueled by the university remaining silent on a series of bigoted incidents, including the student body president being called the n-word and a swastika being drawn on a wall with human feces. The combination of hunger protests, a threat by the football team to forfeit games, and ongoing actions by numerous student organizations created a climate on campus and in the community that was untenable for university administration. Additionally, the fact that the university chose not to address racial strife on a campus less than 150 miles away from Ferguson, Missouri, the site of the 2014 police killing of a young African American man named Michael Brown, and subsequent highly publicized protests of Brown's death, further highlights the unacceptable nature of the university administration's inactivity.

The highly chronicled nature of the events at the University of Missouri as well as the numerous hashtags like #BBUM (being Black at the University of Michigan) or #BeingBlackatLSU that surfaced on college campuses across the nation in response to students of color's perceptions of the racial climate at their institutions, continues a long history of colleges, students, and communities of color struggling with issues of race and racism. The aftermath of the Missouri protests led to the establishment of a system-wide University of Missouri CDO. Following suit, several peer institutions like the Universities of Alabama and Michigan have also established CDOs. Although these and similar issues between university administration and faculty, staff, and students concerning racial justice attracted significant media attention, they are not new. Student activism concerning U.S. involvement in Vietnam in the late 1960s as well as calls for U.S. divestment from South Africa during the apartheid era of the 1980s occurred before the emergence of the CDO. Contrastingly, university responses to the 2017 executive order issued by President Donald Trump concerning a travel ban on individuals from seven countries (Yemen, Iraq, Iran, Somalia, Sudan, Libya, and Syria) presents a new challenge to the current generation of university administrators, which includes CDOs and the support structures and staff that have evolved along with the position.

Building on what we find to be the meaningful insight demonstrated by the executive-level administrator that we opened this section with, armed with a clear recognition of the danger of turning a deaf ear to these issues as in the case of the University of Missouri, we now offer preliminary actions that a university should take under the direction of a CDO to address the challenges associated with the impact of evolving federal immigration-related policies. Gather key constituents—directly impacted students, faculty/staff, and families to clearly define how policy changes will impact the campus community. Actively seek out the input of this same constituent base to brainstorm short- and long-term strategies. Monitor and be prepared to provide mental health and wellness support as needed (i.e., licensed counselors, prayer and meditation locations/space for gathering to build community for impacted constituents). Ensure that university policies associated with registration, housing, summer housing, etc., are flexible enough to accommodate the uncertainty associated with the executive order. Provide adviser/advocacy-related resources for all impacted individuals who come in contact with university- and community-based law and immigration authorities. And finally, even if it means contracting an external communication firm, establishing an ultraresponsive communication system to update the campus on the latest immigration-related information from federal and state authorities.

The overall aim of these actions should be to communicate to students, faculty, and staff that the university values both domestic and international diversity. Further, this message must be steeped in the reality that U.S. higher education cannot meet its core objectives absent participation and exchange by the full-range of local, regional, national, and international constituents. At a base-level, the message that should be sent is that in the simplest terms "the university has its most vulnerable students' backs."

Conclusion

We set out in this chapter to conduct an inquiry into how universities can establish meaningful educational structures for addressing the varied needs of the increasingly diverse community of students, faculty, and staff arriving on 21st-century college campuses. We advanced the argument that far more attention has been paid to boundary crossing students from these traditionally marginalized communities than faculty and staff as a result of notions that students are transient but faculty and staff have more lasting institutional influence. In this regard, we focused specifically on the development of the chief diversity officer position as the physical and institutional embodiment of the executive-level university administrative position established to provide leadership in areas of educational equity.

Despite the fairly logical and straightforward argument we have presented, the undergirding principal that we have struggled with throughout the chapter is the very difficult question: If U.S. university administrators were truly committed to eradicating the vestiges of segregation and the continually evolving types of oppression that fester on college campuses, why have they been so tentative in empowering the CDO with proportional influence to address the issues? As we described in the chapter, a true commitment to empowering the office would include better understanding the skills, knowledge base, background, experiences, and disposition needed for the position. And then once there was consensus on these qualifications there should be more deliberate and measurable movement toward addressing complex issues concerning what existing or newly established infrastructure, policies, protections, academic oversight, financial resources, and employment security practices are needed to in some cases empower and in others inoculate the CDO against the push back, obstruction, and retaliation that they would no doubt experience.

In 2014 the National Association of Diversity Officers in Higher Education started this work by issuing their "Standards of Professional Practice for Chief Diversity Officers in Higher Education" (Worthington, Stanley, and Lewis, 2014) report. The report provides a vivid depiction of the existing landscape for CDOs and U.S. higher education based on data at the turn of the 21st century. Like early students who desegregated U.S. colleges and universities as well as ethnic, gender, and LGBTQ studies departments, the tension between being a part of the institution while not becoming assimilated to the point of not recognizing the existence of pervasive and deeply rooted oppressions within the institution is an ongoing concern for the CDO position. The fact that in three decades the CDO position has grown from the ranks of nonprofessional staff, and in some cases simply concerned community members with no official university standing, to now reside in the executive ranks of the university administration suggests the types of question about preparation, role, and scope that we are asking are central to the field. In the end, as a group of administrators, faculty, and practitioners whose work primarily revolves around equity-related issues, this chapter represents our contribution to the stated need for an expanded professional knowledge base for CDOs.

Notes

1. *Grutter v. Bollinger* is a 2003 court case in which the Supreme Court upheld the University of Michigan Law School's affirmative action policy. The ruling effectively supported a race-conscious admissions process that may favor "underrepresented minority groups," but that also took into account many other factors evaluated on an individual basis for every applicant.

2. *Fisher v. University of Texas* is a 2013 court case that litigated the affirmative action admissions policy of the University of Texas at Austin. Two women,

both White, filed suit, alleging that the University had discriminated against them on the basis of their race.

3. Racial battle fatigue is a concept coined by educational psychologist William A. Smith that asserts that people of color constantly worry, have trouble concentrating, become fatigued, and develop measurable psychological, physical, and emotional trauma when navigating personal and professional spaces that have historically favored White people.

4. Essentialism is the belief that an individuals' race/gender/ethnicity intrinsically endows them with specific traits, characteristics, and understandings. A social constructivist perspective, on the other hand, presents the opposing view, that specific traits, characteristics, and understandings that an individual possesses are the result of social interactions. For the purposes of this chapter, an illustration of racial/ethnic essentialism is the belief that by virtue of being of Mexican descent an individual is somehow *genetically* predisposed to be a Spanish speaker. This is juxtaposed against a social constructivist view that the *socialization* that occurs by growing up in a region where Spanish is the majority language affords an individual the ability to speak the language.

References

Alger, Jonathan. 2013. "A Supreme Challenge: Achieving the Educational and Societal Benefits of Diversity after the Supreme Court's Fisher Decision." *Journal of Diversity in Higher Education* 6(1): 147–154.

Anderson, James. 1988. *The Education of Blacks in the South 1860–1935*. Chapel Hill: University of North Carolina Press.

Ani, Marimba. 1994. *Yurugu an African-Centered Critique of European Culture Thought and Behavior.* Trenton, NJ: Africa World Press.

Anthony Lising Antonio, Mitchell J. Chang, Kenji Hakuta, David Kenny, Shana Levin and Jeffrey Milem. 2004. "Effects of Racial Diversity on Complex Thinking in College Students." *Psychological Science* 1(15): 507–510.

Beeson, Jeffery. 2009. "U.S. Celebrates 40th Anniversary of Black Studies Programs" (January, 3, 2017). http://munews.missouri.edu/newsreleases/2009/02.03.09.brunsma.black.studies.anniversary.php

Bonner, Fred, Aretha Marbley, Robin Hughes, Frank Tuitt, and Petra Robinson. 2015. *Black Faculty in the Academy: Narratives for Negotiating Identity and Achieving Career Success.* New York: Routledge Publishing.

Chief Diversity Officer: Job Duties, Career Outlook and Salary (January). http://study.com/articles/Chief_Diversity_Officer_Job_Duties_Career_Outlook_and_Salary.html

Dancy, Elon. 2010. *Managing Diversity: (Re)visioning Equity on College Campuses.* New York: Peter Lang.

Du Bois, W. E. B. 1903. *The Souls of Black Folk: Essays and Sketches.* Chicago: McClurg.

Edwards, Kirsten. 2014. "Teach with Me: The Promise of a Raced Politic for Social Justice in College Classrooms." *Journal of Critical Thought and Praxis* 2(2): Article 3.

Fasching Varner, Kenneth, Katrice Albert, Roland Mitchell, and Chaunda Allen (eds.). 2014. *Racial Battle Fatigue in Higher Education. Exposing the Myth of Post-Racial America.* Lanham, MD: Rowman & Littlefield.

Fuss, Diana. 2013. *Essentially Speaking: Feminism, Nature and Difference.* New York: Routledge.

Griffey, Trevor. 2016. "Declining of Tenure for Higher Education Faculty." *The Labor and Working-Class History Association* (January 3, 2017). https://lawcha.org/wordpress/2016/09/02/declinetenure-higher-education-faculty-introduction/

Harvey, William. 2014. "Chief Diversity Officers and the Wonderful World of Academe." *Journal of Diversity in Higher Education* 1(7): 92–100.

Hill-Collins, Patricia. 1991. "Learning from the Outsider within the Sociological Significance of Black Feminist Thought." In *Beyond Methodology: Feminist Scholarship as Lived Research,* edited by Mary Fonow and Judith Cook, 35–59. Bloomington: Indiana University Press.

McKenna, Erica, and Scott Pratt. 2015. *American Philosophy from Wounded Knee to Present.* New York: Bloomsbury.

Mitchell, Roland. 2008. "'Soft Ears' and Hard Topics: Race, Disciplinarity, and Voice in Higher Education." In *Voice in Qualitative Inquiry: Challenging Conventional, Interpretive, and Critical Conceptions in Qualitative Research*, edited by Lisa Mazzei and Alicia Jackson, 77–95. New York: Routledge.

Mitchell, R., and J. Rosiek. 2005. "Searching for the Knowledge That Enables Culturally Responsive Academic Advising." *Journal on Excellence in College Teaching* 16(1): 87–110.

Mitchell, Roland, Gerald Wood, and Noelle Witherspoon. 2010. "Considering Race and Space: Mapping Developmental Approaches for Providing Culturally Responsive Service." *Equity & Excellence in Education* 43(1): 294–309.

Nguyen, Thuong, Roland Mitchell, and Chaunda Mitchell. 2016. "Crafting Spaces between the Binary: Renegade Locations for the Radical Re-Visioning of Nontraditional Graduate Advising." *Knowledge Cultures* 4(1): 71–84.

Samuels, Albert. 2004. *Is Separate Unequal? Black Colleges and the Challenge to Desegregation.* Lawrence: University of Kansas Press.

Shahjahan, Riyad. 2005. "Spirituality in the Academy: Reclaiming from the Margins and Evoking a Transformative Way of Knowing the World." *International Journal of Qualitative Studies in Education* 18(6): 685–711.

Sharoff, F. (2011). "Holistic Thought-Forms in Indigenous Societies Indigeneity and Holism." In *Indigenous Philosophies and Critical Education a Reader*, edited by G. Dei, 53–67. New York: Peter Lang.

Thelin, John. 2004. *A History of American Higher Education.* Baltimore, MD: The Johns Hopkins University Press.

Tuck, Eve. 2009. "Suspending Damage: A Letter to Communities." *Harvard Educational Review* 75(3): 409–427.

Tuck, Eve. 2011. "Rematriating Curriculum Studies." *Journal of Curriculum and Pedagogy* 8(1): 34–37.

Vaccaro, Annemarie, and Melissa Camba-Kelsay. 2016. *Centering Women of Color in Academic Counterspaces.* Lanham, MD: Rowman & Littlefield.

Wane, N. (2002) African Women and Spirituality: Connections between Thought and Action. In *Expanding the Boundaries of Transformative Learning: Essays on Theory and Praxis*, edited by E. O'Sullivan, A. Morrell, and M. A. O'Conner, 135–150. New York: Palgrave Macmillan.

Williams, Damon. 2013. *Strategic Diversity Leadership.* Sterling, VA: Stylus Publishers.

Williams, Damon, and Katrina Wade-Golden. 2008. *The Chief Diversity Officer: A Primer for College and University Presidents.* Washington, DC: American Council on Education.

Williams, Damon, and Katrina Wade-Golden. 2013. *The Chief Diversity Officer: Strategy, Structure, and Change Management.* Sterling, VA: Stylus Publishers.

Witt/Kieffer. 2011. "Chief Diversity Officers Assume Larger Leadership Role." (Summer).http://www.wittkieffer.com/file/thought-leadership/practice/CDO%20survey%20results%20August%202011.pdf

Wooten, Sara, and Roland Mitchell. 2015. *The Crisis of Campus Sexual Violence: Critical Perspectives on Prevention and Response.* New York: Routledge.

Worthington, Roger, Christine Stanley, and William Lewis. 2014. "Standards of Professional Practice for Chief Diversity Officers in Higher Education." *National Association of Diversity Officers in Higher Education.* January. http://www.nadohe.org/standards-of-professional-practice-for-chief-diversity-officers

Contemporary Issues Surrounding the College Curriculum and Instructional Delivery

CHAPTER SIX

Prestige, Rankings, and Competition for Status

Jeongeun Kim

Introduction

What characterizes high quality of higher education institutions? Although there is no underlying agreement on what defines quality, one key assumption is that not all universities have it—only a few (Bogue and Hall 2003). This assumption tends to construct a pyramid of *prestige*, defined as an institution's standing, and the widespread respect and admiration felt for it, based on perceptions of its achievements or quality. Although prestige has always been a major goal of higher education institutions (Bowen 1980), over the past decades, various systems in the form of ratings and rankings have emerged to capture and present the standings of academic programs. Despite criticisms on the current systems, ratings and rankings have become popular, and colleges and universities engage in prestige-seeking behaviors based on the systems' mechanisms. As such, it is important to understand why and how institutions respond. The potential consequences of trends and efforts to address concerns with regard to these prestige measures will also be discussed in this chapter.

Defining Prestige

Although prestige is a common word in higher education, the definition is not clear. Prestige refers to the relative standing of an institution and is determined by the acquisition of things that tend to be associated with exceptionally high-quality service (Brewer, Gates, and Goldman 2002). Therefore, what is considered to consist of high-quality academic programs tells us what institutions are seen as prestigious. Although a vague pecking order has always existed within higher education, with the connotations of elite institutions or Ivy League schools, there have been efforts to systematically determine institutions' standings. Generally, the mechanisms that define prestige are based on four factors: graduate outcomes, reputation, research productivity, and resource and student selectivity (Brooks 2005).

In the early 1900s, measures of institutional prestige were outcome based. The first *American College Rankings of Eminent Men*, published by James Cattell (1910), ranked institutions based on the number of eminent scientists who attended as undergraduates or who were employed there. Visher (1928) took a similar approach by listing alumni with bachelor's degrees in *Who's Who* from 1930 to 1951. Other studies attempted to capture the prestige of institutions based on reputation—the opinions generally held regarding the quality of an institution. Raymond Hughes (1925) defined prestige based on faculty ratings of the departments of 36 institutions that granted doctoral degrees; Hayward Keniston (1959) also used this method to compare comprehensive research universities. At this time, reputation rankings were produced mostly for graduate programs or professional schools (for example, see Blau and Margulies 1974; Cartter 1966; Roose and Anderson 1970). Some publications such as *Chicago Sunday Tribune* (Manly 1957) and *The Gourman Report* (Gourman 1967) ranked undergraduate programs based on raters' overall opinions about colleges and universities.

These reputational rankings are popular, but there has been criticism about the subjectivity of the methodology. Raters do not have a common frame of reference, and the judgments of quality are based on what they personally know of an institution or program and how it relates to others they know (Brooks 2005). In recognizing this factor, some rankings added "objective" measures of program characteristics. Solomon and Astin (1981) provided an undergraduate ranking based not only on ratings of perceived quality but also on other factors such as preparation for graduate school, employment, faculty commitment to teaching, scholarly accomplishments of faculty, and innovativeness of curriculum (Bogue and Hall 2003; Webster 1992). In its ranking of research doctorate programs, the National Research Council (NRC) (1982) incorporated other quantitative measures on institutions such as program size, university library size, research support, and characteristics of graduates, along with a reputation survey.

Extensive research activities have become an important criterion for institutional "excellence." In 1973, the Carnegie Foundation for the Advancement of Teaching created a framework to recognize and describe institutional diversity in U.S. higher education in research and policy analysis (Carnegie Classifications n.d.). Despite the original intention and the foundation's repeated statement that the system is not to be used to create hierarchy among higher learning institutions (O'Meara 2007), the Carnegie classification has been a "prestige barometer," because it examined variables linked to normative models of prestige and stature, such as research expenditure, number of research doctorates awarded, and number of research-focused faculty. This practice appears to privilege one element of institutional mission (knowledge production) and by extension certain types of institutions over others (McCormick and Zhao 2005).

Although the attempts to gauge prestige were more of interest to academics and administrators, the practice of rating institutions became more for prospective students as the number of college applicants increased between the 1970s and the 1980s. In this context, the definition of a prestigious institution became more relevant to what consists of a quality student experience. This increased the interest in program characteristics, particularly in selectivity of student body. For example, *Barron's Profiles of American Colleges*, published originally in 1964, classified institutions into six levels: most competitive, highly competitive, very competitive, competitive, less competitive, and noncompetitive. The classification was based on measures of high school class rank, average high school GPA, average SAT scores, and the percentage of students admitted to each institution. Furthermore, the publication of various college viewbooks, such as *The Insider's Guide to the Colleges* and *Peterson's Guide to Four-Year Colleges*, projected the image of prestigious universities to be those with financial resources that could support their collegiate image with a beautiful campus, attentive faculty, and sports teams (Hartley and Morphew 2008).

Development of College Rankings

During the 1980s, college rankings came to the national forefront. Declining application pools, rising costs, and an increased premium for attending an elite school may all have contributed to the explosion of college rankings (Eide, Brewer, and Ehrenberg 1998; Hossler and Foley 1995; Hoxby 1997), which mostly emerged from profit motives of commercial media (Brooks 2005). The first one of its kind and the most influential one is *U.S. News and World Report's America's Best Colleges* (USNWR). USNWR argued that its rankings provide an ideal starting point for families comparing colleges and offer an opportunity to judge the relative quality of the educational experience at schools based on widely accepted indicators of excellence. In 1983, the company published its first ranking by surveying college presidents to name the top five institutions for the respective Carnegie classification categories, and then selecting the top 10 institutions based on the percentage of presidents who listed each institution. The same method was used in 1985.

The success of the first two editions encouraged USNWR to produce its publication annually. Since 1987 (1988 edition), *America's Best Colleges* has been published every year, listing a limited number of "top" colleges for four institution categories—national universities, national liberal arts colleges, regional universities, and regional liberal arts colleges—as defined by the Carnegie classification (prior to 1989, schools were ranked within the five categories of: national universities, national liberal arts colleges, comprehensive universities, regional liberal arts colleges, and smaller comprehensive universities). Because of changes to the Carnegie classification in 1994, 2000, and 2005, some schools were ranked in different categories in later years. Since the start of annual publication in 1987, an institution's ranking has been determined based on reputation (25 percent of the overall score; 22.5 percent in 2010) and the objective measures of input and output (75 percent of the overall score). Data are self-reported. If colleges do not provide data, USNWR uses supplemental data from other sources, such as the American Association of University Professors, the College Board, the National Collegiate Athletic Association, the Council for Aid to Education, and the U.S. Department of Education. In a year's rankings, all data are standardized in the ranking calculation. The top school in each institutional category receives a score of 100, and the relative score is calculated for the rest of the schools based on the rankings. Although USNWR argued that this allows the ranking results to reflect the extent of differences between schools on each ranking component, this practice became controversial as universities assumed it exaggerated minor differences (Sauder and Espeland 2009).

The objective measures of input and output are composed of broad evaluation criteria that are measured through multiple statistics. The broad evaluation criteria include student selectivity, faculty resources, retention and graduation, and educational resources, with a varying degree of emphasis (See Table 6.1.). Student selectivity (12.5 percent of overall score) is measured by the acceptance rate (10 percent), the proportion of freshmen who were in the top 10 percent of their high school (25 percent), and the average SAT/ACT score (65 percent). The yield rate was removed from the selectivity measure in 2003. Financial resources (10 percent of the overall score) is measured by the average spending per student on instruction, research, student services, and related educational expenditures (other/general expenditures per student was removed in 1999). As a last category, faculty resources (20 percent of the overall score) is measured by class size (proportion of classes with fewer than 20 students [30 percent] and with 50 or more students [10 percent]), faculty salary (35 percent), the proportion of professors with the highest degree in their field (15 percent), the student–faculty ratio (5 percent), and the proportion of faculty who are full-time (5 percent). Although the indicators are arbitrary (Hazelkorn 2011) and ranking outcomes are highly sensitive to these indicators and their respective weights

Table 6.1 Changes in *U.S. News* methodology, 1987–2010

Year	Reputation	Student Selectivity	Faculty Resource	Retention and Graduation	Financial Resource	Alumni Giving	Graduation Rate Performance	Numerical Orders
1987	25	25	25	5	20	0	0	Top 25
1989	25	25	25	5	20	0	0	
1990	25	25	25	5	20	0	0	Top 25 + Tier 1, 2, 3, 4
1992	25	25	25	7	18	0	0	
1993	25	25	20	10	15	5	0	
1994	25	25	20	15	10	5	0	
1995	25	15	20	25	10	5	0	Top 50 + Tier 2, 3, 4
1996	25	15	20	20	10	5	5	
1997	25	15	20	25	10	5	5	
1999	25	15	20	25	10[i]	5	5	
2003	25	15[ii]	20	25	10	5	5	Top 120 + Tier 3, 4
2010	22.5[iii]	15	20	25	10	5	7.5	Top 200 + Tier 4

Notes. i. Prior to 1999, expenditure was measured by educational expenditure per student (80%) and other general expenditure per student (20%). Since 1999, only educational expenditure was included in the expenditure.

ii. Since 2003, the category yield rates was dropped from the indicators; weights on the remaining indicators were changed: acceptance rate (from 15% to 10%), % freshmen who graduated in the top 10% of their high school classes (additional 5%), average SAT/ACT (additional 10%).

iii. Since 2010, reputation score is based on the peer survey (66.7%) and high school counselor's rating (33.3%).

(Clarke 2002, 2004; Porter 2000), there has been increasing criticism on the validity and the reliability of the ranking measures. Over time, USNWR added the "value-added" measurement of the graduation rate (5 percent since 1996; 7.5 percent in 2010), while reducing the weights on student selectivity (from 25 percent to 15 percent), financial resources (from 20 percent to 10 percent), and faculty resources (from 25 percent to 20 percent). Retention and graduation rates carried more importance in later periods (from 5 percent to 25 percent), and a measurement of alumni donation (5 percent since 1993) was also added.

Along with measurement changes, the number of institutions ranked expanded over time. For the first annual ranking in 1987, only the top 25 institutions were selected, with no other institutions listed in the publication. In 1990, USNWR created a tiered system: schools not included in the top 25 were divided into four quartiles (tiers). Within each tier, institutions were presented alphabetically without a numerical order. In 1995, USNWR expanded the numerical rankings to the top 50. This placed the first quartile schools in a specific numerical order and the rest of the schools into tiers (Top 50 plus Tiers 2, 3, and 4). In 2003, the magazine started to assign numerical rankings to the top 50 percent of colleges and universities. This resulted in about 125 and 110 universities and colleges being ranked in the national university and liberal arts college categories, respectively. In 2010, USNWR once again expanded the scope of numerical rankings, for which the top 75 percent of institutions received a specific numerical order (Top 200), and the remaining 25 percent (formerly Tier 4) were categorized as Tier 2.

Despite the change, the top 10 schools in each ranking category stayed stable (see Table 6.2). Some analysts argue that these methodological changes reflect a marketing ploy of ranking producers to maintain their popularity by making changes in the forthcoming ranking editions (Federkeil 2008; Stella and Woodhouse 2006). Dichev (2001) found that USNWR's annual rankings have a strong tendency to revert to earlier rankings in the two years following. Year-to-year changes in the positions mostly happened within a small window of ranking points (Grewal, Dearden, and Lilien 2008).

Despite criticisms of its methods, USNWR's ranking has gained popularity among the public. The *America's Best Colleges* issue drove USNWR's typical newsstand sales up by 40 percent, reaching an end audience of 11 million people (Dichev 2001). After the company expanded to the Internet, Web traffic hit an all-time high on the date that rankings were published, with 2.6 million visitors generating 18.9 million page views in a single day (*U.S. News*, September 12, 2013). The success of USNWR led to the expansion of media rankings. USNWR now provides rankings for programs at undergraduate and graduate levels, including specialty program rankings (undergraduate business and engineering), graduate

Table 6.2 Top 10 Institutions in *U.S. News*: 1983–2010

			National Universities		
Rank	1983	1987	1995	2003	2010
1	Stanford University	Stanford University	Harvard University	Harvard University	Harvard University
2	Harvard University	Harvard University	Princeton University	Princeton University	Princeton University
	Yale University		Yale University		
3		Yale University		Yale University	Yale University
4	Princeton University	Princeton University	Stanford University	Massachusetts Institute of Technology	Columbia University
5	University of California, Berkeley	University of California, Berkeley	Massachusetts Institute of Technology	California Institute of Technology	Stanford University
				Duke University	University of Pennsylvania
				Stanford University	
				University of Pennsylvania	
6	University of Chicago	Dartmouth College	Duke University		
7	University of Michigan	Duke University	California Institute of Technology		California Institute of Technology
			Dartmouth College		Massachusetts Institute of Technology
8	Cornell University	University of Chicago,			
	University of Illinois, Urbana-Champaign	University of Michigan			

(*Continued*)

Table 6.2 (Continued)

National Universities

Rank	1983	1987	1995	2003	2010
9			Brown University	Dartmouth College Washington University	Dartmouth College Duke University University of Chicago
10	Dartmouth College Massachusetts Institute of Technology	Brown University	Johns Hopkins University		

Liberal Arts Colleges

Rank	1983	1987	1995	2003	2010
1	Amherst College	Williams College	Amherst College	Williams College	Williams College
2	Swarthmore College Williams College	Swarthmore College	Swarthmore College Williams College	Amherst College	Amherst College
3		Carleton College		Swarthmore College	Swarthmore College
4	Carleton College	Amherst College	Bowdoin College	Carleton College Pomona College Wellesley College	Middlebury College Wellesley College
5	Oberlin College	Oberlin College	Haverford College Wellesley College		
6	Wellesley College	Pomona College			Bowdoin College Pomona College

7	Wesleyan College	Wesleyan College	Middlebury College	Davidson College Middlebury College	
8	Bryn Mawr College	Wellesley College	Pomona College		Carleton College
9	Davidson College Haverford College Pomona College Reed College	Haverford College	Bryn Mawr College	Haverford College	Davidson College Haverford College
10	Grinnell College	Grinnell College	Smith College	Bowdoin College	

rankings on about 12 broad areas (business, education, engineering, law, medicine, nursing, fine arts, public affairs, health, science, library and information studies, and social sciences and humanities), online college rankings, and global rankings.

Many domestic and global successors emerged. Within the United States, media such as *Money, Forbes, Business Week,* and *Wall Street Journal* began to publish college rankings (See Table 6.3.). Globalization increased the need for information about institutions around the world, as international partnerships and cross-border movements of students and faculty increased (Salmi and Saroyan 2007). In particular, governments developed a greater interest in comparing the performance of their countries' higher education institutions to that of other countries. Reflecting these social demands, in 2003, Shanghai Jiao Tong University published the first global Academic Ranking of World Universities (ARWU), and, in 2004, Times Higher Education (THE) and Quacquarelli Symonds (QS) published the top 200 global schools based on reputation, research output, and other quantitative input data. Because comparing institutions situated in unique social and educational systems is a complex task, most of the global rankings focus on reputation and research outcomes, such as numbers of publications and citations.

Ratings and rankings determine and publicize the relative status of institutions based on certain measures. The proliferation and popularity of these measures are thus accompanied by increasing debate about their worth and impact on various constituencies and higher education institutions. In particular, concerns arose that such prestige barometers would have a "corrosive effect" on higher education institutions. Academic programs might pursue prestige by changing policy and reallocating resources in expectation of an improved rank, which neither necessarily enhances the quality of the institution nor the missions of higher education.

Why Does Prestige Matter to Higher Education Institutions?

Prestige is important because it is linked to the highly qualified students and faculty and the financial resources that an institution can obtain (Brewer, Gates, and Goldman 2002). By capturing abstract images of institutions in discrete numbers, measures of prestige such as ratings and rankings shape audiences' perceptions of institutions' relative status. To the public, these measures of prestige suggest which schools are worth attending or supporting, and thus, prestige benefits institutions in terms of admissions, resource attainment, and reputation. Because increases or decreases in these areas affect future prestige as measured by rankings, and because the feedback loop perpetuates, institutions have a keen interest in the pursuit of prestige.

Table 6.3 Media Rankings and Measurements

Name	First Publication Year	Measurements and Weights	Data Sources
U.S. News and World Report: America's Best Colleges	1983, 1987 (annual publication)	Graduation and retention rates (22.5%) Six-year graduation rate (80%), first-year retention rate (20%) Undergraduate academic reputation (22.5%) Faculty resources (20%) Class size (40%), faculty salary (35%), % professors with highest degree (15%), student–faculty ratio (5%), faculty who are full time (5%) Student selectivity (12.5%) SAT/ACT scores (65%), graduated in the top 10% of their high school classes (25%), acceptance rate (10%) Financial resources (10%) Graduation rate performance (7.5%) Alumni giving rate (5%)	Institutional submission
Money's Best Colleges	1990, 2016 (new rankings)	Quality of education (1/3 weighting) Six-year graduation rate (35%), standardized test scores of entering freshmen (10%), yield rate (5%), student–faculty ratio (15%), value-added graduation rate (35%) Affordability (1/3 weighting) Net price of a degree (35%), student debt upon graduation (15%), parent federal PLUS loans (5%), student loan repayment and default risk (15%), value-added student loan repayment measures (15%), affordability for low-income students (15%) Outcomes (1/3 weighting) Early career earnings (10%), mid-career earnings (5%), 10-year earnings (10%), market value of alumni skills (10%), comparative value earnings (15%), career services staffing per 1,000 students (7.5%), presence of a program that connects job seeking students with alumni (7.5%), job meaning (20%)	The U.S. Department of Education (IPEDS and College Scorecard), Brookings Institute, Peterson's, PayScale.com

(Continued)

Table 6.3 (*Continued*)

Name	First Publication Year	Measurements and Weights	Data Sources
Princeton Review	1992	Academics/Administration Classroom experience, out-of-class hours students spend studying, rating on professors, accessibility of professors, science lab facilities, popularity of study abroad program, health services, career services, college library, financial aid, smooth administration, satisfaction with school Quality of life Happiness at school, beauty of campus, campus food, dorms, overall happiness Politics Student composition based on political views, level of political awareness Demographics Race/class interaction, LGBTQ friendly, religious Town life Rating of city/town school is located, town-gown relations Extracurriculars Athletic facilities, intercollegiate sports, intramural sports, college radio station, campus newspaper, theater productions, engagement in community service, student government Social scene Greek life, use of alcohol and drugs	Student survey
Washington Monthly	2005	Social mobility Graduation rate (10%), graduation rate performance (10%), predicted vs. actual % Pell grant recipients (13.33%) and first generation students (6.67%), average net prices paid by first-time, full-time, in-state students with family incomes below $75,000 per year (20%), comparison between the median earnings of a college's former students and predicted earnings 10 years after initial enrollment (20%), student loan repayment rate (raw) (10%), institutional character-adjusted repayment rate (10%)	The U.S. Department of Education (IPEDS and College Scorecard), Corporation for National and

	Year	Indicators	Data sources
		Research Total amount of an institution's research spending, number of science and engineering PhDs awarded, number of undergraduate alumni who have gone on to receive a PhD in any subject, number of faculty receiving prestigious awards, number of faculty in the National Academies Community service (equally weighted) Size of air force, army, and navy ROTC programs, number of alumni currently serving in the Peace Corp, percentage of federal work–study grant money spent on community service projects, percentage students doing community service, number of hours of community service per student, whether any staff were employed in community service, if the institution provides scholarships for community service	Community Service
Forbes: America's Top Colleges	2008	Postgraduate success (32.5%) Salary of alumni (10%), America's leaders list (22.5%) Student debt (25%) Average federal loan debt load (10%), student loan default rates (12.5%), predicted vs. actual percent of students taking federal loans (2.5%) Student satisfaction (25%) Actual (12.5%) and predicted (2.5%) freshmen-sophomore retention rates, Rate my professors (10%) Graduation rate (7.5%) 4-year graduation rate actual (5%), actual vs. predicted rate (2.5%) Academic success (10%) Students win nationally prestigious scholarships and fellowships (7.5%), go on to earn Ph.D. (2.5%)	The U.S. Department of education (IPEDS), PayScale.com, the America's leaders list (Center for College Affordability and Productivity), RateMyProfessors.com
The Economist	2015	Gap in the median earnings of a college's former students and expected earnings calculated based on average SAT scores, sex ratio, race breakdown, college size, control (private/public), and mix of subjects students choose to study, religious	The U.S. Department of education (College

(Continued)

111

Table 6.3 (Continued)

Name	First Publication Year	Measurements and Weights	Data Sources
		affiliation, prevailing wages in its city, wealth of its state, whether it has a ranked undergraduate business school, percentage of students receiving Pell grants, whether it is a liberal arts college, colleges' appearance during the past 15 years on the *Princeton Review's* top-20 lists for political leftism and "reefer madness" (use of marijuana on campus)	Scorecard), Bloomberg's Best undergraduate business schools, *Princeton Review*

The Wall Street Journal and The Times Higher Education	2016	Resources (30%)
		  Finance per student (11%), faculty per student (11%), research papers per faculty (8%)
		Engagement (20%)
		  Student engagement (7%), student recommendation (6%), interaction with teachers and students (4%), number of accredited programs (3%)
		Outcomes (40%)
		  Graduation rate (11%), value added to graduate salary (12%), value added to the loan repayment rate (7%), academic reputation (10%)
		Environment (10%)
		  Percentage of international students (2%), student diversity (3%), student inclusion (2%), staff diversity (3%)
			The U.S. Department of Education (IPEDS, College Scorecard), Bureau of Economic Analysis, THE US Student Survey, THE Academic Survey, Elsevier bibliometric dataset

Sources: https://www.usnews.com/education/best-colleges/articles/how-us-news-calculated-the-rankings
http://time.com/money/4393604/how-money-ranks-best-colleges-2016/
https://www.princetonreview.com/college-rankings/ranking-methodology
http://washingtonmonthly.com/magazine/septemberoctober-2016/a-note-on-methodology-4-year-colleges-and-universities-7/
https://www.forbes.com/sites/carolinehoward/2016/07/06/top-colleges-ranking-2016-the-full-methodology/#2c488e985b82
http://www.economist.com/blogs/graphicdetail/2015/10/value-university
https://www.timeshighereducation.com/world-university-rankings/wall-street-journal-times-higher-education-college-rankings-methodology
All accessed August 27, 2017.

Effect on Admissions

As students cannot evaluate the quality of higher education institutions before their own enrollment and college experience, the prospective students would not have full information about the institutions. In this case, an institution's rank acts as a cue to students of what they can expect from the institution (Fombrun 1996). Also, a higher rank means a better market value of the degrees conferred by the university (Keith 2001). According to the CIRP Freshman Survey, 10.5 percent of the incoming cohort in 1995 responded that rankings in national magazines were very important in their decision to attend their respective institutions. The number nearly doubled in 2015 (20.1 percent) (Eagan et al. 2016). In choosing colleges across national borders, almost 70 percent of prospective students responded that rankings were either "essential" or "very important" (Karzunina, Bridgestock, and Philippou 2014).

In this regard, many empirical studies on rankings have examined how an institution's prestige, defined as its status in rankings, affected admissions. First, the distinction of the top 25 or the top 50—being listed on the front page—results in selective admissions outcomes, with an increase in applications (by about 4 percent), a decrease in acceptance rate (by 3.6 percent to 4 percent), a higher proportion of students in the top 10 percent of their high school (by 1.5 percent to 2.3 percent), and higher average SAT scores (Bowman and Bastedo 2009; Meredith 2004). Studies also found that the impact of rankings is bigger for public and research universities. Moreover, an institution's numerical position matters for admissions outcomes (Alter and Reback 2014), due to the simplicity of the information. Luca and Smith (2013) analyzed institutional data for the period of 1990–2000 and found that a one-rank improvement results in a 2.07 percent increase in applicants and a 3.44 percent decrease in acceptance rate, but no impact was found on yield rate, SAT scores, or high school rank. Sauder and Lancaster's study (2006) on law school admissions indicated that an improvement within the top tier was associated with an increase in the number of applications from students with the highest LSAT scores. Some studies also indicated that full-pay applicants (Griffith and Rask 2007) and students from high-income families who were high achieving and had higher educational motivation (McDonough et al. 1998) were particularly sensitive to rankings.

Resource Attainment

An institution's relative standing affects its opportunities to obtain resources from external sources. When universities are better able to manage their rankings, they can garner greater support for their resource and development efforts from a variety of resource providers (Bastedo and Bowman

2011; Pfeffer and Salancik 1978). Such providers include government and industry, and foundations through public fiscal support, research funding, and private donations. Alumni also donate to their alma mater based on the performance of schools in terms of prestige. Yet research reveals mixed findings. Meredith (2004) found no evidence that rankings influence the amount of gifts—corporate support, research grants, and alumni donations—a university receives, both for public and private institutions. Separating these categories, Bastedo and Bowman (2011) found moderate gains in research and development funding from government and industry, as well as in the proportion of alumni who donate to their university, but found no significant influence on funding from foundations. In addition, the rankings' effect on constituencies and their behaviors may not be immediate; the effect is weaker in a shorter period (two to four years later) than over a longer period (eight years later).

One of the important mechanisms in which prestige affects resource attainment is through political pressure. Under the growing demand for accountability, rankings were folded into state policy to assess university performance (Sponsler 2009). States such as Minnesota (Minnesota Office of Higher Education 2009), Indiana (Indiana Commission for Higher Education 2008), and Texas (UT System 2008) included their state institutions' domestic and global ranking positions in their accountability reports. Jin and Whalley's study (2007) of public institutions noted that exposure to the rankings increased state appropriations, as states made an effort to improve the unfavorable classification of their public colleges by devoting more financial resources. Furthermore, foreign governments use global rankings to decide where to provide scholarships when their students study at foreign institutions. For example, international PhD scholarships (Becas Chile) from Chile's CONICYT are given to candidates accepted into programs in the top 50 of the program's specific area rankings in THE and ARWU (CONICYT 2017); and the Saudi government's scholarship only supports institutions ranked in the top 200 of the ARWU ranking (Redden 2016).

Reputation

Higher ranking positions are important for building reputation. When there is little information about an institution, rankings become a reference point (Bowman and Bastedo 2011). Bastedo and Bowman's (2010) analysis of the USNWR showed that future peer assessments of reputation were substantially influenced by overall rankings, tier level, and changes in tier level, even when controlling for previous peer assessments of reputation and other relevant factors. Even higher education experts, who might normally be expected to have relatively stable assessments of reputation over time, are substantially influenced by the rankings that many of them ostensibly disdain. Stake (2006) found that reputation scores slowly aligned with overall rank, and past rankings were the strongest predictor of an institution's current reputation score.

Another mechanism through which rankings affect the reputation of academic programs is the halo effect. Programs or departments may receive higher evaluations when they are of institutions that have, on the whole, a strong reputation (Cartter 1966; Diamond and Graham 2000). A good example is from Solomon and Astin (1981): even though Princeton had no undergraduate business program, faculty who responded to the researchers' survey gave the nonexistent program top marks because of the university's reputation (Bogue and Hall 2003).

Overall, research and anecdotes suggest that measures of prestige, particularly rankings, influence the admissions, resources, and reputation of an institution. Meanwhile, these are the factors that make up the characteristics of what is considered prestigious in the rankings. The result of this relationship is a Matthew effect, which captures the idea that "the rich get richer and the poor get poorer," from the parable in the biblical Gospel of Matthew (Matthew 13:12) (Merton 1968): colleges that are already privileged in the field make additional gains, while their competitors—which are essentially identical on the most meaningful indicators—fall further behind. In this way, higher education is a winner-take-all market where marginal differences in performance lead to large differences in reputation and resources (Frank and Cook 1995). When prestige is academic currency, the result is a "positional arms race," as institutions engage in behaviors that conform to what rankings measure and consider as prestige.

Institutional Behaviors in Pursuit of Prestige

Despite criticism regarding the volatility and arbitrariness of ranking systems, managerial anxiety about rankings and competition with other universities might lead universities to succumb to the allure of gaming the ranking system (Sauder and Lancaster 2006). In fact, a group of administrators attempted to resist rankings. In June 2007, at the annual meeting of the Annapolis Group, which represents over 100 liberal arts colleges, members discussed the *Presidents Letter* that asked college presidents to refuse to fill out the USNWR reputational survey and to decline using the rankings in any promotional efforts to indicate the quality of their respective institutions. Although 12 presidents signed the letter at the time, followed by more presidents later, the response rate of the reputational survey of the USNWR rankings was at 46 percent in the following spring (2008), which was only a slight decrease from 51 percent in 2007.

Top managers at institutions feel pressure that not "playing the game" hurts their schools (Corley and Gioia 2000) and that engaging in what rankings measure is doing "what's best for the school," since rankings have important effects (Espeland and Sauder 2007). According to the Association of Governing Boards' (2001) survey of college presidents, 76 percent reported that USNWR was somewhat or very important for their institutions, 51 percent attempted to improve rankings, 50 percent used the rankings for internal benchmarks, and 4 percent even launched a task force or committee to address rankings (Levin 2002). At some institutions, presidents criticized rankings and refused to work toward the measures. For example, at Syracuse University, the former chancellor Nancy Cantor (2004–2013) refused to factor rankings into the university's management, criticizing the volatility and mystery of the rankings. Although the school's ranking suffered during the years she served, the new chancellor Kent Syverud, at his arrival, mentioned in an interview that he would pay attention to rankings because rankings affect the decision making of constituencies that matter to universities (Rivard 2014). The pressure on administrators to improve rankings might be higher as some schools link rankings to salary. For example, the Arizona Board of Regents approved a $60,000 bonus for Michael Crow, the president of Arizona State University, as pay for an improved USNWR rating (Jaschik 2007).

The behaviors in the pursuit of prestige within the academic hierarchy (O'Meara 2007) have been tied to rankings, as those systems become powerful influencers. The first step is the institutions' cooperation with rankings by actively providing their institutional data. In 2016, 93 percent of the 1,374 colleges and universities surveyed returned their statistical information to the USNWR. However, universities can strive in a more "active" way, as documented by a number of studies, as well as media that report "successful" institutional cases (e.g., Kutner 2014). Often, changes in practices and policies start from a careful "backward regression"—that is, studying the measurements and figuring out manipulable factors. Institutions then make funding decisions and alter activities within schools to conform to rankings criteria (Espeland and Sauder 2007; Gormley and Weimer 1999). Because ranking measurements heavily depend on reputation, admissions outcomes, expenditure, and faculty resources, institutions' prestige-seeking behaviors are mostly focused on admissions, resource allocation including extensive interest in public relations, faculty hiring, and, at times, even unethical practices.

Admissions and Financial Aid

The pursuit of prestige causes an admissions arms race, as institutions try to increase the number of applications and reduce matriculation rates while attracting more academically selective students. One strategy is the implementation of shorter and/or common applications (Avery et al. 2013; Chaker

2004; Liu, Ehrenberg, and Mrdjenovic 2007) as well as early admissions. Some institutions relax admission standards by dropping SAT/ACT requirements (Kirp 2003), potentially to attract students who are willing and able to pay the full tuition (Brewer, Gates, and Goldman 2002; Stecklow 1995). Avery et al. (2013) insisted that institutions reject some top applicants, knowing they will likely be accepted at other institutions that appeal more to the applicant, who will likely ultimately choose an institution of higher prestige.

The most fundamental element of admissions strategy in creating a selective class is to provide a significant price discount to some of the best students through grants and generous financial aid packages (Leeds and DesJardins 2014; McPherson and Schapiro 1991, 1997; Winston 1997). Specifically, universities and colleges spend more on institutional grants and fellowships, mostly by distributing merit-based financial aid among more students with high test scores, while not changing or reducing need-based aid (Espeland and Sauder 2007; Kim 2016). Because tuition level functions as a "signal" for academic quality (Bowman and Bastedo 2009), schools prefer not to reduce tuition (sticker price) but offer greater price discounts in less visible forms (generous grant aid) (Monks and Ehrenberg 1999).

Resource Allocation

Bowen (1980) explained that the primary goals of institutions are educational excellence, prestige, and influence, and there is virtually no limit to the amount of money an institution could spend for seemingly fruitful educational ends. Each institution raises all the money it can and spends all it raises, which leads to ever-increasing expenditures. In particular, when rankings give a higher mark for institutions with higher levels of expenditure, "new money" would be allocated to improve the "quality" of a program as defined by the institution's ranking (Espeland and Sauder 2007). For example, the 2002 10-year strategic plan for Baylor University outlined goals to move its USNWR position from Tier 2 into the top 100. As of 2007, Baylor spent $200 million on related improvements (Farrell and Van Der Werf 2007). Analyzing institutional expenditure from 1980–2011, Kim (2017) found that the introduction of rankings increased the total amount spent on relevant educational activities: when a national university was ranked, the total expenditure increased by 4.9 percent in the following year, which is about $1,643 per full-time student; similarly, for a national liberal arts college, the expenditure increased by 5.9 percent, which is about $1,900 per student per year.

Intensified efforts to boost institutional prestige not only increase expenditure but also affect the areas of resource allocation. First, in moving up to "Research I" from "Research II" in the Carnegie classification, institutions allocated more resources to research (Iglesias 2014; Zemsky and Massy 1990) and facilities or amenities (Winston 1999) over teaching and learning (Brewer, Gates, and Goldman 2002). As rankings focus only on research universities and national liberal arts colleges, Kim (2017) found that these institutions increased expenditure in instruction, which might be due to efforts to reduce class sizes. Other support activities (instructional support and student services) as well as noneducational services (for example, residential halls, gyms, cafeterias, union buildings) also had significant increases. Rankings also encouraged universities to invest more in marketing. Schools established marketing departments and hired professional directors to head them (Bok 2003; Kirp 2003; Pulley 2003). In Espeland and Sauder's investigation of law schools (2007), many administrators reported that their schools spend more than $100,000 per year on the development of brochures.

As administrators need to support noninstructional activities, such as fund-raising and communications with external agencies (Ehrenberg 2000), the size and the sophistication of administration have increased (Collis 2004). As such, schools research rankings (Kim 2017) to mimic the spending behavior of other prestigious universities and to increase the amount of federal funding received (Morphew and Baker 2004). Those functions further increase expenditure on noninstructional administrative support (Leslie and Rhoades 1995; Zemsky and Massy 1990).

Despite an institution's expensive investment, the chances of moving up the ladder are low. Gnolek, Falciano, and Kuncl (2014) projected that the pursuit of a higher ranking will involve a higher level of costs. The authors simulated the changes in each ranking criterion that would move an institution from the mid-30s to the top 20 in national university rankings. Improving only financial resources per student and average faculty compensation would require a sustained increase of more than $112,000,000 per year, in addition to the expenses of decreasing the class size, increasing the graduation rate, and attracting greater numbers of highly qualified students. Furthermore, moving to the top 20 is impossible without a corresponding change (0.8 points) in undergraduate reputation, which has less than a 0.01 percent probability of occurring.

Faculty Hiring and Promotion

Institutions perceive that prominent faculty can boost their prestige (Grunig 1997; Massy and Zemsky 1994; Melguizo and Strober 2007). Thus, schools make efforts to recruit and retain faculty, and a big part of this effort involves increasing faculty salaries, especially to recruit or *steal* star faculty from other prestigious institutions (Clotfelter 1996; O'Meara 2007). Using the case of a Mid-Atlantic small liberal arts college with lower prestige, in which the school's strategic document called for raising faculty salaries,

Ehrenberg (2003) showed that competition for faculty incentivized universities to increase salary outside of market conditions despite any internal desire to do so. Attracting faculty is also associated with costs for laboratories and facilities or indirect research expenses (Brewer, Gates, and Goldman 2002).

In seeking prestige, institutions emphasize research and publications in academic journals (Massy and Zemsky 1994). Many of these striving institutions lower course loads for faculty so that more time is spent on conducting research (Massy and Zemsky 1994), reflecting the changing priorities of the institution from a teaching culture to a research culture. Clotfelter (1996) compared the arrangement of faculty work at four elite institutions from 1976 to 1992 and found a teaching–research trade-off over the 15 years. He pointed out that this phenomenon occurred at the same time that schools came under pressure to be comprehensive by offering *full service*—that is, offering degrees, conducting research in all or virtually all of the recognized academic fields, and performing many other services. This *academic ratchet* makes institutions hire more part-time or adjunct faculty to both teach courses (Callan 1997; Massy and Zemsky 1994) and reduce the faculty–student ratio (Volkwein and Sweitzer 2006).

It is likely that promotion and tenure requirements reflect this trend. Institutions look to aspirational peers for faculty work norms to raise expectations for tenure (Finnegan and Gamson 1996). When criteria and standards are defined less on the institutional mission but more on the pursuit of prestige, faculty are encouraged to apply the professional standards of research culture (O'Meara 2007) and to produce more publications and garner more research funding (Brewer, Gates, and Goldman 2002; Hazelkorn 2008). Furthermore, as some rankings measure research performance through publication indexes, such as bibliometric and citation practices, such measures then become an unyielding yardstick for tenure (Monastersky 2005; Stergiou and Lessenich 2014).

Unethical and Gaming Behaviors

The pressure to perform well in rankings sometimes pushes institutions to unethical behaviors. Misreporting or fabricating data has been the most common behavior. In 1995, a *Wall Street Journal* article analyzed institutions' statistics submitted to USNWR and other sources such as NCAA. More than a dozen discrepancies in SAT scores, acceptance rates, and other enrollment data were discovered. Similarly, among law schools, 29 out of the 177 USNWR law schools reported a higher median LSAT to the magazine than to the American Bar Association (Carter 1998). To address this concern, since 1999, USNWR has cross-checked data provided by institutions with data from other sources. Yet several universities including Tulane University, University of New Orleans, Bucknell University, Claremont McKenna College,

Emory University, and George Washington University were found to have submitted incorrect test scores or to have overstated the high school rankings of their incoming freshmen (Anderson 2013), although it is impossible to determine if this was done intentionally. Reflecting this trend, a national survey of admissions officers by *Inside Higher Ed* revealed that 91 percent of respondents think other institutions falsified standardized test scores or admissions data, whereas only 1 percent think their own institution misreported them (Jaschik and Lederman 2012).

Meanwhile, some institutions "cut corners" through creative reporting methods. In Espeland and Sauder's study (2007) of law school administrators, administrators described how schools still admit students with lower LSAT scores but reflect the data differently in the reporting. Schools reclassify a portion of admitted students as "part-time" or probationary to exclude their scores from the median LSAT score calculation. Schools also reduce the size of incoming classes by admitting fewer students into the full-time program and more students into the part-time program to improve both the median LSAT score and the student–faculty ratio. For several undergraduate programs, schools were found to exclude international and remedial students (for example, Northeastern University and Boston University) or economically disadvantaged students in special state-sponsored programs (for example, NYU) (Stecklow 1995) to boost the institutions' average verbal or composite SAT scores.

Some institutional practices became controversial as they were interpreted as a gaming strategy for what USNWR measures. In 2006, at the annual conference of the Association for Institutional Research, the former director of institutional research at Clemson University confessed that since 2001, when the former president James F. Barker established the goal of reaching the top 20, the university adopted a policy to "affect every possible indicator to the greatest extent possible." In an attempt to push itself into the top 20 of public research institutions, the university manipulated class sizes and sought to downgrade the academic reputations of other institutions when answering surveys (by rating other institutions below average). Another controversial example comes from Baylor University. In 2008, Baylor University paid admitted freshmen ($300 bookstore credit) to retake the SAT and offered $1,000-a-year merit aid to students whose scores improved by 50 points (Jaschik 2008). Even though the university argued that this was to give out more additional merit-based scholarship, and that ranking is a "factor" but not the "driver" of this policy, the school's average SAT score went up from 1,200 to 1,210. At some graduate programs, schools temporarily hired unemployed graduates to improve their employment numbers, while others solicited more applicants, including obviously unqualified applicants, to boost selectivity numbers (Espeland and Sauder 2007).

Concerns for Striving

The aforementioned strategies can have repercussions for institutions. Institutional responses to rankings might accompany significant financial costs, though there is no clear association between change in expenditure and movement in ranking positions. Furthermore, benefits from a higher ranking might not be sufficient to cover the expanded expenses. Previous research suggested a limited effect of rankings on resource attainment, other than marginal increases in out-of-state tuition and funding from government and industry (Bastedo and Bowman 2011; Grunig 1997; Jin and Whalley 2007; Meredith 2004). Yet the probability of changing an institution's ranking is low, despite the constant increase in expenditures.

In addition, whether more resources would result in better-quality practices at schools is still unclear. Although schools that are highly ranked by USNWR do not necessarily have high retention and graduation rates relative to their student, faculty, and financial resources (Breu and Raab 1994), some studies found significant associations between educational expenditure, institutional grant, and retention and graduation outcomes (Gansemer-Topf and Schuh 2006; Webber and Ehrenberg 1997). Pike (2004) and Kim and Shim (forthcoming) examined the relationships between the six major criteria of USNWR, and student engagement and learning experience, respectively. The studies found that only student selectivity is positively related with students' engagement in enriching educational experiences, while faculty and financial resources measures are positively related with engagement in diversity experiences. How institutional responses to ranking measures relate to institutions' organization and management of core activities and policy values will provide important implications for the methodology and use of rankings in higher education.

Expensive competition for USNWR rankings might influence key institutional missions in affordability and access. As spending increases on institutional fellowships, amenities, and other services under financial constraints, schools might employ a high-tuition, high-aid model (Geiger 2002), as well as establish or increase various fees (Schuh 2003), to compensate for the expenses. Future research should address the extent to which increases in expenditures due to rankings relate to tuition increases (McPherson and Shulenburger 2008). The ranking competition further raises concerns about aggressive student recruiting practices that put more value on positioning the institution and skimming the best students from the applicant pool, and far less value on personal contact, ensuring a good fit, and delivering quality education from admission to graduation (Thacker 2005). The extent to which colleges focus their practices on recruiting certain populations and the effects on student campus composition should be investigated (Rhoades 2014).

Suggestions for Current Practice

The agreement among researchers and professionals in the field is that rankings are here to stay and competition over prestige will be more significant (Teichler 2011). How to improve the current practice of rankings or to reform the way prestige is measured and presented should be discussed among the related interest groups, including higher education researchers and practitioners, ranking providers, and policy makers.

Classifications and rankings have been heavily criticized for the weight they place on some measurement criteria. Although the purpose of rankings is to provide a proxy for institutional quality, the measurements focus disproportionately on reputation and resources (Machung 1998). By choosing a particular set of indicators, rankings set a one-size-fits-all approach in judging institutional performance (Dill and Soo 2005; Usher and Savino 2006, 2007). One solution is to have multiple rankings that measure specific dimensions of an institution (Teichler 2011) in order to promote a diversified definition of prestige. For example, the *Princeton Review* (1992) created their rankings on various dimensions including academics, quality of life, politics, demographics, town life, extracurricular activities, and social scene, as well as the controversial "party school" rankings based on student surveys. Since the mid-2000s, alternative rankings and initiatives have emerged. As tuition has continued to outstrip growth in family income, the increased political pressure on the cost of colleges and universities has made new rankings focus on "return on investment"—the measures of affordability and value of a bachelor's degree in terms of employment outcomes. Since 2008 *Forbes*'s America's Top Colleges ranking has calculated ranking based on postgraduate success as measured by salary, student debt, and loan-related indexes; similarly, *Money* changed their ranking methodology in 2016 by including net tuition price.

Related to this point, some new rankings attempted to address the concerns that previous rankings potentially disadvantaged schools with relatively high proportions of low-income students. *Washington Monthly* (2005) incorporated measures capturing colleges' commitments to educating a diverse group of students, such as the percentage of students receiving Pell Grants and the percentage of first-generation students. Other rankings focus on specific dimensions. The Center for Measuring University Performance measures research productivity; rankings from *The Advocate* and *Black Enterprise* rank the best colleges for gay students and Black students, respectively (Bastedo and Bowman 2010). Economists also seek to create unobtrusive measures of college ranking based on student preferences (Avery et al. 2013). Moreover, stating that rankings' measurement criteria do not reflect the quality of education that students actually receive, some researchers suggest other measurements for judging institutional quality such as the National Survey of Student Engagement (Pike 2004) or the Collegiate Learning Assessment. Whether the perception of prestige will become multidimensional with so many versions of college rankings entering the public consciousness is an interesting question.

Although the above-mentioned rankings attempt to capture different dimensions, in the absence of agreed-upon measures of higher education practice and outcomes, the ad hoc measures employed by the new rankings, such as graduation rates and time-to-degree or cost-of-degree statistics, are likely to be incomplete and misleading (Casper 1996; Massy, Sullivan, and Mackie 2013). Detailed measurements that account for baseline differences and trends in inputs and outputs, as well as information that closely captures the experience of key stakeholders, should be developed over time. In part, this practice is currently limited by data that are mostly reported only at the aggregated level, without information reported for specific activities. For example, instructional expenditure is only provided at the institutional level and is not individualized by departments or academic units. How much is allocated to salary for instructors versus facilities is not reported. Also, the graduation and retention rates of different demographics and the academic characteristics of students are unknown. The disconnect between the data on student learning and outcomes and the measures of a college's performance is another issue (Brooks 2005; Kuh and Pascarella 2004). By incorporating disaggregated measures of input and outcomes as well as longitudinal changes of student experience and learning outcomes into the measurements, ratings and rankings can contain more nuanced information. This will also allow institutions to systematically collect and manage their data to enhance institutional progress.

Also, the diversity among higher education institutions, programs, and students needs to be recognized. A number of studies have found that rankings have varying effects on institutions with different missions and controls (Bastedo and Bowman 2011; Meredith 2004). Different competition strategies develop among the comparison groups, such as research universities and liberal arts colleges (Kim 2016, 2017). For example, in Kim (2017), the two types of institutions increased different resources; research universities increased instructional expenditures, while their liberal arts counterparts increased spending on academic support and student services, in addition to instruction. If these strategies were adopted due to different demands and expectations for colleges of different characteristics, evaluation measurements would better reflect dimensions that recognize the mission and core practices of different types of institutions.

Besides the measurements, the way the results are presented and communicated in the ranking systems is important. A rank order is considered a publicly acceptable method (Sanoff 1998) as it is a less complex way to provide information to stakeholders (Luca and Smith 2013; O'Meara and

Meekins 2012). However, numerical ordering, along with specific cut-offs (tier groups), drives the reactivity of institutions. The significant impact of these mechanisms is alarming, as the numbers tend to exaggerate the differences between institutions (Federkeil 2008; Locke 2011; van Vught and Westerheijden 2010) without scientific precision for distinguishing institutions of close rank (Stella and Woodhouse 2006). Of note, the Carnegie classification, which categorizes universities rather than placing them in a pecking order, also has a similar ramification (McCormick and Zhao 2005) as schools aspire to be research universities (Aldersley 1995; Finnegan and Gamson 1996; Morphew and Baker 2004). For these reasons, the attributes attached to arbitrary groupings, ranking positions, or scores that are related to the vertical stratification of higher education should be considered. How the outputs of particular formats are consumed and by whom, and the consequences of these ranking activities on schools must be investigated.

Moreover, the role of higher education institutions in the process of defining and measuring prestige should be considered. How would colleges and universities take a meaningful part in the process? Since the beginning, the production of prestige measures such as classification and rankings has been led by third parties, with the purpose of generating profit (Locke et al. 2008). Although higher education institutions are requested to submit data to those ranking producers, the ranking producers are not transparent in terms of how the data are used and manipulated to generate rankings (Ehrenberg 2005). In response to this criticism, ranking providers have made efforts to gain legitimacy for their rankings as valid information about institutional quality. Ranking providers insist on frequent dialogue with institutions, college officials, and stakeholders to improve their measures and transparency (Mallette 1995). Furthermore, major ranking providers such as USNWR and THE—with the United Nations Educational, Scientific and Cultural Organization and the Institute for Higher Education Policy—launched the International Rankings Expert Group Observatory on Academic Ranking and Excellence in 2004. The group established the Berlin Principles on Ranking of Higher Education Institutions (2006), emphasizing the ethical practice of data collection, ranking analysis, and information dissemination (Sponsler 2009). Although we do not know specifically if these efforts increased the participation of higher education practitioners and researchers to the enhancement of rankings, and what changes were made to the practice due to their participation, an in-depth conversation on what measures quality and the unintended consequences of those measurements should be continued.

Finally, schools should utilize the current systems of prestige for their own benefit. Although schools are under the pressure to comply with what prestige-measuring systems evaluate, institutions also try to garner some degree of managerial autonomy under the effect of rankings. Administrators and decision makers at colleges and universities need to find strategies to make rankings advantageous for their internal practices. For example, although USNWR measures the total expenditure on educational and relevant activities, liberal arts colleges may focus increased expenditures on areas related to their educational emphasis, such as cooperative learning among peers and faculty-student interaction. Identifying strategies derived from respective core activities, the constitution of the student and faculty body, and institutional missions would allow universities with limited resources to balance the pressure of competition and the needs of their key stakeholders.

References

Aldersley, Stephen F. 1995. "Upward Drift Is Alive and Well: Research/Doctoral Model Still Attractive to Institutions." *Change* 27(5): 51–56.

Alter, Molly, and Randall Reback. 2014. "True for Your School? How Changing Reputations Alter Demand for Selective U.S. Colleges." *Educational Evaluation and Policy Analysis* 36(3): 346–370.

Anderson, Nick. 2013. "Five Colleges Misreported Data to U.S. News, Raising Concerns about Rankings, Reputation." *The Washington Post*, February 6. Accessed February 23, 2017. https://www.washingtonpost.com/local/edu cation/five-colleges-misreported-data-to-us-news-raising-concerns -about-rankings-reputation/2013/02/06/cb437876-6b17-11e2-af53-7b 2b2a7510a8_story.html?utm_term=.8199c021467a

Avery, Christopher N., Mark E. Glickman, Caroline M. Hoxby, and Andrew Metrick. 2013. "A Revealed Preference Ranking of Colleges and Universities." *Quarterly Journal of Economics* 128(1): 425–467.

Bastedo, Michael N., and Nicholas A. Bowman. 2010. "*U.S. News & World Report* College Rankings: Modeling Institutional Effects on Organizational Reputation." *American Journal of Education* 116(2): 163–183.

Bastedo, Michael N., and Nicholas A. Bowman. 2011. "College Rankings as an Interorganizational Dependency: Establishing the Foundation for Strategic and Institutional Accounts." *Research in Higher Education* 52(1): 3–23.

Blau, Peter M., and Rebecca Z. Margulies. 1974. "The Reputation of American Professional Schools." *Change* 6(10): 42–47.

Bogue, E. Grady, and Kimberely B. Hall. 2003. *Quality and Accountability in Higher Education: Improving Policy, Enhancing Performance*. Westport, CT: Praeger Publishers.

Bok, Derek. 2003. *Universities in the Marketplace: The Commercialization of Higher Education*. Princeton, NJ: Princeton University Press.

Bowen, Howard R. 1980. *The Costs of Higher Education*. San Francisco, CA: Jossey-Bass.

Bowman, Nicholas A., and Michael N. Bastedo. 2009. "Getting on the Front Page: Organizational Reputation, Status Signals, and the Impact of *U.S.*

News and World Report on Student Decisions." *Research in Higher Education* 50(5): 415–436.

Bowman, Nicholas A., and Michael N. Bastedo. 2011. "Anchoring Effects in World University Rankings: Exploring Biases in Reputation Scores." *Higher Education* 61(4): 431–444.

Breu, Theodore M., and Raymond L. Raab. 1994. "Efficiency and Perceived Quality of the Nation's Top 25 National Universities and National Liberal Arts Colleges: An Application of Data Envelopment Analysis to Higher Education." *Socio-Economic Planning Sciences* 28(1): 33–45.

Brewer, Dominic J., Susan M. Gates, and Charles A. Goldman. 2002. *In Pursuit of Prestige: Strategy and Competition in U.S. Higher Education.* New Brunswick, NJ: Transaction Publishers.

Brooks, Rachelle. 2005. "Measuring University Quality." *The Review of Higher Education* 29(1): 1–21.

Callan, Patrick M. 1997. "Stewards of Opportunity: America's Public Community Colleges." *Daedalus* 126(4): 95–112.

Carnegie Classification. n.d. About the Carnegie Classification. Accessed August 27, 2017. http://carnegieclassifications.iu.edu/index.php

Carter, Terry. 1998. "Rankled by the Rankings." *ABA Journal* 84:46–52.

Cartter, Allan M. 1966. *An Assessment of Quality in Graduate Education.* Washington, DC: American Council on Education.

Casper, Gerhard. 1996. "Letter to the Editor of US News and World Report." September 23. Accessed March 10, 2017. http://web.stanford.edu/dept/pres-provost/president/speeches/961206gcfallow.html

Cattell, James M. 1910. American Men of Science: A Biographical Dictionary. New York, NY: Science Press.

Chaker, Anne M. 2004. "The Results Are in on Early Admission: As Top Colleges Change Policies, Acceptance Rates Shift; More Openings at Harvard." *The Wall Street Journal*, January 20. Accessed February 25, 2017. https://www.wsj.com/articles/SB107455105768105626

Clarke, Marguerite. 2002. "News or Noise? An Analysis of *U.S. News and World Report's* Ranking Scores." *Educational Measurement: Issues and Practice* 21(4): 39–48.

Clarke, Marguerite. 2004. "Weighing Things Up: A Closer Look at *U.S. News & World Report's* Ranking Formulas." *College and University* 79(3): 3–9.

Clotfelter, Charles T. 1996. *Buying the Best: Cost Escalation in Elite Higher Education.* Princeton, NJ: Princeton University Press.

Collis, David J. 2004. "The Paradox of Scope: A Challenge to the Governance of Higher Education." In *Competing Conceptions of Academic Governance: Negotiating the Perfect Storm,* edited by William G. Tierney, 33–76. Baltimore, MD: Johns Hopkins University Press.

CONICYT. 2017. Rankings Universidades. Accessed August 27, 2017. http://www.conicyt.cl/becas-conicyt/postulantes/donde-estudiar/rankings-universidades/

Corley, Kevin, and Dennis Gioia. 2000. "The Ranking Game: Managing Business School Reputation." *Corporate Reputation Review* 3(4): 319–333.

Diamond, Nancy, and Hugh D. Graham. 2000. "How Should We Rate Research Universities?" *Change* 32(4): 20–33.

Dichev, Iila. 2001. "News or Noise? Estimating the Noise in the *U.S. News* University Rankings." *Research in Higher Education* 42(3): 237–266.

Dill, David D., and Maarja Soo. 2005. "Academic Quality, League Tables, and Public Policy: A Cross-National Analysis of University Ranking Systems." *Higher Education* 49(4): 495–533.

Eagan, Kevin, Ellen B. Stolzenberg, Joseph J. Ramirez, Melissa C. Aragon, Maria R. Suchard, and Cecilia Rios-Aguilar. 2016. *The American Freshman: Fifty-Year Trends, 1966–2015*. Los Angeles: Higher Education Research Institute, University of California, Los Angeles.

Ehrenberg, Ronald G. 2000. *Tuition Rising: Why College Costs So Much*. Cambridge, MA: Harvard University Press.

Ehrenberg, Ronald G. 2003. "Reaching for the Brass Ring: The *U.S. News & World Report* Rankings and Competition." *Review of Higher Education* 26(2): 145–162.

Ehrenberg, Ronald G. 2005. "Method or Madness? Inside the *U.S. News & World Report* College Rankings." *Journal of College Admissions* 189:29–35.

Eide, Eric, Dominic J. Brewer, and Ronald G. Ehrenberg, 1998. "Does It Pay to Attend and Elite Private College? Evidence on the Effects of Undergraduate College Quality on Graduate School Attendance." *Economics of Education Review* 17(4): 371–376.

Espeland, Wendy N., and Michael Sauder. 2007. "Rankings and Reactivity: How Public Measures Recreate Social Worlds." *American Journal of Sociology* 113(1): 1–40.

Farrell, Elizabeth F., and Martin Van Der Werf. 2007. "Playing the Rankings Game." *The Chronicle of Higher Education*, May 25. Accessed March 1, 2017. http://www.chronicle.com/article/Playing-the-Rankings-Game/4451

Federkeil, Gero. 2008. "Rankings and Quality Assurance in Higher Education." *Higher Education in Europe* 33(2–3): 219–231.

Finnegan, Dorothy E., and Zelda F. Gamson. 1996. "Disciplinary Adaptations to Research Culture in Comprehensive Institutions." *Review of Higher Education* 19(2): 141–177.

Fombrun, Charles J. 1996. *Reputation: Realizing Value from the Corporate Image*. Boston, MA: Harvard Business School Press.

Frank, Robert H., and Philip J. Cook. 1995. *The Winner-Take All Society*. New York: Penguin Books.

Gansemer-Topf, Ann M., and John H. Schuh. 2006. "Institutional Selectivity and Institutional Expenditures: Examining Organizational Factors That Contribute to Retention and Graduation." *Research in Higher Education* 47(6): 613–642.

Geiger, Roger L. 2002. "The Competition for High-Ability Students: Universities in a Key Marketplace." In *The Future of the City of Intellect: The Changing American University*, edited by Steven Brint, 82–107. Stanford, CA: Stanford University Press.

Gnolek, Shari L., Vincenzo T. Falciano, and Ralph W. Kuncl. 2014. "Modeling Change and Variation in *U.S. News & World Report* College Rankings: What

Would It Really Take to Be in the Top 20?" *Research in Higher Education* 55(8): 761–779.

Gormley, William T., and David L. Weimer. 1999. *Organizational Report Cards.* Cambridge, MA: Harvard University Press.

Gourman, Jackson. 1967. *The Gourman Report: Ratings of American Colleges.* Phoenix, AZ: Continuing Education Institute.

Grewal, Rajdeep, James A. Dearden, and Gary L. Lilien. 2008. "The University Rankings Game: Modeling the Competition among Universities for Ranking." *The American Statistician* 62(3): 1–6.

Griffith, Amanda, and Kevin Rask. 2007. "The Influence of the *U.S. News and World Report* Collegiate Rankings on the Matriculation Decision of High-Ability Students: 1995–2004." *Economics of Education Review* 26(2): 244–255.

Grunig, Stephen D. 1997. "Research, Reputation, and Resources: The Effect of Research Activity on Perceptions of Undergraduate Education and Institutional Resource Acquisition." *The Journal of Higher Education* 68(1): 17–52.

Hartley, Matthew, and Christopher C. Morphew. 2008. "What's Being Sold and to What End? A Content Analysis of College Viewbooks." *Journal of Higher Education* 76(6): 671–691.

Hazelkorn, Ellen. 2008. "Learning to Live with League Tables and Ranking: The Experience of Institutional Leaders." *Higher Education Policy* 21(2): 193–215.

Hazelkorn, Ellen. 2011. *Rankings and the Reshaping of Higher Education: The Battle for World-Class Excellence.* New York: Palgrave Macmillan.

Hossler, D., and Foley, E. M. 1995. "Reducing the Noise in the College Choice Process: The Use of College Guidebooks and Ratings." In *Evaluating and Responding to College Guidebooks and Rankings,* edited by R. Dan Walleri and Marsha K. Moss, 21–30. San Francisco, CA: Jossey-Bass.

Hoxby, Caroline M. 1997. "How the Changing Market Structure of U.S. Higher Education Explains College Tuition." National Bureau of Economic Research Working Paper no. 6323. Cambridge, MA: NBER.

Hughes, Raymond M. 1925. *A Study of the Graduate Schools of America.* Oxford, OH: Miami University Press.

Iglesias, Kevin. 2014. "The Price of Prestige: A Study of The Impact of Striving Behavior on the Expenditure Patterns of American Colleges and Universities." Doctoral dissertation, Seton Hall University.

Indiana Commission for Higher Education. 2008. *Reaching Higher with Major Research Universities.* Indianapolis, IN.

Jaschik, Scott. 2007. "Battle Lines on 'U.S. News.'" *Inside Higher Ed*, May 7. Accessed March 5, 2017. https://www.insidehighered.com/news/2007/05/07/usnews

Jaschik, Scott. 2008. "Baylor Pays for SAT Gains." *Inside Higher Ed*, October 15. Accessed March 10, 2017. https://www.insidehighered.com/news/2008/10/15/baylor

Jaschik, Scott, and Doug Lederman. 2012. "The 2012 inside Higher Ed Survey of College and University Admissions Directors." *Inside Higher Ed.* Accessed March 10, 2017. http://www.adapt.it/englishbulletin/docs/ihe_2012.pdf.pdf

Jin, Ginger Z., and Alex Whalley. 2007. "The Power of Information: How Do U.S. News Rankings Affect the Financial Resources of Public Colleges?" National Bureau of Economic Research Working Paper no. 12941. Cambridge, MA: NBER.

Karzunina, Dasha, Laura Bridgestock, and Georgia Philippou. 2014. *How Do Students Use Rankings? The Role of University Rankings in International Student Choice.* London: QS Intelligence Unit.

Keith, Bruce. 2001. "Organizational Contexts and University Performance Outcomes: The Limited Role of Purposive Action in the Management of Institutional Status." *Research in Higher Education* 42(5): 493–516.

Keniston, Hayward. 1959. *Graduate Study and Research in the Arts and Sciences at the University of Pennsylvania.* Philadelphia: University of Pennsylvania.

Kim, Jeongeun. 2016. "Colleges Ranked: How Institutions Strategize the Selectivity Game." Unpublished paper, Arizona State University.

Kim, Jeongeun. 2017. "The Functions and Dysfunctions of College Rankings: An Analysis of Institutional Expenditure." *Research in Higher Education.* Accessed August 27, 2017. http://link.springer.com/article/10.1007/s11162-017-9455-1

Kim, Jeongeun, and Woo-jeong Shim. "What Do Rankings Measure? The U.S. News Rankings and Student Experience at Liberal Arts Colleges." The Review of Higher Education (forthcoming).

Kirp, David L. 2003. *Shakespeare, Einstein, and the Bottom Line: The Marketing of Higher Education.* Cambridge, MA: Harvard University Press.

Kuh, George D., and Ernest T. Pascarella. 2004. "What Does Institutional Selectivity Tell Us about Educational Quality?" *Change* 36(5): 52–58.

Kutner, Max. 2014. "How to Game the College Rankings." *Boston Magazine,* August 26. Accessed March 5, 2017. http://www.bostonmagazine.com /news/article/2014/08/26/how-northeastern-gamed-the-college-ran kings/

Leeds, Daniel M., and Stephen L. DesJardins. 2014. "The Effect of Merit Aid on Enrollment: A Regression Discontinuity Analysis of Iowa's National Scholars Award." *Research in Higher Education* 56(5): 471–495.

Leslie, Larry L., and Gary Rhoades. 1995. "Rising Administrative Costs: Seeking Explanations." *The Journal of Higher Education* 66(2): 187–212.

Levin, Daniel J. 2002. "Uses and Abuses of the U.S. News Rankings." *Priorities,* fall. Association of Governing Boards of Universities and Colleges, Washington, DC.

Liu, A.Y.H., Ronald G. Ehrenberg, and Jesenka Mrdjenovic. 2007. "Diffusion of Common Application Membership and Admission Outcomes at American Colleges and Universities." National Bureau of Economic Research Working Paper No. 13175. Cambridge, MA: NBER.

Locke, William. 2011. "The Institutionalization of Rankings: Managing Status Anxiety in an Increasingly Marketized Environment." In *University Rankings: Theoretical Basis, Methodology and Impacts on Global Higher Education,* edited by Jung Cheol Shin, Robert K. Toutkoushian, and Ulrich Teichler, 201–228. New York: Springer.

Locke, William, Line Verbik, John T. Richardson, and Roger King. 2008. *Counting What Is Measured or Measuring What Counts? League Tables and Their Impact on Higher Education Institutions in England*. Bristol: Higher Education Funding Council for England.

Luca, Michael, and Jonathan Smith. 2013. "Salience in Quality Disclosure: Evidence from the U.S. News College Rankings." *Journal of Economics and Management Strategy* 22(1): 58–77.

Machung, Anne. 1998. "Playing the Rankings Game." *Change* 30(4): 12–16.

Mallette, Bruce I. 1995. "Money Magazine, *U.S. News & World Report*, and Steve Martin: What Do They Have in Common?" *New Directions for Institutional Research* 88:31–43.

Manly, Chesly. 1957. Best Colleges: An Analysis of the Nation's Best Men's and Women's Liberal Art Colleges. *Chicago Sunday Tribune*, June 2. Accessed August 27, 2017. http://archives.chicagotribune.com/1957/06/02/page/1/article/haverford-college-its-small-but-its-famous

Massy, William F., Teresa A. Sullivan, and Christopher Mackie. 2013. "Improving Measurement of Productivity in Higher Education." *Change* 45(1): 15–23.

Massy, William F., and Robert Zemsky. 1994. "Faculty Discretionary Time: Departments and the 'Academic Ratchet.'" *Journal of Higher Education* 65(1): 1–22.

McCormick, Alexander C., and Chun-Mei Zhao. 2005. "Rethinking and Reframing the Carnegie classification." *Change* 37(5): 50–57.

McDonough, Patricia M., Anthony L. Antonio, MaryBeth Walpole, and Leonor X. Perez. 1998. "College Rankings: Democratized College Knowledge for Whom?" *Research in Higher Education* 39(5): 513–537.

McPherson, Michael S., and Morton O. Schapiro. 1991. "Paying for College: Rethinking the Role of the States and the Federal Government." *Brookings Review* 9(3): 14–19.

McPherson, Michael S., and Morton O. Schapiro. 1997. "Financing Undergraduate Education: Designing National Policies." *National Tax Journal* 50(3): 557–571.

McPherson, Peter, and David Shulenburger. 2008. "University Tuition, Consumer Choice and College Affordability: Strategies for Addressing a Higher Education Affordability Challenge." National Association of State Universities and Land-Grant Colleges Discussion Paper. Washington, DC: NASULGC.

Melguizo, Tatiana, and Myra H. Strober. 2007. "Faculty Salaries and the Maximization of Prestige." *Research in Higher Education* 48(6): 633–668.

Meredith, Marc. 2004. "Why Do Universities Compete in the Ratings Game? An Empirical Analysis of the Effects of the *U.S. News and World Report* College Rankings." *Research in Higher Education* 45(5): 443–461.

Merton, Robert K. 1968. "The Matthew Effect in Science." *Science* 159:56–63.

Minnesota Office of Higher Education. 2009. *Minnesota Measures*. St. Paul, MN: Accessed August 27, 2017. http://www.ohe.state.mn.us/pdf/minnesotameasures2009.pdf

Monastersky, R. 2005. "The Number That's Devouring Science: The Impact Factor, Once a Simple Way to Rank Scientific Journals, Has Become an Unyielding Yardstick for Hiring, Tenure, and Grants." *The Chronicle of Higher Education*, October 14. Accessed March 10, 2017. http://www.chronicle.com/article/the-number-thats-devouring/26481

Monks, James, and Ronald G. Ehrenberg. 1999. "The Impact of *U.S. News and World Report* College Rankings on Admissions Outcomes and Pricing Policies at Selective Institutions." National Bureau of Economic Research Working Paper no. 7227. Cambridge, MA: NBER.

Morphew, Christopher C., and Bruce D. Baker. 2004. "The Cost of Prestige: Do New Research I Universities Incur Higher Administrative Costs?" *Review of Higher Education* 27(3): 365–384.

National Research Council. 1982. *An Assessment of Research-Doctorate Programs in the United States*. Washington, DC.

O'Meara, KerryAnn. 2007. "Striving for What? Exploring the Pursuit of Prestige." *Higher Education: Handbook of Theory and Research* 22:121–179.

O'Meara, KerryAnn, and Matthew Meekins. 2012. "Inside Rankings: Limitations and Possibilities." NERCHE Working Paper: 2012 Series, Issue 1. Boston, MA: New England Resource Center for Higher Education. Accessed August 27, 2017. http://scholarworks.umb.edu/nerche_pubs/24/

Pfeffer, Jeffrey, and Gerald R. Salancik. 1978. *The External Control of Organizations: A Resource Dependence Perspective*. New York: Harper & Row.

Pike, Gary R. 2004. "Measuring Quality: A Comparison of the *U.S. News* Rankings and NSSE Benchmarks." *Research in Higher Education* 45(2): 193–208.

Porter, Stephen R. 2000. "The Robustness of the Graduation Rate Performance Indicator Used in the *U.S. News and World Report* College Ranking." *International Journal of Educational Advancement* 1:10–30.

Pulley, John L. 2003. "Romancing the Brand." *The Chronicle of Higher Education*, October 24. Accessed March 10, 2017. http://www.chronicle.com/article/Romancing-the-Brand/2712

Redden, Elizabeth. 2016. "Will Saudi Student Boom End?" *Inside Higher Ed*, February 25. Accessed March 6, 2017. https://www.insidehighered.com/news/2016/02/25/will-us-colleges-and-universities-see-decline-saudi-funded-students

Rhoades, Gary. 2014. "The Higher Education We Choose, Collectively: Reembodying and Repoliticizing Choice." *The Journal of Higher Education* 85(6): 917–930.

Rivard, Ry. 2014. "About-Face on Rankings: After Years of Decisions That Increased Diversity But Didn't Help It in the Rankings, Syracuse University Might Start Caring Again." *Inside Higher Ed*, January 6. Accessed March 6, 2017. https://www.insidehighered.com/news/2014/01/06/syracuse-after-refusing-play-rankings-game-may-care-again

Roose, Kenneth D., and Charles J. Anderson. 1970. *An Assessment of Quality in Graduate Education*. Washington, DC: American Council on Education.

Salmi, Jamil, and Alenoush Saroyan. 2007. "League Tables as Policy Instruments: Uses and Misuses." *Higher Education Management and Policy* 19(2): 24–62.

Sanoff, Alvin P. 1998. "Rankings Are Here to Stay: Colleges Can Improve Them." *The Chronicle of Higher Education*, September 4. Accessed March 10, 2017. http://www.chronicle.com/article/Rankings-Are-Here-to-Stay-/9053

Sauder, Michael, and Wendy N. Espeland. 2009. "The Discipline of Rankings: Tight Coupling and Organizational Change." *American Sociological Review* 74(1): 63–82.

Sauder, Michael, and Ryon Lancaster. 2006. "Do Rankings Matter? The Effects of *U.S. News & World Report* Rankings on the Admissions Process of Law Schools." *Law & Society Review* 40(1): 105–134.

Schuh, John H. 2003. "Strategic Planning and Finance." In *Student Services: A Handbook for the Profession* (4th ed.), edited by Susan R. Komives and Dudley B. Woodard, 358–378. San Francisco, CA: Jossey-Bass.

Solomon, Lewis C., and Alexander W. Astin. 1981. A New Study of Excellence in Undergraduate Education: Part One: Departments Without Distinguished Graduate Programs. *Change* 13(1): 22–28.

Sponsler, Brian A. 2009. *The Role and Relevance of Rankings in Higher Education Policymaking*. Washington, DC: Institute for Higher Education Policy.

Stake, Jeffrey E. 2006. "The Interplay between Law School Rankings, Reputations, and Resource Allocations: Ways Rankings Mislead." *Indiana Law Journal* 82:229–270.

Stecklow, Steve. 1995. "Cheat Sheets: Colleges Inflate SATs and Graduation Rates in Popular Guidebooks." *Wall Street Journal*, April 5. Sec A, p. 1.

Stella, Antony, and David Woodhouse. 2006. *Ranking of Higher Education Institutions*. AUQA Occasional Paper, No. 6. Melbourne, Australia: Australian Universities Quality Agency. Melbourne.

Stergiou, Konstantinos I., and Stephan Lessenich. 2014. "On Impact Factors and University Rankings: From Birth to Boycott." *Ethics in Science and Environmental Politics* 13:101–111.

Teichler, Ulrich. 2011. "Social Contexts and Systemic Consequence of University Rankings: A Meta-Analysis of the Ranking Literature." In *University Rankings: Theoretical Basis, Methodology and Impacts on Global Higher Education*, edited by Jung Cheol Shin, Robert K. Toutkoushian, and Ulrich Teichler, 55–72. New York: Springer.

Thacker, Lloyd. 2005. *College Unranked: Ending the College Admissions Frenzy*. Cambridge, MA: Harvard University Press.

University of Texas (UT) System. 2008. *Accountability and Performance Report 2007–08*. Accessed August 27, 2017. www.utsystem.edu/osm/accountability/2007/accountabilityreport07-08.pdf

Usher, Alex, and Massimo Savino. 2006. *A World of Difference: A Global Survey of University League Tables*. Toronto: Educational Policy Institute.

Usher, Alex, and Massimo Savino. 2007. A Global Survey of University Ranking and League Tables. *Higher Education in Europe* 32(1): 5–15.

van Vught, Frans A. and Don F. Westerheijden. 2010. Multidimensional Ranking: A New Transparency Tool for Higher Education and Research. *Higher Education Management and Policy* 22(3): 31–56.

Visher, Stephen. 1928. *Geography of American Notables: A Statistical Study of Birthplaces, Training, Distribution: An Effort to Evaluate Various Environmental Factors.* Indiana University Studies, Vol. XV, Study No. 79. Bloomington: Indiana University.

Volkwein, J. Fredericks, and Kyle V. Sweitzer. 2006. Institutional Prestige and Reputation among Research Universities and Liberal Arts Colleges. *Research in Higher Education* 47(2): 129–148.

Webber, Douglas A., and Ronald G. Ehrenberg. 1997. "Do Expenditures Other Than Instructional Expenditures Affect Graduation and Persistence Rates in American Higher Education." National Bureau of Economic Research Working Paper no. 15216. Cambridge, MA: NBER.

Webster, David S. 1992. "Are They Any Good?" *Change* 24(2): 18–31.

Winston, Gordon C. 1997. "Why Can't a College Be More Like a Firm?" *Change* 29(5): 33–38.

Winston, Gordon C. 1999. "Subsidies, Hierarchy, and Peers: The Awkward Economics of Higher Education." *Journal of Economic Perspectives* 13(1): 13–36.

Zemsky, Robert, and William E. Massy. 1990. "Cost Containment: Committing to a New Economic Reality." *Change* 22(6): 16–22.

CHAPTER SEVEN

Accreditation in the United States

Ryan Thomas Landry

American colleges and universities exist to ensure an educated and enlightened democracy, to further economic development, to impart skills for success, and to discover new cures, methods, and ways of examining life. Simply put, higher education exists for the core purpose of bettering the nation and the world. To ensure institutions of higher education stay true to their missions and maintain quality in all aspects of operations, colleges and universities abide by the rules and regulations of a process called accreditation. If an institution is accredited, it holds emphatic certification that it can be trusted to fulfill its mission and warrants financial support from the federal government for its students. The very nature of accreditation rests on the concept of academic expertise and reliance on judgments of nonbiased, academic peer-scholars. Accreditation provides a vote of confidence in an institution and is critical to an institution's success in today's world.

But over the course of its long history, the American system of higher education quality assurance has faced sharp criticism, perhaps no more so than now. Under this peer-review-based process, many have questioned whether accreditors are adequately policing institutional effectiveness and academic quality. Beyond questioning the efficacy of accrediting agencies, many in government and education have raised significant concerns about the Department of Education's monitoring of accrediting agencies that have been authorized to serve as the gatekeepers to institutional access to federal aid.

A Brief History

The governance model of American colleges and universities can be traced back to colonial times. Although higher education in Europe was born from religious institutions, U.S. higher education, though initially having great influence from the clergy, has long held the hallmark of being subject to the will of the general public. Lay governing boards, many funded from states, were put in charge of governance. The early United States lacked a large class of educated individuals and did not espouse European traditions related to the formation of governance structures (Heller 2011).

American leaders seized opportunities to create new governance mechanisms. "Americans invented their own models. The lay governing board was a key feature, facilitating a neat balance of social accountability and institutional autonomy through the respected influence of the leading citizens, often including clergy, who populated them" (Heller 2011, 174). This combination of laity and clergy being in charge meant that members of the general public, not governmental ministers, were responsible for monitoring success and quality of institutions. More than 130 years ago, leaders of higher education met with leaders of secondary education to seek a better alignment of curricula and admission standards (Thelin 2011). From here was born the modern apparatus of accreditation.

> Unlike in much of the world, in the United States both state and federal governments have historically delegated primary responsibility for certifying academic quality to academics at an arm's length from government. In general, government ministries elsewhere decide what academic quality is and enforce the standards they set, that is, they license and accredit universities directly. In the United States, this type of academic accountability certification is performed, at least at a basic level, by independent accrediting organizations, which in turn depend mostly on teams of academics to examine institutions according to written standards and decide whether they should be accredited (or re-accredited) or not. (Heller 2011, 175)

Enrollments swelled in the late 1940s after World War II with the passage of the GI Bill, which provided education for veterans returning to the United States. Many diploma mills—institutions with little to no rigor and low standards for earning academic credentials—sprang up, targeting veterans with portable GI Bill assistance (Thelin 2011). A need for policing institutions was imminent, but "the federal government really did not want to get into the business of certifying colleges and schools. Nor did college and university officials relish the prospect of the campus being subjected to federal inspection in much the same way as Department of Agriculture representatives scrutinized and then stamped a rating on meat en route to supermarkets" (Thelin 2011, 265).

The demand for higher education saw enrollments increase exponentially. Although old institutions sought to adjust to market forces and accommodate the influx of students, new institutions formed—some better than others. The need for quality assurance was widespread across the country. This saw the increasing prevalence of the concepts of self-study and periodic accreditation reviews. By assuming an active role in monitoring institutions, accrediting agencies allowed the Department of Education to avoid overburdening itself with the task of institutional accreditation review or creating a new bureaucracy (Gaston 2014).

Generous provisions of federal grants extended to proprietary schools despite objections from traditional institutions.

> These gains, however, were continually subjected to scrutiny and attempts at curtailment. Accreditation groups and traditional colleges cited the high default rates among students at some proprietary schools as evidence of lax educational standards and even outright exploitation of at-risk students. The requirement that an institution be accredited provided by itself little assurance that the institution was educationally sound and responsibly operated. By the late 1970s this waning confidence in accreditation as an effective checkpoint had two consequences. First, many state governments undertook their own initiatives to identify and then curb diploma mills. Second, growing dissatisfaction about the efficacy of voluntary accreditation bodies in policing suspect institutions led to the dissolution of the umbrella agency, the Council on Postsecondary Accreditation, or COPA. (Thelin 2011, 340)

Due to the economic recession and reduction of state government spending in the early 1990s, states began to get out of the business of institutional assessment. The Southern Association of Colleges and Schools led the effort for accrediting agencies to pick up the slack as "regional accreditors began pressing colleges and universities for evidence of student academic achievement in a manner similar to the institutional-centered approach previously used by states. In this context, states could relax their mandates and rely on accreditation to do the job" (Heller 2011, 153). In rare cases where a public institution has been threatened with revocation or nongranting of accreditation, state governments have usually intervened to provide necessary resources for remediation (Heller 2011).

How Recognition and Accreditation Work

The U.S. Code of Federal Regulations, the official published record of administrative law, indicates that accreditation "means the status of public recognition that an accrediting agency grants to an educational institution or program that meets the agency's standards and requirements" (The Secretary's Recognition of Accrediting Agencies 2009, 2). It goes on to state that an accrediting agency "means a legal entity, or that part of a legal entity, that conducts accrediting activities through voluntary, nonfederal peer review and makes decisions concerning the accreditation or preaccreditation status of institutions, programs, or both" (The Secretary's Recognition of Accrediting Agencies 2009, 2). Legally, recognition "means an unappealed determination by the senior Department official . . . or a determination by the Secretary [of Education] on appeal . . . that an agency complies with the criteria for recognition . . . and that the agency is effective in its application of those criteria" (The Secretary's Recognition of Accrediting Agencies 2009, 4).

These current regulations remain closely tied to legislation from the 1960s that has significantly shaped and continues to influence American higher education. The Higher Education Opportunity Act of 1965 established the robust program of federal student aid that is still for the most part in effect today. It was reauthorized in 2008 to say of recognized accreditors:

Such agency or association consistently applies and enforces standards that respect the stated mission of the institution of higher education, including religious missions, and that ensure that the courses or programs of instruction, training, or study offered by the institution of higher education, including distance education or correspondence courses or programs, are of sufficient quality to achieve, for the duration of the accreditation period, the stated objective for which the courses or the program are offered. (Higher Education Opportunity Act of 2008)

Accrediting agencies are legitimized by a formal process called "recognition," which is an accrediting agency's own version of a university's institutional accreditation. Accrediting agencies are formally recognized by one of two overarching national entities. The first is the Department of Education, whose official recognition is necessary in order for the accrediting agency to evaluate institutions for the receipt of federal financial aid. The second is the Council for Higher Education Accreditation (CHEA), whose accreditation is focused more on the integrity and standards of the academic enterprise. Many accrediting agencies, including the major regional accrediting agencies in the United States are recognized by both the Department of Education and CHEA (Eaton 2009).

The Code of Federal Regulations defines the Department of Education's role of recognizing which accrediting agencies have the authority to grant accreditation to institutions. The regulation also defines such concepts as "branch campus" as well as "correspondence education" versus "distance education." This delineation is important when considering the rapid expansion of online programs. The regulation requires that accrediting agencies have a certain degree of experience in evaluating institutions of higher education and are generally accepted as valid by stakeholders of institutions (Higher Education Opportunity Act of 2008).

The Higher Education Opportunity Act empowers the National Advisory Committee on Institutional Quality and Integrity (NACIQI) to deliver recommendations regarding the validation of agencies and provides for an appeals procedure to the secretary of education. It mandates that institutions report to agencies any substantive changes to their operations. The act also outlines requirements for institutional self-studies and on-site reviews by accrediting agencies, and it empowers a "senior department official" as a liaison from the NACIQI who reports directly to the secretary and who delivers recommendations to the secretary. The law provides for institutions planning for closure to assist its students in partnership with other institutions until the students complete degree programs. The Code of Federal Regulations (2009) expressly requires institutions seeking accreditation for correspondence or distance education to sufficiently demonstrate the same level of compliance as with traditional modes of instruction.

The mechanics of recognition and accreditation exist within the context of certain shared convictions. Judith Eaton (2009), president of the Council for Higher Education Accreditation purports a core set of values: academic expertise, centrality of mission, academic freedom, and decentralization. According to Gaston (2014), the process has a built-in respect for institutional missions and holds that all institutional activities should be linked to the mission.

> Accreditation is a voluntary process of self-regulation and non-governmental peer review. The education community, in general, supports and legitimizes it so that institutions can state that they possess sound educational practices and the ability for improvement through regular assessment, planning, change, and reassessment. In essence, accreditation provides a benchmark for quality and integrity. The process of accreditation examines the philosophy, goals, programs, facilities, resources, and financial viability of institutions. (Garfolo and L'Huillier 2015, 166)

Several principles are common across all sectors of accreditation in the United States. A generally accepted principle is that institutions should have considerable autonomy in their mission-driven operations. Another widely held tenet is that responsibility for curricula and instruction should rest primarily with faculty. These are in addition to the views that heterogeneity among colleges and universities strengthens higher education as a whole, and, in order to be effective, institutions should safeguard academic freedom (Gaston 2014).

Gaston (2014) outlines five elements most common during an institution's peer review facilitated by an accrediting agency. First is the previsit examination by reviewers of the institution's self-study report. Second, once the reviewers arrive at or near the institution's campus, they divide labor and organize themselves based on specific assignments. They also schedule interviews with institutional personnel and finalize plans for the schedule of the next several of days. Third, they audit the self-study report by examining documents and other evidence produced by the institution, and they appraise components of general campus operations through meetings and on-site inspections. Fourth, team members reconvene with each other to discuss and compare findings and to reach consensus on the group's conclusions and recommendations. Finally, the reviewers meet with institutional leadership and other stakeholders at what is commonly called an exit conference to provide a preview of what will be reported to the accrediting agency (Gaston 2014).

Salina Diiorio (2006) draws upon California State University Monterey Bay's experience of having undergone reaffirmation of accreditation by the Western Association of Schools and Colleges regional accrediting agency. Cal State Monterey Bay was the first institution to be reviewed by WASC under a new scheme. "Rather than relying on a vast checklist of data and documents for institutions to provide, the new model sought to engage institutions in deeper inquiry around educational effectiveness while also reviewing their resources to fulfill their stated mission" (Diiorio 2006, 54).

CSUMB had to reorient institutional reaffirmation leaders from the older audit-like model to the new model focused on assessment and educational effectiveness. Within this context, the administrative structure created by CSUMB is an example similar to many other institutions undergoing reaffirmation of regional accreditation (Diiorio 2006).

CSUMB's provost provided overall leadership to the entire effort and gave committees their charges. A steering committee, chaired by the provost and composed of each divisional vice president and several other key administrators, functioned as a senior oversight committee keeping updated on all reaffirmation efforts. The steering committee ensured that timelines were followed, and it retained approval authority for all final evidentiary information to be submitted to the accrediting agency. Two groups reported to the steering committee: (1) the preparatory review team, responsible for gathering evidence for review, identifying areas needing more information, and assessing the institution's overall capacity to accomplish its stated goals; and (2) the educational effectiveness team, which examined teaching and learning and created scholarly articles and reflective essays to serve as evidence of educational effectiveness. The entire effort was supported by two CSUMB staff who were well versed in accreditation and assessment matters as the accreditation project team. The project team advised all working groups and assembled final review portfolios on behalf of the provost to be submitted to the accrediting agency (Diiorio 2006).

Chief academic officers and their staffs spend a great deal of time on areas related to institutional assessment and accreditation. Aside from the monetary dues paid by institutions to accrediting agencies, the process is labor-intensive (Martin and Samels 2015). Because so much time and effort is spent on accreditation efforts, many in the higher education community and both state and federal government have questioned the real value of the overall process.

Accreditation Today

Performance indicators, especially those related to how students measurably benefit from a college education, could arguably play a greater role in assessing institutional effectiveness. Garfolo and L'Huillier (2015) cite the following areas as needing improvement: currently, there is no requirement for institutions to provide statistics on student retention and graduation rates nor on postgraduation employment rates; no requirement for published benchmarks that must be met by institutions; no clear penalties for institutions that do not meet these benchmarks; and not enough accountability among accrediting agencies to demonstrate how the process affects academic performance.

Although many are concerned with possible conflicts of interest (e.g., an external reviewer might be lenient on a review finding in exchange for leniency when his or her institution is up for review), Gaston (2014) purports that this is rare due to the robust training of reviewers in which they are conditioned to employ evidence-based and objective judgment.

Despite accusations of lax enforcement of accreditation standards, the Department of Education in 2016 exhibited a clear indication of its authority and willingness to sanction. In a rare NACIQI vote, the 18-member federal advisory panel officially recommended stripping recognition from the Accrediting Council for Independent Colleges and Schools (ACICS). The recommendation followed the bankruptcy of Corinthian Colleges Inc. and the soon-to-be bankrupt ITT Educational Services Inc., both for-profit colleges (Kelderman 2016). Acting upon NACIQI's recommendation, then secretary of education John King made the final decision to strip ACICS of its recognition status, citing significant noncompliance issues and a failure to adequately regulate institutions from taking advantage of students and taxpayers (Fain 2016). Although actions of this magnitude are uncommon for the Department of Education, the revocation of ACICS's recognition as an accrediting agency proves that mechanisms are in place to take action against accreditors who fail to meet necessary standards.

The rapid growth of alternative credentialing in recent years has presented a relatively new problem for the American accreditation system. Open e-credentialing, such as open badges, occur in nontraditional ways via online learning and learning in digital social networks. Alternative credentialing often centers on project-based learning by students working at their own pace (Hickey 2017). A white paper issued by the U.S. Senate Committee on Health,

Education, Labor, and Pensions (2015) argues that the well-established regional accreditation system has failed to recognize and adapt to innovative education methods, such as Massive Open Online Courses (MOOCs), stifling innovation and competition. Traditional accreditation standards measure quality, at least in part, through examination of the condition of the physical plant, requirements of tenured faculties, and governance structures. Many, if not most, alternative credentialing mechanisms do not fit into these traditional molds of higher education delivery.

The proliferation of institutions whose academic quality has come into question or whose graduates have high-default loan rates calls for efforts to improve the current accreditation system. Many leaders in higher education and government have called for increased monitoring and enforcement by the Department of Education itself. Nonetheless, measures to completely overhaul the accreditation system could hurt colleges and universities, and ultimately students, more than it could help. The core values of accreditation in the United States, especially the high regard for the peer-review process, has substantial merits. The successes throughout the national higher education landscape are certainly due, not just in part, to this accreditation system.

Garfolo and L'Huillier (2015) acknowledge the benefits of accreditation: the process identifies institutions as having met peer-reviewed established quality criteria; eases transfer of credit; involves faculty in curricular planning and review; provides access to student financial assistance; and provides the public with quality assurance.

Might not a pragmatic approach by the Department of Education, one that retains those meritorious components of accreditation and improves on the current system, yield better results? A stronger process for recognition, one where fewer accreditors are authorized to operate, and a more robust monitoring of accreditor standards and operations could lead to a better controlled and more effective means for ensuring that institutional objectives are met. The old adage "don't throw the baby out with the bath water" seems appropriate. Increased collaboration between the Department of Education and organizations such as CHEA, as well as college and university leaders and heads of accrediting agencies, can bring together divergent opinions and foster increased understanding of what the accreditation process is intended to do and how it can better achieve the goals necessary for success.

Is this a perfect system to ensure that institutions are fulfilling their promises and delivering quality instruction to students? No, it is not. However, its merits are worth applauding. Despite no existence of a large government bureaucracy to directly perform quality control examination, U.S. higher education has employed self-policing as a method that has proven to be efficacious. American colleges and universities, despite being embattled in the public arena of government funding, continue to thrive under this system. The concept of assessment by academic peers has proven to be effective and efficient. As our institutions progress further into the 21st century, a careful analysis of the accreditation process is required in order to address such grave issues as student debt, gainful employment, and efficient use of public dollars. Still, the current system continues to function while seeking to maintain its usefulness and importance within the myriad issues facing society.

References

Diiorio, Salina. 2006. "Preparing for Accreditation: Sowing the Seeds for Long-Term Change." In *Taking Ownership of Accreditation: Assessment Processes That Promote Institutional Improvement and Faculty Engagement*, edited by Amy Driscoll and Diane Cordero de Noriega, 53–71. Sterling, VA: Stylus Publishing.

Eaton, Judith S. 2009. "Accreditation in the United States." *New Directions for Higher Education* 145 (Spring): 79–86. doi: 10.1002/he.337.

Fain, Paul. 2016. "Education Secretary Drops Recognition of Accreditor." *Inside Higher Ed*, December 13. Accessed August 29, 2017. https://www.inside highered.com/quicktakes/2016/12/13/education-secretary-drops -recognition-accreditor.

Garfolo, Blaine T., and Barbara L'Huillier. 2015. "Demystifying Assessment: The Road to Accreditation." *Journal of College Teaching & Learning* 12, no. 4: 151–169. doi: 10.19030/tlc.v12i3.9303.

Gaston, Paul L. 2014. *Higher Education Accreditation: How It's Changing, Why It Must*. Sterling, VA: Stylus Publishing.

Heller, Donald E., ed. 2011. *The States and Public Higher Education Policy: Affordability, Access, and Accountability*. 2nd ed. Baltimore, MD: The Johns Hopkins University Press.

Hickey, Daniel T. 2017. "How Open E-credentials Will Transform Higher Education." *Chronicle of Higher Education*, April 9. Accessed August 29, 2017. http://www.chronicle.com/article/How-Open-E-Credentials-Will/239709.

Higher Education Opportunity Act of 2008, Pub. L. No. 110-315, Sec. 495, 122 Stat. 3324 (2008).

Kelderman, Eric. 2016. "Federal Panel Votes to Shut Down an Accreditor Blamed for Failures of For-Profit Higher Ed." *Chronicle of Higher Education*, June 24. Accessed August 29, 2017. http://www.chronicle.com/article/Federal -Panel-Votes-to-Shut/236907.

Martin, James, and James E. Samels. 2015. *The Provost's Handbook: The Role of the Chief Academic Officer*. Baltimore: Johns Hopkins University Press.

The Secretary's Recognition of Accrediting Agencies, 34 CFR 602 (2009).

Thelin, John R. 2011. *A History of American Higher Education*. 2nd ed. Baltimore, MD: The Johns Hopkins University Press.

U.S. Senate Committee on Health, Education, Labor, and Pensions. 2015. "Higher Education Accreditation Concepts and Proposals." Washington, DC, March 23.

CHAPTER EIGHT

Curriculum Reform: The Aims and Purposes of Higher Education

David W. Robinson-Morris

Curriculum reform, or in many instances curriculum deform—meaning an erosion of educational and intellectual objectives in elementary and secondary schools—has become a much-contested debate in our national and global society. This debate stems from the relatively recent revelation that all curricula, like all research, are political texts. Curricula and schools are never politically neutral. In fact, many scholars argue that schooling, American schooling in particular, is a chief culprit and an active participant in the general system of injustice and suffering (Pinar et al. 2008). Althusser (1971) proffered that educational institutions at every level function as state apparatuses of ideological indoctrination, which acts on, (de/re)forms, and structures the unconscious of students. Included in this indictment of educational institutions by critical theorists is the central role of curriculum within higher education institutions.

Through an ontohistorical analysis of higher education, this chapter seeks to understand how we now find ourselves, within higher education institutions, in a constant state of curriculum (de/)reform or rather within an educational milieu constantly being acted upon by hegemonic neoliberal sociopolitical forces. These very forces coerce all within the environment to decide what knowledge is of most worth and what counts in this space/time.

Beginning with Plato and ending with contemporary debates on higher education curriculum, this chapter explores American higher education curriculum reform through an examination of the aims of higher education and utilizes historical analysis to illuminate the shift of higher education curriculum from holistic education to today's market-driven and vocational-focused higher education environments.

We live in the age of the "multi-versity" (Soo and Carson 2004)[1] that is, "an internally fragmented *Uni*-versity-in-name-only, where the sole communal unity stems from a common grievance about parking spaces" (Thomson 2001, 251). The university has become a fragmented entity that has lost sight of its communal goals of the formation of its students and its aim of knowledge cultivation. As Harvey (2011) and Barnett (2011) assert, the modern university and institutions of higher education serve as socioeconomic classifiers, sorting mechanisms, and ideological filters that impact culture through the (re)production of dominant ideology. The modern American university has always resided in the tensions of espoused principles and the operational realities of its situatedness in a social and political milieu; namely, the university promotes itself as a democratic, egalitarian institution yet practices racism, discrimination, and prejudice. Institutions of higher education, asserts Harvey (2011), have failed on their moral societal obligation to live up to their original aim; they have failed to live up to the principles they espouse. Not only are institutions of higher education failing students on the true aim of education but as I assert within every level of the educational system, we continue to experience the effects of higher education's past cowardice to traverse the terrain of moral injustice.

In tandem with Eric Ashby, I argue, institutions of higher education "must be sufficiently stable to sustain the ideal which gave it birth and sufficiently responsive to remain relevant to the society which it supports" (Altbach, Gumport, and Berdahl 2001, 4), and given the litany of socio-politico-cultural ills from which the world is suffering—they are failing and failing badly.

In essence, today's universities are market-driven institutions composed of siloed "epistemological [sub]regime[s] characterized by fear" (Barnett 2011, 25)—fear of the market, fear of the government, and fear of true education. Institutions of higher education operate in ways dictated by the market for the sake of its own survival. In short, Heidegger's critique of the way in which universities "increasingly instrumentalize, professionalize, vocationalize, corporatize, and ultimately technologize education" (Thomson 2001, 244) has proliferated.

It is true, as Ian Thomson (2001, 250) writes:

Our very 'being-in-the-world' is shaped by the knowledge we pursue, uncover, and embody. There is a troubling sense in which it seems that we cannot help practicing what we know, since we are 'always already' implicitly shaped by our guiding metaphysical presuppositions.

In agreement with Harvey (2011), I argue, the modern university both educationally and socially has failed to live up to its original metaphysical aim: to encounter knowledge, that is, to make strange the familiar and thereby open one up to new modes of being and understanding what it means to be a human being (Barnett 2011). The idea of metaphysics as the base of understanding and function of the university, in agreement with Barnett (2011, 12), is deeply connected to the idea of the university as "the transcendent university," which presupposes the scholar through his or her "own cognitive efforts, . . . can glimpse an entirely new mode of being" (Barnett 2011, 12). Nostalgia in most cases is a lie, this notion of the transcendent university is equally as problematic in some respects as the mess we now find ourselves in; however, the idea of the transcendent university does offer certain possibilities. I argue, we now find ourselves on the extreme end of the spectrum conceiving the university not as a place of higher learning but as an economic engine. (Re)thinking institutions of higher, a *return to* the idea of the transcendent university situated in this space/time may provide the necessary ideological counterbalance to the enterprising multiversity (Barnett 2011; Robinson-Morris 2015; Thomson 2001).

First, this chapter will look back to move forward with a discussion of the aims of education from Plato to Heidegger (Thomson 2001) to the seminal documents that established the American field of student affairs in higher education (American Council on Education 1937, 1949; NASPA 1987). Slattery suggests within education "the slightest perturbation has a significant impact on future patterns" (2013, 271); I am emboldened by Slattery's assertion and hopeful that this perturbation will catalyze a metamorphosis of higher education.

For What Purpose? From Plato to Heidegger

What is the purpose of higher education? What is the idea behind the idea of the university? Dewey would argue the goal of education, in general, is "not knowledge or information, but self-realization, is the goal" (1902, 9). The transformation of self is the goal of education. Thirty years later, Dewey would add: "The history of educational theory is marked by opposition between the idea that education is development from within and that it is formation from without" (1938/1997, 17). This debate regarding the purpose and aims of higher education has been raging since the founding of Harvard in 1636 in the American colonies and continues today (Thelin 2004). I argue that one must look to the past to understand the present and imagine the future; therefore, we begin with a brief history on the idea and of the aims of education first presented in Plato's "Allegory of the Cave" (Plato [360 BCE] 1968). The exploration of Plato's Cave leads perfectly into Heidegger's notion of ontological education (Thomson 2001).

Plato's recollection of the conversation between Socrates and Glaucon in the "Allegory of the Cave" establishes the components, method, and function of education that has proliferated for over two millennia. The classic "Allegory of the Cave" lays the foundation for the aim of education; Plato writes:

> "Next then," I said, "make an image of our nature in its education and want of education, likening it to a condition of the following kind. See human beings as though they were in an underground cave-like dwelling with its entrance, a long one, open to the light across the whole width of the cave. They are in it from childhood with their legs and necks in bonds so that they are fixed, seeing only in front of them, unable because of the bond to turn their heads all the way around. Their light is from a fire burning far above and behind them. Between the fire and the prisoners there is a road above, along which see a wall, built like the partitions puppet-handlers set in front of the human beings and over which they show puppets." (Plato [360 BCE] 1968, 193)

Plato establishes the belief that human beings come to the world chained by ignorance and are plagued with wrong perception. Unable to turn their heads, unable to perceive the world properly, these prisoners are fooled by the shadows cast on the cave wall created by the fire as it burns behind them. These shadows are believed to be other than what they are, which Socrates identifies as:

> human beings carrying all sorts of artifact, which project above the wall, and statues of men and other animals wrought from stone, wood, and every kind material; as is to be expected, some of the carriers utter sounds while others are silent. (Plato [360 BCE] 1968, 193)

Declaring that these prisoners are like us, Socrates avers:

> "For in the first place, do you suppose such men would have seen anything of themselves and one another than the shadows cast by the fire on the side of the cave facing them?"
>
> "How could they," he said, "if they had been compelled to keep their heads motionless throughout life?"
>
> "And what about the things that are carried by? Isn't it the same with them?"
>
> "Of course."
>
> "If they were able to discuss things with one another, don't you believe they would hold that they are naming these things going by before them that they see?" (Plato [360 BCE] 1968, 193–194)

Within the dialogue, Glaucon inquires as to the ability of the prisoners to see, and later their ability to hear as a means of releasing them from the false perception of the shadows as anything other than shadows. This establishes both the importance of the visual and the dialogical in the ability to know and discern truth. If they were able to see and hear, Plato avers, "Then most certainly," I said, "such men would hold that the truth is nothing other than the shadows of artificial things" ([360 BCE] 1968, 194). Through this dialogue between Socrates and Glaucon, Plato then suggests that one aim of education is the revelation of truth through knowledge obtained by the visual and in conversational engagement—the foundations of Western curriculum and pedagogy ([360 BCE] 1968). However, this is not all.

Essentially, Plato asks: At the revelation of knowledge, would the prisoner turn back to the knowing of the cave? Would he bemoan his previous state as prisoner of the cave now that he has revelation of the light? Will the prisoner return to the cave to free the other prisoners and pass on his knowledge? ([360 BCE] 1968) However, this liberation, I argue, from one hell leads to bondage in another. The man now free of the chains of ignorance remains bound in the place of unknowing and once removed from this place he is bound yet again by chains of responsibility to pass on his knowledge and liberate others. Plato asserts if this prisoner now free does return to the cave he is likely to be killed by the shackled cave dwellers, who not knowing any knowledge other than that of the cave will accuse him of being mad ([360 BCE] 1968). This is the allegory of the cave—ignorant of their condition the prisoners take their situation to be the norm; however, armed with knowledge of the light they may free themselves from the bondage of the cave. Liberation—freeing one's soul, then, becomes the metaphysical aim of the educative pursuit.

In the voice of Socrates, Plato writes:

"Then, if this is true," I said, "we must hold the following about these things: education is not what the professions of certain men assert it to be. They presumably assert that they put into the soul knowledge that isn't in it, as though they were putting sight into blind eyes."

[. . .]

"But the present argument on the other hand," I said, "indicates that this power is in the soul of each, and that the instrument with which each learns—just as an eye is not able to turn toward the light from the dark without the whole body—must be turned around from that which is *coming into being* together with the soul until it is able to endure looking at that which *is* and the brightest part of that which *is*. And we affirm that this is the good, don't we?" ([360 BCE] 1968, 197)

Plato ([360 BCE] 1968) conceives of education as not solely about pouring knowledge into an empty soul vessel, but rather education is simultaneously a blossoming of the soul from within and a watering of the soul from without through the exposition of knowledge(s) of "that which *is*" (Plato [360 BCE] 1968)—the real that which is real and not a shadow—or a posteriori knowledge. In essence, Plato ([360 BCE] 1968) rejects the a priori knowledge of intuition, the senses, or embodied knowing and starts the West on the path of rationalism, which a millennium later would splinter into empiricism (Davis 2004). Education, in the Platonic sense, is an ontological aim achieved through a rational epistemological means. More specifically, education of knowledge should "draw men toward being" or cause (wo)men to "rise up out of becoming and take hold of being" (Plato [360 BCE] 1968, 204). Following the "Allegory of the Cave," Book VII of the *Republic* continues to elucidate the components of education, which echo our modern educational curriculum—the arts, gymnasium, astrology, mathematics (Plato [360 BCE] 1968). Additionally, Plato ([360 BCE] 1968) lays out the system of education roughly followed today with the education of children, then establishment of a graduated postsecondary education or university system. He writes:

> "Then, after this time," I said. "Those among the twenty-year-olds who are given preference will receive greater honors than the others. And the various studies acquired without any particular order by the children in their education must be integrated into an overview which reveals the kinship of these studies with one another and with the nature of that which *is*." (Plato [360 BCE] 1968, 216)

The nature of this graduated education is logical argumentation. Additionally, Plato recalling Socrates establishes what we have come to know as graduate or doctoral education, whereby the men and women who are most steadfast in their studies "when they are over thirty, you will give preference among the preferred and assign greater honors" (Plato [360 BCE] 1968, 217). Later, Plato ([360 BCE] 1968, 218) establishes disciplinary procedures for schools. Finally, interpreting this translation of the *Republic*, in addition to teaching, it is the responsibility of the learned men and women[2] to actively engage in the life and leadership of the polis.

Indeed, Plato's ([360 BCE] 1968) *Republic* lays the foundation for our modern concept of education—its aims and purposes. Most notable for this inquiry is Plato's insistence that education or knowledge is the vehicle from which a human being moves from perpetual striving or *becoming* to what reads as a more static state of *being*. Nevertheless, Plato establishes the dominance of rationality over embodied ways of knowing, and the utilization of knowledge as a means to an ontological end ([360 BCE] 1968).

Heidegger's Ontoeducation

Utilizing Plato's conception of education or *paideia*,[3] Heidegger ([1927] 1962;[1942] 1998) deconstructs education and poignantly diagnoses the current state of higher education. As Thomson (2001, 243) avers, Heidegger does not set out to decimate Western educational institutions and neither do I; however, his goal was to "loosen up this hardened tradition and dissolve the concealments it has engendered in order to recover those primordial experiences which have fundamentally shaped its subsequent historical development." In short, Heidegger sought to reform a deformed curricular orientation.

Heidegger's primary goal in his deconstruction of higher education was to shed light on the long-forgotten aspects of education elucidated in Plato's ([360 BCE] 1968) allegory and notion of *paideia* on which the Western conception of education is based. In other words, Heidegger is a advocating for a return to *paideia* or education in the Platonic sense, that is "a pure education [whereby] the soul itself is seized and transformed as a whole, while at the same time man is transplanted to the region of his essence and oriented to it" (Heidegger [1931] 1962, 256). This Platonic notion of *paideia,* for Heidegger, opens up possibilities for the future education that were once unthinkable (Thomson 2001). Namely, reessentializing the being of humans in the higher education milieu or what I term ontoeducation (Robinson-Morris 2015).

So what is Heidegger's conception of education? Heidegger ([1931] 1962) conceptualizes education as *Bildung,* which encompasses two overarching implications:

> It means first of all forming in the sense of developing and molding a character. This "forming" however "forms" (molds) at the same time through its preconceived adaptation to a standard aspect which is therefore called the prototype. Education (*Bildung*) is above all molding and giving direction by means of a form. (Heidegger [1927] 1962, 256)

Education for Heidegger is an ontological endeavor that shapes *being* by leading the learner—the human being—away from and then back to himself. Education is also a moralistic endeavor, a process of unfolding character from within (Thomson 2001). Reaching back to Plato's ([360 BCE] 1968) allegory, education is also the process of revealing unhiddenness in Greek, which is translated as truth Heidegger [1931] 1962). Summarizing Heidegger's connection between truth and education, he asserts if education is liberation and liberation consists of "turning-towards" the unhidden, then the "consummation of the essence of 'education' can therefore take place only in the realm and at the root of the most unhidden [i.e., the most true]. The essence of education is founded in the essence of 'truth'" (Heidegger [1931] 1962, 259–260).

Given my leanings toward postmodernism and its denial of an "essence" of truth, I am at once both gripped by Heidegger's education and truth theorem and proof and ready to reject it. At any rate, he provides an interesting argument and another connection between Plato's ([360 BCE] 1968) allegory and Western education. Much like education, the ancient Greek understanding of truth is much different from the contemporary Western understanding of truth as the congruence of the sign with the signifier—the agreement of concept and thing. Heidegger ([1931] 1962) owes this understanding to Nietzsche who rejects the notion of an essence of truth and conceptualizes truth as always becoming. In critique, Heidegger ([1931] 1962) argues that Nietzsche's metaphysical unthinking alters the truth "from the unhiddenness of beings to the correctness of the glance. The change itself takes place in the definition of the Being of beings as [idea]" (267). This change in conceptualization of the nature of truth from essence to fluidity, according to Heidegger ([1931] 1962), also alters the very idea of *being*. Nietzsche's metaphysical unthought perpetuates a discourse of not being, but perpetual becoming, which implies the lack of a goal beyond the notion of progress; thereby, setting higher education on its current path of technocratic dominance and nihilistic ontotheology[4] (Thomson 2001).

From Being to Entity

Conducting an "ontohistorical"[5] (Thomson 2001, 244) analysis of education, thinking with and through *Bildung* and Plato's *paideia,* Heidegger "seeks to effect nothing less than a re-ontologizing *revolution* in our understanding of education" (Thomson 2001, 254). Born out of his ontohistorical analysis of Western education, Heidegger's understanding that the current ontohistorical epoch is defined by a Nietzschean ontotheology impacts educational institutions, which he avers comes to embody the understanding of *who* and *what* beings *are* (Heidegger 1962; Thomson 2001). Significant to the argument being laid bare, Thomson (2001), interpreting Heidegger's critique of Nietzschean ontotheology, argues Nietzsche's conceptualization of the subject

> clearly demonstrates that he conceptualized 'the totality of beings as such' *ontotheologically,* an 'eternally recurring will-to-power,' that is, as an unending disaggregation and reaggregation of forces without purpose or goal. (Thomson 2001, 249)

Given an Eastern conception of subjectivity, which Nietzsche's conceptualization echoes, I assert the only issue with the Nietzschean concept is the presumed lack of purpose or goal. Being-becoming given it multiplicitous nature is always moving bidirectionally—toward a destination (a goal) and away from—with intentionality. More importantly, Heidegger avers:

> Our unthinking reliance on Nietzsche's ontotheology is leading us to transform all beings, ourselves included, into mere 'resources' (*BestandI*), entities lacking intrinsic meaning which are thus simply optimized and disposed with maximal efficiency. (Thomson 2001, 249)

Our epoch is marked by a technological enframing[6] of subjectivity, that is, the dehumanization of –human beings into expendable commodities– resources (Thomson 2001). Moreover, within this ontotheoretical epoch, human beings are reduced to entities, "programmable information, [and] digitized data" (Thomson 2001, 249). Given Heidegger's critiques of higher education began in 1911, culminated in 1929, and continued into the 1960s, this shift in what beings *are* and for what purpose they should be educated has proliferated over the past 100 years in the West; however, in America the ontohistorical and curricular shift is most evident in 1968 (Berrett 2015).

Educating Entities: Training in Postmodernity

Truly, when our understanding of beings changes, so too must the manner in which we educate them (Thomson 2001). The Cartesian notion of subjectivity of beings as static, individual, and autonomous leaves much to be desired. Higher education institutions have "increasingly instrumentalize[d], professionalize[d], vocationalize[d], corporatize[d], and ultimately technologize[d] education" (Thomson 2001, 244). This change has made possible a technological under-standing of human beings toward the creation of nihilistic, technocratic educa-tional institutions concerned with the production of *widget-beings* (highly skilled flesh robots) rather than the better making of human beings.

What understandings of education have made possible our current reality? Heidegger contends that American higher education has falsely interpreted the Platonic notion of education. More specifically, the misinterpretation of *paideia* has yielded an understanding of education "as the transmission of informa-tion, the filling of the psyche with knowledge as if inscribing a *tabula rasa* or, in more contemporary parlance, 'training-up' a neutral net" (Thomson 2001, 254). Human beings are not blank slates waiting to be filled or written on; we are *always already* being molded by and educated from birth—the home is the first educational environment and mothers our first teachers (Solomon 1985). We are always already caught up in the act of learning. This atrophied under-standing of education as knowledge transmission or acquisition is reflective of the "nihilistic logic of enframing" (Thomson 2001, 254). More concerning is that enframing through discourse has become normalized, so much so that we are unable to recognize we are under its spell. Thomson (2001) writes:

> Yet here again we face a situation in which as the problem gets worse we become less likely to recognize the "impact" of this ontological drift toward meaninglessness can "barely be noticed by contemporary humanity because they are continually covered over with the latest information." (254)

The discourse, which circulates enframing as normal and bombards subjects with quantitative data, is totalizing. The hidden curriculum is always at work.

Today, the purpose of higher education as anything other than workforce training for economic upward mobility is taken for granted and exemplifies the permeation of free market ideas within higher education curriculum (Berrett 2015). The educational milieu, at all levels, has experienced "this ontological drift toward meaninglessness" (Thomson 2001, 254) perpetrated by neoliberal, free-market capitalist evangelizers, who utilize ready-made curriculum to preach an education for economic mobility gospel and use institutions of higher education as their bully pulpits of enculturation. Along with Heidegger via Thomson (2001), I call for an ontoeducational revolution within higher education, a *return to* in this space/time the metaphysical pre-suppositions that undergird our very being-in-the-world. I echo Heidegger's call for a real education or an education that

> lays hold of the soul itself and transforms it in its entirety by first of all leading us to the place of our essential being and accustoming [*eingewöhnt*] us to it. Genuine education leads us back to ourselves, to the place *we are* (the *Da* of our *Sein*), teaches us "to dwell" (*wohnen*) "there" and transforms us in the process. This transformative journey to ourselves is not a flight away from the world into thought, but a reflexive return to the fundamental "realm of the human sojourn" (*Aufenthaltsbezirk des Menschen*). The goal of this educational odyssey is simple but literally *revolutionary*: to bring us full circle back to ourselves, first by turning us away from the world in which we are most immediately immersed, then by turning us back to this world in a more reflexive way [emphasis in original]. (Thomson 2001, 254)

Paideia, or real education, is an ontoeducational endeavor that seeks to make strange the familiar and the familiar strange for the purpose of "turning around the whole human being" (Thomson 2001, 254). In light of Heidegger's notion of real education (Thomson 2001), ontologically (re)thinking higher education sparks a revolution whereby both the being-ness of the institution and ontology of each person that sojourns to the university or within institutions of higher education is metamorphosed.

Heidegger's ([1931] 1962) ontohistorical analysis reaches back to the foundation of the Western idea of education and our contemporary curricular construction, Plato's ([360 BCE] 1968) allegory, to deconstruct Western higher education. Heidegger's deconstruction reveals the unhidden-ness of the disequilibrium between Plato's metaphysical foundation and Nietzsche's postmodern metaphysical unthinking (Thomson 2001). Within the chasm of this edu-onto-theological, disequilibrium has emerged asserts Heidegger ([1931] 1962) and a false interpretation of education and *being*. In fact, the current mess we are in within the higher education milieu is a result of these false interpretations. As opposed to Plato's ([360 BCE] 1968) educational supposition, education is now viewed as training and human beings have been dehumanized—reconceived as widgets, cogs in a wheel, programmable data points to be utilized in the most efficient means possible for maximum economic benefit. Heidegger's critique rings as true today as when he reached the pinnacle of his critiques of higher education in 1929; however, Heidegger wrote primarily of Western university's in Europe. As Hendry (2011) asserts, "History performs incredible epistemological acts" (19) and most often acts of epistemological destructiveness; therefore, to subvert the violence of a unidimensional ontohistorical analysis, we now move to an exploration of an educational ontohistory of the aims and purposes of higher education in America.

The Aims of American Higher Education: 1937–1987

In 1937, the American Council on Education met to take up the issue of student personnel work, or what has come to be known as the field of student affairs in higher education. Experiencing an increase in collegiate enrollment and recognizing the need to professionalize positions that were once the *in loco parentis* responsibility of individual deans of women or men, the American Council on Education (ACE) found it necessary to develop a document that clarified the nature, role, and direction of student personnel work (ACE 1937). Unknowingly, the drafters also delineated the 1937 perspective regarding the central purpose of higher education. The American Council on Education would meet again in 1949 to update the document to fit within the new cultural context and to meet the needs of the second large influx of college students following the passage of the GI Bill (Servicemen's Readjustment Act of 1944) in post–World War II America (Schuh, Jones, and Harper 2011; Thelin 2004). Within the realm of higher education administration and leadership, these are seminal documents and continue to guide general higher education practice. The Student Personnel Point of View documents serve as sites of ontohistorical analysis and interestingly document the (de)evolution of Plato's ([360 BCE] 1968) metaphysical ontotheology within American higher education (ACE 1937, 1949; NASPA 1987; Thomson 2001). More pointedly, these documents lucidly demonstrate the contextual nature of curriculum (de/)reform and signals curricula development as a set of choices.

From Uni- to Multiversity

The 1937 American Council on Education document marks the turn or shift from the *uni*-versity to the *multi*-versity (Thomson 2001). The drafters, experiencing "the impact of a number of social forces upon American society following the Civil War" (ACE 1937, 1), come to recognize the shift in higher education "away from the needs of the individual student to an emphasis, through scientific research, upon the extension of the boundaries of knowledge" (ACE 1937, 1). This shift nearly 70 years after the Civil War marks the first American ontotheological epoch, that is, a marked shift from holistic care of the whole student to the epistemological objective of knowledge production. The document, eerily as relevant today, speaks of the pressures of faculty members to produce knowledge (research) to the detriment of the psychosocial development of their students (ACE 1937). Therefore, the drafters and administrators of higher education institutions felt it necessary to appoint "a new type of educational officer to take over the more intimate responsibilities, which faculty members had originally included among their duties" (ACE 1937, 1)—the field of Student Affairs is born to holistically tend to the well-being of students. What philosophy or understanding of the purposes of education made possible the development of the Student Personnel or Student Affairs professional corps?

Excavating the ontoperspective in the historical, one comes to the realization that a very different discourse regarding the purposes of education was circulating in 1937. Illuminating the basic purposes of higher education, the drafters wrote:

> One of the basic purposes of higher education is the preservation, transmission, and enrichment of the important elements of culture—the product of scholarship, research, creative imagination, and human experience. It is the task of colleges and universities so to vitalize this and other educational purposes to assist the student in developing to the limits of potentialities and in making his contribution to the betterment of society. (ACE 1937, 1)

It appears that the basic purpose of higher education—knowledge production, preservation, and diffusion—to some extent has remained static; however, what has changed to a large degree is the emphasis on the holistic well-being of students alongside their intellectual pursuits. This philosophy of education speaks to the wholeness of students as beings-in-the-world (Heidegger 1931/1962). Higher education, in the perspective of 1937, is aimed at holistic–onto-epistemological development of its students. Prior to 1937, faculty members served as both educators and ontological sherpas tending to both the psychosocial and cognitive needs of their students. The drafters confirm, writing: "Until the last three decades of the nineteenth century interest in the *whole student* [emphasis added] dominated the thinking of the great majority of the leaders and faculty members of American colleges" (ACE 1937, 1). This shift in the philosophy of education would continue and reach an epochal pinnacle following the next American war, World War II.

Four years following the end of World War II, the American Council on Education (1949) would meet again to revise *The Student Personnel Point of*

View report of 1937 and advance the work of student personnel profession-als. More pointedly, *The Student Personnel Point of View* report of 1949 broad-ens the 1937 purposes of higher education to include three new goals:

1. Education for a fuller realization of democracy in every phase of living;
2. Education directly and explicitly for international understanding and cooperation;
3. Education for the application of creative imagination and trained intelli-gence to the solution of social problems and to the administration of public affairs. (ACE 1949, 2)

Putting these additions in their historical context, these goals recontextu-alize higher education curriculum and manifest higher education institu-tions as tools of nation-building and societal growth, while continuing to "affect positively the education and development of each individual student" (ACE 1949, 2). After joining the Allied Forces in the war against Hitler and his vicious assault on humanity, it is no doubt that higher education began to embody the aims of democratic ideals, international understanding, and sociological resolution toward the ultimate aim of, what I argue is, the real-ization of the grand narrative of world peace. Temporality and the political comes to bear on the higher education curricular orientation of 1949.

Placing blame on the proliferation of the modern German research-centric university, the drafters assert that higher education in the early 19th century lost its way, that is, deserted the *being* of its student for epistemological domi-nance (ACE 1949). More directly, "influenced by German models, American educators steered American higher education toward intellectualism" (ACE 1949, 3). Seeking to distance themselves from anything German, they pro-posed a return to a colonial—"European higher education and its American offshoots" (ACE 1949, 2)—holistic perspective of higher education that "gave as much attention to the social, moral, and religious development of students as to their intellectual growth" (ACE 1949, 2). The ontohistorical analysis of American higher education in 1949 is dominated by a philosophy of educa-tion that seeks to holistically develop the humanity and intellect of its stu-dents toward the ultimate goal of the growth of a democratic society (ACE 1949). As the educational philosophy goes, so goes the curriculum. Specifi-cally addressing the being or the being-ness-of-the-student-in-the-world, they write:

The student is thought of as a responsible participant in his own devel-opment and not as a passive recipient of an imprinted economic, politi-cal, or religious doctrine, or vocational skill. As a responsible participant in the societal processes of our American democracy, his full and bal-ance maturity is viewed as a major end-goal of education, and, as well, a necessary means to the fullest development of his fellow citizens. From the personnel point of view any lesser goals fall short of the desired objective of democratic educational processes and is a real drain and strain upon the self-realization of other developing individuals in our society. (ACE 1949, 2)

It seems that higher education, following World War II, becomes a means of nationalist indoctrination, intellectual development, and societal assimilation. Subsequently, an already political curriculum becomes increasingly more racialized and gendered (Pinar et al. 2008). Although I am critical of the dictation of a student's being-ness in the world following the undertaking of an American higher education, I am pleased with the recognition of student as the intersection of multiplicities, an acknowledgment of agency, and a recognition of human interconnectedness in our associated mode of living (Dewey 1916). Theoretically and ontologically, higher education and higher education curriculum in 1949 exhibited the influence of Plato, Heidegger, and Nietzsche and reinforced education as the means through which human beings could develop holistically for the sake of nation-building and peacekeeping.

The second major ontotheological epoch is the shift from the equal privileging of ontology and epistemology to an economic epistemological regime beginning in California and occurring with then governor Ronald Reagan in 1968 in California (Berrett 2015). More succinctly, the 1968 shift marks the beginning of higher education being unconcerned with the epistemological aim of knowledge production, but rather the acquisition of knowledge for economic vitality—the economic epistemological regime in which we are still living. It also is within this second ontotheological epoch that we witness the solidification of the *multi*-versity and the development of education as enterprise (Barnett 2011; NASPA 1987; Thomson 2001).

In 1987, 50 years after the original *The Student Personnel Point of View* was published (1937), the National Association Student Personnel Administrators (NASPA) issued an anniversary statement that did not revise the documents of 1937 and 1949 but served as "perspective written in 1987 to stimulate greater understanding of student affairs among leaders in higher education" (NASPA 1987, 1). Viewing curriculum as historical texts, society from 1949 to 1987 has undergone gargantuan changes such as the Great Society policies of the Johnson era (1964–1965), passage of the civil rights legislation, the women's liberation movement, the Vietnam War, and the height of American protest culture (NASPA 1987; Thelin 2004). Concurrently, changes were occurring within the colleges and universities as well—higher education enrollments doubled in the 1950s and 1960s, faculty member supply was insufficient to meet the demand, and the federal government began its heavy investment in higher education via resources for facilities, research, and federal student aid (NASPA 1987; Thelin 2004). The times have changed and so too must *The Student Personnel Point of View* documents change to reflect a new societal becoming (ACE 1937, 1949; NASPA 1987).

Keeping the additional goals of 1949 *The Student Personnel Point of View* document, NASPA's *A Perspective on Student Affairs* (1987) document enumerates assumptions and beliefs regarding higher education that have formed their own edu-philosophical net. Briefly, they include:

- *The Academic Mission of the Institution Is Preeminent*
- *Each Student Is Unique*
- *Each Person Has Worth and Dignity*
- *Bigotry Cannot Be Tolerated*
- *Feelings Affect Thinking and Learning*
- *Student Involvement Enhances Learning*
- *Personal Circumstance Affect Learning*
- *Out-of-Class Environments Affect Learning*
- *A Supportive and Friendly Community Life Helps Students Learn*
- *The Freedom to Doubt and Question Must Be Guaranteed*
- *Effective Citizenship Should Be Taught*
- *Students Are Responsible for Their Own Lives* (NASPA 1987)

The assumptions and beliefs listed in the NASPA (1987) document illuminate the changes that have taken place in society and higher education since the writing of the 1937 and 1949 documents. The necessity to highlight zero-tolerance for bigotry, and recognize that the personhood of each individual is imbued with dignity, worth, and respect, illustrates a very volatile yet transformative prior 50-year period and reifies curriculum as a historical, political, raced and gendered text. Ontotheologically, the 1987 document signals an increasing role of higher education to fulfill the original aims of higher education and "help individuals cope with significant life transitions—from adolescence to adulthood, from dependence to personal autonomy, from one occupation to another" (NASPA 1987, 7). Today, while the original aims of higher education continue to guide intuitions, I argue that it is the final phrase—"from one occupation to another" (NASPA 1987, 7)—that has taken primacy over ontology and the traditional epistemological function of knowledge acquisition and production.

In agreement with Thomson (2001), when the being-ness of beings changes, then so too must the institutional wombs of being-becoming—colleges and universities, where we become what *are*—transformed.

A Complicated Conversation: Imagining an Ontological Curriculum

Without a doubt, curriculum development and curricular (de/)reform are complicated conversations with multiple aims and enterprises (Pinar et al. 2008). A more holistic approach to education via higher education curriculum reform will provide students with a more balanced curriculum, where higher educational institutions will need to more intentionally address the needs of students or what Noddings (2013) terms the "three great dimensions of contemporary life: home and family, occupational, and civic, both domestic and global" (viii). Educating the whole person serves as educational philosophy and curricular core. The once disembodied notion of curriculum as courses, coursework, and content transforms in a "dynamic discussion that engages multiple voices, views, experiences" (Coe 2016, 55). Curriculum becomes a process of dialogical inquiry, a lived experience, an always becoming, a perpetual doing. Indeed, these are uncomfortable and complicated conversations that move us out of comfort zones, and beyond the safety of the prescriptive nature of curriculum. However, these complicated conversations also inspire hope and lead each of us back to ourselves—exactly what education is intended to be and do.

Notes

1. A term coined by Clark Kerr (1911–2003), chancellor of the University of California (UC) Berkeley between 1952 and 1958, and the 12th president of the UC system (1958–1967) (Soo and Carson 2004).

2. Plato writes: "Don't suppose that what I have said applies any more to men than to women, all those who are born among them with adequate natures" ([360 BCE] 1968, 220).

3. Paideia: "—the classical Greek system of education and training, which came to include gymnastics, grammar, rhetoric, poetry, music, mathematics, geography, natural history, astronomy and the physical sciences, history of society and ethics, and philosophy—the complete pedagogical course of study necessary to produce a well-rounded, fully educated citizen" (Tarnas 1991, 29–30).

4. Thomson (2001) explains ontotheology as Heidegger's argument "that our metaphysicians' *ontological* understandings of what entities are 'as such' ground intelligibility from the inside-out (as it were), while their *theological* understandings of the way in which the 'totality' of beings exist simultaneously secure the intelligible order from the outside-in. Western history's successive constellations of intelligibility are thus 'doubly grounded' in a series of ontotheologically structured understandings of 'the being of beings' (*das Sein des Seienden*), understandings, that is, of both *what* and *how* beings *are*, or of 'the totality of beings as such'" (247). Moreover, each ontotheological positionality grounds the various ontohistorical epochs (Thomson 2001).

5. Ontohistory is "the history of being" (Thomson 2001, 248). Each epoch, asserts Heidegger (1962), is composed of a historical series of "ontotheological understandings of *what* and *how* beings *are* [emphasis in original]" (Thomson 2001, 248).

6. Enframing in the Heideggerian sense is best understood as "a technological understanding of being . . .; an historical 'mode of revealing' in which entities increasingly show up as resources to be optimized" (Thomson 2001, 249).

References

Altbach, Phillip G., Patricia Gumport, and Robert O. Berdahl. 2011. *American Higher Education in the Twenty-First Century: Social, Political, and Economic Challenges*. Baltimore, MD: The Johns Hopkins University Press.

Althusser, Louis. 1971. *Lenin and Philosophy and Other Essays*. Translated by B. Brewser. New York: Monthly Press Review.

American Council on Education (ACE). 1937. *The Student Personnel Point of View*. Washington, DC: Author. http://www.myacpa.org/student-personnel-point-view-1937

American Council on Education (ACE). 1949. *The Student Personnel Point of View*. Washington, DC: Author. http://www.myacpa.org/pub/documents/1949.pdf

Barnett, Ronald. 2011. *Being a University*. New York: Routledge.

Berrett, Dan. 2015. "The Day the Purpose of College Changed." *Chronicle of Higher Education*. http://chronicle.com/article/The-Day-the-Purpose-of-College/151359/

Coe, Heather A. 2016. "Towards a Curriculum of the Heart: Thinking, Growing, Feeling, and Connecting in Contemporary Education." *Transnational Curriculum Inquiry* 13(2): 47–59.

Davis, Brent. 2004. *Inventions of Teaching: A Genealogy*. New York: Routledge.

Dewey, John. 1902. *The Child and Curriculum*. Chicago: University of Chicago Press.

Dewey, John. 1916. *Democracy and Education*. New York: Macmillan.

Dewey, John. (1938) 1997. *Experience and Education*. New York: Touchstone.

Harvey, William B. 2011. *Higher Education and Diversity: Ethical and Practical Responsibility in the Academy*. Commissioned by the Kirwan Institute for the Study of Race and Ethnicity and the Ohio State University Democratic Merit Project.

Heidegger, Martin. 1962. "Plato's Doctrine of Truth." In *Philosophy of the Twentieth Century: An Anthology*, edited by W. Barrett and H. D. Aiken, 251–270. New York: Random House. (Original work published in 1931.)

Heidegger, Martin. 1998. "Plato's Teaching on Truth." In *Pathmarks*, edited by W. McNeill, 155–182. Cambridge: Cambridge University Press. (Original work published in 1942)

Hendry, Petra M. 2011. *Engendering Curriculum History*. New York: Routledge.

Kuhn, Thomas S. (1962) 2012. *The Structure of Scientific Revolutions*. Chicago: University of Chicago Press.

MacIntyre, Alasdair. 2002. "Alasdair MacIntyre in Dialogue with Joseph Dunne." *Journal of Philosophy of Education* 36(1): 1–19.

NASPA. 1987. *A Perspective on Student Affairs.* Washington, DC: Author. https://www.naspa.org/images/uploads/main/A_Perspective_on_Student_Affairs_1987.pdf

Noddings, Nel. 2013. *Education and Democracy in the 21st Century.* New York: Teachers College Press.

Nussbaum, Martha C. 2002. "Education for Citizenship in an Era of Global Connection." *Studies in Philosophy and Education* 21(4–5): 289–303.

Pinar, William F., William M. Reynolds, Patrick Slattery, and Peter M. Taubman. 2008. *Understanding Curriculum: An Introduction to the Study of Historical and Contemporary Curriculum Discourses.* New York: Peter Lang.

Plato. 1968. *The Republic of Plato.* 2nd ed. Translated by A, Bloom. New York: Basic Books. (Original work published in 360 BCE.)

Robinson-Morris, David. 2015. "An Ontological (Re)Thinking: Ubuntu and Buddhism in Higher Education" (Unpublished doctoral dissertation). Baton Rouge: Louisiana State University.

Schuh, John H., Susan R. Jones, and Shaun R. Harper, eds. 2011. *Student Service: A Handbook for the Profession.* 5th ed. San Francisco, CA: Jossey-Bass.

Slattery, Patrick. 2013. *Curriculum Development in the Postmodern Era: Teaching and Learning in an Age of Accountability.* New York: Routledge.

Solomon, Barbara M. 1985. *In the Company of Educated Women: A History of Women and Higher Education in America.* New Haven, CT: Yale University Press.

Tarnas, Richard. 1991. *Passion of the Western Mind: Understanding the Ideas That Have Shaped Our World View.* New York: Random House.

Thelin, John. 2004. *A History of American Higher Education.* 2nd ed. Baltimore, MD: The Johns Hopkins University Press.

Thomson, Ian. 2001. "Heidegger on Ontological Education, or: How We Become What We Are." *Inquiry* 44(3): 243–268.

Further Reading

Cohen, Arthur M. 1998. *The Shaping of American Higher Education.* San Francisco, CA: Jossey-Bass.

Cowley, W. H., and Don Williams. 1991. *International and Historical Roots of American Higher Education.* New York: Garland Publishing.

Cremin, Lawrence A. 1977. *Traditions of American Education.* New York: Basic Books.

Dewey, John. 1904. "The Relation of Theory to Practice in Education." *National Society for the Scientific Study of Education* 3(1): 9–30.

Goodchild, Lester F., and Harold S. Wechsler. 1989. *The History of Higher Education.* 2nd ed. Boston, MA: Pearson Custom Publishing.

Gwynne-Thomas, E. H. 1981. *A Concise History of Education to 1900 A.D.* Washington, DC: University Press of America.

Heidegger, Martin. 1976. *What Is Called Thinking?* Translated by J. G. Gray. New York: Harper and Row. (Original work published in 1954.)

Lucas, Christopher J. 1994. *American Higher Education: A History.* New York: St. Martin's Griffin.

Ramsden, Paul. 1992. *Learning to Teach in Higher Education.* New York: Routledge.

Readings, Bill. 1999. *The University in Ruins.* Cambridge, MA: Harvard University Press.

Rudolph, Frederick. 1962. *The American College & University: A History.* Athens, GA: University of Georgia Press.

Thelin, John. 2004. *A History of American Higher Education.* 2nd ed. Baltimore, MD: Johns Hopkins University Press.

CHAPTER NINE

Under Siege: The Future of the Liberal Arts at State U.

B. Noble Jones and James C. Hearn

Introduction

A conversation has emerged as to whether public institutions of higher education should downsize or even eliminate courses and programs in the liberal arts and/or humanities. State support of higher education has declined over the previous three decades while calls for accountability, performance, efficiency, and value have increased. Governors and legislators in Florida, Wisconsin, North Carolina, Kentucky, and several other states have expressed a desire to abandon the liberal arts to private institutions (which are funded predominantly by students and their families via tuition dollars) rather than to use state allocations to support these fields. This essay examines this debate, considering arguments for and against the privatization of liberal arts offerings in the public sector.

Overview

To fully understand the terms of this debate, it is helpful to first define what is meant by the *liberal arts* or a *liberal education*, and identify its alternatives. Contrary to notions popular among some in the political realm, the word *liberal* in this usage does not refer to a college department's political party or persuasion: a liberal education is neither inclined to the "left" nor "right." Rather, a liberal education is broad-based and far-reaching, grounded in the study of the human condition, and aimed at building an understanding of how members of societies and cultures have arrived where they are and how people relate to one another. The skills acquired in a liberal education can be difficult to assess; indeed, it is often quite challenging to sufficiently and accurately measure the outcomes of higher education in general given the disparate backgrounds and preparations of entering students, and the diversity of students' pathways to college. Despite this challenge, benefits from an education grounded in the liberal arts include the acquisition and refinement of critical thinking skills, analytical acumen and problem solving, and the ability to communicate effectively. Specific coursework, departments, or majors associated with a liberal education might include anthropology, art, history, languages, literatures, music, philosophy, psychology, and sociology, among others.

In contrast to a liberal education is a *practical vocational education*, the content of which is typically associated with applied skills. Such disciplines include areas of knowledge that may be more directly utilized in a career without further instruction required, such as business or marketing, communications, computer science, education, engineering, and health sciences. Study in the practical vocational arts lends itself to the acquisition of more easily measurable, and more immediately practicable, skills in the job market. These fields become the foundation for many professions tied directly to the state or national economy, and thus appeal to policy makers responsible for attracting and retaining new business and industries. Although some science, technology, engineering, and mathematics ("STEM") fields require advanced graduate work prior to entering the job market, other STEM disciplines are sufficient to earn gainful employment in a complementary field upon completion of a bachelor's degree. Regardless of its validity, it has become a popularized notion that practical vocational degrees are the sole avenues to a professional career.

Thus, the current controversy at hand becomes something of a dispute between the immeasurable and the measurable, the qualitative and the quantitative, the experiential and the demonstrable. When coupled with an environment of evermore constrained state and federal budgets, one in which legislators must attempt the judicious appropriation of resources across competing priorities—all of the special interests to various stakeholders (who happen to include taxpayers and voters)—the controversy takes very real shape as it plays out today on public college and university campuses across our country.

Over the course of the past three decades, higher education funding has generally shifted from a public to a private responsibility. Students and their families are now burdened with a larger share of college expenses whereas the federal and state governments once bore the majority of student aid costs

(Mettler 2014). In effect, the responsibility to pay for higher education has been privatized, moving from the taxpayers collectively to individuals themselves. At the same time, legislators have increased calls for accountability and performance assessment by public colleges and universities. Such calls seek to measure the return on the state's investment in a postsecondary degree, requesting evidence that the investment will yield returns to the state's economy in terms of productive, higher earning (and thus higher tax-generating) employees who are attractive to modern businesses and industries.

In concert with these calls for accountability, legislators have initiated a conversation concerning the public value of a liberal arts degree and a liberal education. Some have questioned the rationale behind public subsidization of student financial aid in support of degrees awarded in the liberal arts that, they argue, cost the state more to produce and provide a lower return on investment to the state's resources. In turn, they suggest it would be in the interest of the state to withdraw student aid for those majoring in the liberal arts disciplines. Others have suggested that students studying in liberal arts disciplines could be charged more for their courses. In the same vein, loan forgiveness for "in-demand" degrees has been proposed to incentivize students to major in practical vocational fields as opposed to liberal arts fields. More direct still are calls to withdraw appropriations outright for support of liberal arts departments.

This scenario proposes many questions; a few are included here to lend shape to a debate. Although political leaders may say that they are not dictating the majors of college students, their efforts have the effect of discouraging enrollment in the liberal arts. Should the government incentivize academic majors of college students at the expense of certain departments, particularly when the student attends a public university? When federal or state funds are provided to students to pursue higher education, should the government declare how financial aid is used? Is higher education a private benefit, a public benefit, or both? What should we expect the returns to higher education to be? What is the role of the arts, humanities, and social sciences in a technologically driven modern economy? A brief introduction to the historical relationship between higher education and state and federal governments is helpful to fully frame the modern debate. First, the federal government's historical relationship to colleges and universities is considered, followed by an introduction to the evolving relationship between states and their public higher education institutions.

Brief Context: Higher Education and the Government

For the balance of American history, the content and purpose of higher education in the United States have been generally detached from concerns of the government. The Tenth Amendment of the U.S. Constitution leaves the responsibility for education to the individual states by failing to assign responsibility to the federal government. Despite the expressed desire for a national university by some forefathers, George Washington (1789–1797) among them, no such institution was ever approved by Congress with the notable exception of the military service academies.

Though early colonial colleges were founded in concert between states and churches, debate regarding curriculum was absent. The first institution of higher education in the American colonies, Harvard College, was founded in 1636. Its founders wanted to ensure the proper education of Puritan ministers; thus, students received a liberal education "in the tongues and arts" consistent with "the principles of divinity and Christianity" as preparation for a practical, religious profession (New Englands First Fruits 1643). Those few students fortunate enough to gain access to higher education— typically wealthy, White boys with a few exceptions for others of particular promise earning scholarship—were to be prepared in the liberal arts for their careers as either clergymen, members of government, or businesspersons. As our country expanded, the number of colleges and universities grew both in response to the heightened need for civic leaders and because nascent cities wanted the prestige associated with such institutions. However, the purpose of higher education remained largely unchanged and generally unchallenged.

In the early 19th century, debate in academic circles arose as to what should be taught at university, and the Yale Report of 1828 offered an early glimpse into this contemporary discussion. Written by Yale University professors in response to the 1819 founding of the University of Virginia, which offered both classical and nonclassical curricula, and a controversial 1825 report authored by a Harvard University professor arguing against the teaching of ancient languages, this report has long been interpreted as a reactionary defense of the liberal arts tradition. However, modern historians have readdressed the Yale Report and suggest that it argues instead for a preservation of the core liberal curriculum with needed modernization where appropriate, according to student demands. In short, students desired a classical liberal education, and, given that students provided vital tuition dollars, it was critical that the curriculum appeal to them. Thus, coursework was offered in what was deemed of interest and import by students, not by governments.

The first direct federal intervention in American higher education did not occur until 1862. Enacted by Congress in that year, the Morrill Land-Grant College Act encouraged westward expansion by granting federal land to states; proceeds from sales of these lands were used to found colleges teaching agricultural and mechanical arts. Thus, these public institutions were specifically founded with the goal of preparation for the workforce and the advancement of technology. However, it was not until World War I that the

U.S. government became directly involved in the college curricula with the founding of the Student Army Training Corps, which commissioned men at more than 500 colleges across the country in response to wartime personnel needs. Further, the federal government supplied minimal student financial aid until the Servicemen's Readjustment Act of 1944. Passed in anticipation of the waves of returning servicemembers from World War II, and in light of challenges in reintroducing World War I veterans into daily life following their experiences at war, this congressional act (commonly referred to as the GI Bill) provided grants for veterans to pursue higher education.

Following World War II, federal interest in higher education's aims increased notably with the rise of the Cold War and the Space Race. A functioning democracy required a broadly educated populace, and the nation needed scientists to conduct research. Findings from the 1947 President's Commission on Higher Education (commonly referred to as the Truman Commission) affirmed these positions, followed by the National Defense Education Act (1958) that, in part, strengthened public schooling and encouraged the pursuit of degrees beyond high school. With passage of the Higher Education Act of 1965 and subsequent reauthorizations (see the Educational Amendments of 1972) that included expanded federal financial aid for higher education, the federal government and higher education institutions became permanently intertwined, and governmental interest in higher education fully monetized.

Higher Education and State Governments

Space constraints preclude presenting a comprehensive history of the relationships between state governments and their public colleges and universities in this volume. Writ large, the needs for higher education and the historical support for public institutions vary from state to state and are impacted by population projections and workforce needs. However, a broad introduction to how this relationship generally evolved over the past four decades is vital to framing the current controversy. In short, state governments have drastically reduced funding for public higher education. In the two decades from 1990–2010, state governments decreased funding by 26 percent for state universities and community colleges. To compensate, they raised tuition: "at the average public four-year institution, it skyrocketed by 244 percent in real terms between 1980–1981 and 2010–2011" (Mettler 2014, 10). Though state budgets continue to provide sizable appropriations to public colleges and universities, lawmakers at both the state and federal level have successfully transferred a considerable cost of attendance to students and their families, thus privatizing to a greater extent what is often considered to be a public good (McMahon 2009).

The Current Controversy

Arguments for the privatization of degrees in the liberal arts disciplines revolve around costs and returns. Such programs can be expensive to administer because low enrollments limit economies of scale. What is more, students strapped with debt can have greater difficulty repaying loans with degrees in these fields. Thus, such programs arguably provide lower returns on investment for both governments and students, given graduates' generally lower incomes and subsequent lower tax payments. Advocates argue that because other institutions or online resources can cover these fields more cost-effectively than public colleges and universities, support of such programs may constitute a poor use of state and federal resources. At this time, proponents argue, it is more important to invest in STEM fields that will return greater economic benefits to the state, the nation, and individuals.

Although not a formal prescription, it is helpful to observe that a scale of proposals exists among lawmakers and their approach to funding (or, more accurately, defunding) liberal education. The most modest of these is targeted student aid provided to STEM majors. Those students pursuing degrees in the practical professions would benefit from grants or scholarships as components of their financial aid packages. An alternative to targeted student aid is equally benign relative to other proposals: loan forgiveness. Such programs, already in practice to some extent for particular majors (medical, education) across many states, dismiss a percentage of a graduate's accumulated student debt in exchange for working within the state and sector of interest upon graduation. A related yet somewhat different plan is differential pricing: the costs to provide instruction in STEM fields would be offset to a greater degree than liberal arts fields, such that STEM majors would be charged lower tuition than their liberal arts counterparts. In effect, prospective students would be incentivized to pursue a more affordable option. States, which stand to realize greater immediate returns to their economies, would be willing to shoulder a higher percentage of degree cost. Conversely, liberal arts–inclined students would be disincentivized to pursue their interests in light of cheaper STEM alternatives, though still welcome to major in the liberal arts but at greater expense than their peers. Finally, there is the threat of retracting state support for liberal education programs altogether. Universities would be forced to reduce instruction in or even altogether close non-STEM departments given a lack of funding.

In October 2011, Texas governor Rick Perry introduced an initiative to encourage the state's public universities to offer a $10,000 bachelor's degree "in fields that will provide graduates with the best opportunity for employment" (Hamilton 2012, para. 2). His plan to accomplish this required a redistribution of state appropriations from liberal education disciplines to the prioritization of STEM teaching and funded research (Shinn 2014).

Subsequently, Florida governor Rick Scott announced his intention to pursue public university reforms in the succeeding legislative session. "If I'm going to take money from a citizen to put into education then I'm going to take that money to create jobs. So I want that money to go to degrees where people can get jobs in this state," he stated in an interview to the *Sarasota Herald-Tribune* (Anderson 2011, para. 6). He later elaborated on his campaign to further realign tax expenditures with increased production of STEM degrees, and notably singled out one degree field in particular. He said in a radio interview that Florida does not need "a lot more anthropologists . . . It's a great degree if people want to get it. But we don't need them here" (Bender 2011, para. 3). He continued, "I want to spend our money getting people science, technology, engineering and math degrees. That's what our kids need to focus all of their time and attention on: Those type of degrees that when they get out of school, they can get a job" (Bender 2011, para. 4). Governor Scott proposed an increase in funding to STEM fields at the expense of liberal arts subjects or colleges. The state Senate majority leader expressed his desire to work in concert with the governor, stating that Florida was failing to produce graduates with STEM skills needed to attract corporations. In fact, this same legislator had previously been quite explicit in his desire to redirect state resources to universities in line with corporate interests: "When the No. 1 degree granted is psychology and the No. 2 degree is political science, maybe before we ask $100 million more of taxpayers we should redeploy what we have. That way we make sure we're not sending graduates out with degrees that don't mean much" (Colavecchio 2010, para. 14). In short, curricular offerings at public universities would be correlated with the projected needs of the job market within the state.

The argument for targeted budgeting to particular departments centers on the economic principle of return on investment. Taxpaying citizens entrust that legislators will use their monies efficiently, yielding the highest gains from the public investment in state higher education (among the many competing priorities addressed by a state's budget). Dale A. Brill, president of the Florida Chamber Foundation, argued at the time, "The higher education system needs to evolve with the economy. People pay taxes expecting that the public good will be served to the greatest degree possible. We call that a return on investment" (Alvarez 2012, para. 9). This public battle waged by Florida's legislators on liberal arts disciplines has not subsided. Governor Scott rejuvenated his calls for increased marketability of graduates in January 2016, saying, "Our state-funded universities can and must do more to help graduates get a good-paying job. I am challenging all state universities to better align their degrees with a student's opportunity to get a job when they graduate" (Logue 2016, para. 7).

In 2011, the National Governor's Association released a report asking the question, "Degrees for what jobs?" (Sparks and Waits 2011). This report encouraged state governmental authorities to introduce performance-based funding that would award resources to public institutions that successfully aligned their degree programs with the needs of employers across their respective states. It called for increased dialogue between these employers and public higher education institutions to ensure that graduates were adequately trained for careers in a global economy, as defined by employers. Subsequently, North Carolina governor Patrick McCrory said in regard to such a change to performance-based funding in his own state, "It's not based on butts in seats but on how many of those butts can get jobs" (Kiley 2013, para. 3). McCrory continued his critique by saying that the state should not subsidize liberal arts majors using public funds: "If you want to take gender studies that's fine, go to a private school and take it. But I don't want to subsidize that if that's not going to get someone a job" (Kiley 2013, para. 4). Soon to follow, Wisconsin governor Scott Walker introduced proposed changes to alter the funding formulas for the state's community colleges and the UW system in 2012. This initial proposal sought to reward schools for degrees granted in high demand in the marketplace, as opposed to "degrees that people want to give us," interpreted as a reference to the liberal arts disciplines (Hall and Derby 2012).

A budget memo released by Wisconsin governor Scott Walker in 2015 sought a sizable decrease in funding for the University of Wisconsin system. At the same time, Walker floated the idea of rewriting the mission statement for the University of Wisconsin at Madison, aligning the purpose of the institution with the needs of corporations and businesses across the state and providing workforce preparedness. For perspective, the university had been founded on the notion of the "Wisconsin Idea," the concept that the role of higher education was to improve the lives of the state's citizens in contrast to the needs of its resident corporations.

Carol Geary Schneider, president of the Association of American Colleges and Universities, an organization devoted to representing the interests of nearly 1,500 such institutions united in promoting the tenets of liberal education, countered Governor Walker's proposal. Redirecting the purpose of public higher education toward the interests of employers "is designed for short-term learning and long-term disaster. It's focused on the wrong measures of what actually matters," she stated (Wong 2015, para. 11). Learning outcomes such as critical reasoning and analysis, effective communication, and appreciating persons of different backgrounds—in effect, requisite tools for the functioning of a truly democratic society—cannot be sacrificed in the interests of short-term job placement or salary in the first year after graduation, she noted. A University of Wisconsin at Madison professor, Jo Ellen Fair, added, "To see the university as a technical school is to miss the point of what we do. Our research is all about trying to prepare our students to live in the world" (Wong 2015, para. 14).

In January 2016, Kentucky governor Matt Bevin proposed revisions to the state budget that would reward public colleges and universities for increasing STEM graduates (Cohen 2016). This was not a new idea; indeed, the National Conference of State Legislatures reports that 12 states already have performance-based budgeting plans in place that incentivize STEM degree production. (These states include Arkansas, Hawaii, Illinois, Kansas, Maine, Minnesota, Mississippi, Nevada, Ohio, Pennsylvania, South Dakota, and Texas, as per a NCSL report of July 31, 2015, available at http://www.ncsl .org/research/education/performance-funding.aspx.)

It must be noted that this controversy is not limited to state legislators alone. Indeed, we witness much of the same at the federal level, as well. President Donald J. Trump's higher education platform included a proposal to restrict student loan eligibility by major in order to discourage study in the liberal arts beyond the most prestigious institutions. Former candidates for the Republican presidential nomination have weighed in on the issue as well. Florida senator Marco Rubio claimed that philosophy majors earned less than plumbers, and former Florida governor Jeb Bush complained that psychology majors were only employed at Chick-fil-A. And, in fact, the issue has crossed party lines: President Barack Obama himself entered into controversy in 2014 when he stated, "But I promise you, folks can make a lot more, potentially, with skilled manufacturing or the trades than they might with an art history degree. Now, nothing wrong with an art history degree . . . I'm just saying you can make a really good living and have a great career without getting a four-year college education as long as you get the skills and the training that you need" (Obama 2014).

The Case for Government Support of Liberal Education

Proponents of liberal course offerings herald the nonpecuniary benefits generated by majors in the creative arts and humanities. Put simply, they argue that society requires a full complement of diversely educated individuals, and it benefits from a vibrant community. A liberal education teaches creativity in and appreciation for art, music, and literature. A liberal education allows individuals the opportunity to examine their own culture against those of their peers, to assimilate differences, and identify commonalities. A foundation in the liberal arts allows people to relate to one another, to appreciate uniqueness and individuality, and gives citizens the ability to find a common ground where otherwise there would be misunderstanding. Access to the liberal arts should not be reserved for those students studying in the private institutions or those better positioned to afford a more costly education. All students should have the right to pursue their interests and passions with equal opportunity, to contribute to the intellectual vitality of our society.

Other proponents of the liberal arts champion their vital role in a fully functioning government by and of the people. American philosopher and University of Chicago professor Martha Nussbaum casts a compelling defense of the liberal arts and argues for the preservation of a liberal education. The health and well-being of our American democracy suffers in today's competitive world economy, she argues. "With the rush to profitability in the global market, values precious for the future of democracy, especially in an era of religious and economic anxiety, are in danger of getting lost" (Nussbaum 2010, 6). When we as human beings fail to appreciate the human condition of our neighbors, viewing them narrowly as potential customers or clients, our humanness is sacrificed and the promise of democracy weakened. She continues, "When we meet in society, if we have not learned to see both self and other in that way, imagining in one another inner faculties of thought and emotion, democracy is bound to fail, because democracy is built upon respect and concern, and these in turn are built upon the ability to see other people as human beings, not simply as objects" (Nussbaum 2010, 6). Nussbaum draws upon Harvard president Drew Faust's 2009 editorial in *The New York Times,* who writes, "Higher learning can offer individuals and societies a depth and breadth of vision absent from the inevitably myopic present. Human beings need meaning, understanding and perspective as well as jobs. The question should not be whether we can afford to believe in such purposes in these times, but whether we can afford not to" (Faust 2009).

Faust adds to her argument an indictment of the shortsightedness with which some legislators regard higher education. Acknowledging that there is also a monetary return to a liberal education—though perhaps less immediate than lawmakers might prefer—the fruits of creativity and involved discovery are quite real. "Higher education is not about results in the next quarter but about discoveries that may take—and last—decades or even centuries. Neither the abiding questions of humanistic inquiry nor the winding path of scientific research that leads ultimately to innovation and discovery can be neatly fitted within a predictable budget and timetable" (Faust 2009, para. 15). Complex problems require extensive inquiry that is unlikely to yield solutions in convenient time frames.

However, there is real value within the liberal arts, and degrees are indeed valued by employers. Scientists and businesspersons alike argue that a liberal education is the best preparation for thoughtful, creative, adaptive employees. How does this translate to economic production? Former Apple CEO Steve Jobs (1995–2011) painted a compelling picture for the value of the liberal education in his company: "It's in Apple's DNA that technology alone is not enough—that it's technology married with liberal arts, married with the humanities, that yields us the result that makes our hearts sing" (*Scientific American* 2016, para. 4). Employers in technology fields are seeking innovators, and students grounded in a liberal background are equipped with the cross-disciplinary awareness to make broader connections. Is the role of higher education to make students into efficient workers, or prepare them for an ever-changing and unpredictable world in which nimbleness and creativity are needed in jobs that don't yet exist?

Opponents of heightened tuitions for liberal arts degrees counter that preparation in fields such as psychology reward graduates with flexibility and adaptability. In an ever-evolving marketplace, it becomes more critical that employees be equipped to react to unpredictable circumstances in which their employers may find themselves. Put simply, an institution cannot prepare a student for the job of tomorrow if it doesn't exist today; no amount of skill development will make a future graduate more employable if the skills acquired in college are antiquated and out-of-date shortly after graduation. Proponents of liberal arts argue that students are better prepared for a changing world, one in which the jobs of the future are unknown. Graduates are equipped with the tools to succeed in all tasks precisely because they were not trained to solve a narrow set of preidentified, known problems.

Though liberal arts degree holders may not earn as much as their counterparts in science and engineering fields on average, it is important to acknowledge that humanities degree recipients earn more than those without a college degree (Baum, Ma, and Payea 2013; McMahon 2010). Further, unemployment rates for those holding bachelor's degrees in the humanities are significantly lower than the national average for those individuals with only a high school degree (Baum, Ma, and Payea 2013). A higher percentage of humanities bachelor degree holders are likely to complete graduate education than their peers, resulting in additional earnings that narrow the gap between humanities and applied studies (National Association of Colleges and Employers 2015). Research from the National Science Foundation has revealed that the majority of scientists and engineers reported their highest degree to be in a non–science or engineering field (Finamore et al. 2013). A liberal education may not translate to equitable immediate, short-term financial returns associated with a practical vocational education, but value remains inherent beyond secondary education and as a pathway to professional careers. In short, any college degree holder offers to contribute more to the economy than a non–degree holder.

Beyond the financial returns, there exist other nonquantifiable returns to a liberal education. Research suggests that coursework in the humanities may create better learners in general: language study increases the brain's ability to learn; empathy is acquired through literature and art; and medical students become better at diagnosing illnesses after taking art history courses (Bradburn and Townsend 2016).

In a large sense, liberal arts advocates frame the ongoing curricular debate around the public and private benefits of higher education. One primary purpose of college is to prepare students for a productive, economically fruitful life (as productive taxpaying employees), but is that the sole end of higher education? Some economists argue that there are additional public benefits to higher education (or, positive externalities), including a more informed voting and participatory populous, increased support of cultural organizations, reduced crime rates and pollution, and a citizenry more likely to take advantage of health care and less dependent on public welfare programs. If estimated returns on investment in education fail to account for these other public benefits, the true value of all higher education is underestimated and the full benefits of the liberal arts underestimated. However, even if one is inclined to dismiss these positive externalities, there remains the fact that liberal arts degrees lead to increased individual incomes relative to individuals earning no degrees over the longer term. Immediate returns upon graduation may not equal those in the practical arts, but, over the course of one's lifetime, incomes tend to equalize and may in fact exceed those who are practically educated. In short, the private returns may, in the long run, prove greater for the liberal arts (which translates, naturally, to increased tax revenues).

Finally, outright elimination of liberal arts curricular offerings would be an inefficient use of state resources because of costs associated with tenured faculty in these fields, to whom contractually obligated salaries and employment benefits are due. Additionally, major choices and labor markets tend to cycle (note that the greatest decline in undergraduate humanities degrees occurred in the 1980s; since this time, they have maintained in most fields). Society's interest in the liberal arts has tended to wax and wane relative to current economic and political tenors of the time (Pascarella et al. 2005). For that reason, it is possible that the demand for liberal arts and humanities majors will rebound in the future, leaving public institutions ill-equipped to respond.

References

Alvarez, Lizette. 2012. "Florida May Reduce Tuition for Select Majors." *The New York Times*, December 9. Accessed October 25, 2016. http://www.nytimes.com/2012/12/10/education/florida-may-reduce-tuition-for-select-majors.html

Anderson, Zac. 2011. "Rick Scott Wants to Shift University Funding Away from Some Degrees." Sarasota Herald-Tribune, October 10. http://politics.heraldtribune.com/2011/10/10/rick-scott-wants-to-shift-university-funding-away-from-some-majors/

Baum, Sandy, Jennifer Ma, and Kathleen Payea. 2013. "Education Pays 2013: The Benefits of Higher Education for Individuals and Society." In *Trends in Higher Education Series*. New York: College Board.

Bender, Michael C. 2011. "Scott: Florida Doesn't Need More Anthropology Majors." Tampa Bay Times, October 10. Accessed November 30, 2016. http://www

.tampabay.com/blogs/the-buzz-florida-politics/content/scott-florida
-doesnt-need-more-anthropology-majors

Cohen, Patricia. 2016. "A Rising Call to Promote STEM Education and Cut Liberal Arts Funding." *The New York Times*, February 21. Accessed October 27. http://nyti.ms/20OQKLy

Colavecchio, Shannon. 2010. "Lawmakers Stress Need for Higher Ed but Warn of Cuts." *Tampa Bay Times*, February 26. Accessed October 25, 2016. http://www.tampabay.com/news/lawmakers-stress-need-for-higher-ed-but-warn-of-cuts/1076083.

Faust, Drew Gilpin. 2009. "The University's Crisis of Purpose." *The New York Times*, September 6.

Finamore, John, Daniel J. Foley, Flora Lan, Lynn M. Milan, Steven L. Proudfoot, Emilda B. Rivers, and Lance Selfa. 2013. "Employment and Educational Characteristics of Scientists and Engineers." *National Center for Science and Engineering Statistics, NSF*:13–311.

Hall, Dee J., and Samara Kalk Derby. 2012. "Gov. Scott Walker Unveils Agenda for Wisconsin during Speech in California." *Wisconsin State Journal*, November 19. Accessed October 25, 2016. http://host.madison.com/wsj/news/local/govt-and-politics/gov-scott-walker-unveils-agenda-for-wisconsin-during-speech-in/article_a35a1378-31ed-11e2-bb6c-0019bb2963f4.html

Hamilton, Reeve. 2012. "Perry's $10,000 Degree Challenge Spreads to Florida." *The Texas Tribune*, November 26. Accessed November 30, 2016. https://www.texastribune.org/2012/11/26/perrys-10000-degree-challenge-spreads-florida/

Kiley, Kevin. 2013. "Another Liberal Arts Critic." *Inside Higher Ed*, January 30. Accessed October 25, 2016. https://www.insidehighered.com/news/2013/01/30/north-carolina-governor-joins-chorus-republicans-critical-liberal-arts

Logue, Josh. 2016. "Psych!" *Inside Higher Ed*. Accessed October 25, 2016.

McMahon, Walter W. 2009. *Higher Learning, Greater Good: The Private and Social Benefits of Higher Education*. Baltimore: Johns Hopkins University Press, 2009.

McMahon, Walter W. 2010. "The Private and Social Benefits of Higher Education: The Evidence, Their Value, and Policy Implications." *Advancing Higher Education*. TIAA-CREF Institute.

Mettler, Suzanne. 2014. *Degrees of Inequality: How the Politics of Higher Education Sabotaged the American Dream*. New York: Basic Books.

National Association of Colleges and Employers. 2015. *First Destinations for the College Class of 2014*. Bethlehem, PA: NACE. Accessed March 22, 2017. http://www.naceweb.org/uploadedfiles/pages/surveys/first-destination/nace-first-destination-survey-final-report-05-2015.pdf

National Conference of State Legislatures. 2015. *Performance Based Funding for Higher Education*. Washington, DC: NCSL. Accessed August 16, 2017. http://www.ncsl.org/research/education/performance-funding.aspx

New Englands First Fruits: In Respect, First of the Counversion of Some, Conviction of Divers, Preparation of Sundry of the Indians : 2. of the . . . London. 1643. Sabin Americana. Gale, Cengage Learning. University of Georgia. Accessed March 22, 2017. http://galenet.galegroup.com.proxy-remote.galib.uga.edu/servlet/Sabin?af=RN&ae=CY101072561&srchtp=a&ste=14

Nussbaum, Martha Craven. 2010. *Not for Profit: Why Democracy Needs the Humanities.* Princeton, NJ: Princeton University Press.

Obama, Barack. 2014. *"Remarks by the President on Opportunity for All and Skills for America's Workers."* The White House: Office of the Press Secretary, January 30. Accessed November 29, 2016. https://www.whitehouse.gov/the-press-office/2014/01/30/remarks-president-opportunity-all-and-skills-americas-workers

Pascarella, Ernest T., Gregory C. Wolniak, Tricia AD Seifert, Ty M. Cruce, and Charles F. Blaich. 2005. "Liberal Arts Colleges and Liberal Arts Education: New Evidence on Impacts. ASHE Higher Education Report, Volume 31, Number 3." *ASHE Higher Education Report* 31(3): 1–148.

Scientific American Editors. 2016. "STEM Education Is Vital—But Not at the Expense of the Humanities." *Scientific American*, October 1. https://www.scientificamerican.com/article/stem-education-is-vital-but-not-at-the-expense-of-the-humanities/

Shinn, Larry D. 2014. "Liberal Education vs. Professional Education: The False Choice." *Trusteeship Magazine*, January/February. Accessed November 30, 2016. http://agb.org/trusteeship/2014/1/liberal-education-vs-professional-education-false-choice

Sparks, Erin, and Mary Jo Waits. 2011. *Degrees for What Jobs? Raising Expectations for Universities and Colleges in a Global Economy.* Edited by National Governor's Association Center for Best Practices. Washington, DC: National Governor's Association.

Wong, Alia. 2015. "The Governor Who (Maybe) Tried to Kill Liberal-Arts Education." *The Atlantic*, February 11. https://www.theatlantic.com/education/archive/2015/02/the-governor-who-maybe-tried-to-kill-liberal-arts-education/385366/

Competency-Based Education: A Disruptive Innovation Requiring Demonstrated Performance

Jeffrey C. Sun

Overview and History

Competency-based education is an educational approach in which the learning achievement is manifested by demonstrated competence or mastery of defined learner outcomes. This educational approach is distinguishable from other forms when factoring design elements of curricular content, program delivery and pedagogy, and learner assessments.

Growth and Standardization

Historically, curricular content in postsecondary education derived from designated subject matter. For instance, during the Colonial Era through the 1800s, college curricula evolved into a subject-driven curriculum. The liberal arts, which included logic, grammar, and rhetoric from a Latin perspective, eventually included a reorganization to include the philosophical foundations of the arts and sciences (Rudolph 1993). The subject matter approach was divided into natural philosophy, which included physics, chemistry, biology, and geology, and moral philosophy, which included political science, economics, sociology, and anthropology (Brubacher and Rudy 1997).

Also, during the 1600s through much of the 1800s, program delivery and pedagogy did not change significantly. During that time, the college faculty structured instructional approaches around "three dominant modes—lecture, laboratory, and recitation" (Brubacher and Rudy 1997, 264). As postsecondary education expanded in the United States during the late 1800s and early 1900s, educational leaders were confronted with identifying common measures of learning. The College Entrance Examination Board, which is the predecessor to the College Board's SAT aptitude exam, served as the instrument to standardize measures for college admission. By the early 1900s, the organization now known as the Carnegie Foundation for the Advancement of Teaching proposed instructional time in the form of Carnegie Units, which today are recognized as college credit hours (Silva, White, and Toch 2015).

In short, while new divisions emerged over the years to organize curricular content, they largely remained with a similar structure of subject matter as a standardized format to organizing content. Likewise, program delivery and pedagogy has historically captured standardized approaches to learning, admissions, and instructional measures. Most significantly, measures of learning based on credit hours continues today as a standardized unit of learning.

Professional Education

During the early history of American professional preparation programming, learned professions such as law, medicine, and theology emerged as apprenticeships, not formal educational settings, in which a senior professional or elder would sponsor students through workplace training, and, at times, certify the apprentice into the profession (Sun 2004). Competency evaluation based on the senior professional became the gateway to practice. For instance, in medicine, medical apprenticeships were commonplace during the Colonial Era, and consisted of practical experience much like a preceptorship or clinical experience upon which a doctor would grant recognition of the medical apprentice as an entry point into the profession (Thorne 1973). This approach shifted to formalized education as colleges established professional education and constructed learning through standardized approaches to maintain consistency among the academic fields and sought increased quality and greater accountability through disciplinary accreditation groups such as the American Bar Association (ABA) for law and the Liaison Committee on Medical Education (LCME) for medicine (Sun 2004). Thus, professional preparation evolved from an apprenticeship approach, which presented training similar to a competency-based learning environment, to more formalized professional standards as means to establish professional education.

Learning Objectives and the Outcomes-Based Education Movement

Although the push for standardization largely focused on educational inputs such as subject matter, curriculum, and lessons, curricular theorists such as John Dewey (1938) and Ralph Tyler (1949) began to reshape the narrative about the learning process within the educational system by reexamining the learning encounters. Specifically, Dewey (1938) advanced a progressive examination of education by engaging multiple forms of experience as part of the educational system. Further, in a more practical analysis of curriculum, Ralph Tyler (1949) challenged educator curriculum planning and instruction by designing learning objectives, experiences, and assessments. Building off Tyler's work, Benjamin Bloom, one of Tyler's doctoral students at the University of Chicago, along with a team across the nation, developed a taxonomy of learning to align with the creation of learning objectives and advanced the interest of student mastery of a learning unit (Bloom 1956). Collectively, through building of learning experiences, objectives, and mastery, these events contributed to the outcome-based education movement, specifically one form of outcome-based education, competency-based education.

Emergence of Competency-Based Education

In the late 1960s and early 1970s, early adopters of competency-based education emerged from teacher education programs (Bowles 1973; Schwartz 2001; Semmel and Semmel 1976). Led by the American Association of Colleges for Teacher Education (AACTE), the national focus placed performance at the forefront. As Semmel and Semmel (1976) observed, leaders of teacher education used the terms *competency-based teacher education* and *performance-based teacher education* interchangeably to convey a focus on objectives and demonstrated outcomes. They used these labels to make clear that this approach would be different from past efforts, and it relied on an outcome of demonstrated mastery.

The lever to adopt competency-based education within teacher education largely emerged from grant dollars through the U.S. Office of Education Bureau of Research. The federal government selected 10 teacher education programs, which included Florida State University, University of Georgia, Michigan State University, Teachers College of Columbia University, and the University of Wisconsin. The features of these competency-based teacher education programs included instructional and behavioral objectives, resource information, and criterion-referenced measures. The programs designed the experience as primarily structured as self-paced, individually directed, mastery level achievement, and not as time bounded but rather outcome driven (Bowles 1973; Semmel and Semmel 1976). Put simply, these programs recognized learning inputs and processes, but they were concerned about the mastery of the demonstrated outcomes.

Around the same time as the competency-based teacher education emerged in the 1970s, selected colleges and universities constructed competency-based education designs for adult and professional education programs (Ewell 2002). These programs tended to address vocational and career education fields to advance workforce development or special needs such as nursing. Also spurred-on from a grant sponsored by the U.S. Office of Education (prior to the establishment of the U.S. Department of Education), postsecondary institutions such as Alverno College, DePaul University School for New Learning, Empire State College, Regents College (renamed as Excelsior College), and Thomas Edison State College (later renamed as Thomas Edison State University) developed competency-based programs targeted at adults returning to college (Ewell 2002; Klein-Collins, 2013; Nodine 2016). Nonetheless, the growth of competency-based education remained relatively stagnant through about 2014.

Recent Trends and Developments

Upward Trend with CBE Programs and Enrollments

The growth of competency-based education is evident through several data points. First, the number of institutions designing, building, or offering CBE programs has grown significantly. According to an Eduventures blog, "In 1990, no more than 50 colleges offered CBE programs" (Fleming 2015). Today, the Competency Based Education Network (CBEN), the professional association for this space, estimates that approximately 600 institutions are engaged with CBE programming at various stages such as design, construction, and implementation (Fain 2015).

Second, for this stage in CBE development, the number of students is substantial too. Based on data from nine institutions in which CBE learning design is the primary educational approach and credits are awarded for prior learning (e.g., Charter Oaks, Thomas Edison, and Western Governors), an American Enterprise Institute report calculated enrollments of approximately 140,000 undergraduates and 57,000 graduate students. Of course, because the national datasets are not designed to disaggregate CBE from non-CBE students, this figure does not include institutions with significant traditional enrollments such as Wisconsin, Northern Arizona, and Louisville.

Nonetheless, the data present upward trends. A survey conducted by Public Agenda (2015) of 586 CBE programs in development or implemented yielded 179 individual respondents. Based on that survey report, respondents provided their CBE program stage, which indicate that 64 percent of respondents were in the planning stage (i.e., designing or discussing their model), 11 percent were in the start-up phase (i.e., approved by the administration and beginning to recruit and enroll students), 14 percent were in the implementation stage (i.e., enrolling and educating students), and 17 percent fell within the scale-up stage (i.e., growing and replicating the program). Consistent with these dates, Eduventures forecasts even greater growth of CBE programs by 2020. "By 2020, we estimate that as many as 750 colleges will offer CBE programs and that overall enrollments will exceed 500,000 students, mostly adults learning through self-paced programming offered wholly or mostly online" (Fleming 2015).

Characteristics of CBE College Students Compared to National Data

The characteristics of the CBE students within the nine institutions resembled the national figures of postsecondary students. Taking the same point in time as the American Enterprise Institute (AEI) report, the comparisons display many consistencies. For instance, the nine CBE institutions had slightly more females enrolled than males in fall 2012 with an enrollment of 56 percent female (Kelchen 2015). During the same time period, enrollment was 57.2 percent for women in fall 2012 across all postsecondary institutions. Also, Kelchen reported the racial composition at the nine CBE institutions to have enrolled 64 percent White students, 33 percent students of color, and 3 percent unknown. The national data reports nearly 54 percent as White, 34 percent as students of color, and 10 percent as unknown or nonresident aliens.

The characteristics of the CBE students within the nine institutions are more distinct from national characteristics of college students when considering age, enrollment intensity, and mode of learning. The students at the nine CBE institutions were significantly older. In fact, 51 percent of the students were 35 years and over whereas the national data for a similar time period only reports a total just shy of 17 percent (U.S. Department of Education 2014a). Also, at eight of the nine CBE institutions, more than 50 percent of the students were enrolled part-time in fall 2012 with undergraduate status reported as part-time ranging from 50–100 percent among the institutions. By contrast, during this same period, the national average is approximately 38 percent of postsecondary education students (U.S. Department of Education 2017). The mode in which the students are educated is also different. Among the nine CBE institutions, undergraduate classes were almost exclusively delivered online during the fall 2012 term, whereas the national enrollment trend for this same time period only enrolled 11 percent of all undergraduate students participating exclusively with distance education courses (U.S. Department of Education 2014b).

Type of Institutions Developing or Delivering CBE Compared to National Data

The type of institutions participating in CBE development or implementation illustrates some divergence with the national representation of postsecondary institutions. According to data from a Public Agenda report (2015), institutions represented in the study about CBE programs were overwhelmingly public colleges and universities. Specifically, the distribution was 70 percent public, 23 percent private not for profit, and 6 percent private for profit (Public Agenda 2015). The percentage of postsecondary institutions that award federal student aid is distributed differently with 35 percent public, 37 percent private not-for-profit, and 28 percent private for-profit (U.S. Department of Education 2017). Besides distinctions by institutional control, the characteristics of respondents did not reflect the institutional breakdowns by Carnegie Classification. For instance, respondents from community colleges and comprehensive colleges were 50 percent and 32 percent, respectively, whereas the general population of degree granting postsecondary institutions during this same year, 2015, was 24 percent community colleges and 16 percent of master's comprehensive institutions. In other words, 82 percent of the CBE programmatic representation originated from 40 percent of the institutional landscape.

Arguments in Support of Competency-Based Education

Responds to Learner's Pace

In a typical educational program, time is a constant and locked into a semester or quarter. The learning ends when the term ends, and the measure of learning is credit hours. Correspondingly, learning is less consistent among students. CBE flips learning and time. As Sun (2017) observes, in CBE, "a student must successfully demonstrate competence of a learning outcome before moving onto the next competency lesson, [so] students may take only a few weeks to demonstrate competence or a year" (32). Similarly, in 2013, the U.S. Department of Education established sources for CBE and personalized learning. The department affirmed the idea that CBE offered a new approach in its description: "Transitioning away from seat time, in favor of a structure that creates flexibility, allows students to progress as they demonstrate mastery of academic content, regardless of time, place, or pace of learning" (U.S. Department of Education 2013). Viewed another way, "Under a CBE approach, time represents a variable measure of CBE programs, whereas learning goals and outcomes become a constant measure to one's educational success" (Sun 2017, 32). Thus, the credit hour as a measure no longer becomes the significant indicator (Laitinen 2012; Seymour, Everhart, and Yoshino 2015).

Proponents of competency-based education argue that measures of learning for CBE programs are more responsive to a learner's pace than traditional educational approaches. For instance, in a typical educational program, time is a constant and locked into a semester or quarter. The learning ends when the term ends. Correspondingly, learning is less consistent among students. CBE flips learning and time. As Sun (2017) observes, in CBE, "a student must successfully demonstrate competence of a learning outcome before moving onto the next competency lesson, [so] students may take only a few weeks to demonstrate competence or a year" (32). The structured terms inhibit the learning pace for an individual student's needs.

Supports Degree Attainment

Proponents also posit that competency-based education supports efforts to build the workforce and increase degree attainment (Nodine and Johnstone 2015). As a policy initiative, then secretary of education Arne Duncan has touted CBE as a promising educational design that helps support college students in completing their degrees (Fain 2013). More specifically, Secretary Duncan described CBE as "a key step forward in expanding access to affordable higher education," as he explained, "[w]e know many students and adult learners across the country need the flexibility to fit their education into their lives or work through a class on their own pace, and these competency-based programs offer those features" (Fain 2013).

Evidence also exists that recognizing competencies through prior experiences also increases degree attainment. A study of 62,475 students from 48 institutions revealed the difference between those students who received no prior credit graduated at a rate 2.86 times less than those students who were awarded credit for prior learning (Council for Adult and Experiential Learning 2010). Equally important, the applications of prior learning and life experiences in college learning increased graduation rates significantly for students of color. Specifically, graduation rates for African American students increased from 17 percent to 40 percent and Hispanic students increased even more from 6 percent to 47 percent when prior learning and life experiences were recognized in the degree program (Council for Adult and Experiential Learning 2010).

Indeed, greater degree attainment has a corresponding impact on the workforce by placing graduates in higher skilled jobs with better compensation (Carnevale, Smith, and Strohl 2013; Porter and Reilly 2014). These actions lead to upward mobility for the educated individuals and an improved economy (Carnevale, Smith, and Strohl 2013).

Articulates More Detailed Evidence of Learning

In a *New York Times* article, Fred Hurst, a leader of competency-based education posed the conundrum, "If you look at someone's transcript and it says they have three three-hour courses in history, an employer doesn't know what that means other than someone knows about these time periods in history. If you break it down in a different way and talk about the writing skills that a student got out of those courses, that's a skill someone will need in the workplace" (Kamenetz 2013).

Certainly, student learning outcomes define the "particular levels of knowledge, skills, and abilities that a student has attained at the end (or as a result) of his or her engagement in a particular set of collegiate experiences" (Ewell 2001, 6). Although helpful, even those details of learning are insufficient. Competency-based education moves further so "goals describe not only what is to be learned but also the specific levels of performance that students are expected to master" (Ewell 2001, 6). Further, the implementation of competencies typically requires more authentic assessments and cross validation of the assessments to the competencies. For some areas of study, these competencies are aligned with professional, industry, or other organizational standards or actual defined competencies ensuring consistency within the respective fields or nation. Put simply, CBE offers more validated forms of learning across a curriculum rather than in isolation (Klein-Collins 2013; see, e.g., Frank et al. 2010; Orgill and Simpson 2014).

Demonstrates Significantly Better Performance

In many instances, proponents show evidence that competency-based education is associated with successful learning (see, e.g., Epstein and Hundert 2002; Farrand et al. 2006; Witchger Hansen 2015). For example, Farrand et al. (2006) reported evidence that competency-based outcomes improved performance of nursing students. In that study, there were 139 subjects (121 female, 18 male), who were in their final year of an adult branch nursing program. The study subjects were sorted into two groups depending on their curriculum. Drawing on confidence performance measures such as formulating and documenting a plan of nursing care; taking into account social, cultural, spiritual, legal, political, and economic influences on nursing care; evaluating and documenting outcomes of nursing; and demonstrating skills in literacy, numeracy, information technology, management and problem-solving skills; the students who experienced the competency-based approach performed significantly better when comparing scores through a *t*-test based on statistical significance at a $p < .05$. The conclusion was clearly correlated with the CBE approach.

Arguments in Opposition to Competency-Based Education

Creates an Inappropriate Learning Approach

Critics of competency-based education have questioned the suitability of this approach to all students (Neem 2013; Ward 2016). Neem (2013) posits that "perhaps such an approach makes sense for those vocational fields in which knowing the material is the only important outcome, where the primary goal is certification" (26). He argues, however, that certain learning, especially liberal education "takes seat time" to digest information and create critical arguments (Neem 2013, 26).

The clash between a liberal education and a workforce degree has raised concerns about the actual impact on a learner and the degree's utility. One critic's musings described the CBE movement as an effort "to emphasize marketable skills over a deeper liberal knowledge content" that is in actuality "forcing students (particularly the underserved in lower-tier institutions, whom they claim to be helping) into a 'knowledge-less' version of liberal learning in order to 'hurry things along' and not get in the way of their job training" (Ward 2016, para. 7). Put simply, these viewpoints question whether competency-based approaches are truly useful for a democratic society and whether it can serve as an educational approach or is CBE a form of "cheap, reduced-rate imitations that can only be avoided by those with the right purchasing power" (Ward 2016).

Limits Degree Accessibility

Critics have asserted that access may be limited as costs may preclude students as the CBE design and operational expenditures become clear to institutions. As recently revealed, CBE program designs and similar technology-driven programs present little to no cost savings (Ruff 2016). Estimates of institutional spending on competency-based education programs have ranged from $78,000 to $700,000 to start a single program with an average expenditure of $382,000 (Desrochers and Staislof 2016). Further, institutions have "invested $4.2 million, on average, to develop an array of CBE programs during the initial implementation year, with a variance of $1.5 million across institutions" (Desrochers and Staislof 2016, 5). As reported in a news article, "competency-based programs were priced too low initially, before the business model was developed and start-up costs adequately considered" (Berrett 2016). Because many institutions were priced too low when they first rolled-out, the inferential message is that tuition rates will move up to support these programs. Although technology-driven offerings may be perceived as a cost savings solution to higher education, it has been well established that "adding technology just to add technology isn't a model for saving colleges money" (Ruff 2016).

Equally important, federal financial aid policies do not sufficiently account for competency-based learning that takes place through nontraditional terms. Eligibility and disbursements of funds are still tied to the traditional models of learning, so access to college students is limited when financial aid is not available (Muir and Goldstein 2014; Porter and Reilly 2014).

Lacks Quality Control Measures

Although some evidence exists that competency-based education yields perceived increases in learning or confidence in performing tasks, there is evidence that CBE programs lack sufficient quality control measures. For instance, a report by the inspector general for the U.S. Department of Education (2016) questioned whether even the U.S. Department of Education and one regional accreditor have failed to ensure that institutions maintain a federal financial aid rule requiring for programs to maintain "regular and substantive" interaction between the faculty and the student. Likewise, these programs have been depicted as correspondence programs with little interaction with faculty, and some critics have moved further in their disapproval calling this approach a degree mill in disguise (Ward 2016).

Regional accreditors are charged with the responsibility of reviewing and approving requests for competency-based education programs that wish to offer federal financial aid. Nonetheless, another U.S. Department of Education inspector general's report concluded that "reliance on the accrediting agency is not sufficient to evaluate whether a school is in compliance with Title IV requirements" (U.S. Department of Education 2014c).

Operates with Inconsistent Measures

Critics have drawn attention to the lack of consistent measures and data sources to truly determine the effectiveness of CBE program success (Hawkins et al. 2015). For instance, Hawkins et al. (2015) report that there are "concerns about the lack of consensus and consistency in how competencies are defined, developed, implemented and assessed. There is considerable heterogeneity across countries, along the continuum of education and among [medical] specialties" (1088). These authors also observe that the connection between behavior-derived competencies and program learning goals, objectives, and outcomes are not well articulated. Similarly, Holmboe et al. (2017) highlight the high stakes of misaligning competencies and learning goals to professional expectations, particularly in medical education. Thus, the absence of validated measures along with the presence of inconsistent ones present learning design challenges. Equally important, the inconsistency among competencies from one institution's degree to another created problems for students who wish to transfer from institution to another.

Conclusion

Historically, changes to educational approaches in higher education have met resistance. For instance, the movements that brought forward new areas of study such as science, engineering, business, and agriculture created a stir and raised questions about how these fields would dilute learning and fail to prepare future civic leaders. Similarly, shifts in educational philosophies also challenged the sanctity of a liberal education when educational philosophers such as Thomas Jefferson advocated for secular education, John Dewey offered insights about experiential learning, and critical philosophers—Carol Gilligan, bell hooks, Paulo Freire, and others—challenged our perspectives and redirected the dialogue to omitted, silenced, or overlooked voices and viewpoints. These educational philosophies spurred on debates about the value of essentialism, which advocated for a common core of a prescribed body of knowledge to develop the heritage of intellectual and moral standards once viewed as necessary for society, and perennialism, which called for universal truths to learning and espoused an agnostic view to circumstances of place, time, or person. Likewise, educational delivery of learning has evolved by offering greater access to wider audiences of students. At one time, an educational delivery innovation was learning by correspondence, which the academic community largely shunned as an attempt to advance diploma mills. Then the array of delivery modes continued with programming for part-time college students during the evenings and weekends, with academic offerings available at special sites off-campus, including inside corporate office buildings, and technology-driven options through interactive television and eventually online learning through the Web. Yet, despite opposition—especially during their inception, these educational approaches, philosophies, and modes of delivery have evolved with acknowledgments and, in many cases, adoption of more progressive, complex understandings of curriculum, learning, and students. Most importantly, evidence exists of their successes in educating college students as whole persons with civic responsibilities.

While competency-based education is not new, its capacity for greater adoption has become reified by learning technologies such as more sophisticated learning management systems and artificial intelligence software that have been produced by academic institutions, publishers, professional organizations with certifications, and third-party vendors. In light of these developments, competency-based education has an opportunity to expand more rapidly than online learning had for the past two decades.

Certainly, the expansion of competency-based education presents a disruption to educational practices today. Competency-based education has the capacity to use learning as a driver with authentic assessments to demonstrate mastery of that learning. It also has the capacity to educate in a more personalized manner where performance is at the core, not time. That approach will make the learning more useful and relevant to the students. Further, with technology, competency-based education may be scaled to serve greater numbers of students and at lower costs. In turn, this approach has potential to increase degree attainment. Finally, competency-based education as a curricular design approach has been adopted by many health fields and other professional fields, and these areas of study have demonstrated improved learning successes in terms of cognitive, affective, and behavioral performances (e.g., improved test scores, increased confidence, and higher achievements on entrustable professional activities). Simply put, competency-based education is facing similar opposition to other historical educational approaches, but it has also demonstrated many successes to-date and shows significant promise to improve learning outcomes and scale-up for greater availability.

References

Berrett, Dan. 2016. "Costs of Competency-Based Programs Come into Focus." *Chronicle of Higher Education*, October 18. Accessed on April 22, 2017. http://www.chronicle.com/article/Costs-of-Competency-Based/238092

Bloom, Benjamin S., ed. 1956. *Taxonomy of Educational Objectives: The Classification of Educational Goals (Vol. 1: Cognitive Domain)*. Ann Arbor, MI: Edwards Bros.

Bowles, F. Douglas. 1973. "Competency-Based Teacher Education? The Houston Story." *Educational Leadership* 30(6): 510–512.

Brubacher, John S., and Willis Rudy. 1997. *Higher Education in Transition: A History of American Colleges and Universities* (4th ed.). Brunswick, NJ: Transaction Publishers.

Carnevale, Anthony. P., Nicole Smith, and Jeff Strohl. 2013. *Recovery: Job Growth and Education Requirements through 2020*. Washington, DC: Center on Education and the Workforce at Georgetown University.

Council for Adult and Experiential Learning. 2010. *Fueling the Race to Postsecondary Success: A 48-Institution Study of Prior Learning Assessment and Adult Student Outcomes*. Chicago: Council for Adult and Experiential Learning.

Desrochers, Donna M., and Richard L. Staislof. 2016. *Competency Based Education: A Study of Four New Models and Their Implications for Bending the Higher Education Cost Curve*. Annapolis, MD: rpk Group.

Dewey, John. 1938. *Experience and Education*. New York: Free Press.

Epstein Ronald M., and Edward M. Hundert. 2002. "Defining and Assessing Professional Competence." *Journal of the American Medical Association* 287(2): 226–235.

Ewell, Peter T. 2001. *Accreditation and Student Learning Outcomes: A Proposed Point of Departure*. Washington, DC: Council for Higher Education Accreditation.

Ewell, Peter T. 2002. "An Emerging Scholarship: A Brief History of Assessment." In *Building a Scholarship of Assessment*, edited by Trudy W. Banta, and Associates, 3–25. San Francisco: Jossey-Bass.

Fain, Paul. 2013. "Beyond the Credit Hour." *Inside Higher Ed*, March 19. Accessed on April 22, 2017. https://www.insidehighered.com/news/2013/03/19/feds-give-nudge-competency-based-education

Fain, Paul. 2015. "Keeping Up with Competency." *Inside Higher Ed*, September 10. Accessed on April 22, 2017. https://www.insidehighered.com/news/2015/09/10/amid-competency-based-education-boom-meeting-help-colleges-do-it-right

Farrand, Paul, Mairjam McMullan, Rosalynd Jowett, and Ann Humphreys. 2006. "Implementing Competency Recommendations into Pre-Registration Nursing Curricula: Effects upon Levels of Confidence in Clinical Skills." *Nurse Education Today* 26(2): 97–103.

Fleming, Brian. 2015. "Mapping the Competency-Based Education Universe." *Eduventures Blog*, February 17. Accessed on April 22, 2017. http://www.eduventures.com/2015/02/mapping-the-competency-based-education-universe/

Frank, Jason R., Rani Mungroo, Yasmine Ahmad, Mimi Wang, Stefanie De Rossi, and Tanya Horsley. 2010. "Toward a Definition of Competency-Based Education in Medicine: A Systematic Review of Published Definitions." *Medical Teacher* 32(8): 631–637.

Hawkins, Richard E., Catherine M. Welcher, Eric S. Holmboe, Lynne M. Kirk, John J. Norcini, Kenneth B. Simons, and Susan E. Skochelak. 2015. "Implementation of Competency-Based Medical Education: Are We Addressing the Concerns and Challenges?" *Medical Education in Review* 49:1086–1102.

Holmboe, Eric S., Jonathan Sherbino, Robert Englander, Linda Snell, and Jason R. Frank. 2017. "A Call to Action: The Controversy of and Rationale for Competency-Based Medical Education." *Journal of Medical Teacher* 39(6): 574–581.

Kamenetz, Anya. 2013. "Are You Competent? Prove It." *New York Times*, October 29. Accessed April 22, 2017. http://www.nytimes.com/2013/11/03/education/edlife/degrees-based-on-what-you-can-do-not-how-long-you-went.html

Kelchen, Robert. 2015. *The Landscape of Competency-Based Education: Enrollments, Demographics, and Affordability*. Washington, DC: Center on Higher Education Reform, American Enterprise Institute.

Klein-Collins, Rebecca. 2013. *Sharpening Our Focus on Learning: The Rise of Competency-Based Approaches to Degree Completion*. Champaign: University of Illinois at Urbana-Champaign's National Institute for Learning Outcomes Assessment.

Laitinen, Amy. 2012. *Cracking the Credit Hour*. Washington, DC: New America Foundation.

Muir, Geraldine, and Michael B. Goldstein. 2014. "Establishing Federal Financial Aid Eligibility for Competency-Based Education." *Career Education Review* February (2): 1–8.

Neem, Johann N. 2013. "Experience Matters: Why Competency-Based Education." *Liberal Education* 99(4): 26–29.

Nodine, T. R. 2016. "How Did We Get Here? A Brief History of Competency-Based Higher Education in the United States." *Journal of Competency-Based Education* 1:5–11.

Nodine, Thad, and Sally M. Johnstone. 2015. "Competency-Based Education: Leadership Challenges." *Change: The Magazine of Higher Learning* 47(4): 61–66.

Orgill, Britlyn D., and Deborah Simpson. 2014. "Toward a Glossary of Competency-Based Medical Education Terms." *Journal of Graduate Medical Education* 6(2): 203–206.

Porter, Stephen R., and Kevin Reilly. 2014. *Maximizing Resources for Student Success: Competency-Based Education as a Potential Strategy to Increase Learning and Lower Costs.* Overland Park, KS: National Higher Education Benchmarking Institute.

Public Agenda. 2015. *Survey of the Shared Design Elements & Emerging Practices of Competency-Based Education.* San Francisco: Public Agenda.

Rudolph, Frederick. 1993. *Curriculum: A History of the American Undergraduate Course of Study since 1636.* San Francisco: Jossey-Bass.

Ruff, Corinne. 2016. "Does Technology Ever Reduce the Costs of Teaching?" *Chronicle of Higher Education*, January 26. Accessed on April 22, 2017. http://www.chronicle.com/article/Does-Technology-Ever-Reduce/235046

Schwartz, Stuart E. 2001. "Competency-Based Education: Basic Problems and a Suggested Solution." *Education* 98(1): 57–61.

Semmel, Melvyn I., and Dorothy S. Semmel. 1976. "Competency-Based Teacher Education: An Overview." *Behavioral Disorders* 1(2): 69–82.

Seymour, Deborah, Deborah Everhart, and Karen Yoshino. 2015. *The Currency of Higher Education: Credits and Competencies.* Washington, DC: American Council on Education & Blackboard.

Silva, Elena, Taylor White, and Thomas Toch. 2015. *The Carnegie Unit: A Century-Old Standard in a Changing Education Landscape.* Stanford, CA: Carnegie Foundation for the Advancement of Teaching.

Sun, Jeffrey C. 2004. "Professional: Schools: Research and Assessment Involving Multiple Constituencies." *New Directions for Institutional Research* 124:5–29.

Sun, Jeffrey C. 2017. "Existing Solutions to New Questions on Competency-Based Education." *NASPA Leadership Exchange* (Spring):32–36.

Thorne, Barrie. 1973. "Professional Education in Medicine." In *Education for the Professions of Medicine, Law, Theology, and Social Welfare*, edited by Everett C. Hughes, Barrie Thorne, Agostino M. DeBaggis, Arnold Gurin, and David Williams, 17–99. New York: McGraw-Hill Book Company.

Tyler, Ralph. 1949. *Basic Principles of Curriculum and Instruction.* Chicago: University of Chicago Press.

U.S. Department of Education. 2013. *Competency-Based Learning or Personalized Learning.* Washington, DC: U.S. Department of Education. Accessed on April 22, 2017. https://www.ed.gov/oii-news/competency-based-learning-or-personalized-learning

U.S. Department of Education. 2014a. *Projections of Education: Statistics to 2022* (NCES 2014-051). Washington, DC: National Center for Education Statistics, U.S. Department of Education.

U.S. Department of Education. 2014b. *The Condition of Education* (NCES 2014-083). Washington, DC: National Center for Education Statistics, U.S. Department of Education.

U.S. Department of Education. 2014c. *Direct Assessment Programs: Processes for Identifying Risks and Evaluating Applications for Title IV Eligibility Need Strengthening to Better Mitigate Risks Posed to the Title IV Programs* (Control #ED-OIG/A05N0004). Washington, DC: Office of Inspector General, U.S. Department of Education.

U.S. Department of Education. 2016. *The Western Association of Schools and Colleges Senior College and University Commission Could Improve Its Evaluation of Competency-Based Education Programs to Help the Department Ensure Programs Are Properly Classified for Title IV Purposes* (Control #ED-OIG/A05P0013). Washington, DC: Office of Inspector General, U.S. Department of Education.

U.S. Department of Education. 2017. *National Center for Education Statistics, Integrated Postsecondary Education Data System (IPEDS), Fall Enrollment Component*. Washington, DC: National Center for Education Statistics, U.S. Department of Education. Accessed on April 22, 2017. https://nces.ed.gov/ipeds/Home/UseTheData

Ward, Steven C. 2016. "Let Them Each Cake (Competently)." *Inside Higher Ed*, February 1. Accessed on April 22, 2017. https://www.insidehighered.com/views/2016/02/01/competency-based-education-threatens-further-stratify-higher-education-essay

Witchger Hansen, Anne Marie. 2015. "Crossing Borders: A Qualitative Study of How Occupational Therapy Educators and Scholars Develop and Sustain Global Partnerships." *Occupational Therapy International* 22:152–162.

CHAPTER ELEVEN

Tracing a Troubled Sector: For-Profit Higher Education's Institutional Identity

Constance Iloh

Due to much scandal and speculation, the mainstream image of a for-profit college may resemble anything from a proprietary predator to an innovative leader in higher education (Iloh 2016). Despite continuing debate over the efficacy of for-profit higher education, much less discussion has centered on the features of the sector's educational offerings. As it stands, the increased attention and oversight of for-profit colleges and universities (FPCUs) has arguably not translated into a more coherent picture of the sector's programmatic characteristics and goals. In this chapter, I discuss how for-profit programs can be described, categorized, and differentiated in the broader higher education landscape. The first section includes a background of the for-profit sector, with attention paid to the proliferation and recent decline of FPCUs as well as institutional heterogeneity within the sector. In the next section, I discuss programmatic characteristics typical in the proprietary college sector. The third section illustrates criticisms of the for-profit programs, highlighting recruitment practices, tuition and loans, program quality, and student outcomes. The concluding section discusses ways competing institutions can model how FPCUs utilize institutional research.

For-Profit Higher Education

For-profit colleges are postsecondary education institutions that are privately run and exist, at least in part, to earn money for their owners. The for-profit postsecondary school sector encompasses taxpaying institutions that generate profits by providing post–high school degrees or credentials (Deming, Goldin, and Katz 2012). For-profit providers have highly focused missions targeted to specific segments, particular industries, and are limited to specific fields of study (Ruch 2001). The historic focus of FPCUs has been and remains the employer as a market. In responding to labor demands of numerous employers, trades, and professions, FPCUs develop and offer programs that train students for positions where there is sufficient demand, and for which investment in schooling is likely to be "recoverable" with increased wages they can accrue. Having evolved into an effective competitor to the traditional nonprofit education providers, the for-profit educational sector has grown at a spectacular pace (Chung 2012).

The Rise (and Recent Decline) of the For-Profit Sector

Although regionally accredited FPCUs are relatively new, proprietary vocational education has been in existence since colonial America and is consistent with the entrepreneurial character of the nation (Ruch 2001). Between 1890–1972, for-profit colleges were increasingly marginalized by the growth of highly subsidized public institutions as many reformers argued that education was the business of the state, and society could be improved by strong, publicly backed schools. In the era that followed, the broadened scope of Pell Grants gave rise to an increasing number of for-profit universities offering associates, bachelors, and graduate degrees (Breneman, Pusser, and Turner 2006). Reforms such as the 1972 Higher Education Act recognized for-profit schools as eligible institutions for federal aid programs, which made for-profit postsecondary training a more feasible alternative to public colleges (Heller 2011). Although not all FPCUs are publicly traded, after 1994 FPCUs were considered to be in a Wall Street era where publicly traded corporations drive the expansion of the for-profit sector (Kinser 2006). (See Figure 11.1.)

Most recently, enrollment in the for-profit sector growth has changed. In 2013, four-year, for-profit colleges had the largest enrollment decrease in postsecondary education at 9.7 percent, followed by two-year public colleges at 3.1 percent (National Student Clearinghouse Research Center 2013). In this same year enrollment at four-year public colleges and four-year private, nonprofit colleges actually increased by 0.3 percent and 1.3 percent, respectively (National Student Clearinghouse Research Center 2013). Even with the rise and most recent decline in enrollment at FPCUs, many questions remain

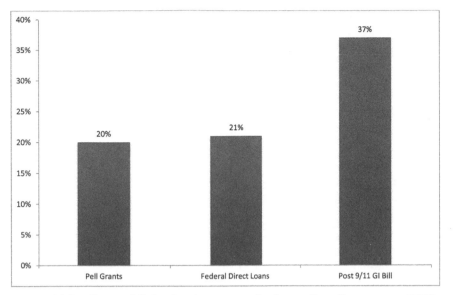

Figure 11.1   Share of federal aid going to the for-profit college sector, 2012–2013 academic year.

unanswered about the role and potential of for-profit colleges and universities (Public Agenda 2014).

Institutional Diversity in the For-Profit Sector

Although the for-profit sector enrolls less than 11 percent of all students in postsecondary education, it contains some of the largest and smallest institutions by enrollment in the country (Deming, Goldin, and Katz 2012). The 15 largest for-profit institutions account for almost 60 percent of for-profit enrollments (Bennett, Lucchesi, and Vedder 2010). The median Title IV-eligible for-profit institution, however, had a fall 2008 enrollment of 172 students as compared with 3,713 for the median community college (two-year public institution), 7,145 for the median four-year public university, and 1,149 for the median four-year private institution (Bennett Lucchesi, and Vedder 2010).

For-Profit Program Characteristics

Financing Model

The essential financial distinction between nonprofit and for-profit universities is not a matter of profitability or profit motive, but one of taxation, as either a source of revenue or form of expenditure. Nonprofit colleges, public and private, are exempt from paying taxes while for-profit institutions are taxpaying. For-profits pursue profits through a combination of growth in volume and growth in unit margins, and these goals and strategies are formulated and monitored by the centralized leadership of the firm. Compared to their counterparts in nonprofits, the senior management at for-profits can more easily: (1) invest personally in their institutions, (2) guide strategies through substantial control of internal operations, (3) direct the strategies through mergers and acquisitions, and by selling off parts of their businesses, and (4) promote growth by attracting added investment capital from private financial markets (Hentschke 2011).

Strategic Expansion and Geographic Variation

The willingness and ability of for-profits to buy and sell facilities (as well as the geographic variation of the for-profit sector) further differentiates them from traditional institutions. FPCUs have fewer resources tied up in buildings and equipment than traditional institutions because they typically lease their facilities. FPCUs pursue the "lease strategy" for three reasons: purchasing does not yield a competitive return; it retards the firm's ability to be nimble and shift locations; and there is a reluctance to mass all fixed assets in one place (Hentschke 2011).

For-profit providers often target states that do not meet the demand of their college-trained workers from within-state capacity. FPCUs also focus on states that have experienced disproportionate increases in their populations, such as California, Colorado, and Arizona, which consequently have the highest increases in for-profit enrollment (Breneman, Pusser, and Turner 2006). Many of the larger for-profit institutions are well dispersed throughout the nation. Three of the largest national chains of FPCUs, Devry University, ITT, and University of Phoenix, have more than three hundred locations in 38 states (Kinser 2006). This geographic variation is different from the concentration of public and private nonprofit institutions, much of which is due in part to history and local politics, rather than student demand and population growth.

Vocational Education

The objective of many for-profit institutions is straightforward in that they exist in order to prepare students for immediate employment in a rather carefully defined occupational field (Shoemaker 1973). Because FPCUs cannot rely primarily on public funding, they must be able to recover nearly all costs associated with the provision of their product in the form of tuition (Bennett Lucchesi, and Vedder 2010). For this reason, FPCUs tend to focus on degree programs with measurable skill outcomes that are more likely to pass a cost–benefit test for students. Moreover, for-profit programs are typically not meant to prepare students to continue to another form of higher education, as is the case with most community colleges, which are also tasked with supporting transfer efforts (Deming, Goldin, and Katz 2012). An analysis of disciplines in which for-profits offer the most degrees reveals that the majority of for-profit students are primarily focused on acquiring skills that will directly increase their value in labor markets. The majority of for-profit colleges provide a small (three to five) assortment of short certificate programs in career-oriented fields, such as culinary services, allied health professions, business support services, computer and IT services, cosmetology, and legal support (Apling 1993). Degree programs offered by most for-profit institutions differ from traditional degree programs by emphasizing skills (versus theory) and practical subjects (versus liberal arts), although programs in all sectors of higher education have become more career-oriented and students are choosing occupational and professional programs in increasing numbers.

Career Services and Job Placement

Most proprietary schools provide students with some type of support services for job placement as most FPCUs attract students by promising an educational experience that will result in a fruitful career. For-profit college connections with employers are usually stronger than those found in traditional institutions (Rosenbaum, Deil-Amen, and Person 2006). Unlike a typical community college offering several vocational programs, a proprietary school is likely to specialize in a single or a few areas, such as health or hospitality, which makes it easier to build strong relationships with regional employers in their fields (Kelly 2001).

Criticism of For-Profit Colleges and Universities

The for-profit higher education sector has been both praised and scrutinized for its impact on 21st-century higher education. Much of the contemporary discussion on FPCUs has reflected the latter rather than the former with the onset of scandals and accusations of corruption overwhelming the proprietary sector. Whether one agrees with the criticism or not, it is fair to say over the past several years, the for-profit higher education industry in the United States has been under withering attack, with much of this criticism rooted in a philosophy that making a profit in education is wrong. Below, I highlight many of the criticisms with regard to the practices and outcomes of their programs.

Quality of For-Profit Programs

The different motives that characterize for-profits (including their pro-growth, antiselectivity, and cost-reduction mind-set) have often been conflated with a presumption that for-profits are inclined to pursue growth at the expense of quality. The roots of this perspective date back to the 1970s when proprietary institutions operated with little oversight, especially over recruiting, instructional, and placement practices (Hentschke 2011). Contemporary scandals arising over unethical recruiting practices, high loan defaults, and low completion and placement rates have further intensified scrutiny of the for-profit sector and have even led to the abrupt closures of some for-profit institutions (Iloh 2016). Those arguing in favor of additional regulation believe that for-profit colleges leave students with insurmountable debt and few skills, while proponents argue that these institutions provide valuable job training for underserved students with both sides often relying on anecdotal evidence.

Over time, resource allocation has been added to the long list of criticisms regarding for-profit quality, as for-profit colleges and universities spend the least amount per student among all sectors of higher education. FPCUs spent on average $9,758 per student in 2008–2009, while public colleges spent almost double that amount and private nonprofit institutions spend nearly four times as much (Bennett Lucchesi, and Vedder 2010). FPCUs also do not support athletic teams, offer residential housing, student centers and clubs, or other functions that provide a climate of student life found at most traditional colleges (Jaeger 1999). And although no evidence illustrates that this stripped-down approach directly lowers quality, it certainly allows for-profit institutions to operate at a fraction of the cost of full-service colleges and universities.

Federal Funding

A disproportionate share of federal financial aid funds is put toward for-profit education. Eighty percent of undergraduates attending for-profit colleges received Title IV aid in the 2011–2012 school year, compared with 57 percent of undergraduates enrolled in postsecondary education generally (ASPCU n.d.). This aid is not only in the form of loans but grants as well. Although for-profit college students comprise less that 15 percent of the higher education population, students enrolled in these schools receive 20 percent of all Pell Grant funds and 21 percent of direct loans to students (Baum and Payea 2013). This amounts to around $33 billion in Title IV aid flowing to the sector each year (Halperin 2014). For-profit students also receive nearly two-fifths (37 percent) of all grants from the post-9/11 GI Bill for those who have served in the military (College Board 2013). This aid serves as the bulk of all revenue that for-profit colleges use for their operations, including marketing, employee compensation, and educational instruction.

Cost and Student Debt

Tuition at FPCUs is substantially higher than at public sector institutions, and students receive less institutional aid to assist them in paying the fees than at nonprofit institutions (Gilpin, Saunders, and Stoddard 2015; Iloh and Toldson 2013). Because the majority of for-profit revenues are derived from tuition, and most students in for-profit schools finance their education through student loans, FPCUs are ultimately reliant on high tuition rates to return a profit. Average annual tuition is nearly five times higher at for-profit colleges than at public community colleges (Baum and Payea 2013). This average tuition at FPCUs is higher than what a public school would charge an out-of-state student, but it is still lower than the average tuition charged by a private nonprofit institution (Bennett Lucchesi, and Vedder 2010).

Consequently, for-profit college students tend to take on more debt than students in any other sector. Ninety-six percent of for-profit students take out student loans (Health, Education, Labor and Pensions Committee 2010). In comparison, 13 percent of students at community colleges, 48 percent at four-year public, and 57 percent at four-year private nonprofit colleges borrow money to pay for school. For-profit schools also enroll far more high-dollar borrowers. Fifty-seven percent of bachelor's students who graduate from a for-profit college owe $30,000 or more (Health, Education, Labor and Pensions Committee 2010). In contrast, 25 percent of those who earned degrees in the private, nonprofit sector and 12 percent from the public sector borrowed at this level (Health, Education, Labor and Pensions Committee 2010). Although students at for-profit colleges represent only about 11 percent of the total higher education population, they are 44 percent of all federal student loan defaults.

Recruitment Practices

In the for-profit sector, there are 10 recruiters for every career services staff member (Health, Education, Labor and Pensions Committee 2010). Further, while just 30 FPCUs hired 35,202 recruiters in 2010, the for-profit higher education industry employed a total of 3,512 career services staff in the same year (Lee 2012). For-profit schools' emphasis on marketing and recruiting raises questions about whether sufficient resources are being devoted to ensure that students receive a quality education that results in increased job opportunities or higher income (Health, Education, Labor and Pensions Committee 2010).

FPCUs lead higher education in marketing and recruiting expenses, spending $4.2 billion on marketing, recruiting, and admissions staffing in the 2009 fiscal year (Lee 2012). Estimates suggest that the average FPCU spends about 15 percent of its revenues on sales and marketing (Tierney and Hentschke 2007). This rate is similar to what is spent by firms in other direct-to-consumer markets (Gallagher and Poroy 2005).

In contrast to traditional institutions, many of which are constrained by state funding and the pursuit of prestige, many for-profit institutions seek to enroll as many "qualified applicants" as they can (Hentschke 2011). Most for-profit institutions (and the federal government) define a qualified applicant as anyone with a high school diploma or GED. Empirical evidence highlights that while for-profit colleges might be more engaging and personable throughout the admissions process, they are less forthcoming with financing and gainful employment information than comparable institutions such as community colleges. For-profits are often criticized for seeking out high-risk students, implying that these students are somehow less astute consumers of education services. Proponents of the for-profit sector often mention that these same students are both underserved by traditional institutions currently and these students must be served if the United States is to significantly increase its proportion of individuals with a college education. Depending on the view, proprietary schools are seen either as taking advantage of uninformed students, or helping these very students to navigate their entry into the labor market (Chung 2012).

For-Profit Student Outcomes

Several studies highlight separate and inadequate satisfaction, earnings, and employment outcomes in the for-profit sector compared with the public and private nonprofit sectors. For example, Deming, Goldin, and Katz (2012) controlled for a wide range of factors and found that, all else being equal, those who attend for-profit colleges are less satisfied with their major or concentration; less likely to report that their student loan debt is a worthwhile investment; less likely to be satisfied with their job; and more likely to be unemployed than those who attend public and private nonprofit schools. Controlling for some of the challenges for-profit students may experience at greater rates, Lang and Weinstein (2012) also found that obtaining a degree or certificate from a for-profit school is less advantageous than doing so from a public or private nonprofit school. Cellini and Chaudhary (2012) measured the before-and-after wage differences between two-year associate's degree enrollees at for-profit and public colleges. The authors found that students who enroll in for-profit associate's degree programs experience wage increases between 6 percent and 8 percent, while community college attendees had no wage growth (Cellini and Chaudhary 2012). However, because for-profit programs are more expensive than those offered at public institutions, the authors concluded that for-profit colleges are still a less-valuable option.

Institutional Research, For-Profit Programs, and New Directions for Nonprofits

Within the higher education context, institutional research (IR) is critical in producing information to meet internal needs and external demands (Zamani-Gallaher 2004). The ability to adapt to the changing higher education market illustrates another difference between FPCUs and the traditional nonprofit sector, particularly in their use of institutional research. Although the previous section emphasizes many concerns with regard to for-profit institutions, this section underscores lessons that competing institutions can adopt from how FPCUs use data. Accordingly, I highlight sector differences but also put forth recommendations for nonprofit institutions in utilizing institutional data.

For-profits often have the use of IR ingrained in the jobs of staff and leaders, whether it is a dean or an admissions counselor. In nonprofit institutions of higher learning, most employees primarily handle academic affairs, and relatively few employees deal with business or economic aspects of the institution (Ruch 2001). This lends itself to an environment in which most employees are insulated from market forces and are consequently unable to pursue the most efficient use of resources (Coleman and Vedder 2008). Accordingly, training staff and leaders to use data relative to their positions might be useful in building a culture where employees are sensitive to utilizing IR in promoting the best institutional practices and outcomes.

Often, for-profit institutions use data to see when there is a shift in student demand for programs. For example, a for-profit leader can look at the financial statements (or enrollment numbers) of his or her college and make a decision to shift resources from one department to another (Ruch 2001). Competing institutions can also use data to analyze what programs are in high demand and those that are less popular. Specifically, institutions can use program enrollment data to guide whether certain programs can be scaled up or down. While community colleges, particularly in urban areas, are often cited as facing capacity issues, expanding and restricting programs based on student demand will help these institutions better structure the few resources they are often given.

For-profits also use IR to identify new niche student markets that are underserved by traditional higher education. This is similar to how many businesses use market research to identify new customers and tailor their products and/or services to them. For-profit institutions have been particularly assertive in using data to create more flexible and responsive programs to address the needs of posttraditional students and adult learners (Bailey, Badway, and Gumport 2001). Today, 85 percent, or about 15 million undergraduates, are a diverse group that includes adult learners, employees who study part-time, low-income students, commuters, and student parents (Soares 2013). Although the budgets for many competing institutions are often restricted, using funds to strategically improve conditions for the highest enrolling demographics will allow institutions to work smarter with their money. For example, better accommodations for parents and commuters might be important directions that enrollment data and student surveys reveal for community colleges.

For-profit institutions not only use IR to be effective, but also to be efficient with their resources. Since responsiveness to data is built into the culture of many mainstream publicly traded for-profit institutions, they can more easily innovate. The bureaucratic decision-making process of shared governance often renders traditional public and private institutions unable to respond quickly enough to necessary changes. Given that many institutions, both nonprofit and for-profit, are now facing rapid declines in enrollments and funding, it will be important that institutions rethink the pace to which they use data-driven insights to survive and thrive fiscally.

Actively and consistently finding ways to use data is another way in which for-profit institutions weave institutional research into the fabric of their institutional behavior. To be sure, competing institutions, such as community colleges, do keep a great deal of data, but it is rarely kept in a form through which it can be easily used as a foundation for program improvement. Although data in the for-profit sector is often used to allow for competitive advantage, the same institutional imperatives could be made for other open access institutional types that serve communities with great need for local postsecondary options.

The goal of this text was to provide a summary unlike that of the traditional higher education narrative that often marginalizes the for-profit higher education sector. I began with a description of the for-profit higher education landscape, paying particular attention to how for-profit programs compare to traditional colleges and universities while also focusing on programmatic criticisms. Ultimately this text reflects the more nuanced question of "how can for-profit higher programs be described, differentiated, and modeled?"— an inquiry necessary for future institutional research, practice, and reform of higher education.

References

Apling, Richard N. 1993. "Proprietary schools and their students." *The Journal of Higher Education* 64:379–416.

Bailey, Thomas, Norena Badway, and Patricia G. Gumport. 2001. *For-profit higher education and community colleges.* Stanford, CA: National Center for Post-secondary Improvement.

Baum, Sandy and Kathleen Payea. *Trends in student aid 2013*. New York: College Board.

Bennett, Daniel J., Adam R. Lucchesi, and Richard K. Vedder. 2010. *For-profit higher education: Growth, innovation, and regulation*. Washington, DC: Center for College Affordability and Productivity.

Breneman, David W., Brian Pusser, and Sarah E. Turner. 2006. *Earnings from learning: The rise of for-profit universities*. Albany: State University of New York Press.

Cellini, Stephanie Riegg, and Latika Chaudhary. 2012. *The labor market returns to a for-profit college education (NBER Working Paper No. 18343)*. Cambridge, MA: National Bureau of Economic Research.

Chung, Anna S. 2012. "Choice of for-profit college." *Economics of Education Review* 31:1084–1101. doi:10.1016/j.econedurev.2012.07.004.

Clowes, Darrel A. 1995. "Community colleges and proprietary schools: Conflict or convergence?" *New Directions for Community Colleges* 1995: 5–15. doi:10.1002/cc.36819959103.

Coleman, James, and Richard Vedder. 2008. *For-profit education in the USA: A primer*. Washington, DC: Center for College Affordability and Productivity.

Deming, David J., Claudia Goldin, and Lawrence F. Katz. 2012. "The for-profit postsecondary school sector: Nimble critters or agile predators?" *Journal of Economic Perspectives* 26:139–164. doi:10.1257/jep.26.1.139.

Gallagher, Sean, and B. Poroy. 2005. *Assessing consumer attitudes toward online education*. Boston, MA: Eduventures.

Gilpin, Gregory A., Joseph Saunders, and Christiana Stoddard. 2015. "Why has for-profit colleges' share of higher education expanded so rapidly? Estimating the responsiveness to labor market changes." *Economics of Education Review* 45:53–63. doi:10.1016/j.econedurev.2014.11.004.

Halperin, David. 2014. *Stealing America's future: How for-profit colleges scam taxpayers and ruin students' lives*. Washington, DC: Republic Report.

Health, Education, Labor and Pensions (HELP) Committee. 2010. *Emerging risk?: An overview of growth, spending, student debt, and unanswered questions in for-profit higher education*. Washington, DC: U.S. Senate.

Heller, Donald E. 2011. "The impact of gainful employment regulations." *Change: The Magazine of Higher Learning* 43:58–64. doi:10.1080/00091383.2011.607074.

Hentschke, Gilbert C. 2011. "Innovations in business models and organizational cultures: The for-profit sector." In B. Wildavsky, A. Kelly and K. Carey (Eds.), *Reinventing higher education: The promise of innovation*. Cambridge, MA: Harvard University Press.

Iloh, Constance. 2016. "Exploring the for-profit experience: An ethnography of a for-profit college." *American Educational Research Journal* 53:427–455. doi:10.3102/0002831216637338.

Iloh, Constance, and William Tierney. 2014. "Understanding for-profit and community college choice through rational choice." *Teachers College Record* 24:1–34.

Iloh, Constance, and Ivory A. Toldson. 2013. "Black students in 21st century higher education: A closer look at for-profit and community colleges." *The Journal of Negro Education* 82:205–212. doi:10.7709/jnegroeducation.82 .3.0205.

Jaeger, David A. 1999. *Proprietary higher education and the labor market: What would we like to know?* University of Virginia: Seminar on For-profit Higher Education.

Kelly, Kathleen F. 2001. *Meeting needs and making profits: The rise of for-profit degree-granting institutions.* ECS Issue Paper. Denver, CO: Economic Commission of the States.

Kinser, Kevin. 2006. *From main street to Wall Street: The transformation of for-profit higher education (ASHE Higher Education Report).* San Francisco, CA: Jossey-Bass Inc.

Kirp, David L. 2003. *Shakespeare, Einstein and the bottom line: The marketing of higher education.* Cambridge, MA: Harvard University Press.

Lang, Kevin, and Russell Weinstein. 2012. "Evaluating student outcomes at for-profit colleges." doi:10.3386/w18201.

Lee, Suevon. 2012. "The For-Profit Higher Education Industry, by the Numbers," August 9.

National Student Clearinghouse Research Center. 2013. *Term enrollment estimates, Fall 2013.* Herndon, VA: National Student Clearinghouse.

Public Agenda. 2014. *Profiting higher education: What students, alumni and employers think about for-profit colleges.* Brooklyn, NY: Public Agenda.

Rosenbaum, James E., Regina Deil-Amen, and Ann E. Person. 2006. *After admission: from college access to college success.* New York: Russell Sage Foundation.

Ruch, Richard S. 2001. *Higher Ed, Inc.: The rise of the for-profit university.* Baltimore, MD: Johns Hopkins University Press.

Shoemaker, Ellwood A. 1973. "Community colleges: The challenge of proprietary schools." *Change* 5:71–72.

Soares, Louise. 2013. *Post-traditional learners and the transformation of postsecondary education: A manifesto for college leaders.* Washington, DC: American Council on Education.

Tierney, William G., and Guilbert C. Hentschke. 2007. *New players, different game: Understanding the rise of for-profit colleges and universities.* Baltimore, MD: Johns Hopkins University Press.

Zamani-Gallaher, Eboni M. 2004. "Proprietary schools: Beyond the issue of profit." *New Directions for Institutional Research* 2004(124):63–79. doi:10 .1002/ir.132.

PART 3

Issues Facing American College Students in the 21st Century

CHAPTER TWELVE

Social Media: Dialogues on Learning, Engagement, Activism, and Identity

Paul William Eaton

Introduction

This chapter presents an overview of some debates related to social media and learning not from deficit or dystopian perspectives, but rather from the perspective of how digital technologies may enhance student learning. The chapter is framed as a series of questions for educators to consider because debates about social media, learning, and education continue and perspectives exist along a continuum. The four central questions discussed center on whether social media enhances or impedes academic learning; how social media is used for cocurricular engagement; the role of social media in student activism; and a questioning of the discourses of identity and development: two central concepts that undergird the work of researchers and educators.

Engaging the Debates on Social Media in Higher Education

The advent and rapid proliferation of social media technologies is perhaps one of the most significant changes to the college student environment and experience within the past decade. Social media platforms are those digital tools that allow users to create a unique profile, actively network, build communities, curate and share information, and disseminate original creative content through digital tools, Web, and phone-based applications (Ahlquist and Cabellon 2016; boyd and Ellison 2007). Colleges and universities have grappled with myriad issues related to social media, the student experience, and the role of institutional accountability.

Much of the discourse and research on social media, college students, and the role of the institution has centered broadly on student learning. Although the discourse of learning can be viewed as a contested issue itself (Biesta 2010), there is fairly broad consensus that one aim of the college and university experience should be learning, defined as "comprehensive, holistic, transformative activit[ies]" (ACPA and NASPA 2004, 4) that occur across a wide range of environments. In "reconsidering learning" for college students, ACPA—College Student Educators International and NASPA—Student Affairs Administrators in Higher Education (2004) clearly articulated learning as a holistic process encapsulating mind, body, and spirit. Thus, learning in this chapter will cover classroom experiences, cocurricular engagement, student activism, and issues of identity. Social media technologies have profoundly impacted each of these aspects of the college student learning experience.

Many of the earliest debates about the impacts of social media on college student learning emphasized technological disruption, focusing on questions of whether new technologies were impeding student learning. Educators expressed concerns about whether students, engaged with Web sites, online gaming, Facebook, other early social media platforms, and blogs were focusing energies to the detriment of academic curricular learning. Many of these earliest discussions were anecdotal, rather than based on any empirical research.

Researchers soon engaged the question. Kirschner and Karpinski (2010) conducted a study to examine whether Facebook use impacted scholastic achievement as measured by grade point average. In their study, students who self-reported spending significant time engaged with Facebook also reported lower GPAs. The researchers suggested that such evidence might point to the negative impacts of social media on academic achievement. However, Ahn (2011) criticized this study, noting that although there may be a relationship between Facebook use and academic achievement, there is little to suggest direct causality. In other words, Facebook may or may not be the reason students underperformed academically in comparison to their non-Facebook using peers.

Debates about the implications of social media also occurred in higher education and student affairs. Connolly (2011) discussed drawbacks of social media use, including "weaker critical thinking skills" (128) and difficulties with "concentration, reasoning, and reflection" (129). However, Martinez

Aleman (2011) countered this argument, citing her 2009 study with Wartman in which they found "students use Facebook to hone their cognitive skills to create new or alter existing connections of real-life and data" (136). Recognizing the dramatic shift occurring as a result of social media, Martinez Aleman (2011) advocated that college student educators "examine whether traditional constructs and norms for learning . . . are adequate" (138).

Although the early years of social media also raised concerns about student–educator interaction, privacy, trolling, bullying, and digital citizenship (Guidry and Ahlquist 2016), there is growing recognition that social media and digital technologies should be examined for their potential to *enhance*, *redefine*, or *reimagine* learning. Although researchers might still be concerned about potential impediments to traditional constructs of learning as measured by grade point average or measures of cognitive ability, what is increasingly evident in the literature is recognition that social media platforms offer new alternatives for our understanding of learning. In aligning with the definition of learning offered earlier, college student educators are now embracing social media platforms as environments where critical learning can and does occur. Following a brief overview on the growth of social media use, this chapter will focus on four trends, debates, or controversies in social media use and learning, which I am framing as dialogues: the influences of social media on classroom learning; cocurricular engagement; student activism; and identity.

Growth of Social Media Use

Understanding how ubiquitous social media use is within the world's population can be discovered by visiting the Pew Research Center Internet, Science, and Technology Web site. The center's 2015 study on trends in social media use notes that 65 percent of adults in the United States engage with some form of social media (Perrin 2015). The trend line for those aged 18–29, what is still commonly encapsulated as the traditional college aged student, shows a stark growth in the use of social media over the past decade. In 2005, the first year in which data is available and one year after the launch of Facebook, only 12 percent of 18–29 year olds were engaged in social media. By 2006, just one year later, that number jumped to 41 percent. This rapid growth might be explained by remembering the early history of Facebook. Still the most popular and widely adopted social media platform, Facebook was initially only available to college students. Users needed an .edu e-mail address in order to obtain access to the platform. This requirement was removed in 2006, and thereafter the social media platform grew exponentially among all age demographics. In addition, social media platforms and phone-based applications began proliferating rapidly in the first decade of the 21st century. As digital technologies became increasingly accessible, tools for content creation, integration of "sharing" features between Web sites and social media platforms, innovative start-up companies, and diverse users exponentially multiplied the social media landscape. Qualman (2013) noted that there were more than 300 social media Web sites, a number that clearly has grown in the three years since publication of his book *Socialnomics*. The variety and veracity of social media platforms means that as of 2015, 90 percent of 18–29 year olds were engaged on one or several social media platforms.

Beyond age, data now shows that social media use is similar among other demographic groups. For example, Perrin (2015) reports that there are no differences in adoption patterns between White, African American, and Hispanics, although data on Asian Pacific American or native and indigenous populations is not reported (Rowan-Kenyon et al. 2016). Gender also appears to make little difference in social media adoption, with both men and women engaging in some form of social media at similar rates. Appreciable differences do tend to appear based on income level, with Perrin (2015) noting higher adoption patterns among individuals with more income. Educational background also appears to influence social media adoption, with college-educated individuals adopting use at higher rates than those who have not attended college, a data snapshot with implications for this chapter.

Finally, while good data on platform specific use among college students is unavailable, the most recent report from the *Pew Research Center* (Duggan 2015) does provide some insight into popular social media platforms and Web sites within the broader population. Facebook continues to outpace other social media platforms in terms of adoption, with 72 percent of social media users reporting having an account. However, the most rapid growth in recent years has been among platforms such as Instagram, Pinterest, Twitter, and LinkedIn. What is not reported in Duggan's analysis (2015) is Snapchat, a recent addition to the popular mix of social media platforms that is gaining prominence among youth and college-aged students (Dukes and Spinozzi 2016). It is also important to note that in terms of specific platform adoption, there are slight differences based on demographic variables. Hispanics, African Americans, and women are using Instagram, Pinterest, and Twitter more frequently than their White or male counterparts.

Does Social Media Enhance or Impede Academic Learning?

As noted in the introduction, some of the earliest research and conjecture regarding social media in higher education centered on whether digital technologies would impede student learning. There is evidence regarding potentially negative impacts of social media on student GPA, attention span, academic honesty, and privacy, many of which are reviewed in Rowan-Kenyon et al. (2016). Although these studies are important to consider, particularly in the realm of how educators might respond, they also advance deficit perspectives, viewing technological disruption from what Reynol Junco (2014) calls adult-normative perspectives. It is not uncommon for technological innovation to cause such concerns among educators, with similar conversations happening throughout history. The advent of writing, mass printing, radio, and television were similar technological disruptions in history that caused consternation among educators (Gleick 2011).

Presently, the debate regarding social media and other digital technologies' impact on learning have shifted away from dystopian dialectics toward more utopian, pragmatic, and innovative dialogues. Most campuses, faculty, and educators realize that given the ubiquity of social media and other digital technologies, adjustments need to be made in our approaches to student learning within the classroom. Many campuses have adopted various models of online learning, be that total distance education, hybrid models, or at minimum the adoption of various learning management platforms, such as Blackboard or Moodle, to supplement information dissemination, facilitate assignment completion, or help students in formal learning spaces develop personal learning networks.

Part of the debate about whether social media enhances or impedes classroom practices is centered on precisely how educators might view the very concept of learning. A key question that should be asked by faculty or classroom instructors is "how do I conceptualize, understand, or define learning?" In the realm of this debate, one must also consider the importance of the formalized classroom environment as a site or space of learning. For much of the formal history of colleges, universities, and primary school education, the classroom has been viewed as the space of learning. Concomitantly, the teacher or professor has been seen as a necessary agent in the learning that occurs within such spaces (Aviram 2010; Biesta 2010; Gerber et al. 2017; Pinar et al. 1995). Digital social media spaces are radically altering these approaches to formal curricular learning. Professors' attitude toward learning, how they conceptualize the type of learning that can, will, or should occur within an academic course or curriculum, as well as how they conceptualize their own role in controlling or guiding learning, will define how they may choose to integrate social media into the formalized learning structures of a classroom, course, or curriculum.

Part of the reticence for incorporating such technologies into formalized classroom environments centers on the language of social media. The "social" nature of such platforms implies a level of engagement that is sometimes misunderstood within the walls of formal academic spaces. Whereas there are certainly social aspects to social media, platforms and phone-based applications have evolved beyond spaces where people simply socialize. As highly connected spaces, social media are not solely viewed as individual platforms but as third space ecologies where people are living and learning through multiple social intra-actions and via broad information sharing and content creation processes.

How we conceptualize learning, as an individual act of cognition, a change of behavior, or a socially performed or enhanced activity, will largely dictate the particular attitude and approaches of incorporating social media into formalized learning spaces. Gerber et al. (2017) discuss the importance of viewing digital spaces as learning spaces across a continuum of involvement. Some spaces are truly designed for individual use, production, or consumption. However, other social media spaces allow for robust intra-action, content creation, and the sharing of information. These spaces might shift perception of learning away from an individual act toward one rooted in intra-active communities of practice; or as spaces of connected learning, where students' academic and personal interests converge with peer culture to enhance learning as social and community-based phenomena (Gerber et al. 2017).

Thus, as educators begin conceptualizing whether or how to incorporate social media into formalized learning spaces, it is important to begin by envisioning learning activities that can occur across a continuum of involvement. In some cases, social media might be used in order to enhance individual cognitive and behavioral changes in students, for example, utilizing social media as spaces for individuals to respond to questions, share information, or track their progress for purposes of comparison with other students. In other cases, educators might harness the community- and network-based powers of such sites in order to engage students in collective learning processes, such as solving difficult problems, cowriting papers and reports, or creating educationally relevant content through digital tools (such as creating infographics, videos, games, or Web sites). Gerber et al. (2017) provide substantial examples of how to conceptualize learning across these continuums.

Rowan-Kenyon et al. (2016) provide a thorough snapshot of current, albeit limited, understanding of social media integration into the classroom environment. Their review of the literature notes that social media integration often impacts four key areas important to student learning: the enrichment of course content; the facilitation of discussion beyond the classroom; the completion of collaborative projects; and the sustaining of formal and informal learning communities. Although Rowan-Kenyon et al. (2016) do not parse out faculty–student interactions, student perceptions of faculty as a fifth area of impact appears to be an important outcome of effectively integrating social media into the formal learning environment.

One point becomes clear: it is more important to think about *how* one integrates social media into the formal learning environment, rather than *whether* one integrates social media into the environment. One should not add a social media component to a course without thinking through the ways that its integration might impact student learning, engagement, community building, or collaboration. This requires some recognition on the part of faculty and instructors about the unique uses of various functions of social media. In other words, what can various platforms and applications do and what are their limitations. Further, integrating social media into the formal structure of a class may require some level of sustained intra-action from the faculty members or members of the instructional team. This is not always the case, as Rowan-Kenyon et al. (2016) report on several studies where informal learning communities developed around courses without direct interference or guidance from faculty members or instructors.

Faculty who are interested in integrating social media into their classroom environments should recognize that these digital tools are not a panacea, nor should they be totally dismissed. Given the ubiquity of social media use among much of the population, particularly youths, faculty could consider the ways that social media might enhance their course objectives toward the end of enhancing student learning. There is still reticence among most faculty to actively experiment with social media integration (Rowan-Kenyon et al. 2016), and yet the still very early understanding of social media and classroom integration demonstrates both possibilities for new approaches to engaging students in learning, and limitations for how to ensure applicability of such learning across the broad population of digitally connected students. Further, as social media technologies continue to proliferate and change rapidly, faculty will need to remain attuned to trends in platform use and familiarity among college-age students, as well as be open to learning new tools, platforms, and applications.

What seems clear about social media and formal learning is that possibilities exist to enhance the learning that occurs in classroom environments if faculty pay attention to several key questions: attitudes and understanding of learning; perception of the role faculty must play in facilitating such learning; and willingness to learn and experiment with new and constantly shifting forms of digital social media technologies.

What Is the Role of Social Media in Cocurricular Learning and Engagement?

The holistic approach to learning that has been embraced by members of campus communities working in student affairs emphasizes the importance of student involvement (Astin 1984) and engagement (Quaye and Harper 2015) beyond the classroom. Although the terms have often been used interchangeably, Quaye and Harper note that there is a qualitative difference between the two. First, "it is entirely possible to be involved in something without being engaged" (Quaye and Harper 2015, 4); and second, while involvement often places the onus of responsibility on the individual student, engagement is more conceptually broad-based. Campus policies, procedures, attitudes, and dispositions toward engagement and learning will greatly impact the levels of engagement in educationally purposeful activities.

Little empirical research examines the impact of social media on levels of student involvement and engagement beyond the classroom. Thus, campuses continue to grapple with questions about precisely how to measure and account for the influence of social media on cocurricular learning, as well as how to implement practices that lead to educationally beneficial outcomes for students and campus organizations on and through digital social media environments. A major indicator of this difficulty is recognized by Gross and Meriwether (2016) who indicated that the National Survey of Student Engagement (NSSE) only began experimenting with the inclusion of questions measuring social media impacts on student engagement in 2014.

There are studies demonstrating the impact of social media on enhancing student social capital and sense of belonging. For example, Ellison, Steinfield, and Lampe (2007), in one of the earliest studies of how social media impacts college students, found that new college students were utilizing platforms such as Facebook in order to maintain social capital accrued earlier in life (precollege) while also bridging into their new college and university environment (a concept they refer to as bridging social capital). In this study, the use of maintained and bridging social capital was found to positively influence student transition to college, potentially easing stress and assisting students as they learned to navigate their new physical environment. Ellison et al. (2014) have continued this research. Strayhorn (2012) also researched the impacts of social media on a student's sense of belonging within campus communities. These research studies indicate the importance of social media in providing digital spaces for students to maintain personal and family networks while forging new friendships as they learn to navigate the college campus experience.

As with formal classroom learning experiences, how educators envision the concept of learning in the cocurricular environment impacts the ways they might incorporate social media into spaces such as student organizations, college athletics, or arenas such as career services and residence life. For example, campuses often promote student engagement as a means of cultivating one's leadership skills. Leadership, which is a broad and amorphous concept can imply individual leadership skill and attitude development, as well as teamwork and leadership geared toward larger social change (Komives, Wagner, and Associates 2016; Northouse 2015). Ahlquist (2015) conducted her dissertation research on the ways that campus leaders were utilizing social media platforms within their own personal leadership learning processes. She suggests that although student leaders had some understanding of the impacts social media may have on their development, there needs to be more intentional educational programming from campuses to help students develop their digital leadership skills, understand online self-presentation, and positively promote their organizations.

Ahlquist (2016a, 2016b) has also written about the impacts of social media on relationships between college administration and students. Strong relationships between campus administrators and students can help to enhance the student learning experience beyond the classroom. Highlighting the many ways senior campus administrators have used social media in their professional practices on campus, Ahlquist has noted that there are ways that social media enhances what might be termed bidirectional learning. Campus administrators can effectively serve as role models and educate students about important resources, activities, and leadership skills through social media; and administrators can learn from students the "pulse" of the campus, including potential issues that need to be addressed. In addition, senior campus administrators can demonstrate their passion and commitment to their roles on campus, celebrate students and their accomplishments, and help foster an increased sense of belonging and integration. This is what Ahlquist (2016a) refers to as the "heartware" of social media, the positive impacts of using social media to build authentic relationships rooted in an ethic of care.

One of the key challenges for educators is how to harness the power of social media to increase dialogue and learning across differences. In the earliest days of the Internet, one of the great hopes was the potential for increasing interaction and engagement across social differences, including cross-racial, ethnic, gender, sexual orientation, and religious interactions. It was thought that the potentially democratizing design of the Internet might facilitate such cross-cultural engagements in much the same way that campuses hoped diversification of the student body would enhance intra-action among diverse students. What has become increasingly evident, however, is that campuses must do much more to facilitate such interactions (Quaye and Harper 2015), and this includes more intentionality in digital spaces. Rowan-Kenyon et al. (2016) report that although some students who are traditionally marginalized on campus, students of color on predominantly White campuses, for example, have used social media to build social support, there are troubling trends of using social media to create hostile environments. Incidents of racism, sexism, homophobia, Islamaphobia, classism, ethnocentrism (Rowan-Kenyon et al. 2016), and xenophobic neoracism (Glass, Wongtrirat, and Buus 2015) are all concerns that must be addressed by campuses.

The need to facilitate intentional learning through social media must be balanced with the ongoing questions about how campuses should respond to incidents of bias and discrimination. These are perhaps some of the most difficult questions for campuses to address presently, as they merge questions of privacy, free speech, and the blurring of boundaries between physical and digital spaces. In addition, given the highly litigious society and times within which we work, many campuses are concerned about protecting students and the campus from lawsuits or bad press. Finally, and, perhaps most important, campus educators are concerned about the potential short- and long-term consequences of bias, discrimination, and harassment on social media on individuals' mental and physical health (Rowan-Kenyon et al. 2016).

College athletics is one area where we see these conflicts occurring. In many ways, college athletics offices continue to have a negative attitude toward student athlete use of social media (Rowan-Kenyon et al. 2016). The monitoring and social media policies enacted by college athletics departments has raised concerns about privacy and free speech for student athletes, in addition to questions about whether colleges and universities are harnessing social media toward educational ends, particularly in relation to student athletes. Further, placing certain restrictions on the use of social media might inadvertently "create negative perceptions of social media usage" among student athletes, rather than "showcas[ing] positive conceptualizations of social media usage" (Rowan-Kenyon et al. 2016, 87) such as networking, personal branding, or creating an educational dialogue and promoting the importance of physical and mental wellness.

College athletics departments are also dealing with the implications of social media on student athlete wellness. For example, Rowan-Kenyon et al. (2016) report that many campuses have to protect college athletes from social media users who have taken to platforms such as Twitter in order to harass or threaten college athletes for their performances. Incidents such as these might also be of concern to other students on campus who are working in various campus organizations, especially those that may advocate for certain communities or political positions.

The central question appears to be: how can college campuses harness social media toward educational ends in cocurricular environments while also protecting students from the potentially deleterious impacts of certain social media functions? College student educators must be thinking more strategically and intentionally about harnessing social media for the purposes of educational benefit for students. This will require a great deal more experimentation and research, as there is little that has been examined in the literature about the educational impacts of social media practices on student engagement beyond the classroom. At the same time, there needs to be much more open dialogue about issues such as social media policies on college campuses. How can campuses craft policies to protect students from harassment, discrimination, and bias, without also limiting dialogue and engagement across differences? Additionally, how do campuses write policies that take account of the constantly shifting and dynamic nature of social media platform proliferation?

How Are Social Media Redefining Campus and Student Activism?

Campuses have always been sites where social activism occurs (Chatterjee and Maira 2014; Linder et al. 2016). Some of the new challenges associated with social media and student activism for campuses appears to center on precisely how to define "activism" in the digital age, and how to encourage a campus environment that responds appropriately to student use of social media toward ends of creating campus and social change. Campuses, fearing potential backlash and negative press from students who raise awareness about issues on campus through social media, can respond negatively (which involves backlash, minimization, or demonization of student activists) or with a more student and activist centered mind-set (such as partnering with students, learning from students, and utilizing social media to better explicate and respond to student concerns).

Broadly, the use of social media tools by college students toward ends of enacting specific practice or policy changes is a form of cyberactivism (Linder et al. 2016). The benefits of social media for enacting social change on campus, and within broader national and global networks, is an area of increased focus for researchers. Although there have been critics of social media activism (which some refer to as slacktivism), increasingly researchers are observing how students use social media tools to enhance their own learning or to raise consciousness about topics of concern; to build communities of solidarity across geographically dispersed spaces; to create nonhierarchical leadership structures; and to provide counternarratives within activist communities (LaRiviere et al. 2012; Linder et al. 2016).

Hashtag activism, as it is sometimes called, has developed around a number of issues directly related to colleges, universities, and the student experience. Many are familiar with #blacklivesmatter, but hashtags have also developed around specific campus incidents, or to raise awareness about particular issues impacting campus communities. At the University of Missouri, #concernedstudent1950 was utilized to discuss ongoing systemic oppression, racism, and discrimination faced by African American students and other students of color. Similarly, #therealuw has been used to raise awareness about racist incidents at the University of Wisconsin at Madison (Nashrulla 2016). Linder et al. (2016) refer to these, and many other examples, about the power of social media to provide counterspaces for marginalized students to share their stories and build communities of solidarity across geographically dispersed individuals. Such communities can provide support and validation for issues a student may be facing on campus, such as discrimination, bias, or harassment. Social media activism can expose such issues.

Social media also provides spaces for educational action and what Linder et al. (2016) call consciousness-raising. In their study of how sexual violence activists utilize social media, Linder et al. describe the important role that social media played in helping sexual violence activists raise awareness about the issue of campus sexual violence in communities that were previously difficult to educate. Part of what makes social media powerful is its varied nature. Activists are able to harness the different technological functions of various spaces—Twitter, Instagram, Pinterest, Tumblr, and Facebook—in order to spread information, education, and elicit participation from people engaging across the vast distributed social media landscape. The unique functions of various platforms also means students can find creative and impactful means of raising such consciousness. How one utilizes visual imagery to raise awareness in Instagram is quite different from how one might utilize blogs or YouTube to raise consciousness. Yet, in the landscape of digital social media, all these tools become important in harnessing educational endeavors toward raising awareness of issues.

Educators on college campuses can utilize these social movements, enacted or spread through social media, in order to educate about broader issues of power, systemic inequalities, or the connections between various forms of oppression. For example, Godrej (2014) discusses the implications of the University of California's various responses to student protest and organizing against tuition increases in recent years. In a now infamous incident at UC Davis, police officers pepper-sprayed peaceful student protesters who were assembled in protest against the ongoing tuition hikes. This image soon went viral on news outlets and social media platforms. Recently, it was discovered that UC Davis attempted to "scrub" the Internet and digital social media sites of news about this incident, in an attempt to quell the negative public relations impacts the campus was feeling in years since the incident (Schmidt 2016).

Many questions emerge from incidents such as these. How do we educate students about their civil rights? What role do campuses play in their response to such protests? This is part of the hidden curriculum of colleges and universities, and it has direct implications for how we educate college students to be active and civically minded individuals in a diverse democracy and global society. Godrej (2014) argues that incidents such as those at UC Davis should be used to better educate students about the entanglement of colleges and universities with corporate, military, and prison–industrial complexes. Responses to peaceful campus protests have become increasingly militarized, and thus educators should be thinking about critical educational questions regarding protecting student civil rights, educating about democracy, and protecting student safety.

Godrej (2014) also goes on to discuss the disproportionate impact that such physical protests can have on particular marginalized communities—including people of color, the poor, or the queer community. This is a concern also raised by Linder et al. (2016). As social media exposes students to these incidents nationally and globally, educators can think about the important complicated conversations with students about the impact of translating social media activism into physical activism. In addition, campuses can use these incidents to better educate themselves about more fair-minded and appropriate responses to student protests. Increasingly, there are efforts under way to undermine student activism in higher education (Chatterjee and Maira 2014). Campus administrators and faculty should be engaging students in these important dialogues and determining how to use social media in order to understand the issues students are raising and respond in an ongoing and proactive manner.

Simultaneously, educators should be encouraged by the rise of youth activism and should seek to foster environments that grow movements for social change. In many cases, this means learning from students who have the creative and intellectual capacity to harness the functions of social media to raise awareness about the issues that are important to them. If the aim is to foster spaces of critical dialogue and engagement, then partnering with and learning from students about social media can also increase the likelihood that educators model the role of activism and citizenship in the digital age (Linder et al. 2016).

In what ways can educators assist students in learning how to use social media to impact change? Understand issues of power? Or provide exposure to ideas rooted in the activist, community engagement, and civically minded nature of a democratic society?

Should Educators Think Differently about Identity Development?

Digital social media has challenged normative conceptualizations of identity development in ways that college student educators are still unable to fully grasp. College has traditionally been viewed as a time of developmental importance, and there are more than a few theories examining the impacts of college on cognitive, psychosocial, moral, racial, sexual, spiritual, ethnic, and other social identities (Patton et al. 2016). Many, if not all, of these theories were developed, conceptualized, and researched in a predigital age. Although there are a mix of psychological and sociological foundations for these theories, few explicitly account for the role that largely disembodied digital spaces might play in the development of students.

Thus, a major debate is whether to think differently about issues of identity, and, in particular, conceptualizations of "development" altogether. A few early career scholars have begun examining and conducting research on student use of social media in relation to issues of identity, and there is growing awareness that language and foundational conceptualizations might need to change. For example, Paul Gordon Brown (2016) has articulated the importance "for educators to remain open to the possibility that college students may be living their lives in radically different spaces with opportunities and challenges that are unique to their growth and development" (70).

Brown is one theorist who has begun reenvisioning traditional identity theories inclusive of digital technologies. In his more postmodern approach, Brown (2016) articulates a difference between *digital identity*, which he defines as the "the various presentations, personas, and constructions of an individual in online space" (62), and *digitized development*, which he defines as "the psychological process of growth and self-learning that occur when digital contexts are introduced" (62). Brown also articulates the importance of recognizing that an individual can have more than one digital identity, and that these identities are neither static nor fully controlled by the individual user due to various functions and digital traces that may occur for a user in online space. One way to think about Brown's new conceptualization is that digital identity is the many ways one self-presents across distributed social media spaces; whereas digitized development is how one changes psychologically, and potentially cognitively, through the use of digital social media tools. In this way, Brown's digitized development aligns well with earlier discussions of learning as an individual cognitive process (Gerber et al. 2017).

Traditional student development theory is also being challenged by critical scholars writing in what has been defined by Jones and Stewart (2016) as the third wave. Like postmodern theories, third wave theorists challenge many of the foundations of student development theory, including normative conceptualizations of development, the centering of the human as the unit of measurement, and the very concept of student. Third wave theorists are working to achieve these ends by focusing on issues of power and systemic oppression. Thus, perspectives such as critical race theory or intersectionality theory afford researchers new ways of researching issues around identity from discursive, organizational, and ecological perspectives.

Some of the critical research and work that must be accomplished lies in merging third wave perspectives with digital spaces in order to examine the complicated nature of power dynamics in digital spaces. In my 2016 article "Tag-Untag: Two Critical Readings of Race, Ethnicity, and Class in Digital Social Media" I attempt to begin bridging this gap by highlighting how the act of tagging or untagging oneself from photos in social media might be read as a response to issues of racial, ethnic, and class power between digital and physical spaces (Eaton 2016). There is little work in higher education that examines such power dynamics in social media, although researchers in media, communication, and technology studies have been examining such power dynamics for at least the past decade (Nakamura 2002, 2008; Nakamura and Chow-White 2012).

This leads to the final point and question. In order to effectively think differently about the role social media plays in students' lives, ways of being, and educational systems, researchers need to continue pushing the incorporation of transdisciplinary perspectives into the field of higher education. Simultaneously, researchers must question whether to abandon, or at least consistently challenge, development and identity altogether (Eaton 2015). Both concepts, which undergird much of the work in higher education and student affairs, are rooted in notions of control, stasis, and linearity and center on the human subject. Digital technologies have profoundly altered any notions that development (and learning) occur linearly, or that we can totally control such learning through prescriptive processes rooted in normative constructs and outcomes. In my own work, I have largely given up on utilizing the language of development, centering the notion of *becoming* as a more ethical and open process occurring through entanglements of human and nonhuman actors (Braidotti 2011; Masny and Cole 2014).

Further, digital technologies enact agency upon humans, just as humans enact agency upon digital technologies. Thus, there is a need to better account for entanglements (Barad 2007) between the human and other material and nonmaterial entities. This includes physical materials, such as phones, computers, and wearable technologies, but also nonphysical forces, such as discourse and energy fields. Theorists and philosophers writing in posthumanisms (Braidotti 2013; Snaza and Weaver 2015), assemblage theory (Weheliye 2014), and new materialisms (Coole and Frost 2010; Snaza et al. 2016) are actively pursuing these questions. Embracing these new theoretical and philosophical perspectives means researchers and educators must become comfortable with giving up notions of control that often align with the educational concept of "development." It also requires researchers and educators to break outside of what has become comfortable reading boundaries, sometimes tackling work that is difficult to understand, challenging to read, or complicated to think with. Yet, doing so will assist in rethinking practices and how to better engage and intra-act with digital technologies, while pushing the boundaries of our knowledge.

Conclusion

Social media technologies are challenging the boundaries of how researchers and educators conceptualize college learning experiences. As Gerber et al. (2017) state, "Learning in a digital age involves the layering of literacies, the intersection of multiple tools and spaces, and the necessity of individual learners' movement across and between multiple components of field sites" (30). When educators view learning in college from holistic perspectives, it becomes possible to recognize that critical engagements occur in classrooms, in cocurricular environments, around issues of public importance, and across spectrums of identity. There are, as has been explored in this chapter, many debates about the various impacts of social media technologies on college student learning within these and many other areas of importance.

My own position in this debate cannot be unaccounted for. In my estimation, digital technologies certainly can be viewed as a disruptive and dangerous force in our society; however, this is not how I choose to view them. Rather, as with most tools in life, I believe researchers and educators should view the possibilities and limitations of digital social media technologies. The more I read and think about digital social media, the more I recognize that the ongoing proliferation of social media is providing new ways to learn and engage the world; new networks and communities of practice; and new challenges for educators. Further, social media is providing space for alternative conceptualizations of the world and the work we do as researchers and educators, opening access to information, resources, and ways of seeing, knowing, and reading about the world (Freire [1992] 2014) previously unavailable to us. In this way, researchers and educators have much to rethink about the imaginative and creative ways to engage and learn about the world.

References

ACPA, and NASPA. 2004. *Learning Reconsidered: A Campus-Wide Focus on the Student Experience.* Washington, DC: ACPA and NASPA.

Ahlquist, Josie. 2015. *Developing Digital Student Leaders: A Mixed Methods Study of Student Leadership, Identity, and Decision Making on Social Media.* Doctoral dissertation, California Lutheran University.

Ahlquist, Josie. 2016a. "Digital Leadership: The Heartware of Tech in Higher Education." Josie Ahlquist Blog. Accessed October 29, 2016. http://www.josieahlquist.com/2016/04/21/heartware/

Ahlquist, Josie. 2016b. "The Digital Identity of Student Affairs Professionals." In *Engaging the Digital Generation,* edited by Edmund T. Cabellon and Josie Ahlquist, 29–46. San Francisco, CA: Jossey-Bass. doi: 10.1002/ss.20181

Ahlquist, Josie, and Edmund T. Cabellon, eds. 2016. *Engaging the Digital Generation.* San Francisco, CA: Jossey-Bass.

Ahn, June. 2011. "The Effect of Social Network Sites on Adolescents' Social and Academic Development: Current Theories and Controversies." *Journal of the American Society for Information Science* 62(8): 1435–1445. doi: 10.1002/asi.21540

Astin, Alexander W. 1984. "Student Involvement: A Developmental Theory for Higher Education." *Journal of College Student Personnel* 25:297–308.

Aviram, Aharon. 2010. *Navigating through the Storm: Reinventing Education for Postmodern Democracies.* Boston, MA: Sense Publishers.

Barad, Karen. 2007. *Meeting the Universe Halfway: Quantum Physics and the Entanglement of Matter and Meaning*. Durham, NC: Duke University Press.

Biesta, Gert. 2010. "Learner, Student, Speaker: Why It Matters How We Call Those We Teach." *Educational Philosophy & Theory* 42(5/6): 540–552. doi: 10.1111/j.1469-5812.2010.00684.x

boyd, danah m., and Nicole B. Ellison. 2007. "Social Networking Sites: Definition, History, and Scholarship." *Journal of Computer Mediated Communication* 13(1): 210–230.

Braidotti, Rosi. 2011. *Nomadic Theory: The Portable Rosi Braidotti*. New York: Columbia University Press.

Braidotti, Rosi. 2013. *The Posthuman*. Malden, MA: Polity Press.

Brown, Paul Gordon. 2016. "College Student Development in Digital Spaces." In *Engaging the Digital Generation*, edited by Edmund T. Cabellon and Josie Ahlquist, 59–74. San Francisco, CA: Jossey-Bass. doi: 10.1002/ss.20183

Chatterjee, Piya, and Sunaina Maira, eds. 2014. *The Imperial University: Academic Repression and Scholarly Dissent*. Minneapolis: The University of Minnesota Press.

Connolly, Mark R. 2011. "Does Social Networking Enhance or Impede Student Learning? Social Networking and Student Learning: Friends without Benefits." In *Contested Issues in Student Affairs: Diverse Perspectives and Respectful Dialogue*, edited by Peter M. Magolda and Marcia B. Baxter Magolda, 122–134. Sterling, VA: Stylus Publishing.

Coole, Diana, and Samantha Frost, eds. 2010. *New Materialisms: Ontology, Agency, and Politics*. Durham, NC: Duke University Press.

Duggan, Maeve. 2015. "Mobile Messaging and Social Media 2015," August 19. Pew Research Center Internet, Science, and Tech Blog. Accessed October 29, 2016. http://www.pewinternet.org/2015/08/19/mobile-messaging-and-social-media-2015/

Dukes, T., and A. Spinozzi. 2016. "Snap(chat) to It! Building Community on a Commuter Campus." Conference presentation. *TACUSPA Conference*. Austin, TX.

Eaton, Paul William. 2015. "Beyond Development: Post-Secondary Ethical Responsibilities in College Student Identity and Subjectification" Paper Presentation, American Educational Research Association Conference, Chicago, IL.

Eaton, Paul William. 2016. "Tag-untag: Two Critical Readings of Race, Ethnicity, and Class in Digital Social Media." *Journal of Critical Scholarship on Higher Education and Student Affairs* 3(1): 61–78.

Ellison, Nicole. B., Charles Steinfield, and Cliff Lampe. 2007. "The Benefits of Facebook Friends: Social Capital and College Students' Use of Online Social Network Sites." *Journal of Computer-Mediated Communication* 12(4): 1143–1168.

Ellison, Nicole B., Jessica Vitak, Rebecca Gray, and Cliff Lampe. 2014. "Cultivating Social Resources on Social Network Sites: Facebook Relationship

Maintenance Behaviors and Their Role in Social Capital Processes." *Journal of Computer-Mediated Communication* 19(4): 855–870.

Gerber, Hannah R., Sandra Schamroth Abrams, Jen Scott Curwood, and Alecia Marie Magnifico. 2017. *Conducting Qualitative Research of Learning in Online Spaces.* Thousand Oaks, CA: Sage.

Glass, Chris R., Rachawan Wongtrirat, and Stephanie Buus. 2015. *International Student Engagement: Strategies for Creating Inclusive, Connected, and Purposeful Campus Environments.* Sterling, VA: Stylus.

Gleick, James. 2011. *The Information: A History, a Theory, a Flood.* New York: Vintage Books.

Godrej, Farah. 2014. "Neoliberalism, Militarization, and the Price of Dissent: Policing Protest at the University of California." In *The Imperial University: Academic Repression and Scholarly Dissent*, edited by Piya Chatterjee and Sunaina Maira, 125–143. Minneapolis: University of Minnesota Press.

Gross, Liz, and Jason L. Meriwether. 2016. "Student Engagement through Digital Data." In *Engaging the Digital Generation*, edited by Edmund T. Cabellon and Josie Ahlquist, 75–89. San Francisco, CA: Jossey-Bass. doi: 10.1002/ss.20184

Guidry, Kevin R., and Josie Ahlquist. 2016. "Computer-Mediated Communication and Social Media." In *The Handbook of Student Affairs Administration*, edited by George S. McClellan, Jeremy Stringer, and Associates, 595–612. San Francisco, CA: Jossey-Bass.

Jones, Susan R., and Dafina-Lazarus Stewart. 2016. "Evolution of Student Development Theory." In *Critical Perspectives on Student Development Theory*, edited by Elisa S. Abes, 17–28. doi: 10.1002/ss

Junco, Reynol. 2014. *Engaging Students through Social Media: Evidence-Based Practices for Use in Student Affairs.* San Francisco, CA: Jossey-Bass.

Kirschner, Paul A., and Aryn C. Karpinski. 2010. "Facebook and Academic Performance." *Computers in Human Behavior* 26(6): 1237–1245.

Komives, Susan R., Wendy Wagner, and Associates. 2016. *Leadership for a Better World: Understanding the Social Change Model of Leadership Development.* San Francisco, CA: Jossey-Bass.

LaRiviere, Kristin, Jeanette Snider, Alison Stromberg, and Kerry Ann O'Meara. 2012. "Protest: Critical Lessons of Using Digital Media for Social Change." *About Campus* 17(3): 10–17. doi: 10.1002/abc.21081

Linder, Chris, Colleen Riggle, Jess S. Myers, and Marvette Lacy. 2016. "From Margins to Mainstream: Social Media as a Tool for Campus Sexual Violence Activism." *Journal of Diversity in Higher Education* 9(3): 231–244. doi: 10.1037/dhe0000038

Martinez Aleman, Ana M. 2011. "Social Media and Learning: A Profile." In *Contested Issues in Student Affairs: Diverse Perspectives and Respectful Dialogue*, edited by Peter M. Magolda and Marcia B. Baxter Magolda, 135–140. Sterling, VA: Stylus Publishing.

Masny, Diana, and David R. Cole, eds. 2014. *Education and the Politics of Becoming.* New York: Routledge.

Nakamura, Lisa. 2002. *Cybertypes: Race, Ethnicity, and Identity on the Internet.* New York: Routledge.

Nakamura, Lisa. 2008. *Digitizing Race: Visual Cultures of the Internet.* Minneapolis: University of Minnesota Press.

Nakamura, Lisa, and Peter Chow-White, eds. 2012. *Race after the Internet.* New York: Routledge.

Nashrulla, Tasneem. 2016. "Students at the University of Wisconsin-Madison Are Using #TheRealUW to Expose Racism on Campus," April 4. Buzzfeed News. Accessed October 29, 2016. https://www.buzzfeed.com/tasneem nashrulla/students-at-the-university-of-wisconsin-madison-are-using -th?utm_term=.hwLZnE4GYJ#.qxn6Q7rvzA

Northouse, Peter G. 2015. *Leadership: Theory and Practice.* Thousand Oaks, CA: Sage.

Patton, Lori D., Kristen A. Renn, Florence M. Guido, and Stephen John Quaye. 2016. *Student Development in College: Theory, Research, and Practice.* San Francisco, CA: Jossey-Bass.

Perrin, Andrew. 2015. "Social Media Usage: 2005–2015," October 8. Pew Research Center Internet, Science, & Tech Blog. Accessed October 29, 2016. http://www.pewinternet.org/2015/10/08/social-networking-usage-2005 -2015/

Pinar, William F., William M. Reynolds, Patrick Slattery, and Peter M. Taubman. 1995. *Understanding Curriculum.* New York: Peter Lang.

Qualman, Erik. 2013. *Socialnomics: How Social Media Transforms the Way We Live and Do Business.* Hoboken, NJ: John Wiley & Sons.

Quaye, Stephen John, and Shaun R. Harper, eds. 2015. *Student Engagement in Higher Education: Theoretical Perspectives and Practical Approaches for Diverse Populations.* New York: Routledge.

Rowan-Kenyon, Heather T., Ana M. Martinez Aleman, Kevin Gin, Bryan Blakely, Adam Gismondi, Jonathan Lewis, Adam McCread, Daniel Zepp, and Sarah Knight. 2016. *Social Media in Higher Education.* Hoboken, NJ: John Wiley & Sons.

Schmidt, Peter. 2016. "UC-Davis Was Ridiculed for Trying to Sway Search Results. Many Other Colleges Do the Same." *The Chronicle of Higher Education*, April 21. Accessed October 29, 2016. http://www.chronicle.com /article/UC-Davis-Was-Ridiculed-for/236188

Snaza, Nathan, Debbie Sonu, Sarah E. Truman, and Zofia Zaliwska, eds. 2016. *Pedagogical Matters: New Materialisms and Curriculum Studies.* New York: Peter Lang.

Snaza, Nathan, and John A. Weaver, eds. 2015. *Posthumanism and Educational Research.* New York: Routledge.

Strayhorn, Terrell L. 2012. "Exploring the Impact of Facebook and MySpace on First Year Students' Sense of Belonging and Persistence Decisions." *Journal of College Student Development* 53(6): 783–796.

Weheliye, Alexander G. 2014. *Habeas Viscus: Racializing Assemblages, Biopolitics, and Black Feminist Theories of the Human.* Durham, NC: Duke University Press.

CHAPTER THIRTEEN

The Struggle for Equity in Intercollegiate Athletics

Joy Blanchard

The NCAA was founded in 1906 not only to enforce rules of fair play but also to ensure that intercollegiate athletics remained a game of amateurs (Smith 1988; Suggs 2004). Just as commercialization was a threat to college sports in the late 1800s and early 1900s, the lure of profits has permeated the contemporary collegiate game—with unfortunate consequences for the college athlete who still is classified as "amateur." From student-athletes' quest to unionize, expand athletic scholarships, and even equally expand participation to women, the bottom line seems to drive many of the decisions made today by universities and the NCAA alike.

Overview of the Issue

The notion of "big time" college sports is not new. In the 1800s, college games often featured cash prizes for participants, "phantom" students who were professional athletes paid to compete for the institution, and highly paid professional coaches. In fact, the first paid professional head football coach was at Harvard University, and in 1905 he was earning nearly double the salary of what a full professor then averaged (Branch 2011).

Today, enormous payouts almost seem the norm. In 2010, the CBS network and the NCAA entered into a 14-year, $10.8 billion contract to broadcast the annual "March Madness" men's basketball tournament (Fram and

Frampton 2012). During the 2014 season, the five largest and most powerful athletic conferences (also known as the Power Five) received more than $1 billion from football television contracts. The University of Alabama alone reported $143.4 million in athletic revenues during the 2012–2013 academic year—greater than the annual revenue of 25 NBA and all 30 NHL teams, and the head football coach's annual salary approaches $7 million (Edelman 2014). The combined collegiate athletic revenues for the 2010–2011 academic year was $12.6 billion; the National Football League (the most profitable professional sports league in the United States) made $7.6 billion in revenues (Monks 2013).

Despite the hefty revenues for many intercollegiate programs, student-athletes have not seemed to benefit from the flourishing collegiate sport enterprise, because: (1) student-athletes have not been able to leverage their power to collectively bargain for increased benefits; (2) college coaches are allowed to capitalize on the marketplace generated by their sports, though student-athletes are prohibited from doing so; and (3) as college sports programs invest heavily in lucrative (or potentially lucrative) sports like football and men's basketball, a business-type model has prevented many institutions from adequately expanding participation opportunities to female student-athletes, arguably because their sports do not generate large ticket revenue or garner lucrative television contracts.

Recent Developments

Unionization of Student-Athletes

In 2014, football players at Northwestern University, represented by the College Athletes Players Association (CAPA), sought to unionize in order to bargain for scholarships that covered the full-cost of attendance, assistance with degree completion, and better medical treatment. At the time, NCAA regulations prohibited student-athletes from receiving scholarships beyond tuition, room and board, and books—even though federal financial aid regulations recognized a broader definition of "full-cost of attendance." Nationally, the gap between the true cost of attendance and the amount covered by an athletic scholarship was estimated between $3,000 and as much as $6,000 (Fram and Frampton 2012).

According to research conducted by the National College Players Association, 85 percent of "full" scholarship student-athletes could be categorized as living under the federal poverty level (National College Players Association 2011). In fact, the NCAA specifically has provisions in its compliance manual allowing for student-athletes to receive food stamps. Yet the NCAA strictly prohibited student-athletes from receiving benefits beyond the athletic scholarship, even special meals.

The student-athletes' case was reviewed by a regional director of the National Labor Relations Board (NLRB), who was presented with evidence that student-athletes struggle to cover the costs of weekend meals, travel home, and uncovered medical expenses—contrasted with the fact that during the 2012–2013 academic year, the football program at Northwestern University made a net profit of approximately $8.4 million (Brief for Petitioner 2014). The university generated revenue from ticket sales, broadcast contracts, and team memorabilia and merchandise. Northwestern University sold replica player jerseys, used players' likenesses in promotional and marketing material, and requested that student-athletes sign memorabilia to be auctioned or sold at the benefit of the institution. However, in the name of amateurism, student-athletes were not allowed to share in those profits.

In order for the football players to win the right to unionize, the student-athletes first had to successfully argue that they fell under the legal definition of an employee. Ironically, the term student-athlete was first introduced as a means to avoid having student-athletes be classified as employees for the purposes of receiving workmen's compensation (Branch 2011; Byers 1995). Under interpretations from the U.S. Supreme Court and the National Labor Relations Board, an employee is "a person who performs services for another under a contract of hire, subject to the other's control or right of control, and in return for payment" (Brief for Petitioner 2014, 13). The NLRB previously had recognized the commercial nature of universities after reviewing a case brought by librarians at Cornell University. There, the institution made $4,890 from selling microfilms and the "Germanic and Romanic Reviews" (Fram and Frampton 2012). In the Northwestern case, obviously the institution profited exponentially more from the labor of its student-athletes. The NLRB director in this case found that the student-university relationship was not an educational but rather an economic one. He did not find that the football players were "primarily students" and that participation in football was not linked to the educational mission of the institution (*Northwestern University v. College Athlete Players Association* 2014).

Despite the positive 2014 ruling from the regional labor director, the NLRB in 2015 declined to review the football players' petition to be certified to form a labor union. This decision effectively ended the student-athletes' efforts. However, the regional NLRB decision cited many issues of concern for those making policies regarding student-athletes. It cited Northwestern University's immense control over playing and practice conditions, as well as the power coaches and staff exerted in controlling and monitoring student-athletes' private lives. A student-athlete's scholarship is linked to performance as an athlete and not as a student, and the scholarship can be revoked if the student is dismissed from the team. The regional director noted that many of the rules that student-athletes were subjected to were not regulations that the regular student body had to abide by, such as preapproval of any off-campus lease, permission to obtain outside employment, restrictive social media policies, attendance at mandatory study halls and training tables, submission of flight itineraries when leaving campus to visit home, prohibitions against participation in media interviews unless otherwise directed, prohibitions against the use of profanity in public, and required drug testing.

The regional NLRB director also exhaustively recapped the time requirements placed on student-athletes, especially the extensive amount of time spent during the football season and during the off-season in practice and training sessions. For example, during the football season, football players spent approximately 40 to 50 hours per week on team-related activities. Though the NCAA limits "countable athletically related activities" to 20 hours per week, those guidelines do not account for travel, training meetings, strength training, medical attention, watching game tapes, or attendance at mandatory training tables. To avoid violating NCAA practice rules, evening practices are not officially sanctioned by the coaches but instead organized by the quarterback. Required activities continue throughout the year after the postseason bowl game, including spring conditioning and summer workouts. (Spring training camp requires approximately 60 hours per week of mandatory drills, meetings, and activities.) The record indicated that football players only have approximately two to three weeks of discretionary time throughout the year to leave campus to return home.

However, in its request for appeal, Northwestern University argued, "If football student-athletes are allowed to unionize, the patch-work of labor laws that govern colleges playing Division I Football Bowl Subdivision (FBS) football would have a chaotic impact on the sport and the respective universities' administration of the sport" (Request for Review 2014, 39). This indeed could pose problems, as there are more than 100 public institutions—not under the purview of the NLRB and federal labor law—in the NCAA Division I Football Bowl Subdivision, and only 17 private institutions—which would be the only institutions subject to a ruling by the NLRB. And that is the reason why the NLRB declined to decide the issue. However, public institutions are governed by their respective state labor laws, and several states have construed the student-institution relationship to be not just academic but economic in nature (Fram and Frampton 2012)—which could bode well for student-athletes at public institutions wishing to unionize.

And though the NLRB declined to certify a possible labor union in 2015, there may still be life to the student-athletes' quest, as in January 2017 the Office of the General Counsel of the NLRB issued an opinion indicating that football players at Division I FBS schools are employees under the National Labor Relations Act and that efforts to collectively bargain for payment beyond the athletic scholarship, increased medical care, and other interests should not be denied. The opinion noted that the U.S. Supreme Court and the NLRB have endorsed broad interpretations of statutory definitions of an "employee" and that football players and students are not among the few enumerated exceptions mentioned by law. The general counsel went on to opine that football players should be considered employees because "they perform services for their colleges and the NCAA, subject to their control, in return for compensation" (Memorandum 2017, 19) and that they generate immense profits for the institution, which have arguably "immeasurable positive impact to Northwestern's reputation, which in turn undoubtedly boosted student applications and alumni financial donations" (Memorandum 2017, 19).

Though promising to those who favor paying collegiate athletes, it is important to note the limited weight of this opinion, as it is not representative of the full National Labor Relations Board nor does it decide the issue beyond that of Division I FBS scholarship football players. The opinion noted, "We cannot conclusively determine the employee status of other kinds of student athletes in cases that may arise in the future" (Memorandum 2017, 22). It did, however, encourage private institutions "to comply with their obligations under the Act" (Memorandum 2017, 23).

Antitrust Challenges to NCAA Regulations

Antitrust laws were established in America to protect consumer rights and prevent cartels from controlling the prices of goods within the free marketplace (Sherman Antitrust Act 1890). When antitrust claims have been brought against the NCAA, courts analyze whether the intent of the contested restrictions are meant to preserve the amateur status of intercollegiate athletics or serve to promote the commercial interests of the NCAA and its member institutions (Greene 2000). The NCAA at times has been able to ward off such challenges by demonstrating that the procompetitive effects of its regulations outweigh the anticompetitive effects of the rule. Conversely, those who have challenged NCAA regulations have been able to prevail in court by demonstrating that any such procompetitive benefits may be achieved in a less restrictive manner. The most notable example—and a case that permanently altered the nature of college sports—was *NCAA v. Board of Regents of the University of Oklahoma* (1984).

Before the U.S. Supreme Court ruling in the *Regents* case, the NCAA controlled how many times—and for how much money—college football games could be broadcast. Though this restriction limited the amount of games fans could enjoy, the NCAA was fearful that too many televised games would dilute the "product" and reduce ticket sales. In 1976, frustrated that such restrictions prohibited them from capitalizing on their popularity within the market, 63 college teams broke away from the NCAA and formed the College Football Association (CFA). The CFA collectively began to negotiate its own contracts with NBC, and the University of Notre Dame later independently negotiated its own contract with NBC. The NCAA responded by prohibiting CFA teams from participating in any NCAA-sanctioned contests in any sport (Hunter and Mayo 1999; Porto 2012; Schmit 2007).

As members of the CFA, the University of Oklahoma and the University of Georgia filed suit, claiming that the NCAA restrictions violated antitrust laws. At trial the court ruled that the NCAA's restrictions over football television contracts violated the Sherman Act by fixing prices, threatening boycotts through exclusive network contracts, and placing artificial limits on the number of televised games (*Board of Regents of University of Oklahoma v. National Collegiate Athletic Association* 1982). The court compared the NCAA restrictions to a "classic cartel" that caused the prices television networks were forced to pay for broadcasting rights to artificially soar, thus creating a pricing structure that was unresponsive to viewer demand (Hunter and Mayo 1999).

That decision was ultimately upheld by the 10th Circuit Court of Appeals (*Board of Regents of University of Oklahoma v. National Collegiate Athletic Association* 1983) and the U.S. Supreme Court. Justice Byron White (a famed college and professional football player himself) foretold in his dissenting opinion, however, that "permitting a small number of colleges, even popular ones, to have unlimited television appearances, would inevitably give them an insuperable advantage over all others and in the end defeat any efforts to maintain a system of athletic competition among amateurs who measure up to college scholastic requirements" (Porto 2012, 81). The decision in *Regents* arguably can be labeled as the start of an "arms race" in relation to coaches' salaries, student-athlete recruiting, and conference realignments. Although the NCAA had tried to keep media exposure and revenue equitable among its member institutions, the changes after the decision in *Regents* began a clear bifurcation of the "haves" and "have nots" (Dennie 2012).

Although other antitrust lawsuits have been brought against the NCAA since the *Regents* case, from challenging restraints on assistant coaches' salaries to disputing the terms of athletic scholarships and myriad other regulations, the next most notable antitrust suit came in 2010 when former UCLA basketball standout Ed O'Bannon took the lead challenging regulations that prevented student-athletes, both current and former, from profiting from the use of their image and likeness through video games. As a condition of play, the NCAA requires all student-athletes sign an agreement that relinquishes their rights to profit from their image and likeness from collegiate athletic participation in perpetuity.

The NCAA had a contract with video game producer Electronic Arts Inc. (also known as EA Sports) to create video games that included the likeness of current and former football and basketball players. O'Bannon, who played for UCLA from 1991 to 1995, was prominently featured in one of the video

games but had never been asked permission from EA Sports to use his likeness, nor had he been compensated. EA Sports ceased to produce the video
games and in September 2013 settled a lawsuit brought by a group of current
and former student-athletes for $40 million (Berkowitz 2014).

However, the NCAA refused to concede that student-athletes were owed a
portion of the revenue generated by the video games. The student-athletes'
lawsuit did not seek "pay for play" in a way that would offend the senses of
those who vehemently embrace the amateur ideals of intercollegiate sports,
but instead it sought to utilize the proceeds from video games and other
media licensed by the NCAA to bridge the gap between what an athletic
scholarship covers and what it truly costs a student-athlete to attend college.
When the *O'Bannon* case went to district court in California, the judge found
that the "challenged NCAA rules unreasonably restrain trade in the market
for certain educational and athletic opportunities offered by NCAA Division
I schools. The procompetitive justifications that the NCAA offers do not justify this restraint and could be achieved through less restrictive means" (7 F.
Supp. 3d at 2).

The district court recognized that a similar market for profitable sport
video games existed in the professional ranks—in 2010, EA Sports paid the
NFL players union more than $35 million in royalties (Branch 2011)—and
ruled that the NCAA was prohibited from enforcing regulations that
restricted member institutions from offering full grant-in-aid. It called for
Division I FBS institutions to deposit in trust no less than $5,000 for every
year that each student-athlete was academically eligible for competition. The
amount of money that could be deposited in trust could fluctuate, but an
institution could not offer a recruit more or less money than the amount
offered to other student-athletes recruited for the same year for the same
team.

The NCAA filed for appeal before the 9th Circuit Court of Appeals, and in
2015 a three-judge panel affirmed the district court's ruling that NCAA regulations prohibiting student-athletes from profiting from their image and likeness in perpetuity equated to a price-fixing agreement and that college sports
programs "behave as a cartel—a group of sellers who have colluded to fix the
price of their product" (802 F.3d at 1058). The panel, however, overturned
the aspect of the previous ruling that would allow institutions to deposit in
trust funds to be accessible to student-athletes, asserting that it did not serve
to promote the NCAA's historic mission of promoting and preserving
amateurism.

Thanks to the persistence of dogged student-athlete advocates, additional
legal challenges have since been brought forth, and in February 2017 the
NCAA reached a $208.7 million settlement in a class action lawsuit that
would provide student-athletes the difference between the value of the athletic scholarship they received and the actual full cost of attendance at the

time of their enrollment (which was projected to be approximately $6,800 per student-athlete). This settlement is the second-largest in the NCAA's history and follows a similar agreement the NCAA brokered for $230 million, which also challenged provisions that prohibited athletic scholarships from covering the full cost of attendance. Those eligible to receive compensation under the settlement include athletes in Division I men's basketball, Division I women's basketball, and Bowl Subdivision Football who were on athletic scholarship in the 2009–2010 school year or any time between then and 2015, when the NCAA changed its regulations to allow Division I institutions to begin offering scholarships that covered the full cost of attendance, or who were on athletic scholarship at an institution that chose not to expand its scholarship offerings but have since begun to or plan to do so (Berkowitz 2017).

Gender Equity in Intercollegiate Athletics

Title IX of the Education Amendments of 1972 states, "No person in the United States shall, on the basis of sex, be excluded from participation in, be denied the benefits of, or be subjected to discrimination under any education program or activity receiving Federal financial assistance." Courts have ruled that all programs at institutions receiving federal funding—including extracurricular organizations and athletics teams—are subject to these nondiscrimination regulations.

In the context of intercollegiate athletics, the application of Title IX frequently refers to gender equity in opportunity and funding, including equity in equipment, practice time, travel accommodations, compensation of coaches, facilities, housing, and publicity (Kaplin and Lee 2014). The U.S. Department of Education developed a three-prong test to measure equity: (1) opportunities must be "substantially proportionate" to the overall male-to-female student enrollment; (2) the institution must continually expand opportunities for female student-athletes; and (3) the interests and abilities of female students must be fully and effectively accommodated (*Title IX 1979 Policy Interpretation on Intercollegiate Athletics*, 44 Fed. Reg. 71,413).

That three-prong standard was fleshed out in the 1990s via a series of cases that questioned practices within Brown University's athletic department. A more recent challenge has, however, illustrated that not only is gender equity in intercollegiate athletics still an issue, but institutions' willingness to address the issue from a good-faith perspective also seems to be in question.

A lawsuit was filed against Quinnipiac University in 2009 shortly after the university attempted to cut women's varsity volleyball, men's golf, and men's outdoor track and field and in its place establish a women's competitive cheerleading team, which the U.S. Department of Education's Office of Civil

Rights had ruled could not be counted as a sport for purposes of Title IX compliance. A district court blocked the proposed cuts, finding that the university could not seek to satisfy the proportionality prong by eliminating men's teams (*Biediger v. Quinnipiac University* 2012). Shockingly, evidence indicated that the participation numbers for women's track and field were inflated, as all female student-athletes were required to participate in cross country, outdoor events, and indoor events—and that their participation was counted three times in the university's overall tally of female student-athletes. Though the difference between female student-athletes and the overall female undergraduate student population was less than 4 percent, the court still found that the opportunities afforded to women were not equal.

Following that ruling, the institution added women's golf and women's rugby (of which only four other institutions in the country sponsored an intercollegiate team), continued to cultivate the competitive cheerleading squad, and developed a policy that female runners were not required to participate in all three track squads. In order to establish cheerleading/acrobatics as a recognized NCAA sport, Quinnipiac developed the National Competitive Stunt and Tumbling Association, of which seven other institutions joined.

When Quinnipiac filed to lift the previous court injunction, the district court pointed out that participants in these new sports were unable, in contrast to every men's varsity team, to participate in postseason competition and, thus, were not provided a substantive athletic opportunity per Title IX. The NCAA provides emerging sports a 10-year window to become a championship sport, otherwise they are discontinued. Sports with nearly 50 intercollegiate squads have failed to garner official status, and in the case of Quinnipiac, women's rugby, with only four intercollegiate teams and nearing the end of the 10-year window, could not be considered a sport for Title IX purposes.

The court established a new standard for measuring gender equity in intercollegiate athletic participation: levels of competition. Less than 2 percent of men's competitive opportunities at Quinnipiac were against teams outside of Division I, while 7.5 percent of women's competitive contests were against institutions below Division I. (The women's rugby team played the majority of its contests against nonvarsity club sport teams.)

Possible Solutions

In August 2014 the NCAA established the "Power Five" subdivision in Division I intercollegiate athletics, allowing teams in the Big Ten, Pac-12, Big 12, Atlantic Coast, and Southeastern conferences to develop some of their own governance regulations (NCAA 2014). In making this announcement, the NCAA asserted that it would allow institutions greater flexibility in deciding benefits for student-athletes. In an op-ed article published shortly after its adoption, however, former executive director of the NCAA Cedric Dempsey predicted that the new governance system "will deepen the gap between institutions with self-sustaining sports programs and those without, depriving athletes at lower-tier institutions the chance to compete at the highest level" (Dempsey and Suggs 2014) and deepen the rift between the "haves" and "have nots" that Justice White warned about in his *Regents* dissent. That prediction seemed to prove correct, as the Power Five recorded $6 billion in profits in 2015, approximately $4 billion more than all other NCAA institutions combined (Lavigne 2016). Unless the NCAA or Congress intervenes[1] to get a handle on the disproportionate share of profits enjoyed by some institutions, not only will competition continue to be unequal but so will opportunities for gender equity and equitable scholarship grants for student-athletes.

Note

1. In exchange for an antitrust exemption, Congress has intervened before to regulate issues in sport (via the Sports Broadcasting Act of 1961).

References

Berkowitz, Steve. 2014. "Proposed Video Game Settlement Could Help Current NCAA Players." *USA Today Sports*, May 30. Accessed May 9, 2017. http://www.usatoday.com/story/sports/college/2014/05/30/ed-obannon-ncaa-name-and-likeness-lawsuit-settlement/9789605/

Berkowitz, Steve. 2017. "NCAA Agrees to $208.7 Million Settlement with Athletes." *USA Today Sports*, February 3. Accessed May 9, 2017. https://www.usatoday.com/story/sports/college/2017/02/03/ncaa-settlement-lawsuit-compensation-athletes-cost-attendance-scholarships/97446676/

Biediger v. Quinnipiac University, 691 F.3d 85 (2nd Cir. 2012).

Board of Regents of University of *Oklahoma v. National Collegiate Athletic Association*, 546 F.Supp. 1276 (W.D. Okla. 1982).

Board of Regents of University of *Oklahoma v. National Collegiate Athletic Association*, 707 F.2d 1147 (10th Cir. 1983).

Branch, Taylor. 2011. "The Shame of College Sports." *The Atlantic*, September 7. Accessed May 9, 2017. http://www.theatlantic.com/magazine/archive/2011/10/the-shame-of-college-sports/308643/

Brief for Petitioner, Northwestern University and College Athletes Players Association, Case 13-RC-121359 (N.L.R.B. 2014).

Byers, Walter. 1995. *Unsportsmanlike Conduct: Exploiting College Athletes*. Ann Arbor: University of Michigan Press.

Dempsey, Cedric W., and David Welch Suggs Jr. 2014. "An Opportunity to Redefine College Sports." *Chronicle of Higher Education*, August 10. Accessed

May 9, 2017. http://www.chronicle.com/article/An-Opportunity-to-Re define/148347/

Dennie, Christian. 2012. "Changing the Game: The Litigation That May Be the Catalyst for Change in Intercollegiate Athletics." *Syracuse Law Review* 62:15–51.

Edelman, Marc. 2014. "The Future of Amateurism after Antitrust Scrutiny: Why a Win for the Plaintiffs in the NCAA Student-Athlete Name & Likeness Licensing Litigation Will Not Lead to the Demise of College Sports." *Oregon Law Review* 92:1019–1055.

Fram, Nicholas, and T. Ward Frampton. 2012. "A Union of Amateurs: A Legal Blueprint to Reshape Big-Time College Athletics." *Buffalo Law Review* 60:1003–1078.

Greene, Stephanie M. 2000. "Regulating the NCAA: Making the Calls under the Sherman Antitrust Act and Title IX." *Maine Law Review* 52:81–95.

Hunter, Richard J., Jr., and Ann M. Mayo. 1999. "Issues in Antitrust, the NCAA, and Sports Management." *Marquette Sports Law Journal* 10:69–85.

Kaplin, William A., and Barbara A. Lee. 2014. *The Law of Higher Education: Student Version (5th ed.).* San Francisco: Jossey-Bass.

Lavigne, Paula. 2016. "Rich Get Richer in College Sports as Poorer Schools Struggle to Keep Up." *ESPN.com*, September 6. Accessed May 9, 2017. http://www.espn.com/espn/otl/story/_/id/17447429/power-5-conference -schools-made-6-billion-last-year-gap-haves-nots-grows

Memorandum by Richard F. Griffin Jr. 2017. *General Counsel's Report on the Statutory Rights of University Faculty and Students in the Unfair Labor Practice Context.* Washington, DC: National Labor Relations Board.

Monks, James. 2013. "Revenue Shares and Monopsonistic Behavior in Intercollegiate Athletics." Cornell Higher Education Research Institute working papers. Accessed May 9, 2017. http://stage.ilr.cornell.edu/sites/ilr.cornell .edu/files/WP155.pdf

National College Players Association. 2011. "The Price of Poverty in Big-Time College Sport." Accessed May 9, 2017. http://assets.usw.org/ncpa/The-Price -of-Poverty-in-Big-Time-College-Sport.pdf

National Collegiate Athletic Association v. Board of Regents of University of Oklahoma, 468 U.S. 85 (1984).

NCAA, 2009–2010 DIVISION I MANUAL: Constitution, Operating Bylaws, Administrative Bylaws, Art. 15.2.2.5.

NCAA. 2014. "Board Adopts New Division I Structure." Accessed May 9, 2017. Accessed May 9, 2017. http://www.ncaa.org/about/resources/media-center /news/board-adopts-new-division-i-structure

Northwestern University v. College Athletes Players Association, Case 13-RC-121359 (N.L.R.B. 2014).

O'Bannon v. National Collegiate Athletic Association, 7 F. Supp. 3d 955, (N.D. Cal. 2014).

O'Bannon v. National Collegiate Athletic Association, 802 F.3d 1049 (9th Cir. 2015).

Porto, Brian L. 2012. *The Supreme Court and the NCAA: The Case for Less Commercialism and More Due Process in College Sports.* Ann Arbor: University of Michigan Press.

Request for Review, Northwestern University and College Athletes Players Association, Case 13-RC-121359 (2014).

Schmit, Jude D. 2007. "A Fresh Set of Downs? Why Recent Modifications to the Bowl Championship Series Still Draw a Flag under the Sherman Act." *Sports Law Journal* 14:219–254.

Sherman Antitrust Act, 15 U.S.C. §§ 1–7.

Smith, Ronald A. 1988. *Sports and Freedom: The Rise of Big-Time College Athletics.* New York: Oxford University Press.

Suggs, Welch. 2004. "Football, Television, and the Supreme Court." *Chronicle of Higher Education,* July 9. Accessed May 9, 2017. http://www.chronicle.com/article/Football-Televisionthe/2342

Title IX 1979 Policy Interpretation on Intercollegiate Athletics, 44 Fed. Reg. 71,413.

Title IX of the Education Amendments of 1972, 20 U.S.C. §1681.

CHAPTER FOURTEEN

Unfinished Business for Student Veterans: Gaps in Policy and Practice

David DiRamio

Introduction

The past decade's research studying student veterans focused primarily on describing transition from military service to civilian life and college campus. Many studies, based mostly on small samples and qualitative methods, were data rich and of high quality, but nongeneralizable, mostly speculative, and not empirically tested. In 2014, the Million Records Project released findings showing veterans' completion rates were better than other posttraditional student groups and similar to rates for traditionally aged college students. This signaled a shift to investigating academic success. With 95 percent of post-9/11 GI Bill student veterans likely exhausting benefits by 2020, it's time to resolve long-standing issues and craft policies to ensure high-quality veterans' education survives going forward.

Overview

Early in 2016, I had the privilege of delivering a keynote speech at a student success conference hosted by a university located in Michigan. While preparing to give that talk, it suddenly dawned on me that, although efforts to support student veteran success on college campuses across the nation are continuing along at a business-as-usual pace, we find ourselves at a turning point of sorts. The critical juncture that I have sensed is occurring not only because post-9/11 student veteran enrollment likely peaked sometime in fall 2014 but, perhaps more importantly (barring another scandal at the level of the 2015 VA health care debacle, which saw veterans waiting many months to receive care), advocacy and support on behalf of veterans is fading as the subject moves off of the general public's "radar." If my perceptions are accurate and interest in veterans is waning, what are the implications for the remainder of the cohort of student veterans through 2020—some of whom are just starting to use their military educational benefits? Moreover, what should the higher education community be doing in terms of policy and practice?

In this chapter, seven areas of concern are identified and labeled as "unfinished business." Efforts to address these seven items should continue, resume, or, in some cases, begin in order to provide support for current and future veterans in college, particularly while there is still authentic support from senior administrators, trustees, and policy makers. Skeptics may have concluded that the general public will always support veterans, and on the surface such assumptions are true. Few people are "against" veterans or veterans' issues, but tepid support is very different than the type of support needed to sustain genuine advocacy and to influence policy formation or changes. History tells us this is true; lack of support for Vietnam veterans comes to mind as an extreme example. As the focus on supporting student veteran success fades at your institution, don't be surprised if veterans issues receive glad-handed faux support, empty promises, and little resource allocation for new or, sometimes, even existing programming. With that in mind, here are the seven areas of unfinished business in student veteran affairs:

- Adequately address the needs of student veterans in terms of manpower and collaborative efforts;
- Faculty and staff training;
- Fair evaluation of military schooling for college credit;
- Workforce preparedness and transition for undergraduates;
- Reach out to related subpopulations;
- Wake-up call regarding traumatic brain injury, mental health, and substance abuse; and
- Address educational inequity.

Manpower Needs

It has been nearly a decade since the first veterans of the wars in Iraq and Afghanistan began enrolling in college using new GI Bill educational benefits, and yet many schools still have inadequately staffed veterans affairs offices (McBain et al. 2012). Of course, if enrollment numbers don't necessitate the need for a physical space or office, then low staffing is under-standable. However, at institutions with hundreds of veterans enrolled and receiving GI Bill and other educational benefits, we are past the point of excuses like, "We're all set at our school. We've got a VA benefits certifying official and she handles everything." It has been firmly established that the needs of student veterans go well beyond the processing of financial aid paperwork to include academic, social, and health-related support (Elliott, Gonzalez and Larsen 2011; Whiteman et al. 2013). Responsibility for pro-cessing VA educational benefits at a typical college or university is extremely challenging and the paperwork required to support each student is complex and tedious. Frankly, the onerous duty of certification each semester (and during the semester) could easily take up all the time of a competent staffer, thus leaving little time for the other important support services that can and should be offered to student veterans.

If understaffing remains a problem at college or university, serious discus-sions about staffing should be attempted with the institution's president, senior student affairs officer, and/or other senior officials involved in hiring decisions. One benchmark to keep in mind is the "tipping point" ratio (stu-dent veteran enrollment to total student enrollment) and the recommenda-tion by the American Council on Education that—when a school reaches the 1 percent to 3 percent range—support services for student veterans should be provided (Cook and Kim 2009). Moreover, support services should be evidence-based, empirically tested in the research literature, and from prom-ising practices in the field.

Another reason that staffing needs can be so variable is related to how effective collaboration is among campus units. When units such as financial aid, career services, registrar's office, academic support, and the counseling clinic partner to support student veteran success in a unified manner, this synergy can have a significant positive effect on easing the workload of the veteran support staff and may have implications for staffing requirements. Community colleges and others who routinely face tight budgetary con-straints should consider how a collaborative approach might work effectively to support the efforts of their VA benefits certifying official.

Faculty and Staff Training

Most of the research literature about student veterans published during the past decade included recommendations for colleges and universities to conduct faculty and staff training for working with veterans (American Council on Education 2010). Less than half (47 percent) of the schools sur-veyed in *From Soldier to Student II* had conducted faculty–staff training and another 20 percent pledged to do so in the next five years (McBain et al. 2012). No more recent published updates about the number of colleges that are implementing training programs are available to date and, anecdotally from my most recent observations and information, I suspect the percentage of schools providing training for faculty and staff has not increased as promised and, in some instances, actually waned. That is why it is unfinished business and it is important. Training done well provides faculty and staff with important information about the student veteran population's transitional and educational needs, as well as best practices for supporting them both in and out of the classroom. For example, differences exhibited by veterans when compared with younger, traditionally aged students are not considered deficits and an inclusive atmosphere can bolster a welcoming environment, which is helpful to many veterans.

There is an adage in the student veteran support community: When designing training, appeal to faculty members through their hearts and administrators through their wallets. The financial appeal to administrators is simple and straightforward: In a sense, each student veteran using GI Bill benefits is a mini–federal grant with up to 36 months of continuous funding. Faculty members, on the other hand, are less concerned about tuition and educational benefits. In my experience, most faculty want to know why there is an "edge" to many of the veterans in their classes and how can they set aside their ambivalent, sometimes fervent, opposition to war to present a welcoming attitude to the war veteran.

I emphasize two related themes for faculty members to consider as part of the training curriculum that I use. First, I reassure professors that the edgy disposition they have sensed may indeed be the way that a student who comes from a military culture expresses the need for help, whether it be for academic assistance or other matters including frustration with school, difficulties transitioning to civilian life, psychological challenges, or most likely a blend of multiple factors. In military culture, one does not ask for help except within the close-knit unit in which he or she serves. Asking for help is, with few exceptions, a sign of weakness and, as one can imagine, weakness is not a virtue highly regarded in the military. Second, I make faculty members aware that a majority of the student veterans I have worked with and interviewed over the years view their professors as officers and that comes with a mixed bag of connotations ranging from deep respect to high expectations.

Of course, as a tenured faculty member myself, I strongly support my fellow faculty member's efforts to conduct her or his classes in a manner that is deemed best by each individual, regardless of pedagogy and classroom management. However, a professor's style may clash with the student veteran's "professor-officer" expectations and lead to frustration or confrontation, all of which are also components of the typical edgy disposition that my colleagues report and students may express. There are no pat answers to resolve these sorts of issues, but in my experience, training to make faculty aware of the dynamics at play certainly seems to help. There is much more to faculty/ staff training than the two items mentioned above but, above all else, if professors would investigate and make themselves aware of the resources available for assisting student veterans, that will go a long way to allowing them to make informed referrals for students who are facing a crisis and are having trouble asking for help.

Transfer Credit for Military Schooling

Of all the unfinished business items, this may be thorniest of issues. At the institutional level, each academic program reserves the right to accept or reject transfer credits regardless of the source. For most of the student veterans with whom I have spoken, the bottom line is that a veteran will accept whatever decision is made regarding the applicability of their military schooling as long as he or she feel that officials from the program, college, and/or university have made a good faith attempt to fairly evaluate the military transcript. Experiential credit is another matter and beyond the scope of this chapter, but it is certainly on the minds of registrars and their staffs across the nation.

Good faith and fair evaluation is the key, as suggested by a 2011 Memorandum of Understanding (MOU) issued by the Department of Defense (DoD) to all colleges and universities that receive DoD-funded tuition remittance for active duty military personnel that attend these schools. One of the tenets of the MOU reads, "Participating institutions must review, and where possible, accept transfer credits for military training and experience" (U.S. Department of Defense 2011). This MOU is for active duty personnel only and does not apply to student veterans using educational benefits administered by the Department of Veterans Affairs, but I have long suspected that federal officials are looking into the same issue as it applies to veterans education and as a cost-saving strategy for a post-9/11 GI Bill program that exceeded expenditures of $42 billion in 2014.

Consortium building among institutions and states appears to be a worthy top-down strategy to attack this issue of military credit. For example, the accrediting body known as the Midwestern Higher Education Compact (MHEC), with funding from the Lumina Foundation, is supporting the Multi-State Collaborative on Military Credit (MCMC), which is an:

> Interstate partnership of 13 states (Illinois, Indiana, Iowa, Kansas, Kentucky, Michigan, Minnesota, Missouri, Nebraska, North Dakota, Ohio, South Dakota, and Wisconsin) to advance best practices . . . with special reference to translating competencies acquired through military training and experiences into milestones toward completing a college degree or earning a certificate or license. (Midwestern Higher Education Compact 2016, 1)

Again, this is a thorny issue, but MCMC has made headway, particularly in the areas of licensure and certification by working with licensing boards and industry associations to make it easier for military servicemembers and veterans to translate their training and experience directly into a license or an industry certificate, thereby streamlining the process and removing the postsecondary schools, many that are community, technical, and vocational colleges, that offer licensure and certification from the precarious position of interpreting each student's military record of training and experience (American Council on Education 2015).

For larger institutions, my advice, drawn from firsthand experience, is to select one college within your university (i.e., Liberal Arts or Business) and work with that college's associate dean for academics to see if any programs within that college would be amenable to a more standardized approach to evaluating student veteran military transcripts and a willingness to consider accepting some military schooling for credit toward a major(s), not simply as general elective credits that would not likely help a student veteran's educational attainment goals. Share with the dean the ACE College Credit for Military Service Web site and its online resources (American Council on Education 2016). Perhaps take the time to go through an example from the ACE guide of an official military course and the recommendations that are made for appropriate application of credit toward a program's major. What you are doing is setting up a cooperative effort, a pilot program of sorts, with a particular college and select programs within that college in order to give your student veterans the option to select a major that is more credit-friendly toward accepting their military schooling. Again, in my experience, student veterans are looking for a good faith attempt from the institution to offer more credit-friendly programs and, should a student choose to stick with a major like engineering that will not typically accept any military schooling for credit, he or she will be satisfied with that choice and be appreciative of the effort by the institution to offer alternatives. Please keep your university's registrar informed of your efforts. It will pay off in the end because cooperation and support from the registrar is vital to the success of an initiative like this one.

Workforce Preparedness

When a servicemember is discharged from the military, enrolls in college soon after, and then proceeds to complete courses as quickly as possible without participating in any of the cocurricular or out-of-the-classroom experiences offered by a college, what is the quality of his or her transition to civilian life and employment after graduation? The answer is, of course, "it depends," but just as likely no substantive transition at all from the perspective of a student affairs educator who knows the possibilities that exist for students (veteran and nonveteran) to develop socially, cognitively, and a "civilian version" of the transferable skills that employers are looking for when they hire a veteran.

Many companies listed in the Fortune 100 have some form of an initiative to hire veterans because they possess skills, abilities, and attributes only found in military service. It turns out, however, that employers—many who prefer to hire veterans because it makes for smart business sense and shows good corporate responsibility—are underwhelmed with the preparedness of our veteran population turned civilian. In fact, 50 percent of the 429 hiring professionals surveyed by the Society for Human Resource Management (SHRM) reported making specific efforts to hire veterans, but a surprisingly high 60 percent in the same study indicated that many veterans have difficulty adapting to workplace culture (Society of Human Resource Management 2010). In my experience, many veterans attending college today need to learn to adapt themselves to a civilian corporate culture, which is markedly different from military culture, particularly during a time of war. A student veteran will likely say that he or she needs no training for transferable skills development and corporate culture preparedness, perhaps even citing examples of experiences, some gritty and very intense, that he or she experienced during active duty.

The student does not realize that there is a civilian version of the skills, attributes, and lessons learned that got them through those gritty experiences. One way that the higher education community, especially those in the career counseling and academic advising fields, can assist student veterans to acquire the requisite skills needed in preparation for employment and career is to create opportunities for a "civilian" academic and social development in the broader campus community. I know that the benefits clock is ticking (most students have only 36 continuous months to use their military educational benefits) but veterans affairs staff should counsel students, particularly those veterans who are lower division undergraduates, that reasonable efforts be made to get involved and engaged in some form beyond the college classroom. For example, a reasonable level of participation in the student veterans organization on campus is ideal for honing the skills needed in the civilian workplace. Frankly, it is part of what employers want: The dynamic and dedicated military servicemember as a fully transitioned civilian with a bit of the military cultural "edge" shaved off in order to perform capably in private business, global industry, public service, and a civilian corporate culture.

Related Subpopulations

Beyond the veterans themselves, there is an interest developing to learn more about the children of veterans who are attending college using military educational benefits transferred from their parents. Their enrollment numbers are impressive and at some schools they exceed the number of actual veterans enrolled. Research findings suggest that because of their experiences living in a military family, these "military brats" (a term that should only be used by the dependents themselves) have characteristics that are different from a typical undergraduate student. One theme that seems to resonate with this student group is that they do connect well with each other and veterans affairs staff should help them do so. Several schools have student organizations formed by these dependent children of military families, and they reap the benefits of participation in cocurricular activities, including social and philanthropic efforts, just as nonveteran students in the general population do.

For many, the stereotypical image of a military veteran is purely male. My own coauthored research confirmed that gender is of paramount significance in military culture and is structured along the lines of two factors: gender and whether or not one had served in combat (DiRamio et al. 2016; Iverson, Seher, DiRamio, Jarvis, and Anderson 2016). Most of the women we interviewed simply wished to be called veterans, with no distinction by gender.

This nuanced language serves as an illustration of the subtle gender bias (that can sometimes manifest itself as outright misogyny) that many of the women who have served—280,000 returning from deployments in Iraq and Afghanistan in the past decade—bring as part of their narratives to our campuses. For example, Molina and Morse (2015) discovered that female undergraduate veterans accrued significantly more debt in school than their male counterparts. Clearly, supporting this important student group, including research investigating financial need and other disparities, is a top priority as veterans move off the nation's radar. However, a more serious issue looms.

Sexual assault statistics reported in both the military and higher education are alarming and I wonder how our female students are experiencing their undergraduate journey in an era of ramped up Title IX enforcement and nationally reported debacles at prestigious schools such as Stanford University (D'Onofrio 2016), Baylor University (Braziller 2016), and Wesleyan University (Barthel 2015). As part of the higher education ethos of rallying against the marginalization of student subpopulations and ensuring a safe campus environment that is free of oppression and threat (real or perceived), I challenge the higher education community to give extra consideration and thoughtfulness to this noteworthy group of women.

Mental Health and Substance Abuse

With all due respect to those who have been injured in service to our country, the signature injury of the wars in Iraq and Afghanistan is traumatic brain injury (TBI) due to a concussive blast. Unfortunately, the signature "cure" for many veterans who have returned with a variety of untreated problems (both physical and psychological injuries) is substance abuse and self-medication using drugs and alcohol. Findings from a survey conducted by Peer Advisors for Veteran Education (2014), a national peer support program found at dozens of campuses across the nation that connects incoming student veterans with student veterans already on campus in order to help them navigate college life, revealed that an alarming 52 percent of student veterans reported hazardous drinking behavior. The lack of leadership and an absence of effective mental health policy in our society, in general, and higher education, specifically, are making addressing the matter of substance abuse among veterans serious and disconcerting. Clearly, this is a critical piece of our unfinished business. We must continue to sound the alarm by requesting campus policies and student programming that emphasize increased resources for treatment and education.

Educational Equity

Educational opportunity is an important theme in the American narrative. Our nation's colleges and universities strive to empower students through their educational journey to pursue a pathway to socioeconomic opportunity. However, our nation continues to struggle with inequity to opportunities that persist along socioeconomic and demographic lines. One would think that the post-9/11 GI Bill (providing funding for full tuition at a public college or university, a monthly stipend based on the military's pay scale, and a textbook allowance) could mitigate the educational inequities that veterans might face, but their college-going profile is remarkably similar to that of traditionally underserved populations and minority students, with overrepresentation in the for-profit sector and underrepresented in the private nonprofit sector. Moreover, student veterans are graduating with more debt than anticipated because, although the new GI Bill is deservedly generous, unmet financial need is an issue for many.

In terms of different sectors in postsecondary education, Cate (2014) found that nearly 13 percent of student veterans graduated from proprietary (for-profit) institutions, which is closer to the 2013 enrollment patterns of African American students in the for-profit sector (15.8 percent) and nearly 60 percent higher than the general population of all students (8.1 percent). Similarly, while 19.5 percent of all students, in general, attended private, nonprofit colleges and universities, only 10.7 percent of student veterans did so, which is actually lower than the lowest underrepresented Latino student population who have 11 percent attending private schools.

The debt accrued by student veterans based on their unmet financial need, despite receiving military educational benefits, is alarming. Molina and Morse (2015) found that 40 percent of Latino student veterans accrued loan debt that averaged $5,275 and more than 53 percent of African American student veterans accrued loan debt that averaged $7,459. Compare these numbers with White student veterans who averaged $4,246 in loan debt. Before interest in the challenges facing veterans in college fades, more should be done to assist student veterans with the unmet financial need that extends beyond what the post-9/11 GI Bill provides. Many student veteran organizations have established scholarships for veterans as part of their philanthropic efforts.

Conclusion

It is important to put policies in place before issues fade out and veterans move "off the radar." I encourage the higher education community to act now and reach out to senior administrators and policy makers with considerations for what will be needed to support student veteran success for the next 5 to 10 years. Remember that student veterans are their own best advocates and, while still partially in the limelight, their requests resonate with our top officials with more influence than the voices of faculty members and staffers. Keep in mind that, as with any new student program or support initiative in today's assessment and evaluation environment, one needs data to support policy making. Finally, in a cynical sense, nobody wants to be on the wrong side of a veterans' issue in the current sociopolitical climate. However, setting cynicism aside, supporting the postsecondary pursuits of this generation of men and women who have served our country in war, helping to preserve the freedoms that we all enjoy remains the proper thing to do.

References

American Council on Education (ACE). 2010. *Service members in school: Military veterans' experiences using the Post-9/11 GI Bill and pursuing postsecondary education.* Washington, DC: Steele, Salcedo & Coley.

American Council on Education (ACE). 2015. "Quick hits: Credit mobility and postsecondary attainment." Accessed December 17, 2016. http://www .acenet.edu/news-room/Pages/Quick-Hits-Credit-Mobility-and-Postsec ondary-Attainment.aspx

American Council on Education (ACE). 2016. "College credit for military service." Accessed December 17, 2016. http://www.acenet.edu/news-room/Pages /Military-Guide-Online.aspx, 2016

Barthel, Margaret. 2015. "Where all the frat houses are coed." *The Atlantic Monthly,* May 31. Accessed December 22, 2016. https://www.theatlantic .com/education/archive/2015/03/wesleyan-coed-frats/389177/

Braziller, Zach. 2016. "Horrifying details of Baylor sexual assault scandal revealed." *New York Post,* October 28. Accessed January 3, 2017. http://nypost .com/2016/10/28/horrifying-details-of-baylor-sexual-assault-scandal -revealed

Cate, Chris. 2014. *Million Records Project: Research from student veterans of America*. Washington, DC: Student Veterans of America.

Cook, Brian J., and Young Kim. 2009. *From soldier to student: Easing the transition of service members on campus*. Washington, DC: American Council on Education.

DiRamio, David, and Kathryn Jarvis. 2011. *Veterans in higher education: When Johnny and Jane come marching to campus*. San Francisco, CA: Wiley.

DiRamio, David, Kathryn Jarvis, Susan Iverson, Kristen Seher, and Susan Anderson. 2016. "Out of the shadows: Female student veterans and help-seeking." *College Student Journal* 49(1): 49–68.

D'Onofrio, Kaitlyn. 2016. "Campus rape culture: Outrage over light sentence in Stanford sexual assault." DiversityInc, June 8, 2016. Accessed on December 22, 2016. http://www.diversityinc.com/news/stanford-rape-brock-turner/

Elliott, M., C. Gonzalez, and B. Larsen. 2011. "U.S. military veterans transition to college: Combat, PTSD, and alienation on campus." *Journal of Student Affairs Research and Practice* 48(3): 279–296.

Iverson, Susan, Christin L. Seher, David DiRamio, Kathryn Jarvis, and Rachel Anderson. 2016. "Walking a gender tightrope: A qualitative study of female student veterans' experiences within military and campus cultures." *NASPA Journal about Women in Higher Education* 9(2): 152-168.

McBain, Lesley, Young M. Kim, Bryan J. Cook, and Kathy M. Snead. 2012. *From soldier to student II: Assessing campus programs for veterans and service members*. Washington, DC: American Council on Education.

Midwestern Higher Education Compact (MHEC). 2016. "Multi-state collaborative on military credit." Accessed January 17, 2017. http://www.mhec.org/multi-state-collaborative-on-military-credit

Molina, Dani, and Andrew Morse. 2015. *Military-connected undergraduates: Exploring differences between National Guard, reserve, active duty, and veterans in higher education*. Washington, DC: American Council on Education and NASPA Student Affairs Administrators in Higher Education. Accessed June 3, 2016. http://www.acenet.edu/news-room/Documents/Military-Connected-Undergraduates.pdf

Peer Advisors for Veteran Education (PAVE). 2014. *About PAVE*. Accessed June 3, 2016. http://paveoncampus.org/about-pave/

Society of Human Resource Management. 2010. *Employing military personnel and recruiting veterans*. Accessed January 11, 2017. www.shrm.org/Research/SurveyFindings/Documents/10-0531 Military Program Report_FNL.pdf

U.S. Department of Defense. 2011. *Department of Defense (DoD) voluntary education partnership memorandum of understanding (MOU)*. Accessed February 27, 2005. http://www.dantes.doded.mil/educational-institutions/dod-mou.html#sthash.vTz5NXgB.dpbs

Whiteman, Shawn, Adam Barry, D. Mroczek, and Shelley MacDermid Wadsworth. 2013. "The development and implications of peer emotional support for student service members/veterans and civilian college students." *Journal of Counseling Psychology* 60(2): 265–278.

CHAPTER FIFTEEN

Guns on Campus: Are They Helping or Hurting?

Mercy Roberg

Introduction

From the time when settlers needed arms to hunt for their food and protect their families and livelihoods through the Industrial Revolution and into today's high-tech weapons world, the words of the Second Amendment have allowed the citizens and noncitizens of the United States to own firearms (with a few exceptions). This chapter will provide an overview of the general history of gun regulation in the United States, focusing on four significant court cases, *United States v. Cruikshank, Presser v. State of Illinois, District of Columbia v. Heller,* and *McDonald v. City of Chicago.* This chapter will then discuss recent trends and developments regarding guns on campus in the contexts of federal law, state legislation, and university policies. This chapter will close with two leading policy proposals regarding the possession of guns on the campuses of institutions of higher education.

General History of Federal and State Regulation

"A well regulated Militia, being necessary to the security of a free State, the right of the people to keep and bear Arms, shall not be infringed" (Second Amendment, U.S. Constitution). One sentence, yet so much controversy. In 2008, *District of Columbia v. Heller* became the first Supreme Court decision regarding the Second Amendment since 1939. The *Heller* opinion stated, "The meaning of this sentence is not self-evident, and has given rise to much commentary but relatively few Supreme Court decisions."

In *United States v. Cruikshank* (1875), the Supreme Court specifically stated that "the Second Amendment declares that it shall not be infringed; but this, as has been seen, means no more than that it shall not be infringed by Congress." The decision goes on to distinguish the Second Amendment as one of the amendments "that has no other effect than to restrict the powers of the national government" and essentially returns the regulation of arms back to the states (1875, 533).

In another key case, *Presser v. State of Illinois* (1886), a court upheld the ruling in *Cruikshank*, but looked at the concept of preemption arguing that the rights of states are "confided by the Constitution to Congress, when it acts upon the subject, and passes a law to carry into effect the constitutional provision, such action excludes the power of legislation by the State on the same subject" (1886, 261).

The *Presser* case confirmed that in regard to the Second Amendment the states had control. "But a conclusive answer to the contention that this amendment prohibits the legislation in question lies in the fact that the amendment is a limitation only upon the power of Congress and the National government, and not upon that of the States. . . . It is only the privileges and immunities of citizens of the United States that the clause relied on was intended to protect. A State may pass laws to regulate the privileges and immunities of its own citizens, provided that in so doing it does not abridge their privileges and immunities as citizens of the United States" (*Presser v. Illinois* 1886, 265–266).

From 1886 onward, litigation regarding private firearm ownership continued, but for more than a century, it had little impact on the legal issues regarding the Second Amendment, states' rights, and federal regulation of private firearms.

Until *District of Columbia v. Heller* in 2008, the Supreme Court ruled in favor of individual rights. The crux of that case involved the District of Columbia's alleged excessive regulation of guns in the form of a law forbidding private possession of handguns. The Supreme Court conducted an in-depth historical analysis of the Second Amendment and concluded, "In sum, we hold that the District's ban on handgun possession in the home violates the Second Amendment, as does its prohibition against rendering any lawful firearm in the home operable for the purpose of immediate self-defense" (*District of Columbia v. Heller* 2008, 2822). This case illustrated the holding in *Presser* that the states had a legitimate role to play in regulating firearms, but that those regulations could not interfere with an individual's constitutional rights.

Two years later, in *McDonald v. City of Chicago* (2010), the Supreme Court once again took up the issue of federal and state rights to regulate firearms, but went even further to look at city authority. The conclusion in *McDonald v. City of Chicago* resulted in city ordinances regulating guns declared unconstitutional, establishing the federal government's right to regulate. "In *Heller*, we held that the Second Amendment protects the right to possess a handgun in the home for the purpose of self-defense. We therefore hold that the Due Process Clause of the Fourteenth Amendment incorporates the Second Amendment right recognized in *Heller*" (*McDonald v. Chicago* 2010, 3050).

State regulation of firearms has fluctuated wildly from state to state. Each year state legislatures and public institutions of higher education litigate the authority of the state to regulate guns on campus. The outcome has varied across the United States of America. The state regulations regarding guns on campus were born out of states adopting concealed weapons legislation. Concealed weapon legislation allowed concealed weapons to be carried, so the next question became establishing boundaries as to where people could carry concealed weapons. Private universities have had the discretionary power to write their own policies regarding weapons on campus and have done so continuously throughout the years.

Recent Trends and Developments

There are essentially two trends regarding guns on campus. Members of a campus community may argue to ban guns on campus with the rationale being campus safety. Alternatively, there is an argument for state legislation to allow guns on campus for personal safety. Florida and Texas are key examples with regard to the argument to keep guns off campus versus allowing campus carry.

In December 2016, Florida State president John E. Thrasher told the FSU faculty that he was steadfastly opposed to a Republican bill that would allow guns on campus in the state. "I opposed it. I killed it. I have worked against it since then . . . And you have my promise that I will work against it this year also" (CBSMiami 2016). Thrasher's outspoken criticism of the bill illustrated that the debate over guns on campus sometimes crosses party lines. He is a strong Republican, including formerly holding the position of chair of the Republican Party. But when it comes to guns on campus, he splits from his party's traditional progun stand. Florida has continuously introduced legislation to allow guns on campus, but as of the summer of 2017 still does not allow guns on college campuses. It is expressly prohibited in Florida Statute section 790.06(12).

The state of Texas in 2016 passed a law, "which Republicans pushed in the name of personal protection, allowing the licensed carrying of concealed handguns in most public university buildings. Unlike public schools, private colleges and universities can opt out of the law—and all but one have done so" (Benning 2016). Although private colleges could opt out, state schools were required to adopt the new law, despite the opposition of senior administration. Gregory Fenves, the president of the University of Texas at Austin, opposes guns on campus, but must follow the law. When the fall semester started in 2016, the university faced protests from students on campus. The protest, run by an organization named "Cocks not Glocks" formed out of a group that discovered it was illegal to carry a dildo in public but not a concealed weapon on campus. The firearms law does allow for a few caveats. Faculty members have the option of keeping their offices gun-free and there are certain parts of the campus where firearms are not permitted, such as "labs with hazardous materials, some areas of dormitories, day-care centers, football games, mental health facilities and the top of the University of Texas Tower, where 50 years ago an engineering student shot 49 people" (Philipps 2016).

As the national landscape regarding guns has changed, more and more states are passing legislation allowing guns on campus. Supporters say that these changes show public support for both personal safety and state authority. Critics, though, argue that these laws will make campuses more dangerous. Everytown, a watch-dog group that heavily advocates against guns on campus, identified 160 school shootings across 38 states that took place from 2013 to 2015. According to Everytown, about 53 percent of the identified shootings took place at K-12 schools, while 47 percent took place on college or university campuses. Such data is often used by gun control advocates, but these statistics have also been used by proponents of guns on campus to argue that they show the need for students and faculty to have personal protection.

In 2012, the Colorado Supreme Court ruled in *Regents of the University of Colorado v. Students for Concealed Carry on Campus* to divest the Regents of the University of Colorado of their right to regulate concealed carry weapons on campus. The University of Colorado at Boulder then implemented the following as part of its weapons policy: "Those who are age 21 and over and possess a valid concealed carry weapons permit (CCW) may have concealed weapons on campus. This is in accord with a March 2012 Colorado Supreme Court ruling" (University of Colorado Boulder 2017). In addition, "University of Colorado Boulder housing regulations do not permit the storing of weapons in residence halls. As a convenience, the University Police Department provides weapons storage facilities with 24-hour access for university-housed students" (University of Colorado Boulder 2017).

Reforms

As the pendulum swings from one side to the other, the idea of reform in the ongoing debate regarding guns on college campuses would look completely opposite from each end of the barrel. We will look at reform from two perspectives, campus safety and personal safety: Campus safety, those who advocate reforming current legislation and moving the issue of guns on campus back to campus control, and those who advocate for personal safety and push for continued legislative control over campus weapons policies.

Campus Safety

Opposition to guns on campus comes from a wide array of voices. "Most college administrators, law enforcement personnel, students, gun-control advocates and editorial boards have expressed serious reservations about allowing concealed weapons on campus. Foremost in their reasoning is that the challenges that are often inherent in college life (including drug use, alcohol abuse, stress and social obstacles), when overlapped with weapons, could have potentially lethal consequences for all people in the campus community" (Harnisch 2008, 5).

Many gun control advocacy groups formed following tragic campus shootings such as the Virginia Tech massacre and Northern Illinois University shooting. One such group, Students for Gun Free Schools (SGFS), states that our colleges and universities should be safe sanctuaries for learning, and that campuses are endangered by the presence of concealed handguns for the following reasons:

1. Concealed handguns would detract from a healthy learning environment;
2. More guns on campus would create additional risk for students;
3. Shooters would not be deterred by concealed carry permit holders;
4. Concealed carry permit holders are not always "law-abiding" citizens, and
5. Concealed carry permit holders are not required to have law enforcement training (Students for Gun Free Schools 2008, 1).

One of the strongest arguments against weapons on campus is couched in law enforcement training. The scenario involving a campus shooter and multiple people pulling their weapons on campus plays out with law enforcement not knowing who the "shooter" might be. This scenario was contemplated by the Virginia Tech Review Panel, which commented: "If numerous people had been rushing around with handguns outside Norris Hall on the morning of April 16, [2007,] the possibility of accidental or mistaken shootings would have increased significantly. The campus police said that the probability would have been high that anyone emerging from a classroom at Norris Hall holding a gun would have been shot" (Virginia Tech Review Panel 2007, 75).

The idea of guns on college campuses and the harm that can occur can be summarized by the 2015–2017 incidents reported by Everytown. From February 2015 to January 2017, there were approximately 50 incidents of a firearm being discharged, with incidents ranging from accidental injuries to active shooter incidents. "Incidents were classified as school shootings when a firearm was discharged inside a school building or on school or campus grounds, as documented by the press or confirmed through further inquiries with law enforcement. Incidents in which guns were brought into schools but not fired, or were fired off school grounds after having been possessed in schools, were not included" (Everytown 2015).

Advocates argue that as the right to carry on campus has increased, the numbers of gun-related incidents on campus have increased. Opponents of this argument state that as the number of incidents have increased on campus, the need for personal safety measures—including campus carry—has become even more evident.

Personal Safety

The personal safety argument arose out of the Virginia Tech massacre, an incident in which college campuses around the nation began to analyze their active shooter policies, and legislation began to swing from no guns on campus to state rights trumping campus rights in order to set weapons policy. Personal safety advocates were granted a big win when *Regents of the University of Colorado* was decided in the Colorado Supreme Court in 2012. The court held that Colorado's Concealed Carry Act preempted the campus policy against guns. The court stated that "comprehensive statewide purpose, broad language, and narrow exclusions [of the concealed carry legislation] show that the General Assembly intended to divest the Board of Regents of its authority to regulate concealed handgun possession on campus" (*Regents v. Students for Concealed Carry* 2012, 497).

Although the schools that do allow guns on campus make a lot of headlines, the reality is that only a small percentage of states allow guns on campus. But both advocates and critics of guns on campus agree that legislative efforts to allow firearms on campus have intensified in the past 10 years. A push in legislation regarding personal safety and the argument for guns on campus correlate with the number of incidents on campus. In addition, the U.S. Supreme Court, following its ruling in *Heller*, ruled in favor of the Second Amendment applying to state rights in *McDonald v. City of Chicago, Illinois*. The case involved a municipal ban on handguns, and the Court held the Second Amendment right of individuals to keep and bear arms in self-defense applied against state and local governments as well as the federal government. Personal safety was at the heart of the argument in *McDonald*. Multiple amicus briefs (legal documents filed in appellate court cases by nonlitigants with a strong interest in the subject matter) were filed arguing that Chicago's handgun laws denied citizens the right of self-defense against criminals. With the changes in *Heller* and *McDonald*, states began introducing legislation for personal safety.

In 2016, Texas passed legislation enabling students with valid firearms licenses to carry firearms on campus. "Concerns arose over student and faculty safety with the potential of more guns being allowed on campus. After one semester with the new laws in place, most of the concerns have been put to rest according to campus officials and law enforcement at West Texas A&M. Campus carry is now being described as a 'non-issue' during its first semester" (Balaskovitz 2016). Opponents of right to carry often argue that the presence of guns on campus will hinder academic freedom and the health of the classroom-learning environment. Advocates of right to carry counter with the following: "Ask anyone in a 'right to carry' state when he or she last noticed another person carrying a concealed handgun. The word 'concealed' is there for a reason. Concealed handguns would no more distract college students from learning than they currently distract moviegoers from enjoying movies or office workers from doing their jobs" (Students for Concealed Carry 2017).

The state of Texas currently agrees with gun advocates. Judge Lee Yeakel rejected the argument that the presence of guns in a classroom affects the discussion of controversial topics (Jaschik 2016). As the legislation unfolds in the next five years, we will see if the political climate remains the same with regard to gun laws, or if we begin to see the pendulum swing back to a more restrictive view of the Second Amendment.

Conclusion

From one end of the barrel to another, the gun controversy remains a national, state, and local issue. As the political climate changes, so do the gun laws. The idea of campus safety over personal safety is, at the end of the day, a personal choice. A student who is comfortable around guns may have no issue with campus carry, while another student may decline to enroll in a school over the issue. One of the greatest things about America is our freedom to choose, and guns on campus is an example of such a choice.

References

Balaskovitz, Ronald. 2016. "WT Transitions Smoothly to First Semester of Campus Carry," December 2016. Accessed March 23, 2017. http://amarillo.com/news/2016-12-18/wt-transitions-smoothly-first-semester-campus-carry

Benning, Thomas. 2016. "Texas Schools Said Campus Carry Would Cost $15m This Year But Have Spent Less Than $1m So Far," September 2. Accessed March 23, 2017. http://www.dallasnews.com/news/politics/2016/09/02/texas-schools-said-campus-carry-cost-15m-year-far-less-1m

CBSMiami. 2016. "Thrasher Takes Aim at Guns on Campus," December. Accessed March 23, 2017. http://miami.cbslocal.com/2016/12/07/thrasher-takes-aim -at-guns-on-campus/

District of Columbia v. Heller, 128 St. Ct. 2783 (2008).

Everytown. 2015. "Analysis of School Shootings," December 31. Accessed March 23, 2017. https://everytownresearch.org/reports/analysis-of-school -shootings/

Harnisch, Thomas L. 2008. "Concealed Weapons on State College Campuses: In Pursuit of Individual Liberty and Collective Security." American Association of State Colleges and Universities. Accessed September 5, 2017. http://www .aascu.org/policy/publications/policymatters/2008/gunsoncampus.pdf

Jaschik, Scott. 2016. "Judge: Academic Freedom Doesn't Bar Campus Carry," August. Accessed March 23, 2017. https://www.insidehighered.com /news/2016/08/23/federal-judge-rejects-academic-freedom-challenge -campus-carry-law

McDonald v. City of Chicago, 130 St. Ct. 3020 (2010).

Philipps, Dave. 2016. "What University of Texas Campus Is Saying about Concealed Guns," August. Accessed March 23, 2017. https://www.nytimes .com/2016/08/28/us/university-of-texas-campus-concealed-guns.html

Presser v. State of Illinois, 2 U.S. 542 (1875).

Regents of the University of Colorado v. Students for Concealed Carry on Campus, 497 CO 17 (2012) Students for Concealed Carry. 2017. "Common Arguments." Accessed March 23, 2017. http://concealedcampus.org/common -arguments/

Students for Gun Free Schools. 2008 "Why Our Campuses Are Safer without Concealed Handguns." Accessed March 23, 2017. http://www.students forgunfreeschools.org/SGFSWhyOurCampuses-Electronic.pdf

United States v. Cruikshank, 92 U.S. 542 (1875).

University of Colorado Boulder. 2017. "Weapons on Campus." Accessed March 23, 2017. http://www.colorado.edu/police/services-faqs/weapons-campus

Virginia Tech Review Panel. 2007. "Mass Shootings at Virginia Tech: Report of the Review Panel Presented to Governor Kaine," August. Accessed March 27, 2017. https://governor.virginia.gov/media/3772/fullreport.pdf

PART 4

Legal and Regulatory Issues Facing the 21st-Century American University and Students

CHAPTER SIXTEEN

Sexual Violence on College Campuses

Joy Blanchard

Beginning in earnest with the Barack Obama administration, the issue of college campus sexual violence has gone from a regulatory and disciplinary issue to one of great national concern. The presidentially commissioned report "Not Alone" issued practical recommendations to higher education institutions, and the social norming campaign "It's On Us" sought to raise awareness of the role of bystanders in preventing date rape and sexual assault. The U.S. Department of Education's Office of Civil Rights since then has increasingly expanded its Title IX enforcement efforts, and as of April 2017 had 318 active investigations (Chronicle of Higher Education 2017). But what more needs to be done? Have recent efforts been successful?

Overview of the Issue

Unlike other criminal offenses, like murder or arson, federal law requires that educational entities undertake their own investigations into reports of sexual assault, separate from criminal court proceedings.[1] This mandate comes from Title IX of the Education Amendments of 1972, which states

No person in the United States shall, on the basis of sex, be excluded from participation in, be denied the benefits of, or be subjected to discrimination under any education program or activity receiving Federal financial assistance (20 U.S.C. § 1681).

Though often enforcement of Title IX falls to the U.S. Department of Education's Office of Civil Rights, the rights of students who have been sexually assaulted or sexually harassed has been taken up by the highest courts—and forms the basis for contemporary regulatory enforcement and campus practice.

In 1992, the U.S. Supreme Court unanimously ruled that monetary damages could be recovered for violations of Title IX. In *Franklin v. Gwinnett County Public Schools*, a student filed suit when a school district failed to take action after she reported being repeatedly harassed by her high school teacher. The school district went so far as to encourage the student not to file charges against the teacher, and the school district closed its investigation into the harassment after the teacher resigned his position.

In a 1998 ruling, the Supreme Court established the judicial standard for Title IX liability that is still used today: actual knowledge (or notice) and deliberate indifference. (It is important to note that this is the current judicial standard, though the "Dear Colleague" letter issued by the Office of Civil Rights in April 2011 enacted some broader guidelines.) In a 5–4 decision, the Court ruled in *Gebser v. Lago Vista Independent School District* that a school district could not be held liable for harassment it was not made aware of. In that case a female high school student engaged in a consensual sexual relationship with a teacher. When the two were discovered having sex on school property, the teacher was arrested and subsequently fired. Though the school district was in violation of federal law by not having an antiharassment policy in place, nor a policy by which harassment could be reported, the Court ruled that the school district could not be held liable for harassment that it had no knowledge of.

In the last major case regarding Title IX harassment decided by the U.S. Supreme Court, in 1999 the Court established that educational institutions could be held liable for student-on-student harassment. In *Davis v. Monroe County Board of Education*, a fifth-grade student suffered repeated and pervasive taunting and sexual harassment from a classmate. The student and parent reported the behavior numerous times to school officials, but nothing was done to remedy the harassment. Noting the severe and systematic nature of the harassment, the Court agreed that the student had been deprived of an educational benefit, per the language of Title IX.

Though the issue of Title IX sexual harassment has not appeared before the highest court in nearly 20 years, there have been major developments at the federal level regarding enforcement—namely the "Dear Colleague" letter issued in April 2011 by the U.S. Department of Education's Office of Civil Rights (OCR). Most notable is OCR's guidance that institutions be responsible for harassment or assault that they know or "reasonably should know about." This is in stark contrast to the Supreme Court's test of actual knowledge or notice. Institutions continue to struggle with determining what behavior they should know about in order to avoid Title IX-related investigations.

Per OCR guidance, an institution is on notice when a "responsible employee knew, or in the exercise of reasonable care should have known about the sexual violence" (Brown 2016). A responsible employee is someone in a position of authority to redress the behavior in question; or a person who has been charged with reporting such incidents; or a person a student could reasonably believe has such authority or duty.

Other recommendations laid out in the Dear Colleague letter include that institutions should separate the parties involved in a complaint, protect the victim from retaliation, prevent recurrence, and remedy the effects of the alleged harassment or assault—such as providing counseling, housing support, or even changing course schedules. Additionally, institutions must investigate incidents involving students that occur off campus and should not wait for the conclusion of criminal proceedings to commence their investigations. The OCR's guidance offers 60 days as a guide to complete a timely investigation, though some cases may require more time. The guidance letter also calls for increased and improved training for staff and administrators regarding reporting and investigative procedures and calls on institutions to designate a Title IX coordinator, separate from the person who will adjudicate the campus proceedings, to lead fact-finding inquiries.

Recent Developments

Despite changes in guidance regarding the implementation of Title IX regulations on campus, one cannot lose sight of the overarching issue—and that is whether or not campus sexual violence has decreased. Enacting new policies, providing more trainings, and expanding federal oversight seemingly still have yet to ameliorate the key pressing issue. The April 2011 Dear Colleague letter itself included some startling statistics: one in five women are victims of completed or attempted sexual assault while in college.

Following recommendations from the Obama administration that campuses conduct "climate surveys" among the student body to get a clearer picture of the prevalence of sexual assault, some startling statistics came to light. In October 2014, the University of Oregon released results from a survey of nearly 1,000 of its students. Thirty-five percent of female respondents indicated that they had a sexual encounter at least once without consent; for men that rate was 14 percent. More disturbing was that one-in-seven indicated that they had not reported these incidents to authorities (Thomason 2014). In a separate study released by the White House (2014), only approximately 12 percent of victims of campus sexual assault indicated that they reported the abuse (Harvey 2014).

A national survey conducted by the Association of American Universities (2015) confirmed similar trends. This study was conducted on 27 campuses and included 150,072 responses, examining rates of rape and sexual touching along with physical force, drugs and alcohol, coercion, and absence of affirmative consent. Less than 28 percent of assaults were reported to campus organizations or law enforcement agencies.

Beyond the issue of victims being reluctant to report sexual crimes to authorities, campuses also seem to be failing in their duty to report such crimes. The Jeanne Clery Disclosure of Campus Security Policy and Campus Crime Statistics Act (or Clery Act) requires all higher education institutions receiving federal funding to report statistics regarding crimes that occur on or near their campuses. A study conducted by the American Association of University Women found that of the colleges that disclosed annual crime statistics, 91 percent of campuses indicated zero incidences of rape in 2014—which is highly unlikely (American Association of University Women 2015).

According to a U.S. Department of Education Web site, 14,726 sexually related offenses were reported in 2015 across 6,701 institutions. This breaks down to an average of 2.2 sexually related crimes per campus per year. However, this figure is a notable increase from 12,232 incidences reported in 2014. One must question whether the numbers are indicative of trends in sexual assault occurring on campus, or are institutions feeling the pressure to more accurately report their crime data? (The Department of Education can fine an institution $35,000 per infraction for misrepresenting Clery data.) Yung (2015) found that reports of campus sexual assault increase by 44 percent when an institution is engaged in a Clery audit by the U.S. Department of Education, while preaudit and postaudit figures are statistically indistinguishable. However, the Department of Education has only conducted 54 audits to date—which points to lax enforcement.

Factors Affecting Campus Sexual Violence

Sexual Assault and Substance Use

Approximately half of sexual assault cases involve alcohol (Abbey 2002). In one study of nearly 6,000 college female students, researchers found that most sexual assaults occurred when the women voluntarily consumed alcohol (Krebs et al. 2009). However, administrators are reticent to link alcohol and sexual assault, out of fear that victims will blame themselves and not report the crime (Wilson 2014).

Greek-letter organizations have been linked in the research to higher rates of alcohol and sexual assault (Murnen and Kohlman 2007). Sorority women experience sexual assault at higher rates than the general female student body (Barrick et al. 2012). Fraternity men drink significantly more often and with greater intensity (DeSimone 2009)—which has been linked to higher rates of sexual assault. A study by United Educators (2015), a risk management firm, examined statistics from 305 claims of sexual assault it received from 104 campuses between 2011 and 2013. Ten percent of accused perpetrators were members of a Greek-letter fraternity. Of the cases involving multiple perpetrators, 13 percent involved fraternity men. Twenty-four percent of repeat offenders were members of a fraternity.

Additionally, campus geography can breed party culture and drinking. For example, there are approximately 60 establishments that serve alcohol within a quarter mile of the universities at Georgia and Wisconsin, and 100 such establishments lie within a quarter-mile radius of the University of Nebraska at Lincoln (Myers and Narayanswamy 2014).

Student-Athletes and Sexual Assault

The link between intercollegiate athletics and campus sexual misconduct has been growing stronger at an alarming pace. Nearly a third of college sexual assaults are reported to be committed by student-athletes (National Coalition against Violent Athletes 2012). In its own study of claims reported between 2011 and 2013, United Educators found 15 percent of accused perpetrators were student-athletes. Of the cases involving multiple perpetrators, 40 percent involved student-athletes. Twenty percent of repeat offenders were student-athletes (United Educators 2015).

Several of the institutions investigated by the OCR for Title IX infractions have been found to fail to report or act on allegations of sexual misconduct by student-athletes. The investigation at the University of Montana—in which the settlement with the U.S. Department of Education has become a "blueprint" for institutions to model policy and practice—was first begun after two students claimed that the institution failed to fully investigate their claims that they had been sexually assaulted by members of the football team. Other high-profile cases have occurred at Florida State University (involving Heisman Trophy winner Jameis Winston), University of Colorado, and Arizona State University, in which the university paid $850,000 to a female student who was raped by a football player who had been expelled yet reinstated at a coach's request after "groping, threatening, and exposing himself to women" (Munson 2009)—to name a few.

Similarly startling is the apparent role college sports has played in creating a culture among the student body permissive of excessive partying, substance use (particularly alcohol), and sexual assault. Using the National Incident Based Reporting System, a voluntary reporting system of municipal law enforcement agencies collected by the Federal Bureau of Investigation,

Lindo, Siminski, and Swensen (2015) analyzed crime statistics from 96 institutions that participate in Division I football. While controlling for variance across days of the week and times of the year, the researchers found a 28 percent increase in reported rape among 17- to 24-year-old victims on college football game day—a 41 percent increase during home games and a 15 percent increase during away games. The researchers found there were more reports of other crimes as well on game day—disorderly conduct (54 percent), DUI (20 percent), drunkenness (87 percent), and liquor law violations (102 percent).

Potential Reform

Two separate legal and regulatory issues intersect campus sexual violence: Title IX and the Clery Act. One relates to campus adjudication and prevention; the other relates to reporting. Have either been successful in achieving the results by which they were created? Has Title IX been successful in reducing the number of sexual assaults occurring on campus, and has Title IX been enforced properly? Has Clery been a reliable tool in reporting campus sexual violence? Critics would say no on both accounts.

A somewhat controversial argument has entered the debate: adjudicating sexual assault should be left to the courts, not colleges (Intelligence [2] Debates 2016; Yoffe 2014). Part of this argument is that campus administrators are ill-equipped and trained to adjudicate the complexities of such charges, and, particularly with the push for enforcement from OCR, that campus proceedings are biased against the accused and campus definitions of assault, including the promulgation of affirmed consent[2] regulations, are overbroad and overreaching.

Since 2011 approximately 150 lawsuits brought by male students who were sanctioned (typically expelled) via campus proceedings were pending across the country (New 2015) and nearly a dozen of those in the past two years have been successful (New 2016; Shapiro 2017). In those lawsuits, litigants claimed that they had been unfairly targeted and presumed guilty because of Title IX enforcement (a version of reverse gender discrimination, so to speak) or that their constitutional due process rights had been violated. It is important to note that OCR guidance requires institutions to utilize a "preponderance of the evidence" standard when deciding cases of sexual harassment and sexual assault, which means that a hearing panelist must decide if it is more likely than not that the offense occurred. This is the lowest threshold of proof in contemporary law.

In *Doe v. Alger* (2016) a male student sued George Mason University after the president upheld a campus appeals board's decision to suspend him, contrary to the determination of the original hearing board, which after five hours of testimony and deliberation determined that he was not responsible for sexual misconduct.

In *Doe v. University of Southern California* (2016), a male student was accused of violating the student code of conduct after he engaged in a group sexual encounter with a female student at an off-campus party. The sexual contact between the accused and the victim was consensual, but that was not the case with the other parties. Though the campus hearing board did not find the male student engaged in rape, they did find that he violated the student code of conduct by encouraging or allowing other students to slap the victim on the buttocks and by "endangering" her by leaving her alone in a bedroom after the last sexual encounter ended. In the lawsuit, the accused student claimed that the university had not provided him the same due process protections as the victim during the course of the proceedings. The trial court found that the university had not provided the accused student information regarding the sections of the student code that ultimately formed the basis of his suspension from the university. An appellate court agreed that he had not been afforded a fair hearing and that the evidence did not support the findings of the preliminary campus adjudication board.

In a case alleging deprivation of due process rights, a male student who was expelled from Washington and Lee University presented in his lawsuit that the Title IX officer in his case argued that "regret equals rape," citing an article from a Web site titled *Total Sorority Move* that reasoned "sexual assault occurs whenever a woman has consensual sex with a man and regrets it because she had internal reservations that she did not outwardly express" (*Doe v. Washington and Lee University* 2015, 10). The court, siding with the student, found that the university altered its policies and practice in order to gain more convictions to satisfy pressures to comply with Title IX, something it called "a practice of railroading accused students" (10).

This trend has become disturbing to some in the higher education community. In their thought-provoking, if not controversial, 2016 essay, Harvard Law professors Jacob Gersen and Jeannie Suk argued that laws like Title IX have created a "sex bureaucracy," evolving from first prohibiting institutions from engaging in sex discrimination to now compelling schools and universities to affirmatively expand and create internal structures "to respond, prevent, research, survey, inform, investigate, adjudicate, and train" (881) regarding sexual conduct that often includes voluntary and willing sexual acts. In fact, as late as 2005 OCR advised an institution "that it 'was under no obligation to conduct an independent investigation' of an allegation of sexual assault if 'it involved a possible violation of the penal law, the determination of which is the exclusive province of the police and the office of the district attorney'" (Gersen and Suk 2016, 901). Fast-forward to the post-2011 Dear

Colleague guidance, and campuses must now investigate conduct it "should have known" occurred.

Gersen and Suk point out the overbreadth of certain regulatory language. The 2013 reauthorization of the Violence Against Women Act includes among its violations "any sexual act," which according to Gersen and Suk differs from sexual contact or sexual touching and could be construed to include verbal, nonverbal, and electronic communication (e.g., "a text message expressing sexual desire" [894])—all of which are not criminal offenses but potential violations on any college campus.

Gersen and Suk allege that the Department of Education has overreached in its enforcement and has "no legal authority to force colleges to do anything that the law—whether a statute or regulations—does not mandate" (Gersen and Suk Gersen 2017). Citing one institution's Title IX policy that set the standard for sexual harassment as the "perspective of a reasonable person within the campus community" Gersen and Suk Gersen (2017) asked whether that functioned as de facto[3] sexual discrimination by using a standard contrary to what has been decided via sexual harassment, civil tort, and criminal law.

The authors go on to claim a "definitional overinclusiveness makes it difficult for both colleges and students to distinguish serious cases of sexual assault and harassment from cases in which the absence of affirmative or enthusiastic agreement nonetheless accompanied a genuinely voluntary decision to engage in sexual conduct" (Gersen and Suk Gersen 2017). Referencing policies from institutions such as Yale University and Georgia Southern University that define permissible sex as imaginative, enthusiastic, and creative, Gersen and Suk argue that higher education is "in the business of formulating and providing sex and relationship instruction and advice, and regulating it bureaucratically" (2016, 929).

Another position gaining traction in the higher education community is that the Clery Act does not accomplish its proposed intent—and that is to capture accurately how crime impacts members of a campus community. The Jeanne Clery Disclosure of Campus Security Policy and Campus Crime Statistics Act was passed in 1990 after the rape and murder of a student at Lehigh University and mandated that all institutions of higher education receiving federal funding compile, file, and make public statistics related to crime on or near their campus. An inherent flaw in Clery data is that it only captures crime that occurs on campus or on contiguous property.

Another flaw is inaccurate reporting or even nonreporting. Clery regulations and definitions can be quite complicated and convoluted, not just for campus administrators but even for attorneys. In his 2014 dissertation, Michael DeBowes designed eight scenarios and tested survey respondents to determine their level of comprehension of Clery mandates. Participants were drawn from the membership of the Association of Student Conduct

Administrators, the leading national organization in the student conduct field; 99.3 percent of respondents could not properly categorize the Clery-related factors in the scenarios. Interestingly, when DeBowes presented the same scenarios to attorneys from the Department of Education, even their interpretations varied. If thousands of campuses must participate annually in crime reporting, and rightfully assuming that the knowledge and training among those responsible for such reporting varies widely, how reliable can Clery data be expected to be?

In addition to inaccurate reporting, there is widespread belief that some institutions engage in nonreporting. To illustrate what some believe to be a widespread phenomenon, the *New York Times* compared Clery data to statistics kept by a Tallahassee rape crisis center. The study found that between 2011 and 2013, 16 on-campus rapes were reported at FSU and no forcible sex offenses from 2007–2013 (which is what would appear in Clery data), but 63 FSU students sought treatment at area hospitals for sexual assault during that same time period (Perez-Pena and Bogdanich 2014). In open court, the head of the FSU Victim Advocate Office testified in 2014 that 113 students reported sexual assault yet the university only included nine cases in its crime statistics (Jaschik 2015). The story from Florida State is merely one example. Janosik and Plummer (2005) reported that 16 percent of campus victim advocates believed that senior administrators attempt to cover up campus sexual assault.

Institutions take advantage of a potential loophole that exempts medical and mental health professionals from reporting Clery-related crimes (e.g., rapes and sexual assault) to campus officials. But some institutions engage in a practice in which no employees of a victim advocacy office or health center, even nonmedical professionals, must report—which is contrary to Clery regulations. Also, one should note, it does not violate patient privilege to report anonymous, aggregate data. Senator Claire McCaskill (D-Mo.), who has been leading congressional efforts to shore up enforcement of campus sexual assault laws, commissioned a study in which 40 percent of 236 responding institutions indicated that they had not conducted any sexual assault investigations during the past five years (U.S. Senate Subcommittee 2014)—a number difficult to believe is accurate.

No clear solutions emerge to mitigating the issue of college sexual violence. What does appear clear, however, is that efforts would be better spent focusing on changing the culture surrounding sexual violence rather than expanding reporting, adjudications, and other bureaucratic measures.

Notes

1. Title IX also requires that institutions investigate sexual harassment, which is not a criminal offense but a civil one.

2. Affirmed consent requires the person initiating a sexual encounter to gain oral affirmative permission from any partner participating in such act.

3. A term to describe a practice that has some effect not specified by law.

References

Abbey, Antonia. 2002. "Alcohol-Related Sexual Assault: A Common Problem among College Students." *Journal of Studies on Alcohol Supplement* 14: 118–128.

American Association of University Women. 2015. "91 Percent of Colleges Reported Zero Incidents of Rape in 2014." Accessed November 3, 2016. http://www.aauw.org/article/clery-actdata-analysis/

Association of American Universities. 2015. "Report on the AAU Campus Climate Survey on Sexual Assault and Sexual Misconduct." Accessed May 1, 2017. https://www.aau.edu/sites/default/files/%40%20Files/Climate%20 Survey/AAU_Campus_Climate_Survey_12_14_15.pdf

Barrick, Kelle, Christopher P. Krebs, Christine H. Lindquist, Carolyn Moore, and Diane Plummer. 2012. "Factors Associated with Incidents of Sexual Assault among Undergraduate Women at Historically Black Colleges and Universities." *Victims & Offenders: An International Journal of Evidence-Based Research, Policy, and Practice* 7: 185–207.

Brown, G. Anthony. 2016. "Highlights from OCR's Guidance on Title IX and Sexual Violence." Paper presented at the Annual Meeting of the Education Law Association, Orlando, FL, November 2016.

Chronicle of Higher Education. 2017. "Title IX: Tracking Sexual Assault Investigations." Accessed May 1, 2017. https://projects.chronicle.com/titleix/

Davis v. Monroe County Board of Education, 526 U.S. 629 (1999).

DeBowes, Michael Matthew. 2014. "Student Conduct Administrator Knowledge of the Statistical Reporting Obligations of the Jeanne Clery Disclosure of Campus Security Policy and Crime Statistics Act." PhD diss., Old Dominion University. ERIC (ERIC Number ED556977).

DeSimone, Jeffrey S. 2009. "Fraternity Membership and Drinking Behavior." *Economic Inquiry* 47: 337–350.

Doe v. Alger, 175 F.Supp. 3d 646 (W.D. Va. 2016).

Doe v. University of Southern California, 200 Cal. Rptr.3d 851 (Cal. Ct. App. 2016).

Doe v. Washington and Lee University, Case No. 6:14-cv-00052 (W.D. Va. 2015).

Franklin v. Gwinnett County Public Schools, 503 U.S. 60 (1992).

Gebser v. Lago Vista Independent School District, 524 U.S. 274 (1998).

Gersen, Jacob, and Jeannie Suk. 2016. "The Sex Bureaucracy." *California Law Review* 104: 881–948.

Gersen, Jacob, and Jeannie Suk Gersen. 2017. "The Sex Bureaucracy: To Fight Assault, the Feds Have Made Colleges Clumsy Monitors of Students' Sex Lives." *Chronicle of Higher Education*, January 6. Accessed May 1, 2017. http://www.chronicle.com/article/The-College-Sex-Bureaucracy/238805

Harvey, Taylor. 2014. "To Curb Sexual Assault on Campuses, Surveys Become a Priority." *Chronicle of Higher Education*, May 12. Accessed May 1, 2017. http://chronicle.com/article/To-Curb-Sexual-Assault-on/146475/

Intelligence[2] Debates. 2016. "Courts, Not Campuses, Should Decide Sexual Assault Cases." Accessed April 20, 2017. Accessed May 1, 2017. http://www.intelligencesquaredus.org/debates/courts-not-campuses-should-decide-sexual-assault-cases

Janosik, Steven M., and Ellen Plummer. 2005. "The Clery Act, Campus Safety and the Views of Assault Victim Advocates." *College Student Affairs Journal* 25: 116–130.

Jaschik, Scott. 2015. "New Questions on Sex Assaults at Florida State." *Inside Higher Ed*, November 30. Accessed May 1, 2017. https://www.insidehighered.com/quicktakes/2015/11/30/new-questions-sex-assaults-florida-state

Jeanne Clery Disclosure of Campus Security Policy and Crime Statistics Act, 20 U.S.C. § 1092.

Krebs, Christopher P., Christine H. Lindquist, Tara D. Warner, Bonnie S. Fisher, and Sandra L. Martin. 2009. "College Women's Experiences with Physically Forced, Alcohol- or Other Drug-Enabled, and Drug-Facilitated Sexual Assault before and since Entering College." *Journal of American College Health* 57: 639–647.

Lindo, Jason M., Peter M. Siminski, and Isaac D. Swensen. 2015. "College Party Culture and Sexual Assault." Working paper from National Bureau of Economic Research. Accessed November 3, 2016. Accessed May 1, 2017. http://www.nber.org/papers/w21828

Munson, Lester. 2009. "Landmark Settlement in ASU Rape Case." ESPN.com, January 30. Accessed May 1, 2017. http://m.espn.go.com/general/story?storyId=3871666&src=desktop&wjb

Murnen, Sarah K. and Marla H. Kohlman. 2007. "Athletic Participation, Fraternity Membership, and Sexual Aggression among College Men: A Meta-Analytic Review." *Sex Roles* 57: 145–157.

Myers, Justin, and Anu Narayanswamy. 2014. "6 Campuses and the Booze That Surrounds Them." *Chronicle of Higher Education,* December 1. Accessed May 1, 2017. http://www.chronicle.com/interactives/alcohol_campuses/

National Coalition Against Violent Athletes. 2012. "The Stats Tell the Story." Accessed April 29, 2017. Accessed May 1, 2017. http://www.ncava.org/statistics

New, Jake. 2015. "More Students Punished Over Sexual Assault Are Winning Lawsuits against Colleges." *Inside Higher Ed*, November 5. Accessed May 1, 2017. https://www.insidehighered.com/news/2015/11/05/more-students-punished-over-sexual-assault-are-winning-lawsuits-against-colleges

New, Jake. 2016. "Out of Balance." *Inside Higher Ed*, April 14. Accessed May 1, 2017. https://www.insidehighered.com/news/2016/04/14/several-students-win-recent-lawsuits-against-colleges-punished-them-sexual-assault

Perez-Pena, Richard, and Walt Bogdanich. 2014. "In Florida Student Assaults, an Added Burden on Accusers." *New York Times*, September 14. Accessed

May 1, 2017. http://www.nytimes.com/2014/09/15/us/in-florida-student-assaults-an-added-burden-on-accusers.html?_r=0

Shapiro, T. Rees. 2017. "Expelled for Sex Assault, Young Men Are Filing More Lawsuits to Clear Their Names." *Washington Post*, April 28. Accessed May 1, 2017. https://www.washingtonpost.com/local/education/expelled-for-sex-assault-young-men-are-filing-more-lawsuits-to-clear-their-names/2017/04/27/c2cfb1d2-0d89-11e7-9b0d-d27c98455440_story.html?elq=d4413e40cf8b41c18b78606a3b3a0948&elqCampaignId=5708&elqTrackId=f62d804201664de899ad16e7cd028c24&elqaid=13722&elqat=1&utm_term=.12cd714dd514

Thomason, Andy. 2014. "Local Police to Alter Rape Reporting after High-Profile Case at Florida State." *Chronicle of Higher Education*, June 13. Accessed May 1, 2017. http://chronicle.com/blogs/ticker/local-police-to-alter-rape-reporting-after-high-profile-case-at-florida-state/79849

Title IX of the Education Amendments of 1972. 20 U.S.C. § 1681.

United Educators. 2015. "Confronting Campus Sexual Assault: An Examination of Higher Education Claims." Accessed November 3, 2016. Accessed May 1, 2017. https://www.edurisksolutions.org/Templates/template-article.aspx?id=2147484744&pageid=94&_ga=1.217350544.762351057.1493512469

U.S. Department of Education. 2011. "Dear Colleague Letter." Accessed October 10, 2014. https://www2.ed.gov/about/offices/list/ocr/letters/colleague-201104.html

U.S. Senate Subcommittee on Financial and Contracting Oversight. 2014. "Sexual Violence on Campus: How Too Many Institutions of Higher Education Are Failing to Protect Students." Accessed October 10, 2014. Accessed May 1, 2017. http://www.mccaskill.senate.gov/SurveyReport withAppendix.pdf

White House (Obama administration). 2014. "Not Alone: The First Report of the White House Task Force to Protect Students from Sexual Assault." Accessed October 10, 2014. https://www.justice.gov/ovw/page/file/905942/download

Wilson, Robin. 2014. "Why Campuses Can't Talk about Alcohol When It Comes to Sexual Assault." *Chronicle of Higher Education*, September 4. Accessed May 1, 2017. http://chronicle.com/article/Why-Campuses-Can-t-Talk/148615/

Yoffe, Emily. 2014. "The College Rape Overcorrection." Slate, December 7. Accessed May 1, 2017. http://www.slate.com/articles/double_x/doublex/2014/12/college_rape_campus_sexual_assault_is_a_serious_problem_but_the_efforts.html#section-8

Yung, Corey Rayburn. 2015. "Concealing Campus Sexual Assault: An Empirical Examination." *Psychology, Public Policy, and Law* 21: 1–9.

CHAPTER SEVENTEEN

"Open" Campus Areas and Students' First Amendment Speech Rights

Neal H. Hutchens and Kerry Brian Melear

Overview

Legal disputes involving the constitutional speech and expressive rights of public college and university students occur on a consistent basis. One issue routinely contested involves the type of access that institutions must provide to students to open campus areas such as walkways, courtyards, or plazas. This chapter explores public college students' First Amendment rights relative to such open spaces to engage in speech and expressive activities, including handing out flyers or soliciting signatures for petitions.

At the University of Cincinnati in 2012, members of a university student group sought to gather signatures at various campus areas for a petition aimed at placing a "right to work" amendment on the Ohio ballot for voter consideration (*University of Cincinnati Chapter of Young Americans for Liberty v. Williams* 2012). University officials notified the students that institutional policy required them to limit such "spontaneous" signature gathering activities to a designated free speech area. The students received a warning that collecting signatures outside the designated speech zone could result in their arrest. They initially complied with the order to restrict their petition gathering activities to the designated space but only managed to interact with six students due to low pedestrian traffic. As a result of the restrictions, the students initiated a lawsuit in federal court challenging university administrators' authority to limit their efforts to a designated campus area absent prior approval. The students' legal challenge dealt with an issue that regularly arises at public colleges and universities, namely the extent of institutional authority to regulate college students' speech and expression in ostensibly "open" campus areas.

As discussed further in the chapter, courts commonly look to what is termed forum analysis in analyzing students' speech rights and corresponding institutional regulatory authority over student speech in open campus spaces. Under forum analysis, a key step involves classifying the type of forum under consideration and the applicable First Amendment standards for the forum in question. Designating a particular open campus area as a *traditional public forum* or a *designated public forum* places important legal constraints on institutional authority to regulate or limit student speech and expressive activity. In contrast, classifying an open campus space as a type of *limited public forum* or *nonpublic forum* results in greater legal control for college and university officials over student speech and expression. Legal cases reveal skepticism from multiple courts—though not necessarily all—concerning arguments that a public college or university possesses legal discretion to designate all or the overwhelming majority of open campus spaces as a limited public forum or a nonpublic forum in relation to students.

Recent Trends and Developments: Forum Analysis and "Open" Campus Areas

U.S. Supreme Court and lower court decisions establish that public college and university students possess First Amendment speech rights on campus. Students do not shed their constitutional rights at the "schoolhouse gate" (*Tinker v. Des Moines Independent Community School District* 1969, 506). But, the specific contours of a student's First Amendment rights in a public educational environment depend on several factors. The way in which a court construes a student's constitutional speech rights in particular instances turns not only on the setting in which the speech arises, but potentially on the nature or type of speech as well. In some situations, a public college or university may exercise heightened control over student speech. For instance, court decisions support that, in general, greater institutional control exists over student speech occurring in class-related or instructional contexts in comparison to student speech outside formal instructional settings (Sun, Hutchens, and Breslin 2013). Or, a college or university may take action against students on the basis of threatening or harassing speech. Especially outside of an instructional context, however, institutions often possess less authority over student speech, even if such speech offends or is hurtful to other members of campus or beyond.

The Supreme Court has long recognized that public college and university students possess important First Amendment rights on campus. In *Healy v. James* (1972), the Supreme Court rejected the argument that a group of students suffered no First Amendment deprivation in being denied the same opportunity to meet on campus as afforded to other students as long as the excluded students could still meet off campus. The case provided important notice to public colleges and universities on their responsibilities to uphold students' First Amendment rights on campus. Along with confirming that public college students possess significant constitutional speech rights, the Supreme Court in *Healy* also stated that campus officials possess authority to restrict speech and expressive activities that "infringe reasonable campus rules, interrupt classes, or substantially interfere with the opportunity of other students to obtain an education" (189).

Other Supreme Court decisions articulated limits on institutional authority over student speech and expression in campus forums available for student use. In *Widmar v. Vincent* (1981), for instance, the Court held that a public university could not deny access to a student religious organization to institutional facilities generally made available to student groups. The Supreme Court stated that once the institution opted to open certain campus areas for student use, it could then not favor particular viewpoints in granting or denying access. The university "assumed an obligation to justify its discriminations and exclusions under applicable constitutional norms" (267–268). At the same time, however, the Supreme Court discussed that First Amendment standards applicable to the university should be determined based on the "special characteristics of the school environment" (267n5). It noted that a public university campus "differs in significant respects from public forums such as streets or parks or even municipal theaters" (267n5). As such, public higher education institutions retain discretion to "impose reasonable regulations compatible with that mission upon the use of its campus and facilities" (267n5). According to the Court, a public college or university operates under no legal obligation to "make all of its facilities equally available to students and nonstudents alike, or that a university must grant free access to all of its grounds or buildings" (267n5).

As pointed out, in analyzing students' constitutional speech rights in open campus areas, courts routinely rely on forum analysis. The forum concept applies to all governmental property, including public colleges and universities (*Christian Legal Society v. Martinez* 2010). Some types of governmental property, referred to as nonpublic forums, are generally not open or available for citizen speech (*Perry Education Association v. Perry Local Educators' Association* 1983). In contrast, other property, such as public parks or sidewalks, constitute traditional public forums, spaces marked by history and custom as accessible for citizen speech (*Cornelius v. NAACP* 1985). Along with traditional public forums, the government may create designated public forums for speech and expressive activity. With either a traditional or a designated public forum, a governmental restriction on the content of speech must survive a stringent judicial test known as strict scrutiny.

Under strict scrutiny, any content-based regulation must be narrowly tailored to serve a compelling governmental interest. A strong legal presumption exists against content-based restrictions in a traditional or a designated public forum. In both forums, the government may impose content-neutral regulations affecting speech and expressive activities related to time, place, or manner. Such restrictions, however, must be narrowly tailored to serve a significant governmental interest and must leave open ample alternative channels for communication (*Clark v. Community for Creative Non-Violence* 1984). Under time, place, and manner standards, the government may, for example, restrict the use of sound amplification devices in a public park (*Ward v. Rock against Racism* 1989).

Between the traditional and designated public forums and the nonpublic forum, there also exists a middle forum. Not always uniform in the terminology used to describe this type of forum, some courts refer to a limited public forum—the name adopted for this chapter—while others describe it as a limited designated public forum. With a limited public forum, government may open a space to certain groups (e.g., students) or for specific types of speech or expressive activities. In this middle forum, governmental restrictions must be reasonable in relation to the purpose served by the forum and must adhere to viewpoint neutrality (*Christian Legal Society v. Martinez* 2010, 2984). The reasonableness standard does not leave governmental actors, including public colleges and universities, with unfettered authority over speech, but it provides more discretion than the legal rules governing traditional or designated public forums. Significantly, if a public college or university creates a limited public forum, then it must not engage in viewpoint discrimination, such as favoring the College Republicans over the College Democrats or vice versa, in allowing access to the forum.

Rather than only a single forum, multiple forums exist on public college and university campuses. Under forum standards, public institutions possess greater legal authority to restrict speech in nonpublic campus forums, such as offices, classrooms, libraries, and locations for performances or athletic events. In considering a particular campus location and the resulting forum, it is important to recognize that some campus spaces serve multiple purposes, with the type of forum potentially shifting depending on use. An auditorium, for instance, might constitute a limited public forum at times for students eligible to reserve the space to engage in speech or expressive activities. At other times, the same auditorium's use for performances or lectures would likely receive designation as a nonpublic forum. Similarly, many institutions make classroom spaces available to student organizations when not being used for instructional purposes.

As with institutional buildings, open campus areas may accommodate several types of forums. Legal disputes periodically arise regarding students' constitutional speech rights in seemingly open or public areas of campus, such as sidewalks, courtyards, or plazas. Students may reason these areas are generally open and available for various speech and expressive activities, but, as the University of Cincinnati case shows, this is not necessarily how institutions classify such spaces in relation to students. In fact, students and institutional officials regularly clash regarding students' First Amendment rights in open campus spaces versus institutional authority to disallow student speech or expressive activity or to impose various rules such as prior notice requirements. In litigation, institutions often contend that the legal standards associated with the limited public forum or the nonpublic forum should apply to open campus areas in question. Unsurprisingly, students and prominent speech organizations such as the Foundation for Individual Rights in Education (FIRE) counter that the legal rules associated with the traditional or designated public forum should govern students' speech and expressive rights in open campus areas. The chapter now turns to cases involving legal disputes over students' speech rights in such open campus spaces.

Cases Involving Open Campus Areas

Apart from areas not available for student speech activities unless by special institutional invitation—such as classrooms, auditoriums, libraries, and offices—what about the legal status of open campus spaces such as sidewalks, courtyards, or plazas? Although not demonstrating complete uniformity, cases reveal a resistance on the part of courts to uphold institutional rules and policies deemed overly restrictive in terms of students' speech rights in open campus areas. In litigation, several public colleges and universities have argued that the legal standards associated with limited or nonpublic forums should apply to all open campus spaces. Such a classification, as noted, generally vests institutional officials with greater legal authority to regulate student speech and expression compared to traditional or designated public forums. In contrast, students have contended in these cases that courts should view open campus areas as generally subject to the constitutional rules governing traditional or designated public forums, at least in relation to students.

In the case discussed to open the chapter, *University of Cincinnati Chapter of Young Americans for Liberty v. Williams* (2012), the university imposed rules that limited demonstrations, picketing, and rallies to an area constituting 0.01 percent of the campus. Additionally, the students claimed that university's prior notice requirements served to prohibit all spontaneous speech activities, even if they were not involving large numbers of students or otherwise potentially disruptive. In framing its analysis, a federal district court first discussed the existence of three types of public forums, namely the traditional public forum, the designated public forum, and the limited public forum. The *Williams* court discussed that forum classification depended on "the traditional use of the property, the objective use and purposes of the space, the government intent and policy with respect to the property, and its physical characteristics and location" (*University of Cincinnati Chapter of Young Americans for Liberty v. Williams* 2012, 3). The students argued that the institution's designated free speech zone constituted a traditional public forum and that other contested areas comprised designated public forums for students. The university contended that legal review of its policies should be subject to a reasonableness standard, contending that all of the campus areas in question represented limited public forums. The court faced a choice between these competing assertions of the nature of the forums at issue in the case.

In considering how to categorize the university's free speech area, the court stated an important difference existed between the university's "*subjective*" intent to restrict access versus its adoption of "*objective* criteria [that] demonstrate that the University has traditionally made the Free Speech Area available to students as a designated public forum" (*University of Cincinnati Chapter of Young Americans for Liberty v. Williams* 2012, 4). The court found it significant as well the designation of the area by the university as the "main free speech area" and the fact that the university limited demonstrations, rallies, and pickets to that area but disallowed them in other campus locations (4). Having determined that the university made the free speech area available to students "as a matter of course," the court held that the space constituted a designated public forum for students (4). Along with the free speech zone, the court looked to new university policies adopted during the course of litigation as a basis to categorize additional open campus areas under review in the case as designated public forums for purposes of students.

Deciding that the free speech area, like other campus spaces under consideration, constituted a designated public forum—at least for students—the court did not analyze the students' assertion that the free speech area represented a traditional public forum. In limiting its analysis to the issue of designated public forum, this legal decision, like others, leaves open the pivotal question of whether at least some portion of a public college or university campus must be classified as an open forum for students. In *Williams*, the court interpreted the university's policies and actions as creating various designated public forums on campus. Could the university have responded to the decision by electing to amend policies and practices to make all open campus areas some type of limited or nonpublic forums? Unlike a traditional public forum, the government ostensibly possesses legal discretion to recategorize a designated public forum. Although not directly addressing the issue, the court in *Williams* characterized the level of authority over student speech in open campus spaces requested by the institution as "anathema to the nature of a university" as a marketplace for ideas (*University of Cincinnati Chapter of Young Americans for Liberty v. Williams* 2012, 5). Furthermore, the court noted its unawareness of any previous cases establishing that a public college or university "may constitutionally designate its entire campus as a limited public forum *as applied to students*" (5). Such language suggests potential limits on institutional authority to classify all open campus areas as limited or nonpublic forums in relation to students. Other cases also reveal skepticism by courts regarding policies and practices viewed as unduly restrictive on student speech and expressive activities in open campus spaces.

Similar to the outcome in *Williams*, in a case involving the University of Texas at Austin, *Justice for All v. Faulkner* (2005), a federal appeals court held that multiple open campus areas at the university constituted designated public forums in relation to students. The court rejected the university's arguments that such locations should be construed as, at most, limited public forums and subject to greater institutional control than a traditional or designated public forum. The university contended that designating particular campus areas as a limited public forum for students also meant that the institution would have to provide the same level of access to the general public. The federal appeals court proved unmoved by this argument, stating that rather than deciding campus access in relation to the general public, "our task is simply to determine whether outdoor open areas of the University campus, accessible to students generally, have been designated as a forum for *student* expression" (767).

Upholding a lower federal court's decision in the case, the appeals court determined that the university, as expressed in institutional rules and statements and practice, gave "its students too broad a guarantee of expressive freedom now to claim it intended its campus to function as a limited public forum" (*Justice for All v. Faulkner* 2005, 769). Under the standards applicable to a designated public forum, the appeals court decided that a prohibition on anonymous leafleting proved an unreasonable regulation on the part of the university as applied to students.

Although not directly addressing potential limits on institutional authority to categorize all campus spaces as limited or nonpublic forums for students, the courts in both *Williams* and *Justice for All* looked unfavorably on officials' efforts to interpret all open campus areas as, at most, limited public forums for students. The courts relied on both stated policies and, notably, actual institutional practices in making their determinations. Courts in other cases have also placed considerable importance on institutional practices in addition to the stated policy in making forum determinations for particular open campus areas. In litigation involving the University of Houston, for instance, a federal district court concluded that the university "purposefully opened" a campus plaza as a place for student expressive activity over a long time period on roughly a bimonthly basis (*Pro-Life Cougars v. University of Houston* 2003, 582). Interpreting the plaza as a designated public forum meant that the court employed the heightened standards associated with traditional and designated public forums. In its opinion, the court did not directly address the issue of under what conditions, if any, a public college or university could permissibly recategorize a designated public forum to a limited public forum or nonpublic forum in relation to students. But, the court rejected an attempt by the university, once legal challenges to its policy had begun, to restrict all expressive activity from the plaza and essentially attempt to convert it to a nonpublic forum absent an express declaration to do so.

Other legal decisions reinforce not only the importance of actual practice in forum determinations, but also the need to appropriately publish and publicize institutional policies and to enforce standards in a uniform manner. In a case arising at Oregon State University, for instance, a federal appeals court determined that a group of students had sufficiently established a claim that the university violated the First Amendment in restricting the placement of news bins for the distribution of an alternative student newspaper (*OSU Student Alliance v. Ray* 2012, 1066–1067). Looking to the university's own administrative rules, the court determined that public areas of campus constituted a designated public forum for students. Furthermore, the court characterized the rule enforced against the student organization and its newspaper as unpublished and unpublicized and applied selectively to only this one publication.

The cases examined thus far suggest a preference on the part of multiple courts to conclude the existence of at least a designated public forum in relation to students when interpreting institutional policies and practices. At the same time, legal opinions reveal limited discussion regarding the level of access public institutions must provide under the First Amendment to students in open campus areas. In a case involving Texas Tech University, a federal district court did take up this topic (*Roberts v. Haragan* 2004). Specifically, the court considered whether a public college or university possesses a First Amendment obligation to make at least some open campus areas available to students as an open forum, whether classified as a designated or a traditional public forum. In considering this issue, the court took into account two "axioms" regarding the campus and forum analysis: (1) "the entire University campus is not a public forum subject to strict scrutiny" (860) and (2) the "campus of a public university, at least for its students, possesses many characteristics of a public forum" (861). Considering together both of these directives, the court offered the "preliminary assumption" that "to the extent the campus has park areas, sidewalks, streets, or other similar common areas, these areas are public forums, at least for the University's students, irrespective of whether the University has so designated them or not" (861).

In a footnote, the court reflected more on classifying various open campus areas for purposes of students. Such spaces, according to the court, could in "one sense" be viewed as traditional public forums (*Roberts v. Haragan* 2004, 861n8). At the same time, however, "there is a sense in which they might more properly be referred to as designated forums nonetheless, because they are part of a campus that neither serves nor is open to the public at large, but which is designated almost exclusively for the use of its students" (861n8). The court offered a potential rationale for making such areas designated forums in relation to students. It suggested that institutions may create open forums when it comes to students through campus design that results in open areas that fulfill roles equivalent to public streets or parks, that "correspond directly" to "traditional public forums outside the campus" (861n8).

Having determined that at least some parts of campus constituted open forums in relation to students, the court in *Roberts* offered the following: "These areas comprise the irreducible public forums on the campus. Of course, the University, by express designation, may open up more of the residential campus as public forums for its students, but it can not designate less" (*Roberts v. Haragan* 2004, 862). This meant that any institutional regulations on student speech and expression in such areas were subject to the standards governing traditional and designated public forums. Although indicating that some open campus areas must be classified as traditional or public forums for students, the court discussed that "not all places within the boundaries of the campus are public forums" (862). Thus, while rejecting that a university could make all its campus a limited or nonpublic forum in terms of students, the court also emphasized that not all open campus areas must be categorized as a traditional or a designated public forum.

The cases discussed so far in this section demonstrate how multiple courts would likely view with skepticism a public college or university's efforts to argue that all open campus areas constituted limited or nonpublic forums for purposes of students. To date, the Supreme Court has not issued a definitive guiding precedent on the issue. As such, the legal status of open campus areas likely will continue as a subject of litigation in lower court cases. Some courts may prove amenable to institutional assertions of legal discretion to treat all or most open campus areas as limited public or nonpublic forums in relation to students.

In one notable case of a court showing deference to a university, a student organization at the University of South Alabama sought to distribute flyers and signs and engage in "peaceful demonstrations" and other expressive activities at various campus locations (*Students for Life USA v. Waldrop* 2016, 1219). The university limited the students' activities to a free speech zone near the student center, which the institution identified in policy as the only campus location for such student speech. Later, the university adopted a revised policy that expanded the available locations for student speech but still continued to disallow student speech activity in an area—known as the "Perimeter"—that included "most spaces between the street side of campus buildings and the public sidewalks paralleling [two streets through campus]" (1220).

The court rejected the students' contention that the Perimeter constituted a traditional public forum. Alternatively, the students contended that a campus area such as the Perimeter could constitute a designated public forum for students while only a limited public forum for the general public. Although not "endorsing" this proposition, the court accepted the position that the Perimeter "could theoretically be a designated public forum in relation to students despite being a limited public forum as to the general public" (*Students for Life USA v. Waldrop* 2016, 1224). Even assuming this position for its analysis, the court concluded that the university's policies and practices failed to result in the Perimeter becoming a designated public forum for students. The court looked to institutional policy, which contained a clear expression that the Perimeter was not open to students for expressive activity. It dismissed the students' efforts to rely upon general statements in the student handbook regarding the university as a community of scholars and place for the open exchange of ideas. The court viewed such language as insufficient to override the policy directly applicable to the Perimeter. Alongside a clear policy statement, the court discussed that the students proved unable to demonstrate that the university had engaged in sufficient practices related to the Perimeter that resulted in the creation of a designated public forum. According to the court, the students "failed to show a consistent or even sporadic practice by the University of authorizing, contrary to its formal policy, indiscriminate use of the Perimeter for general student discourse" (1225). At most, stated the court, the Perimeter could be considered a limited public forum for students.

As occurred in the University of South Alabama case, other courts may look to guidance from previous legal decisions involving nonstudents where courts have permitted institutions to classify open campus areas as limited or nonpublic forums. For example, in litigation involving Lehman College in New York, a nonstudent challenged his exclusion from the campus to engage in leafleting in support of vegetarianism (*Hershey v. Goldstein* 2013). The individual claimed that the campus' main walkway represented a traditional public forum or, at a minimum, a designated public forum. The court rejected the traditional public forum argument, stating that courts had consistently declined to classify public college campuses as traditional public forums. Additionally, the court rebuffed the assertion that the walkway constituted a designated public forum. According to the court, the college maintained and enforced a policy that prohibited leafleting by nonmembers of the campus community. As such, the walkway did not exist as a type of open forum available for leafleting by members of the general public.

In support of its determination in favor of Lehman College, the court discussed that public higher education institutions differ from other governmental properties, such as airport terminals. Namely, public colleges and universities possess a distinct educational mission. Making arguments potentially applicable to the treatment of students along with nonstudents, the court discussed the need to afford discretion to public institutions in managing their campus environments to maintain competitiveness with private higher education. To that end, the court stated that the judiciary should provide appropriate latitude to public institutions regarding decisions of campus access for speech and expressive activities by nonmembers of the campus community.

Another representative case comes from a legal decision involving Georgia Southern University (*Bloedorn v. Grube* 2011). An itinerant preacher challenged a university policy that required him to obtain a permit to gain access to the campus free speech area. With the directive in mind that a university campus contains multiple forums, the court categorized the free speech area, per university policy and actions, as creating a designated public forum in relation to those who are a part of and those who are external to the university community. In regard to areas only open to members of the campus community, the court rejected the claim that these areas constituted some kind of open forum for nonstudents as well. According to the court, the university incurred "no obligation to open its campus to outside, non-sponsored speakers; the First Amendment does not guarantee access to speech activities simply because the property is government-owned" (1233). Additionally, the court stated that the physical characteristics of the property did not transform it into some type of open forum for individuals not associated with the university.

Future legal cases provide the potential opportunity for courts to further delineate the contours of students' constitutional speech rights in open campus areas. Such litigation could clarify whether and to what extent a public college or university must treat some portion of campus as an open forum, at least for students. Alternatively, cases could result in judicial determinations that institutions possess discretion in the designation (or not) of open campus forums, including in relation to students. At a minimum, the cases reviewed in this chapter indicate a preference by some judges to favor the creation of designated public forums for students when interpreting institutional policies and practices.

Proposed Responses

Public college students periodically clash with institutional officials over access to open campus areas to engage in speech and expressive activities. Cases indicate that public colleges and universities are not required to classify all open campus areas as traditional or designated public forums in terms of students. Thus, institutions possess substantial legal control over such campus areas, even in relation to students. At the same time, legal decisions reveal a wariness on the part of multiple courts to characterize all or most open campus areas as limited or nonpublic forums when it comes to students. Legal decisions considered in this chapter showed instances of courts not predisposed to look favorably upon institutional policies perceived as unnecessarily restrictive of student speech and expressive activities in open campus areas. Additionally, discussion in some cases suggests that public colleges and universities are barred under the First Amendment from declaring all or most open campus as limited or nonpublic forums in relation to students. But, legal cases have not provided undisputed guidance on this issue. As pointed out, future legal cases are likely to continue to push courts to address the limits of institutional authority in the categorization of open campus spaces for forum purposes and students' First Amendment rights to engage in speech in such areas.

In managing student speech and expression in open campus areas, colleges and universities are faced with more than parsing out specific legal standards for given situations. At its best, the higher education experience provides a unique time and place for students to stretch their intellectual boundaries and to engage in a process of discovery about themselves and the larger world. As part of this journey of intellectual examination and growth, an accompanying function of the collegiate experience is to help strengthen the ability of students to participate in and contribute to democratic society and institutions. Although public colleges and universities need to prevent undue disruptions to the educational process and to maintain safe campus environments, officials should question the appropriateness of constrictive speech policies applicable to student speech in open campus. Overly restrictive speech standards and practices are at odds with the academic mission of higher education. No matter the legal discretion ultimately provided by courts, institutions should seek to craft policies and practices for student speech in open campus areas that promote rather than inhibit the exchange of ideas.

References

Bloedorn v. Grube, 631 F.3d 1218 (11th Cir. 2011).

Christian Legal Society v. Martinez, 130 S. Ct. 2971 (2010).

Clark v. Community for Creative Non-Violence, 468 U.S. 288 (1984).

Cornelius v. NAACP Legal Defense Fund, 473 U.S. 788 (1985).

Healy v. James, 408 U.S. 169 (1972).

Hershey v. Goldstein, 938 F. Supp. 2d 491 (S.D. N.Y. 2013).

Justice for All v. Faulkner, 410 F.3d 760 (5th Cir. 2005).

OSU Student Alliance v. Ray, 699 F.3d 1053 (9th Cir. 2012).

Perry Education Association v. Perry Local Educators' Association, 460 U.S. 37 (1983).

Pro-Life Cougars v. University of Houston, 259 F. Supp. 2d 575 (S.D. Texas 2003).

Roberts v. Haragan, 346 F. Supp. 2d 853 (N.D. Texas 2004).

Students for Life USA v. Waldrop, 162 F. Supp. 3d 1216 (S.D. Ala. 2016).

Sun, Jeffrey C., Hutchens, Neal H., and Breslin, James D. 2013. "A (Virtual) Land of Confusion with College Students' Online Speech: Introducing the Curricular Nexus Test." *University of Pennsylvania Journal of Constitutional Law* 16: 49–96.

Tinker v. Des Moines Independent Community School District, 393 U.S. 503 (1969).

University of Cincinnati Chapter of Young Americans for Liberty v. Williams, No. 1:12-CV-155, 2012 WL 2160969 (S.D. Ohio June 12, 2012).

Ward v. Rock against Racism, 491 U.S. 781 (1989).

Widmar v. Vincent, 454 U.S. 263 (1981).

CHAPTER EIGHTEEN

Substance Abuse Policies on College Campuses: Is Practice in Line with the Law?

Joy Blanchard and Frank A. Rojas

Overview

Since the late 1990s, Congress has passed numerous pieces of legislation to address the issue of drug and alcohol abuse on college and university campuses. The Higher Education Reauthorization Act of 1998 (Pub. L. No. 105-244) not only allowed for institutions to notify parents in instances of underage alcohol violations (20 U.S.C. § 1232g) but also mandated that institutions implement and assess programs to reduce drug and alcohol abuse among students. Provisions of the Collegiate Initiative to Reduce Binge Drinking and Illegal Alcohol Consumption (20 U.S.C § 1011 (h)) require that all institutions of higher education receiving federal funding create a student/faculty taskforce and town/gown alliance to reduce the culture of drinking on campus, as well as provide alcohol-free campus programming and enforce a strict code of student conduct related to substance abuse on campus. (See Table 18.1.)

Institutions must not only implement but also assess and certify to the U.S. Department of Education that they have developed programs to educate students and employees about the dangers of drugs and alcohol (34 C.F.R. 86 [hereafter referred to as Part 86]). Noncompliance could lead to loss of

Table 18.1   20 USC §1011h: Binge Drinking on College Campuses

[I]n an effort to change the culture of alcohol consumption on college campuses, all institutions of higher education should carry out the following:

(1) The president of the institution should appoint a task force consisting of school administrators, faculty, students, Greek system representatives, and others to conduct a full examination of student and academic life at the institution. The task force should make recommendations for a broad range of policy and program changes that would serve to reduce alcohol and other drug-related problems. The institution should provide resources to assist the task force in promoting the campus policies and proposed environmental changes that have been identified.

(2) The institution should provide maximum opportunities for students to live in an alcohol-free environment and to engage in stimulating, alcohol-free recreational and leisure activities.

(3) The institution should enforce a "zero tolerance" policy on the illegal consumption of alcohol by students at the institution.

(4) The institution should vigorously enforce the institution's code of disciplinary sanctions for those who violate campus alcohol policies. Students with alcohol or other drug-related problems should be referred for assistance, including on-campus counseling programs if appropriate.

(5) The institution should adopt a policy to discourage alcoholic beverage-related sponsorship of on-campus activities. It should adopt policies limiting the advertisement and promotion of alcoholic beverages on campus.

(6) The institution should work with the local community, including local businesses, in a "Town/Gown" alliance to encourage responsible policies toward alcohol consumption and to address illegal alcohol use by students.

federal funding, though no such sanctions have been given out to date. In March 2012 the U.S. Department of Education issued a report finding that oversight of Part 86 regulations was nonexistent from 1998 to 2010. Since oversight was delegated to the Office of Federal Student Aid in 2010, the process has been sporadic at best with no ramifications for noncompliance (U.S. Department of Education 2012).

The minimum requirements of the federal drug and alcohol abuse prevention regulations set forth in Part 86 state that institutions must annually distribute information to employees and students regarding substance abuse risks, prevention programs, and sanctions as well as biennially submit a report to the U.S. Department of Education outlining compliance with the regulations and results of assessment efforts. In its 2012 report, the U.S. Department of Education audited 28 of the reviews previously conducted by the Office of Federal Student Aid (FSA). Of those 28 reports, only five

Table 18.2   Drug and Alcohol Abuse Prevention: 34 C.F.R. 86.100: What Must the IHE's Drug Prevention Program Include?

The IHE's drug prevention program must, at a minimum, include the following:

(a) The annual distribution in writing to each employee, and to each student who is taking one or more classes for any type of academic credit except for continuing education units, regardless of the length of the student's program of study,

(1) standards of conduct that clearly prohibit, at a minimum, the unlawful possession, use, or distribution of illicit drugs and alcohol by students and employees on its property or as part of any of its activities;

(2) a description of the applicable legal sanctions under local, State, or Federal law for the unlawful possession or distribution of illicit drugs and alcohol;

(3) a description of the health risks associated with the use of illicit drugs and the abuse of alcohol;

(4) a description of any drug or alcohol counseling, treatment, or rehabilitation or reentry programs that are available to employees or students; and

(5) a clear statement that the IHE will impose disciplinary sanctions on students and employees (consistent with local, State, and Federal law), and a description of those sanctions, up to and including expulsion or termination of employment and referral for prosecution, for violations of the standards of conduct required by paragraph (a)(1) of this section. For the purpose of this section, a disciplinary sanction may include the completion of an appropriate rehabilitation program:

(b) a biennial review by the IHE of its program to—

(1) determine its effectiveness and implement changes to the program if they are needed; and

(2) ensure that the disciplinary sanctions described in paragraph (a)(5) of this section are consistently enforced.

institutions were correctly identified and reported as not being in compliance. However, of the remaining 23, 10 institutions had been labeled as compliant but documentation indicated otherwise. In four reviews, the institutions were reported as being noncompliant but nothing in the program review report issued by FSA indicated such (U.S. Department of Education 2012). (See Table 18.2.)

The extent to which federal regulations aimed at curbing substance abuse on college campuses have been successful in their intent is undetermined. Building off of previous studies examining the effectiveness of federal law aimed at curbing alcohol abuse among college students (e.g., exceptions to federal privacy laws that allow for institutions to contact the parents of students who violate campus drug and alcohol policies, also known as "parental notification policies") (Lowery, Palmer, and Gehring 2005; Palmer et al. 2001), this study examined whether the Drug and Alcohol Abuse Prevention regulations are being effectively and uniformly utilized among chief student conduct administrators. Most specifically this study sought to determine whether chief student conduct administrators are aware of the various provisions of this act, whether they are complying with its provisions, and whether there is evidence of the law's success in reducing substance abuse on college campuses.

Recent Trends and Developments

The problem of underage drinking—and the corollary crime, debauchery, and disruption to academics—are not new to American higher education (Rudolph 1990; Thelin 2011). Sadly, more than 15 years after federal law aimed at reducing campus substance abuse was enacted, the majority of campus conduct violations still involve alcohol (Bernat et al. 2014). According to a report issued by the Commission on Substance Abuse at Colleges and Universities, one-third of college students report that they drink to get drunk regularly, and approximately 40 percent of college women and more than 50 percent of college men engage in binge drinking (National Center on Addiction 2007). The number of hospitalizations from excessive drinking rose by 67 percent from 1999 to 2008 (Bendlin 2015).

With alcohol advertisements adorning college stadiums and featured in campus newspapers, and city zoning laws that allow for bars and restaurants profiting from cheap beer and liquor specials aimed at the college student clientele, many college environments "actively promote drinking, or passively promote it, through tolerance, or even tacit approval, of college drinking as a rite of passage" (National Institute on Alcohol 2007, 1). Because most college students overestimate the prevalence of drinking on campus and perceptions of drinking norms—particularly on large campuses where the norm is not widely known among students—researchers argue that ignorance influences underage students to drink and to feel that their actions are socially acceptable. "The social context in which individuals place and otherwise find themselves can influence the likelihood of using drugs [or alcohol] . . . [and] can provide social modeling and social norms for either use or abstention from use" (Johnston et al. 2013, 292).

Alcohol also is correlated with academic issues, criminal arrests, and vandalism (Bernat et al. 2014; National Institute on Alcohol 2007). Nearly 1,500 college student deaths each year can be linked to alcohol consumption, and nearly 3.5 million college students reported driving under the influence of alcohol (National Institute on Alcohol 2007). Alcohol can been linked to approximately 100,000 sexual assaults or rapes annually among college students (Abbey 2002; National Institute on Alcohol 2007). The rise in drug-related issues on college campuses has been even more alarming. In 2012, the rate of use of illicit drugs was nearly 25 percent among college men and 20 percent among college women (U.S. Department of Health 2013). Between 1997 and 2007, the number of college students that abused pre- scription drugs nearly tripled, and the number of college students using hard drugs such as cocaine and heroin rose more than 50 percent (National Cen- ter on Addiction 2007).

From a liability standpoint, colleges and universities are increasingly being challenged to proactively address the known culture of substance abuse among students (Peters 2007). The "bystander era," as labeled by Bickel and Lake (1999), in which courts refused to extend liability to colleges and uni- versities in favor of viewing students as adults responsible for their own actions, has given way to an era of increased duty of reasonable care, ushered in by the decision in the hazing case of *Furek v. University of Delaware* (1991). Though for decades institutions enjoyed insularity from liability under the theory of in loco parentis (a Latin term that translates to "in place of the par- ent"), courts increasingly are less likely to unilaterally place the blame on students for injuries associated with substance abuse and, instead, are recog- nizing "shared responsibility . . . in the college culture and . . . legal responsi- bility to create a more responsible . . . culture" (Lake and Epstein 2000, 616).

Millennial students and their parents have come to expect that institu- tions will play a greater role in ensuring campus safety, and as this consumer- like attitude expands from the classroom to out-of-class experiences, some commentators predict courts' interpretations of the student-institution relationship will evolve as well. "The reliance that today's students have on their parents, and their parents' corresponding willingness to intervene in college-student affairs, will help persuade colleges and judges to redefine the college-student relationship in terms more appropriate to modern Ameri- can culture" (Peters 2007, 460).

Peters (2007) proposed the Millennial Model, under which "this paradigm does not make the college 'an insurer of the safety of its students,' but instead gives rise to an affirmative duty when a student reasonably relies on some act by the college that has a tangential relationship to the college's overall mis- sion" (467). It should be noted, however, that though courts have broadened the landscape as it relates to institution liability since the early 1990s, many remain hesitant to establish that institutions owe students a duty of care— the first requirement for a negligence lawsuit to proceed to trial—as it relates to drug use (e.g., *Bash v. Clark University* 2007) and alcohol, even when administrators could foresee such harm or were even present at an event (e.g., *Coghlan v. Beta Theta Pi Fraternity* 1999) (Bendlin 2015). Because negligence law varies from state to state, and because negligence cases rely incredibly on the nuanced facts of each case, there are no definitive precedents by which to rely.

Prior Research Regarding Campus Policies and Federal Regulations

Though there has been no research into the compliance and effectiveness of Part 86, there has been some research into the implementation and effectiveness of the parental notification provisions of the Higher Education Amendments. A group of researchers at Bowling Green State University surveyed 189 higher education institutions to gauge the rate of implementation of parental notification policies, how the policies were utilized, and the effectiveness of the policies among parents and students (Palmer et al. 2001). By 2001, 44 percent of those institutions surveyed had implemented a parental notification policy, while another 15 percent did not have a formal policy but did so in practice and 25 percent were considering adopting a policy. Those not considering policies stated that the reasons were either because of institutional philosophy, demographics (a large over-21 population), or state privacy laws.

Among campuses included in the survey, 40 percent of all alcohol-related cases resulted in notification of a parent or guardian. Fifty-two percent of survey respondents said that alcohol violations and recidivism have been reduced since parental notification policies were implemented on their respective campuses. Though 72 percent of respondents indicated that parents or guardians who were contacted following their student's alcohol violation were very supportive, only 12.7 percent of institutions indicated that the implementation of a parental notification policy aided in significantly lowering the number of alcohol violations on their campus, and 28.6 percent indicated that the policy had no effect whatsoever.

In 2005, Lowery, Palmer, and Gehring published a follow-up study and out of 349 institutional respondents, 35 percent indicated that parental notification had no impact in deterring students from violating alcohol policies on their respective campuses. However, when parental notification was utilized for repeat violations, 74 percent of respondents indicated that the policy could be attributed with slightly or significantly reducing the number of alcohol violators.

In 2013, Gehring, Lowery, and Palmer published a report funded by the Century Council, in conjunction with the Association for Student Conduct Administration and the National Judicial College, which explored college students' views of what worked in deterring them from drinking and violating campus alcohol policies. The pilot study included 154 students and the full study included 777 students who had been found responsible for violating campus alcohol policy within the previous six months. The researchers found that the most commonly used sanctions tend to be least effective (i.e., alcohol education programs, warnings and probations, and fines—which typically are a tax on the parents and not the students). The students surveyed indicated that they were aware of institutional policies, as well as the negative effects of alcohol use, but nonetheless still chose to drink. This study indicated that the most successful means of deterring such behavior were alcohol assessments, treatment programs, involvement with the criminal justice system, or parental notification.

Gehring, Lowery, and Palmer (2013) noted that many institutions fail to follow-up with students and their guardians after the conclusion of the student conduct process and, thus, lose out on the educational opportunities presented there. They also recommended that institutions should become more creative in educating students about campus substance abuse policy and that to assume students read the handbook (usually posted online and briefly mentioned during orientation) is foolish. These recommendations are salient, as Part 86 requires that institutions educate students and employees about campus substance abuse policy and programs, as well as become more proactive in creating and assessing effective programming to reduce the problem on campus.

Effectiveness of Federal Regulations

The earlier research into the effectiveness of federal regulations aimed at curbing substance abuse at colleges and universities indicated that not all campuses were taking full advantage of the provisions articulated through legislation. Based on the report indicating that federal oversight of the requirements of Part 86 was lacking—and in some instances nonexistent (U.S. Department of Education 2012)—we posited that nationwide implementation of these regulations also had not been administered consistently. The guiding research questions for this study were

1. Are chief student conduct administrators knowledgeable of the requirements set forth by Part 86?
2. Are institutions fully implementing the requirements set forth by Part 86?
3. Is there evidence that the intent of the regulations, to reduce substance abuse on campuses, has been successful?

We submitted a request to the Association of Student Conduct Administrators (ASCA) to survey a portion of their membership. The survey was reviewed and validated by the organization's research committee, and questions were clarified and refined based on their feedback. We wanted to survey only chief student conduct administrators so as to eliminate duplicate answers from the same institution, as well as gauge knowledge and compliance of the regulations at the highest level within the division of student affairs. Because ASCA's database was unable to narrow down the query in that way (namely because different titles at different institutions serve in the same capacity) the survey was sent out to the entire membership, which at the time consisted of 2,121 members. We asked that only chief student conduct administrators respond. (Based off of job titles, the executive director was able to approximate our target sample at 770: 328 directors; 202 deans of students; 119 assistant deans; 121 associate deans.)

Of the 141 responses received, 95 indicated that they were the chief student conduct administrator for their campus. Because of the anonymous nature of the responses, we could not ascertain if some of the surveys completed by those who indicated that they were not the chief student conduct administrator were also completed by colleagues at the same institution. For that reason, we based our analysis off of the responses of only those 95 that indicated that they were the chief student conduct administrator for their campus. Therefore, with an adjusted target sample of 770, the response rate was 12 percent (*n*=95). Though this is lower than desired, this is not an uncommon trend in higher education research (Dey 1997). When Palmer, Lohman, Gehring, Carlson, and Garrett (2001) surveyed members of ASCA, after removing duplicate responses from the same institution, their final sample included 189 respondents of the 815 members surveyed (response rate 23 percent).

The survey included 40 questions. The first set of questions asked respondents whether they served as the chief student conduct administrator for their campus and at what type of institution they worked (e.g., private or public institution; two-year or four-year institution; largely residential campus or not). (A list of survey questions is included in Table 18.3.)

The next 19 questions asked whether information regarding substance abuse was disseminated to employees and students, how often, by what means, and with whom did that responsibility rest. The next set of questions related to campus substance abuse education programs and assessment methods, two of which were open-ended questions that asked participants to explain their campus substance abuse programming as well as their assessment methods. (A summary of those responses are included later in this discussion.) The next questions inquired into reporting and certification with the Department of Education. Three questions then inquired into knowledge of penalties for noncompliance. One of those three questions was open-ended and asked respondents if they knew of instances in which an institution could be penalized or investigated for noncompliance and are discussed later in this section. The final six questions attempted to gauge the relative success of the regulations' intent and asked about rates of substance abuse infractions and recidivism on campus.

Table 18.3   Survey Items

1. Chief student conduct administrator (Yes/No)
2. Institutional affiliation (Public/Private)
3. Institutional type (Four-year/Two-year)
4. Institution receive federal funds (Yes/No)
5. Number of students enrolled (<2,999/3,000–10,000/More than 10,000)
6. Students living on campus (None/<1,000/1,001–2,499/More than 2,500)
7. Does your institution distribute to employees information regarding alcohol/drug use and associated legal penalties? (Yes/No/Not sure)
8. If yes, how often? (Yearly/Every 2–5 years/Never)
9. Who is responsible for disseminating this information? (Campus police/ Human resources/Student conduct office/Other/Not sure)
10. Does your institution distribute to employees information regarding health risks associated with alcohol/drug use? (Yes/No/Not sure)
11. If yes, how often? (Yearly/Every 2–5 years/Never)
12. Who is responsible for disseminating this information? (Campus police/ Human resources/Student conduct office/Other)
13. Does your institution distribute information regarding treatment and counseling programs available to university employees? (Yes/No/Not sure)
14. If yes, how often? (Yearly/Every 2–5 years/Never)
15. Who is responsible for disseminating this information? (Campus police/ Human resources/Student conduct office/Other/Not sure)
16. Does your institution distribute to students information regarding alcohol/drug use and associated legal penalties? (Yes/No/Not sure)
17. If yes, how often? (Yearly/Every 2–5 years/Never)
18. Who is responsible for disseminating this information? (Campus police/ Human resources/Student conduct office/Other)
19. Does your institution distribute to students information regarding health risks associated with alcohol/drug use? (Yes/No/Not sure)
20. If yes, how often? (Yearly/Every 2–5 years/Never)
21. Who is responsible for disseminating this information? (Campus police/ Human resources/Student conduct office/Other/Not sure)
22. Does your institution distribute information regarding treatment and counseling programs available to university students? (Yes/No/Not sure)
23. If yes, how often? (Yearly/Every 2–5 years/Never)
24. Who is responsible for disseminating this information? (Campus police/ Student conduct office/Other/Not sure)
25. How do you distribute information regarding drug/alcohol use to your campus community? (Web site/Hard copy/Social media/Student and employee handbook/Not sure)

Table 18.3   (*Continued*)

26. Has your institution implemented a program to prevent unlawful drug and alcohol distribution on your campus? (Yes/No/Not sure)

27. Describe your campus program to educate and reduce alcohol and drug use

28. How often do you assess these programs? (Every year/Every other year/3–5 years/Never)

29. Describe your assessment methods.

30. How often does your institution forward a certification and evaluation of this prevention program to the U.S. Department of Education? (Every year/Every two years/3–5 years/Never/Not sure)

31. Who is responsible for your campus assessment and reporting for drug/alcohol reduction programs? (Campus police/Student conduct office/Other/Not sure)

32. Have you ever been penalized or investigated by the Department of Education for failure to comply with alcohol/drug education and prevention guidelines? (Yes/No/Not sure)

33. Are you aware of in what instances you could be penalized or investigated by the Department of Education for failure to comply with alcohol/drug education and prevention guidelines? (Yes/No)

34. If you answered yes, please briefly describe those instances known to you.

35. Approximately what percentage of campus conduct cases involve alcohol? (0–10 percent/ 11–25 percent/26–50 percent/51–over)

36. Focusing only on the issue of repeat violators of your campus alcohol policy, which response best approximates what you have observed on your campus over the past 10 years? (Repeat violators have increased/Repeat violators have decreased/Not sure)

37. If you answered that you have seen a reduction in the number of alcohol-related offenses and/or instances of recidivism, to what would you attribute it? (Parental notification/Alcohol and drug education/Campus judicial process/Alternative campus programs/Other/Not sure)

38. Approximately what percentage of campus conduct cases involve drugs? (0–10 percent/11–25 percent/11–25 percent/26–50 percent/51-over)

39. Focusing only on the issue of repeat violators of your campus drug policy, which response best approximates what you have observed on your campus over the past 10 years? (Repeat violators have increased/Repeat violators have decreased/Not sure)

40. If you answered that you have seen a reduction in the number of drug-related offenses and/or instances of recidivism, to what would you attribute it? (Parental notification/Alcohol and drug education/Campus judicial process/Alternative campus programs/Other/Not sure)

The mix of institutional affiliations was relatively even, with approximately 53 respondents coming from public institutions. The sample skewed largely toward four-year institutions (92 percent), and nearly all respondents indicated that their campus received federal funds. The respondents worked at institutions of varying size: institutions of less than 3,000 students (28.4 percent), less than 10,000 students (36.8 percent), and more than 10,000 students (34.8 percent). Though some campuses had no or relatively few residential students, 36.8 percent of respondents worked at institutions with between 1,001 and 2,499 residents and 31.6 percent of respondents worked at institutions with more than 2,500 residents.

In regard to implementation of Part 86, the participating institutions overall complied with the notification prong. More than 65 percent of respondents indicated that their institution distributes to employees information about the legal ramifications of illegal substance use; more than 93 percent of responding institutions distribute information related to the health risks; nearly 67 percent of the institutions distribute information related to available treatment programs. The majority of institutions distribute information annually and delegate this responsibility to human resources.

Under Part 86, institutions are required to share the same information with students. More than 80 percent of participating institutions notified students annually of the legal penalties and risks associated with substance abuse, as well as available treatment and counseling programs. A large number of campuses distributed this information through the student conduct office, but the majority of institutions indicated that this information was distributed through some "other" office (other than student conduct, campus police, or human resources). Many institutions rely on the institution's Web site (35.7 percent) or the student/employee handbook (42.9 percent) to disseminate this information.

Regarding the other mandatory requirements of Part 86, some institutions fell short or seemed to perhaps be unaware of the totality of its components. Nearly 51 percent of respondents indicated that their campus had implemented programming to prevent substance abuse, yet 34.6 percent of respondents indicated that they had failed to do so and 14.8 percent were not sure. (This does not necessarily indicate that no programming occurs at these institutions; perhaps this falls under the purview of another office for which the respondents were not aware.) Participants were asked to describe the type of programming that had been implemented at their respective institutions. The most common responses included MyStudentBody or other online modules, peer education, orientation programming, residence hall programming, speaker series, social media, social norming, and memorandums of understanding with local law enforcement to monitor students living off campus. Some institutions address substance abuse as part of their sexual assault programming. Religious colleges and universities indicated that they used the mission of the institution to enforce a substance-free policy. One institution indicated that because it was not residential, substance abuse programming was not a priority. Still some respondents indicated that their programming was only geared toward violators of the substance abuse policy.

Nearly 42 percent of responding institutions were in compliance regarding assessment of substance abuse programming, yet nearly 30 percent indicated that they never assessed these programs. When asked to explain how they assessed the effectiveness of their programming, some respondents indicated that they looked at the posttest results of online modules, while others indicated that they looked at the statistics related to student hospitalizations each year. A few campuses used focus groups, follow-up surveys, or tracked recidivism rates or trends in the number of violations from year to year. For some offices assessment is a more informal process; one respondent indicated their campus used a roundtable discussion.

The U.S. Department of Education requires a biennial report: 6.3 percent of respondents indicated that they prepare reports yearly and 24.1 percent indicated that they do this biennially, but a staggering 20.3 percent indicated that they never forward these reports and an additional 48.1 percent are unsure. This is in line with the congressional audit (U.S. Department of Education 2012), which indicated that compliance and oversight of Part 86 and its mandates has been overwhelmingly lax and nonexistent since its inception.

Approximately 18 percent of respondents indicated that the office of student conduct was responsible for assessing and reporting campus substance abuse programs; 49 percent of respondents indicated that it was another office and nearly 24 percent were not sure which office was responsible for this portion of the Part 86 mandates. Though nearly 84 percent of respondents indicated that they had never been penalized or investigated for Part 86 compliance (the rest were not sure), a staggering 53.7 percent indicated that they were unaware of the instances in which they could be penalized or investigated for noncompliance. Of those that were aware of the instances in which their institution could be penalized or investigated, respondents correctly identified failure to have substance abuse programming, failure to conduct assessment, or failure to provide a biennial report as the reasons for such penalties. Commenting on the perceived effectiveness of Part 86 among the student conduct administrator community, one respondent indicated that it was "unlikely-to-unheard of for the feds to take action"—which indicates that there is a perception that many federal regulations lack the "teeth" to be vigorously enforced.

The third research question sought to answer whether the intent of Part 86 to mitigate substance abuse on campus had been successful. Nearly three-fourths of respondents indicated that alcohol cases comprised more than a quarter of campus conduct cases (with nearly 39 percent of respondents indicating that alcohol was involved in more than half of all campus conduct cases). The number was lower for drug-related cases, with 74.2 percent of respondents indicating that these were involved in less than 10 percent of campus conduct cases. Though 44.2 percent of respondents indicated that there had been a decrease in repeat violators of campus alcohol policy, sadly 42.7 percent indicated that there had been an increase in recidivism among drug users. The majority of respondents indicated that any noticeable changes in substance abuse on their campus could be attributed to the campus conduct process or alcohol and drug education.

Proposed Responses and Reforms

This study attempted to illustrate that some of the legislation promulgated to mitigate substance abuse on campus, namely Part 86, has not been as effective as Congress had intended. After the U.S. Department of Education (2012) issued a report finding that federal oversight of Part 86 had been relatively nonexistent for more than a decade, we posited that the same regulations held little weight on college campuses as well. What we found was that institutions overwhelmingly comply with the requirement to make available information regarding substance abuse, but compliance with the requirement to assess alcohol and drug education programming and report these efforts to the U.S. Department of Education have been sparse. Additionally, though 44 percent of respondents did report a decrease in recidivism rates among students who violate alcohol policies, that trend did not occur among students who violated campus drug policies. As higher education has increasingly become litigious and regulated (Carlisle 2014), this study furthers the argument that congressional bureaucracy, such as Part 86, has not had an overwhelming effect in reducing college substance abuse and, instead, arguably has become yet another regulation that campus administrators are not fully educated on and bureaucrats are not effectively monitoring.

The implementation of Part 86, as well as knowledge of its provisions, seems to be lacking on many campuses. Still, the issue of substance abuse continues to be a pressing one for campus administrators and one in which more innovative practices and policies must be developed. Of the themes we discovered in this study, insufficient communication appeared to be among the most prevalent: communication from the administration to the campus community, communication among campus administrators, and communication from the federal agencies in charge of enforcing regulations aimed at reducing campus substance abuse.

- *Communication between campus administration and campus communities needs to be more effective and innovative.* Many respondents indicated that their campus electronically disseminates its annual substance abuse policy. Though this practice is permitted by law, institutions must be able to demonstrate that this method is effective (DeRicco 2006). Considering the abundance of information disseminated during new student orientation, or the profusion of mass e-mails sent to the campus community on a nearly daily basis, it would be naive to believe that faculty, staff, and students are carefully reading—or even reading at all—the information contained in institutional substance abuse policies as well as the information regarding counseling services and programs.

- *Interdepartmental communication must be improved to ensure Part 86 reporting compliance.* Many respondents indicated that they were "not sure" as to what office was responsible for carrying out varying reporting aspects of the requirements of Part 86. Blanchard (2014) found that frequent staff turnover and waning institutional memory affected the consistency and effectiveness with which campus policies and federal regulations were enacted. As staff shift over time, campuses need to implement centralized systems to ensure continued compliance and effectiveness, particularly as it relates to Part 86.

- *The federal government needs to better articulate the requirements of Part 86.* Requirements of the biennial review are ambiguous and do not prescribe the date upon which reviews are due, what dates to include in the self-study, how the self-study should be conducted, or in what format the results should be reported (DeRicco 2006). In turn, as evidenced by this study, the requirements of Part 86 remain somewhat unclear among administrators.

In addition to improving communication channels, administrators should improve the assessment methods used on their campuses to monitor the effectiveness of drug and alcohol programming (National Institute on Alcohol 2007; National Research Council 2003). Students have been educated as to the dangers of substance abuse since elementary school, and research shows that the traditional methods of deterrence have not been effective (Gehring, Lowery, and Palmer 2013). Some innovative recommendations for practice include increasing both parent-focused programming and use of parental notification policies (Cosden, Gauthier, and Hughes 2013; Cosden and Hughes 2012). Institutions lose the opportunity to create lasting parental partnerships by not regularly following-up after the conduct process has ended.

Further recommendations include changing the culture on campus that allows substance abuse to be viewed as a socially acceptable norm, creating alcohol-free events, and reducing the means by which alcohol and drugs are available to students (DeRicco 2006). Campuses also should work with municipalities to alter zoning laws to limit the availability of alcohol around the campus, especially those establishments that sell cheaply to target the college demographic (Nelson et al. 2005).

Any efforts to address environmental factors must be coupled with buy-in from the campus president as well as community leaders. Blanchard (2014) found that some administrators met resistance when they tried to alter municipal zoning laws, tailgating rules, and other policies that affected constituents beyond the student body. Possible future research includes examining the link between campus substance abuse and sexual assault and how campus traditions, such as football, may contribute to these problems (Cohen and Rogers 1997).

Though measures to mitigate substance abuse on campus—from educational sanctioning to federal regulations—have not achieved the desired effects, the charge remains the same: educators and administrators must remain diligent in enforcing policy and creative in formulating programming that cuts at the pervasive, historical culture of substance abuse among college students. Perhaps instead of promulgating more regulations, Congress should convene hearings that could provide guidance on how institutions can implement practices that are successful for their respective campuses.

References

Abbey, Antonia. 2002. "Alcohol-Related Sexual Assault: A Common Problem among College Students." *Journal of Studies on Alcohol Supplement* 14: 118–128.

Bash v. Clark University, 22 Mass L. Rep. 399 (Mass. 2007).

Bendlin, Susan S. 2015. "Cocktails on Campus: Are Libations a Liability?" *Suffolk University Law Review* 48:67–108.

Bernat, Debra H., Kathleen M. Lenk, Toben F. Nelson, Ken C. Winters, and Traci L. Toomey. 2014. "College Law Enforcement and Security Department Responses to Alcohol-Related Incidents: A National Study." *Alcoholism: Clinical and Experimental Research* 38:2253–2259. doi: 10.1111/acer.12490.

Bickel, Robert D., and Peter F. Lake. 1999. *The Rights and Responsibilities of the Modern University: Who Assumes the Risks of College Life?* Durham, NC: Carolina Academic Press.

Blanchard, Joy. 2014. "Institutional Response to the Changing Legal Environment Regarding Student Safety: A Multi-Campus Case Study." *Kentucky Journal of Higher Education Policy and Practice* 2(2): Article 5.

Carlisle, Brian A. 2014. "The 'Legalization' of Student Affairs." *The Chronicle of Higher Education*, June 2. Accessed April 14, 2017. http://www.chronicle.com/blogs/conversation/2014/06/02/the-legalization-of-student-affairs/

Coghlan v. Beta Theta Pi Fraternity, 987 P.2d 300 (Idaho 1999).

Cohen, Fran, and David Rogers. 1997. "Effects of Alcohol Policy Change." *Journal of Alcohol and Drug Education* 42:69–82.

Collegiate Initiative to Reduce Binge Drinking and Illegal Alcohol Consumption, 20 U.S.C. §1011i (2000).

Cosden, Merith, Justin R. Gauthier, and Jennifer B. Hughes. 2013. "College Students' Perspectives on Parental Notification and Parent–Student Communication on Student Alcohol Use." *Journal of Student Affairs Research and Practice* 50:416–431. doi: 10.1515/jsarp-2013-0029.

Cosden, Merith, and Jennifer B. Hughes. 2012. "Parents' Perspectives on Parental Notification of College Students' Alcohol Use." *Journal of Student Affairs Research and Practice* 49:51–64. doi: 10.1515/jsarp-2012-6356.

DeRicco, Beth. 2006. *"Complying with the Drug-Free Schools and Campuses Regulations."* Accessed April 14, 2017. http://www.higheredcompliance.org/resources/resources/dfscr-hec-2006-manual.pdf

Dey, Eric L. 1997. "Working with Low Survey Response Rates: The Efficacy of Weighting Adjustments." *Research in Higher Education* 38:215–227. doi: 10.1023/A:1024985704202.

Drug and Alcohol Abuse Prevention, 34 C.F.R. 86 (1990).

Furek v. University of Delaware, 594 A.2d 506 (Del. 1991).

Gehring, Donald D., John W. Lowery, and Carolyn J Palmer. 2013. "Students' Views of Effective Alcohol Sanctions on College Campuses: A National Study." Century Council. Accessed April 14, 2017. http://responsibility.org/sites/default/files/files/Effective%20Sanctions%20Study%20Final%20Report.pdf

Higher Education Reauthorization Act of 1998, Pub. L. No. 105-244, §952, 112 Stat. 1581, 1836 (codified as amended at 20 U.S.C. §1232g).

Johnston, Lloyd D., Patrick M. O'Malley, Jerald G. Bachman, John E. Schulenberg, and Richard A. Miech. 2013. "Monitoring the Future: National Survey Results on Drug Use 1975–2013." National Institute on Drug Abuse at the National Institutes of Health. Accessed April 14, 2017. http://monitoringthefuture.org/pubs/monographs/mtf-vol2_2013.pdf.

Lake, Peter F., and Joel C. Epstein. 2000. "Modern Liability Rules and Policies Regarding College Student Alcohol Injuries: Reducing High-Risk Alcohol Use through Norms of Shared Responsibility and Environmental Management." *Oklahoma Law Review* 53:611–630.

Lowery, John W., Carolyn J. Palmer, and Donald D. Gehring. 2005. "Policies and Practices of Parental Notification for Student Alcohol Violations." *NASPA Journal* 42:415–429. doi: 10.2202/1949-6605.1533.

National Center on Addiction and Substance Abuse at Columbia University. 2007. "Wasting the Best and the Brightest: Substance Abuse at America's Colleges and Universities." Accessed April 14, 2017. National Center on Addiction and Substance Abuse. http://www.casacolumbia.org/addiction-research/reports/wasting-best-brightest-substance-abuse-americas-colleges-universitys

National Institute on Alcohol Abuse and Alcoholism. 2007. "College Drinking—Changing the Culture." Task Force of the National Advisory Council on Alcohol Abuse and Alcoholism. Accessed April 14, 2017. http://www.collegedrinkingprevention.gov/niaaacollegematerials/taskforce/taskforce_toc.aspx

National Research Council and Institute of Medicine of the National Academies. 2003. "Reducing Underage Drinking: A Collective Responsibility." Accessed April 14, 2017. National Academies (Committee on Developing a Strategy to Reduce and Prevent Underage Drinking). http://www.iom

.edu/~/media/Files/Report%20Files/2003/Reducing-Underage-Drinking
-A-Collective-Responsibility/ReducingUnderageDrinking.pdf

Nelson, Toben F., Timothy S. Naimi, Robert D. Brewer, and Henry Wechsler. 2005. "The State Sets the Rate: The Relationship among State-Specific College Binge Drinking, State Binge Drinking Rates, and Selected State Alcohol Control Policies." *American Journal of Public Health* 95:441–446. doi: 10.2105/AJPH.2004.043810.

Palmer, Carolyn J., Gretchen Lohman, Donald D. Gehring, Sarah Carlson, and Olan Garrett. 2001. "Parental Notification: A New Strategy to Reduce Alcohol Abuse on Campus." *NASPA Journal* 38:372–385. doi: 10.2202/1949-6605.1145.

Peters, Kristen. 2007. "Protecting the Millennial College Student." *Southern California Review of Law and Social Justice* 16:431–468.

Rudolph, Frederick. 1990. *The American College and University: A History.* Athens, GA: University of Georgia Press.

Thelin, John R. 2011. *A History of American Higher Education* (2nd ed.). Baltimore, MD: Johns Hopkins University Press.

U.S. Department of Education. 2012. "The Department of Education's Process for Ensuring Compliance by Institutions of Higher Education with the Drug and Alcohol Prevention Programs" (ED-OIG/I13L0002).

U.S. Department of Health and Human Services, Substance Abuse and Mental Health Services Administration, Center for Behavioral Health Statistics and Quality. 2013. "Results from the 2012 National Survey on Drug Use and Health: Summary of National Findings." Accessed April 14, 2017. http://www.samhsa.gov/data/nsduh/2012summmnatfinddettables/nationalfindings/nsduhresults2012.htm#ch2.9

PART 5

The Impact of the Economy and Financial Policy on Contemporary Universities

CHAPTER NINETEEN

Current Trends and Issues in College and University Endowments

Kenneth E. Redd, Lindsay K. Wayt,
and Lesley McBain

Introduction

This chapter explains the mechanics of endowments (e.g., how they work) and then explores current endowment trends and issues, including policy proposals to institute mandatory endowment spending policies, impose new taxes on endowments, eliminate donor tax deductions for gifts to endowments and other nonprofit charities, and encourage institutions to divest from fossil fuel investments.

Overview

College and university endowments are designed to provide a reliable revenue stream to help institutions meet long-term planning and other needs. However, as college tuition sticker prices have risen, policy makers, students, and many others have asked various questions and expressed concerns about institutions' endowed funds: Should policy makers be doing more to make colleges and universities spend more from their endowments on financial aid for low- and middle-income families? Are colleges and universities investing in socially responsible ways? These questions highlight the complexities of understanding college and university endowments. This chapter first describes how endowments work and the size of endowed funds at higher education institutions. Second, we consider the recent trends and issues facing institutional endowments. We also explore a number of policy options that would affect college and university endowed funds; these include proposals to institute mandatory spending policies on institutions' endowments, tax college and university endowments, eliminate tax deductions for donors to college and university endowments and all other nonprofit charities, and encourage institutions to divest from fossil fuels as part of their mission to serve the public good.

What Are Endowments?

As MaryFrances McCourt (2015), former senior vice president and chief financial officer at Indiana University, explains, an endowment is "a collection of funds provided by donors to secure long-term institutional strategic goals" (7). That is, at nearly all universities, the "endowment" is a collection of hundreds of individual funds that range in size from below $10,000 to more than $1 million. Most of these individual funds have a specific, donor-directed purpose (for example, research, teaching, or student financial aid). These endowed funds represent the institution's promise to donors to use income and investment gains generated by their gifts to support an aspect of the university's mission, usually in perpetuity (that is, forever). Like all nonprofit tax-exempt organizations, educational institutions create endowments and retain their earnings without any tax liability. These endowed funds are designed to provide long-term support for a charitable purpose that would otherwise have to be carried out by federal or state governments.

Endowed funds are normally established by donations provided to higher education institutions from alumni. The donors would, as part of legally binding gift agreements with the institutions, require that any income or investment gains generated by the financial contributions be used for only one specific purpose. That purpose could be student financial aid, faculty research (through "endowed chairs"), facilities maintenance, or any other aspect of the institution's mission.

When choosing to accept donors' endowed gifts, colleges and universities are legally bound to act in the donors' best interests. In nearly all states, schools must follow guidelines established by the Uniform Prudent Management of Institutional Funds Act (UPMIFA), which addresses fiduciary relationships established between donors and nonprofit institutions. UPMIFA sets standards for investment management, establishes fundamental rules for the investment of endowment funds, and provides criteria to guide annual spending distribution decisions (Greene 2016).

Endowments serve a dual purpose; they must generate immediate income that serves current students and faculty, while at the same time they must generate growth over and above any income spent and the rate of inflation so that additional funds are available for future generations. This dual purpose is known as generational equity and, generally, in order to meet this goal, endowment managers must invest the funds so that they generate a 10-year average annual return on investments of 7 percent to 8 percent. This long-term return target includes an annual spending of roughly 4 percent to 5 percent of endowment assets to support financial aid and other campus operations, 1 percent to 2 percent of assets to pay investment management fees and expenses, and 2 percent of growth in the endowment funds to account for inflation, spending, and fees.

Nearly all American colleges and universities have endowed funds, but most are held by a relatively small number of campuses, as Table 19.1 shows. Of the 805 institutions that responded to the 2016 NACUBO[1]-Commonfund

Table 19.1 Number of Respondents* to the 2016 NACUBO-Commonfund Study of Endowments, and Total Endowment Market Values,* by Endowment Size and Institution Type

Type of Institution	Number of Respondents	% of Total	Total Endowment Value ($1,000)*	% of Total
Over $1 Billion	91	11.3%	$382,538,589	74.3%
$501 Million to $1 Billion	75	9.3%	$54,064,633	10.5%
$101 Million to $500 Million	264	32.8%	$60,472,069	11.7%
$51 Million to $100 Million	163	20.3%	$12,078,690	2.3%
$25 Million to $50 Million	121	15.0%	$4,545,969	0.9%
Under $25 Million	91	11.3%	$1,409,177	0.3%
Total (All Institutions)	**805**	**100.0%**	**$515,109,128**	**100.0%**
Type of Institution				
All Public Institutions	**299**	**37.1%**	**$165,100,708**	**32.1%**
Public College, University, or System	*71*	*8.8%*	*$89,525,248*	*17.4%*

(Continued)

Table 19.1   (*Continued*)

Type of Institution	Number of Respondents	% of Total	Total Endowment Value ($1,000)+	% of Total
Institution-Related Foundations	*169*	*21.0%*	*$32,872,251*	*6.4%*
Combined Endowment/ Foundation	*59*	*7.3%*	*$42,703,209*	*8.3%*
All Private Colleges and Universities	**506**	**62.9%**	**$350,008,420**	**67.9%**

Due to rounding, details may not sum to 100%.
*Includes U.S. colleges, universities, and affiliated foundations only.
+Total endowment value as of June 30, 2016.

Source: Reprinted from 2016 Nacubo-Commonfund Study of Endowments © 2016 National Association of College and University Business Officers (NACUBO). Available online at http://www.nacubo.org/Research/NACUBO-Commonfund_Study_of_Endowments/Public_NCSE_Tables.html. Used by permission.

Study of Endowments (NCSE), just 91 schools had total endowment assets of more than $1 billion. But these 91 schools held more than 74 percent of all endowed assets among these higher education institutions. In contrast, nearly 47 percent of schools had endowments of $100 million or below, and these schools collectively accounted for only 3.5 percent of total higher education endowment assets.

Collectively, the colleges and universities that participated in the 2016 NCSE held a total of $515 billion in endowment assets as of June 30, 2016. The average endowment among all the participating schools was $639.9 million while the median was $116.2 million.

Recent Endowment Trends and Developments

Over the past several years, college and university endowments have faced three major challenges: lower investment returns, sharply higher spending in order to support financial aid and other important functions, and more complex investment strategies used to generate greater returns. This section summarizes each of these three major challenges.

Much Lower Returns, Regardless of Endowment Size

Historically, endowments have returned on average about 9 percent (net of investment fees and expenses) each year (Redd 2015). However, in the past two years, annual returns have been far below average. In FY 2015, on average, endowments returned just 2.4 percent, and FY 2016 endowments returned an average –1.9 percent return. Schools with the largest endowments—those with more than $1 billion in endowed assets—reported an average FY 2016 loss of –1.9 percent compared with a 4.3 percent gain in FY 2015. The changes among endowments valued between $501 million and $1 billion were nearly as great (–12.2 percent in 2016 versus a 2.8 percent gain in 2015), while schools with the lowest endowments—total endowed assets of under $25 million—saw their average FY 2016 returns drop to –1.0 percent compared with a gain of 2.3 percent the year prior.

Although the negative one-year returns have captured headlines, the more important number for endowment managers is the 10-year average annual return figures. As we mentioned previously, most schools have to realize a long-range return of between 7 percent and 8 percent in order to achieve their generational equity goal; that is, endowment managers need to meet their return target in order to both provide spending from their endowments to support current students and operations *and* achieve growth after spending, inflation, and fees to support future generations.

In 2016, the overall average 10-year return was 5.0 percent, down from 6.3 percent in FY 2015. The smallest endowments achieved an average FY 2016 long-term return average of only 5 percent.

The across-the-board negative returns of FY 2016 combined with FY 2015's lower returns, if they persist over time, may adversely affect institutions' ability to maintain their endowments' purchasing power. Endowments may become unable to meet their primary function of providing income for today's students and faculty while generating inflation-adjusted growth for future generations.

Endowment Spending Up Sharply

Typically, universities spend about 4 percent of their endowment assets annually to fund student scholarships, faculty research, patient care at university hospitals, community service programs, and many other important aspects of life on college campuses. On average, endowments provided roughly $22 million in funding for school operations in the fiscal year, according to the 2016 NCSE.

Lower endowment returns make it much more difficult to use endowment earnings to fund financial aid and other operations. Nonetheless, because these services are vital to college and university missions, many institutions continue to increase withdrawals from their endowments to support these and other vital programs.

As a result, a large share of NCSE survey participants indicated that they increased their endowment withdrawals for campus-related programs. In FY 2016, 74 percent of schools increased their endowment spending; 82 percent of schools with total endowments over $1 billion raised their endowment draws. In FY 2016, the median increase in spending dollars for those who withdrew additional endowment funds was 8.1 percent. The median spending growth was 7.7 percent for the largest endowments; for the smallest, it was 12.5 percent. (Larger institutions' endowments have much higher dollar amounts, so any increases in spending amounts will be lower in percentage terms for larger endowments than for smaller ones.)

Rising endowment spending has benefited student scholarships and other programs on campuses. It has also been critical for stabilizing colleges' funding at a time when other revenue sources have declined.

Endowments have provided schools with the flexibility and resources they have needed to preserve access to college for students and to support cutting-edge research by faculty. Endowment funds remain a key ingredient for schools to meet their goals now and in the future. However, at the same time, as returns have been lower, schools may be spending from the principal balances of their endowed funds (that is, they are not just spending investment gains, they are also spending funds from their original endowed gifts). Such spending, called "eating into the corpus" of endowments, would make it much more difficult for schools to rely on endowed assets in the future.

More Complex Investment Portfolios

Lower investment returns have also influenced endowment managers' decisions to adopt new ways to invest their assets. In fiscal year 1974, the first year of the NACUBO endowment study series, the typical endowment portfolio had 60 percent of its funds invested in U.S. and foreign stocks, 22 percent in bonds (U.S. and non-U.S.), and 18 percent in cash equivalents and other asset types. Less than 1 percent of assets were invested in "alternative" investment vehicles, such as hedge funds, private equity, and commodities. By 2016, however, portfolios on average had 29 percent of total assets in alternative strategies, 48 percent in stocks, 16 percent in bonds, and just 7 percent in cash.

Although schools with both large and small endowment sizes have adopted alternative strategies, the largest endowments have been the most likely to use these investment vehicles. In FY 2016, on a "dollar-weighted" basis (that is, data weighted by size of schools' total endowment assets), institutions with total endowment funds of more than $1 billion had 58 percent of their endowed assets invested in alternative strategies, compared with 10 percent at schools with endowments below $25 million.

Many investment analysts believe their alternative strategies benefit most schools, regardless of endowment size, because they provide added opportunities for generating higher returns with lower overall investment risk. "Over the years, expert investment managers have more successfully employed venture capital, private equity, and hedge fund strategies, as well as investments in real estate, oil and gas, and other commodities," says John S. Griswold, former executive director for Commonfund Institute, NACUBO's partner in the annual NCSE endowment study (Redd 2015, 32).

However, more complex investment strategies have some disadvantages. They potentially drive up investment management costs because universities have to hire higher priced consultants in order to gain access to these strategies. Additionally, as the lower returns since the 2008–2009 financial crisis demonstrate, many alternatives can have sharp declines that cause schools to incur steep losses. For example, in FY 2016, due to the decline in oil and gas prices, endowments' investments in energy and natural resources suffered a –7.5 percent return, according to the 2016 NACUBO-Commonfund Study of Endowments.

Therefore, endowment managers' greatest future challenge may be to find new investment opportunities in an era where even alternative strategies may not help performance. "In the past, endowment managers have been able to deploy more of their assets into alternatives to help generate higher returns," Griswold points out. "Safe harbors may be harder to find in the future" (Redd 2015, 34).

Proposed Reforms to Endowments

Despite trends in college and university endowments over the past decade—lower investment returns coupled with higher spending—many policy makers are calling for reforms regarding endowment policies. Reform proposals relate to college access and affordability, equity between high- and low-income individuals in treatment of tax deductions for charitable giving, and the role of higher education institutions in practicing socially responsible investment strategies. In this section, we will consider various proposals that would institute mandatory spending policies on institutions' endowments, tax college and university endowments, eliminate tax deductions for those who donate to college and university endowments and all other nonprofit organizations, and divest from fossil fuels as a way to reduce the effects of climate change.

Endowments and College Affordability

Because the first three proposals discussed all relate to the general idea of reforming college and university endowment policies to address the issue of college affordability, we first consider the pros and cons of the concept as a whole. We then consider the specifics of each proposal—including details about the proposed policy reforms and specific pros and cons cited by various stakeholders.

These three proposals (mandatory spending, taxing endowments, and eliminating the charitable tax deduction for donors) have similar roots, each stemming from calls for higher education institutions to use more of their endowments to address concerns about the rising cost of college. As Table 19.1 indicates, 91 higher education institutions have total endowment assets over $1 billion, and many of these reform proposals would be aimed at these schools.

Most of the schools with large endowments tend to be doctoral-granting research-intensive universities with very high sticker prices. According to the College Board's 2016a *Trends in College Pricing* report, the average annual price of tuition, fees, room, and board for undergraduates attending full-time at a private nonprofit research university reached $54,560 in 2016–2017; at public research institutions, average annual published price reached $21,350. Students and their families, particularly those from low- and middle-income backgrounds, have thus perceived college affordability slipping away, at least in regard to published sticker prices. Yet the College Board's 2016b *Trends in Student Aid* report shows that both private and public doctoral research universities provide the largest average amounts of institutional grant aid to low- and moderate-income students.

Nonetheless, this dichotomy of wealthy institutions with large endowments and high sticker prices has led policy makers to scrutinize the role of colleges and universities in keeping college affordable for low- and middle-income students and their families. As congress member Rep. Tom Reed of New York posited, "It is a disservice to the next generation of students that colleges continue to stock pile large sums of money that are tax exempt, and for which donors receive tax deductions, while tuition costs continue to rise. We need to shed some sunshine on how endowments are being used and really get to the bottom of why the cost of college continues to skyrocket" (Reed 2016).

These comments and similar sentiments led the House Ways and Means Committee to hold a hearing on tax-exempt university endowments in fall 2016, during which concerns about rising sticker costs were expressed and policy makers questioned whether institutions were doing enough to use their endowments to address these concerns. This was not the first hearing of this nature; a similar hearing was held in fall 2015 and another in 2008 prior to the recession. In the 2016 hearing, some committee members questioned institutions' use of endowment funds and depicted at least some institutions as the "haves" that spend money on luxuries such as climbing walls and lazy rivers, pay exorbitant salaries to athletic coaches, and contribute to administrative bloat—with some institutions paying seven-figure presidential salaries.

However, as many higher education policy analysts often point out, the dichotomy of wealthy institutions with endowments worth billions of dollars that also charge ever-rising sticker prices cannot be considered without further context. For example, Sandy Baum (Hearing/Baum 2016), a senior fellow at the Urban Institute, stated in her congressional hearing testimony that state funding of public colleges has declined by almost 30 percent on a per-student basis over the past decade. This decline can be linked to college and university decisions to both increase sticker prices and withdraw more funds from their endowments.

In addition, previous congressional testimony provided by MaryFrances McCourt (Hearing/McCourt 2015) demonstrated that although endowment spending may not always be directly applied to institutional student aid (although large amounts are, especially at institutions with larger endowments), spending not specifically directed to aid often is used to fund institutional operational budgets. This use also cuts down on costs that would otherwise be incurred by students and their families.

It also must be noted that although many universities support efforts to increase financial aid for low- and moderate-income students, they must follow UPMIFA and donors' wishes when they accept endowed gifts. Donors often direct their financial contributions to support teaching, research, libraries, public service, academic facilities maintenance, and other aspects of campus life not directly related to student scholarships. Thus, using endowed funds dedicated to other priorities to increase spending on financial aid would potentially violate UPMIFA and other legally binding donor gift agreements.

Mandatory Spending

Under current federal law, private nonprofit foundations are required to spend 5 percent of their assets to support charitable causes. College and university endowments, however, currently do not have a minimum required spending rate. Thus, one specific reform that has been proposed is a mandatory spending policy for college and university endowments, similar to the 5 percent payout requirement that currently exists for private nonprofit foundations.

Proposals for minimum spending rates have been around for a number of years. In 2008, Senator Charles Grassley of Iowa, along with Senator Max Baucus, then chairman of the Senate Finance Committee, wrote to 136 colleges and universities with endowments of $500 million or more requesting information about endowment payouts. In a "Point of View" piece in *The Chronicle of Higher Education*, Grassley indicated, "Legislation to require the wealthiest institutions to have an annual 5 percent endowment payout remains a possibility."

Although no specific congressional proposals for a mandatory spending rate surfaced at the time, likely because of the economic recession, and because many institutions have voluntarily increased endowment payouts since 2008, Grassley and others have continued to advocate for mandatory spending requirements for college and university endowments—at least for institutions with the largest amounts of endowed funds. Some other spending rate proposals that have been discussed include tying a payout requirement to investment earnings (which would allow more flexibility in down years), having a payout requirement determined on a rolling basis (for example, 5 percent over a 3-year period rather than a strict annual 5 percent payout requirement), or linking the spending percentage to other metrics (for example, tuition levels or number of Pell Grant recipients). These policies could apply to all college and university endowments or only those that meet a certain threshold of wealth (Sherlock et al. 2015).

Those in favor of a mandatory spending policy have argued that it would both make payout requirements consistent across all endowment size categories and would make colleges and universities do their part in using tax-exempt funds to support students. As Senator Grassley (2010) said, "The thinking is that since these organizations are allowed to accumulate money tax-free for their charitable purpose, they should have to spend at least a small amount fulfilling that purpose."

On the other hand, institutions already use much more than a "small amount" of their endowed funds to fulfill their charitable purposes. In fiscal 2016, institutions withdrew $16.7 billion from their endowments to support financial aid, research, and other aspects of their missions, according to the NCSE. From 2015 to 2016, nearly three quarters of endowment study participants increased their endowment spending amounts; the median spending increase was nearly 9 percent.

A number of organizations have expressed concerns about institutions' endowment spending rates despite these spending increases. A study conducted by The Education Trust considered the spending rates of 67 private nonprofit universities that have total endowment assets of $500 million or more and found that the median spending rates among these institutions in fiscal years 2012 and 2013 were 4.6 and 4.9 percent, respectively (Nichols and Santos 2016). The authors of this report estimated that if all these schools increased their spending rate to 5 percent, an additional $418 million in endowed funds would have been generated for spending, enough to cover the tuition of an additional 2,376 low-income students.

However, the Education Trust study also revealed weaknesses in using a mandatory payout rate for college and university endowments. Their calculations indicating the increased numbers of low-income students whose tuition could be covered assumed that none of these funds were restricted for other uses by donors. However, as the 2015 NACUBO-Commonfund Study of Endowments demonstrates, 90 percent of the new gifts to endowments in FY 2015 had donor restrictions—which suggests a minimum payout requirement would not necessarily be directed toward student financial aid. UPMIFA and donor gift agreements may require that funds drawn from particular endowed funds go toward faculty research or maintenance of a particular building on campus, rather than for student financial assistance.

Even if one assumed that an increase in spending on operational costs from endowments as a result of a mandatory payout rate would decrease overall costs to students, this still may not hold true across all campuses. If the policy implemented does not consider endowment size, there is a concern about whether a mandatory spending minimum is appropriate for all institutions, and whether some institutions would view 5 percent as a ceiling and not a floor (Sherlock et al. 2015)—meaning the policy may actually encourage some institutions to decrease spending from endowment funds while at the same time financially straining other, less endowed institutions.

In addition, mandatory payout rates, if applied to all institutions without regard to endowment size, could disparately affect institutions' spending. As Wolf (2011) noted, "Wealthy universities are the exception, not the norm: they represent a tiny fraction of the institutions in the country and educate a tiny fraction of the country's students" (606). When Bennett (2015) considered the potential impacts of a mandatory 8 percent spending rate, he noted vast differences on per-student spending based on institutions' endowment sizes. Although per-student spending could increase, on average, by $13,000, this figure is vastly skewed by institutions with larger endowments. For more than 10 percent of schools, spending increases would amount to less than $1,000 per student, and at some institutions spending per undergraduate would only increase by about $200.

These findings suggest that even if endowments did not have donor restrictions, a mandatory spending policy may have limited impact on per-student spending for low- and middle-income students. In addition, students from low- and middle-income families who attend the wealthiest institutions already receive generous support. A number of public and private colleges with large endowments already have policies in place to ensure that students whose family income is $60,000 or less get scholarships that cover the total costs of tuition, fees, room, and board, as Wolf (2011) points out. These scholarship programs are often funded in whole or in part by endowment income. Mandatory spending policies thus may not generate substantially more financial aid dollars for these targeted populations.

A Tax on Endowments

Some believe that endowments have become too large—that is, they are "hoarding" cash that could be used to achieve other societal goals. Some members of Congress, such as Rep. Peter Roskam of Illinois and Rep. Tom Reed of New York, have argued that college costs to students and families have increased while wealthy institutions maintain a tax benefit. As such, these representatives believe a tax on large endowments could be used to generate additional revenue without doing any harm to campuses' educational quality.

As with mandatory payout requirements, there are various ideas on how to tax college and university endowments. Under one option, a tax on endowments would apply to universities with larger total funds (i.e., those with endowments over either $500 million or $1 billion), or only to institutions that have recently raised tuition. This tax could be similar to the current tax on net investment income of private foundations, or only endowment earnings could be subject to a tax—similar to the current maximum rate of 35 percent imposed on tax-exempt entities for unrelated business income tax (UBIT) (Sherlock et al. 2015). Another proposal would apply an endowment tax as a penalty on institutions that do not meet a certain spending threshold or certain spending criteria (such as spending below a specified amount on student financial aid). However, it is unclear whether funds generated from these taxes would be earmarked for student aid or if they would be treated as general funds that could be used for other, non-education-related purposes.

One policy proposal based on collaborative work by the American Institutes for Research (AIR) and the Nexus Research and Policy Center was designed specifically to address concerns of inequalities in taxpayer subsidies for institutions. Mark Schneider of AIR explained, "Since endowments are not taxed, students at well-endowed private schools enjoy public subsidies that are far greater than those for students at the public two- and four-year schools responsible for educating most working- and middle-class Americans" (Hearing/Schneider 2016, 3). The groups propose that Congress levy an excise tax (at rates of 0.5 percent to 2.0 percent, varying based on endowment size) on endowments that are more than $500 million. Their proposal also includes language that would allow the tax to be offset each year based on the amount an institution allocates toward financial aid for students eligible to receive federal Pell Grants, a program designed to provide financial aid to students from the lowest-income families. Additionally, the AIR study proposes that revenues raised from this tax *only* be used to benefit students at community colleges; money would be made available in the forms of grants for qualified purposes at community colleges. This proposal, in a sense, reallocates wealth *internally* by encouraging more institutional grant aid awards to low-income students and *externally* by reallocating money from wealthier universities to less wealthy colleges that currently receive less subsidy support but have a larger focus on access to higher education for low-income students.

Another proposal, from Rep. Reed, aims to increase the amount of endowment income devoted to student financial aid. Reed's proposal, which as of this writing has yet to be introduced as legislation, would require institutions with more than $1 billion in endowed funds to use at least 25 percent of their endowments' investment gains to lower the cost of college for students from middle- and lower-income families. Under Reed's plan, higher education institutions that do not meet this spending requirement would be subject to a tax of at least 30 percent against their investment income, and (for continued violations) the loss of eligibility to receive any charitable contributions.

Proposals to tax endowments are not without drawbacks. Notably, there is no guarantee that the funds from these taxes would be earmarked specifically to address concerns about college affordability. And because a tax of any amount would lower endowment current values, institutions would have to lower their total endowment spending amounts in order to meet their intergenerational equity goals. One study estimated that wealthier institutions in particular would see declines in endowment payments—with schools in the third quartile seeing a 2.6 percent decrease and those in the top quartile seeing a 17 percent drop in endowment spending dollars (Milton and Ehrenberg 2014).

Further, as MaryFrances McCourt noted in her testimony for the Ways and Means hearing in 2015, these proposals could adversely affect institutions' abilities to address other funding concerns. "The single most challenging financial constraint we've faced in recent years at Indiana University is the fact that the state has not been able to appropriate adequate funds to keep up with inflation and enrollment growth," McCourt said (2). Endowments are one tool institutions have to address declining state support, and a tax on endowments could undermine this purpose.

Eliminate Tax Deductions for Contributions to Endowments

In addition to taxing endowments, some policy makers and education analysts have also proposed eliminating the deductibility of financial contributions to college endowments as a way to create greater fairness and make the federal tax code less confusing. According to the 2016 NCSE, colleges and universities received roughly $7.7 billion in new gifts and donations to their endowments; about 60 percent of these gifts went to schools with endowments of more than $1 billion. Under current tax law, such gifts are provided tax free to the universities because they are tax-exempt entities. The people who donate funds or financial assets (such as stocks and bonds) to these endowments can claim a deduction on their federal tax returns for at least a portion of the total amount donated.

Critics of large higher education endowments claim that these tax benefits provide an unfair advantage to the wealthy. One study found that, on average, college and universities with endowments of more than $1 billion receive a tax subsidy of $41,100 per student, while community colleges receive an average subsidy of just $5,100 per student (Klor de Alva and Schneider 2015). This subsidy, the authors claim, flows mostly to students from wealthy families, who are much more likely to attend schools with large endowments and are more likely to have made large donations to private schools that qualify for tax exemptions. Wealthy schools also have additional tax incentives that help them achieve greater wealth because, as nonprofits, their investment gains are not taxed, which allows them to keep more of their growth (Weissmann 2015).

Schools with large endowments counter that such arguments overlook or ignore the fact that investment gains used by higher education institutions are used to meet various charitable purposes, such as providing financial aid for low-income students and health care and other services to the indigent in their communities. And, as economist Ronald Ehrenberg (2013) points out, many wealthy private colleges already make voluntary payments in lieu of taxes (PILOTs) to their local communities; these PILOTs are in addition to the economic development, employee and employer taxes, and other economic gains generated by private higher education institutions.

Nonetheless, policy makers have expressed concern about the amount of tax benefits given to nonprofit institutions generally, and the amount of tax savings provided to wealthier Americans specifically due to the current treatment of charitable deductions. The Trump administration has thus proposed limiting all itemized deductions, including those for charitable donations, to $100,000 for individuals and $200,000 for married couples.

Although such a limit could increase tax equity by raising the effective amount paid in income taxes by the wealthy, it could also severely limit the funds colleges, universities, and other nonprofits would be able to raise each year. How higher education generally, and wealthy institutions specifically, would meet additional fund-raising challenges if donations were no longer tax deductible is not clear.

Divestment of Fossil Fuels

In addition to the tax and mandatory spending issues, many campuses have faced demands from students and others to divest their endowments from investments in oil, gas, coal, and other fossil fuel companies. Fossil fuels have been identified by the Union of Concerned Scientists (n.d.) as one of the leading causes of global warming and climate change. Student groups believe campus endowments should divest from all stock, bond, and other fossil fuel investments as a way to reduce global warming and improve the environment. However, many endowment managers believe these restrictions will be very costly and will hurt long-term investment performance.

According to the 2016 NCSE, direct energy and natural resources investments accounted for about 6 percent of the $515 billion in college and university endowments (an unknown percentage of assets were indirectly invested in energy-related investments that were commingled with other funds). Most of these energy investments were in oil, gas, and other fossil fuels; a very small share was invested in wind, solar, and other non–fossil fuel sources.

The American student movement to convince colleges to sell their fossil fuel assets was broadly organized in 2012 by the advocacy group 350.org, an international environmental advocacy organization, through its "Fossil Free" campaign. This campaign calls for schools at all levels, religious institutions, governments, and other nonprofit organizations to eliminate any investments in fossil fuel companies from their endowments, foundations, and pension portfolios. Harvard University, Swarthmore College, and many other schools with large endowments have seen student petitions, sit-ins, teach-ins, and other actions that seek to convince campus leaders to commit to a timetable for reducing oil and other energy-related holdings.

Student support for divestment is widespread. The divestment campaign at Harvard University, for instance, received 72 percent of support from the student body, according to *The Nation* (Welton 2012). Students argue that the dangers of climate change are real; that the oil, coal, and gas industries have not done enough to limit their greenhouse gas emissions; and that it is hypocritical of nonprofit higher education institutions to receive benefits from fossil fuels that threaten the health and future well-being of their students. Or, as Bill McKibben (2013), best-selling author and environmental activist, put it: "The logic of divestment couldn't be simpler: if it's wrong to wreck the climate, it's wrong to profit from that wreckage . . . The hope is that divestment is one way to weaken those [fossil fuel] companies—financially, but even more politically. If institutions like colleges and churches turn them into pariahs, their two-decade old chokehold on politics in DC and other capitals will start to slip."

Some institutions have partially or fully divested from energy-related investments as a result of these student campaigns. Stanford University, for instance, announced in 2014 that it would eliminate all coal-related holdings from its endowment (Stanford News 2014). Yale University announced that it had eliminated $10 million in investments from two publicly traded fossil fuel producers (Schick 2016). But for the most part, universities with large endowments plan to continue fossil fuel investments, arguing that complete divestment would harm endowment performance in both the short and long term, and that any investment restrictions would harm their ability to achieve generational equity.

Swarthmore College, which declined to divest from fossil fuels in 2015, stated it "manages the endowment to yield the best long term financial results, rather than to pursue other social objectives" (Kemp 2015). The institutions also pointed out that limiting access to investments outside of energy would be very costly. Swarthmore College estimates its endowment would lose $10 million to $20 million each year if full divestment were instituted, while complete divestment would cost Yale University's endowment roughly $51 million annually (DivestmentFacts 2016).

How each campus decides on divestment could have broad implications for future asset allocation and investment returns. These divestment decisions, as well as policy makers' actions on mandatory spending policies, taxes, and limitations on tax benefits for charitable gifts, also could have wide-ranging implications for college students and faculty. These and other proposals to adjust campus endowed funds will likely continue into the future.

Note

1. National Association of College and University Business Officers

References

Bennett, Daniel. September 20, 2015. "Another Bad Idea—Mandatory Endowment Spending." *Minding the Campus*, accessed August 2, 2016: http://www.mindingthecampus.org/2015/09/another-bad-idea-mandatory-endowment-spending/

College Board. 2016a. *Trends in College Pricing 2016*. Washington, DC: College Board, accessed November 9, 2016: https://trends.collegeboard.org/sites/default/files/2016-trends-college-pricing-web_0.pdf

College Board. 2016b. *Trends in Student Aid 2016*. Washington, DC: College Board, accessed November 9, 2016: https://trends.collegeboard.org/sites/default/files/2016-trends-student-aid.pdf

DivestmentFacts.com. April 13, 2016. "5 Things to Know about Yale's 'Divestment' Announcement." *DivestmentFacts* (blog), accessed November 8, 2016: http://divestmentfacts.com/5-things-to-know-about-yales-divestment-announcement/

Ehrenberg, Ronald G. September 8, 2013. "Should Colleges and Universities Be Taxed?" *Minding the Campus*, accessed August 2, 2016: http://www.mindingthecampus.org/2013/09/should_colleges_and_universiti/

Grassley, Senator Chuck. May 29, 2008. "Wealthy Colleges Must Make Themselves More Affordable." Chuck Grassley: United States Senator for Iowa, accessed August 2, 2016: http://www.grassley.senate.gov/news/news-releases/wealthy-colleges-must-make-themselves-more-affordable

Grassley, Senator Chuck. January 27, 2010. "Grassley: Students, Families Shouldn't Bear Brunt of College Endowment Losses." Chuck Grassley: United States Senator for Iowa, accessed August 2, 2016: http://www.grassley.senate.gov/news/news-releases/grassley-students-families-shouldn%E2%80%99t-bear-brunt-college-endowment-losses

Greene, R. L. 2016. College and University Business Administration (CUBA). 2016 Endowment Management. NACUBO: National Association of College and University Business Officers, accessed August 2, 2016: http://www.nacubo.org/Products/Online_Publications/CUBA_7.html

Hearing on Rising Costs of Higher Education and Tax Policy, House Committee on Ways and Means. October 7, 2015 (Serial No. 114-OS08) (statement of MaryFrances McCourt), accessed October 14, 2016: https://waysand means.house.gov/event/39840295/

Hearing on Tax-Exempt College and University Endowments, House Committee on Ways and Means. September 13, 2016 (statement of Dr. Sandy Baum), accessed October 14, 2016: https://waysandmeans.house.gov/event /hearing-tax-exempt-college-university-endowments/

Hearing on Tax-Exempt College and University Endowments, House Committee on Ways and Means. September 13, 2016 (statement of Mark Schneider), accessed October 14, 2016: https://waysandmeans.house.gov/event /hearing-tax-exempt-college-university-endowments/

Kemp, Gil. May 2, 2015. "Sustainability and Investment Policy." Swarthmore College Board of Managers, accessed November 14, 2016: http://www .swarthmore.edu/board-managers/sustainability-and-investment-policy

Klor de Alva, Jorge, and Mark Schneider. 2015. *Rich Schools, Poor Students: Tapping Large University Endowments to Improve Student Outcomes*. San Francisco, CA: Nexus, accessed October 14, 2016: http://nexusresearch.org /wp-content/uploads/2015/06/Rich_Schools_Poor_Students.pdf

McKibben, Bill. February 22, 2013. "The Case for Fossil-Fuel Divestment." *Rolling Stone*, accessed November 14, 2016: http://www.rollingstone.com /politics/news/the-case-for-fossil-fuel-divestment-20130222

Milton, Ross T., and Ronald G. Ehrenberg. 2014. "University Endowment Growth: Assessing Policy Proposals." ILR School, Cornell University, accessed August 2, 2016: https://www.ilr.cornell.edu/sites/ilr.cornell .edu/files/WP162.pdf

NACUBO and Commonfund Institute. February 2016. 2015 NACUBO-Commonfund Study of Endowments. Washington, DC.

NACUBO and Commonfund Institute. February 2017. 2016 NACUBO-Commonfund Study of Endowments. Washington, DC.

Nichols, Andrew Howard, and Jose Luis Santos. 2016. "A Glimpse inside the Coffers: Endowment Spending at Wealthy Colleges and Universities." Washington, DC: Education Trust, accessed August 4, 2016: https:// edtrust.org/wp-content/uploads/2016/08/EndowmentsPaper.pdf

Redd, Kenneth E. November 2015. "Forever Funds." *Business Officer Magazine*, accessed November 14, 2016: http://www.nacubo.org/Business_Officer _Magazine/Magazine_Archives/November_2015/Forever_Funds.html

Reed, Tom. February 29, 2016. "Reed Demands Lower College Costs." Tom Reed: 23rd District of New York, accessed on October 14, 2016: https://reed .house.gov/media-center/press-releases/reed-demands-lower-college -costs

Schick, Finnegan. April 12, 2016. "Yale to Partially Divest from Fossil Fuels." Yale News (blog), accessed November 14, 2016: http://yaledailynews .com/blog/2016/04/12/yale-begins-divestment-from-fossil-fuels/

Sherlock, Molly F., Jane G. Gravelle, Margot L. Crandall-Hollick, and Jeffrey M. Stupak. December 2, 2015. "College and University Endowments: Overview and Tax Policy Options." Congressional Research Service, accessed August 2, 2016: https://www.fas.org/sgp/crs/misc/R44293.pdf

Stanford News. May 6, 2014. "Stanford to Divest from Coal Companies." Stanford News, accessed November 14, 2016: http://news.stanford.edu /news/2014/may/divest-coal-trustees-050714.html

Union of Concerned Scientists. n.d. "Global Warming 101." accessed October 17, 2016: http://www.ucsusa.org/global_warming/global_warming_101#.WC t6udUrJph

Weissmann, Jordan. Sept. 7, 2015. "Is It Time to Tax Harvard's Endowment?" Slate, accessed August 4, 2016: http://www.slate.com/articles/business /moneybox/2015/09/harvard_yale_stanford_endowments_is_it_time _to_tax_them.html

Welton, Alli. November 20, 2012. "Harvard Students Vote 72 Percent Support for Fossil Fuel Divestment." The Nation, accessed October 17, 2016: https://www.thenation.com/article/harvard-students-vote-72-percent -support-fossil-fuel-divestment/

Wolf, Alexander M. 2011. "The Problems with Payouts: Assessing the Proposals for a Mandatory Distribution Requirement for University Endowments." *Harvard Journal on Legislation* 48:591–622.

Further Reading

Commonfund Institute. May 31, 2016. Striking the Balance: A Fiduciary Approach to Risk and Investment Policy. Wilton, CT.

CHAPTER TWENTY

Incorporating Innovation and Entrepreneurship in STEM Programs: The Challenges of Universities as Engines of Economic Growth

Beth-Anne Schuelke-Leech

Introduction

Research universities are viewed by many policy makers, business leaders, and university executives as a key driver in economic growth. Research commercialization, university start-ups, spinoffs, and new business ventures, as well as technology transfer to existing businesses, are all viewed as essential components to economic prosperity and job creation. STEM programs are the target of new innovation and entrepreneurship programs. These changes are challenging the existing norms of higher education. This chapter explores the issue of incorporating innovation and entrepreneurship into STEM programs and the challenges that it creates.

Overview

Technology transfer between the public sector and industry, research commercialization, and entrepreneurship are often viewed as the key to economic development and use of new knowledge. The U.S. federal government has pushed for increased use of government-funded inventions and discoveries, from both government and university labs. In recent years, there has been widespread interest in understanding the knowledge creation and dissemination processes that occur in a country's innovation system. To understand these processes, it is necessary to understand the institutions in which they occur and the actions and values of the individuals within them. From a broad perspective, a nation's innovation system is composed of a complex array of organizations—small businesses, large industrial organizations, universities, start-up companies, research centers, joint ventures, think tanks, government laboratories, financial institutions, private investors, and venture capitalists (Crow and Bozeman 1998). These institutions interact and collaborate for the purpose of generating, disseminating, and utilizing knowledge and technology (OECD 1996). The goal of these activities is to promote economic activity and prosperity through the transformation of scientific knowledge into commercial products.

This innovation system has undergone profound changes in the past 30 years, which has given rise to new institutions and new activities. With the adoption of Vannevar Bush's proposal for post–World War II research and development (R&D) funding in *Science, the Endless Frontier* (Bush 1945), research universities became central to innovation in the United States. Private firms focused on applied research, while universities focused on building foundational, curiosity-driven knowledge. Government laboratories covered a range of activities, consistently focused on strategic or classified research projects. The vast majority of the funding for scientific research was through the public sector.

Declining national competitiveness in the 1970s and 1980s in the global manufacturing sector pushed policy makers to look for ways to assist industry. Numerous initiatives were launched to try to link universities and industrial innovation and to encourage collaboration between the sectors (Mowery and Sampat 2001; Mowery et al. 1999). Legislation[1] was enacted to permit contractors of federally funded research to patent and license inventions in the hopes that they would be in a better position for exploiting scientific discoveries. Government and university labs alike were viewed by policy makers as "treasure chests"—repositories—of technology and knowledge that had direct applicability to private industry (Ham and Mowery 1998). At the same time, citizens began to question the public expenditures and sought accountability and minimization of government spending (Schein 1996). Public research labs have faced additional pressures from elected officials who sought to reduce public expenditures by reducing funding. With an ability to patent and license their intellectual property, university administrators began to look to the work done in their labs as holding potential for substantial revenues—a treasure chest of another sort.

The rise of commercialization in public labs occurred at the same time that there was a decrease in corporate research and commercialization. For much of the 20th century, U.S. firms kept strategic R&D in house (Mowery 1983). Faced with declining competitiveness, rising costs, and resource shortages, private sector organizations in the 1970s and 1980s began to look to improve efficiencies and operations.

Rising costs of production, increased pace of technology development and diffusion, and intensified globalization of markets have changed the nature of competition for most businesses (Bettis and Hitt 1995; Johnson 2006; Porter 1986). It is difficult for most organizations to operate in complete isolation. Even small businesses are affected by the costs of manufacturing overseas. Businesses have tried to reduce their R&D expenditures; many firms eliminated in-house basic research aimed at creating knowledge that directly fed into their commercial entities (Crow and Bozeman 1998; Johnson 2006). At the same time, the pace of business and of knowledge creation made it essential for firms to acquire new knowledge, technologies, and processes to incorporate into their operations and products. While businesses have been divesting themselves of unnecessary internal expenditures and outsourcing everything from production to accounting to reduce costs, they have also been looking for ways to integrate external sources of knowledge and technology (Cockburn 2005) because there is an increasing need to be innovative (Johnson 2006); and the complexity of knowledge needed for the design, development, and manufacturing of products makes it impossible to have it in-house (Brusoni, Prencipe, and Pavitt 2001).

Coupled together, these factors led to an increase in the pressures for both private firms and public research organizations to work together. University–industry collaborations have become crucial to successful global competition and new product development for many firms. Mansfield (1998) calculated that 10 percent of all new products and processes introduced in the drug and medical device, information processing, chemical, electrical, instruments, metals, and machinery industries could not have been developed without academic research. University–industry collaborations have brought biotechnology, lasers, recombinant DNA, liquid crystals, synthetic polymers, and a large array of computer technologies to the marketplace (Owen-Smith and Powell 2003; Rosenbloom and Spencer 1996). Innovation, technology transfer, and university–industry collaborations have become almost synonymous with global competitiveness and economic development. At the same time, entrepreneurship has become the cornerstone of job creation and new industries. Universities have increasingly been expected to create entrepreneurial environments, in which students and faculty can generate new start-ups and commercialize their research (see, for example, Christensen and Eyring 2011; Thorp and Goldstein 2010; U.S. Department of Commerce 2013).

This chapter discusses these changes and explores the challenges that they present to colleges and universities.

Recent Trends and Developments

Scientific research and development has become a major national policy focus (NRC 1999). Science and technology are viewed as essential to creating sustained economic growth and improving the living standards of U.S. citizens (NRC 1999). Science has been tied to economic development and global competitiveness (Augustine 2005; NRC 1999). Universities have become a major focal point, since a substantial amount of publicly funded research and development is performed in universities. In a survey conducted of manufacturing firms, Cohen, Florida, and Walsh found that two-thirds of the firms believed that academic research was at least "moderately important" to their own internal R&D efforts (Cohen, Florida, and Walsh 1996). In addition, university research has proven essential for product development in some industries, such as the pharmaceuticals and biotechnology industries (Cohen et al. 1998). Governments in many countries now view universities as key drivers of economic growth and critical for achieving global economic competitiveness (Laredo and Mustar 2001).

Universities in turn have been encouraged to improve their connections and research relevance to industry in order to advance commercial technologies and products (Cohen et al. 1998; Lee 1997). Thus, science and technology policy in the United States in the past 40 years has aimed to promote collaboration between universities and industry through legislative reforms (e.g., Bayh-Dole Act, Economic Recovery Tax Act of 1981 and 1986, National Cooperative Research Act of 1984), subsidized partnerships (Behrens and Gray 2001), funding requirements (Landry and Amara 1998), and new research institutions (Cohen, Florida, and Goe 1994). These policies are based on the assumption that collaboration results in improved transfer of scientific knowledge and increased economic competitiveness through the development of innovative technologies (Behrens and Gray 2001; Fluckiger 2006), while decreasing the overall costs of innovation (Katz and Martin 1997) by allowing facility and equipment sharing, as well as reducing duplication of research efforts.

Organizational culture plays a critical role in establishing the standards and conventions for behavior for the members of an organization or group. The concept of culture was originally adopted by organizational researchers from cultural anthropologists who were studying whole societies (Schein

1996). Organizational culture became a useful concept for researchers trying to explain the relatively poor performance of American companies compared to Japanese ones (Schein 1996). Researchers proposed that the strength of the shared conventions in Japanese organizations led to superior performance in achieving organizational goals (Denison 1990; Knapp 1998; Lai and Lee 2007; Ogbonna and Harris 2001). Thus, organizational culture can provide a competitive advantage (Lai and Lee 2007; Scholz 1987). At the same time, a culture can provide obstacles to organizational change and reform.

Universities, private firms, and government operations each have distinct cultures that determine how things get done and how success is measured. Private sector companies are primarily driven by owners seeking to maximize their return on investments. The profits of a firm are routinely distributed to the owners, who have assumed the risk of the success or failure of the business. Performance is measured quantitatively, typically through profits, market share, share price, and earnings (Frumkin and Galaskiewicz 2004). Businesses must necessarily focus on short-term financial success and tangible goals (Mueller 2006), as there is no guaranteed long-term funding or cash flow. The focus is on getting readily applicable knowledge that will assist the organization in meeting its goals (Mueller 2006). Knowledge is thus viewed as an input to production (Brusoni and Prencipe 2006). The cost and timeliness of the knowledge is crucial. Management is also viewed as a productive input (Perry and Rainey 1988), contributing to the efficient use of resources.

Due to their profit maximization imperative, businesses will seek to acquire their resources as efficiently as possible. More successful firms will build relationships with their suppliers and customers to improve knowledge transfer and efficiencies (Schraeder, Tears, and Jordan 2005), including to university researchers and students when these are viewed as production inputs. Innovation and research is often done on a team (i.e., collaborative basis) (Chesbrough 2003; Hargadon 2003; Van de Ven et al. 1999), both for timeliness and enhanced results.

Universities, on the other hand, are not beholden to a profit motive or limited by the need for timely results in the same way businesses are. They are loosely coupled bureaucracies, with shared decision making power and poorly defined power structures (Cohen and March 1974). University organizations can seem much more disorganized and difficult to navigate and change.

Researchers within the public science system primarily undertake research for the purpose of knowledge creation and dissemination, mainly through publication of the results (Bozeman and Boardman 2003; Whitley 2003). Researchers follow their own research agenda. They are primarily motivated by the pursuit of their own and their organization's reputation and prestige within their academic disciplines (Link and Siegel 2005; Whitley 2003), with little concern for the commercial potential or postdiscovery development. Most researchers have little patience with administration and accounting procedures (Bozeman and Boardman 2003). Tenured faculty members enjoy lifetime employment (Dill 1982) and are not generally concerned with the overall administration of the institution.

Though technology transfer and intellectual property exploitation have become part of the mission of many universities, university researchers and administrators typically have little incentive to accelerate the commercialization process. Researchers are not driven to meet externally imposed deadlines, nor is scientific discovery a process that necessarily lends itself to a prescribed timeline (Kantorovich 1993; Kantorovich and Ne'eman 1989). Administrators want to ensure that they have followed all the appropriate rules and procedures to maximize the potential return on the intellectual property (Link and Siegel 2005). Thus, there is a disconnect between the expectations and the needs of private sector organizations and public sector ones.

There is no evidence that the increase in commercial activities at universities have yet affected the research culture so as to bias research toward industrial applications and away from basic discovery (Owen-Smith and Powell 2003). However, the rapid pace of knowledge creation and the demands of the global marketplace have put pressures on public sector research organizations to adopt new roles in the innovation system.

Technology transfer efforts are founded on the belief that scientific discoveries can be leveraged to create products and services that have real-world applications. These scientific discoveries are often viewed as coming from scientists, working alone in laboratories. The application of these scientific discoveries by engineers and technicians is believed to be relatively straightforward and not particularly noteworthy. However, the innovation process is not linear (Kranzberg 1967; Price 1965, 1963; Rosenberg 1982; Wise 1985; Zuckerman 1988). Scientific innovation is complex and requires the cooperation and understanding of different disciplines, particularly if scientific knowledge residing in universities is to be leveraged more effectively and quickly.

Innovation and technology transfer policies often try to unite scientific discoveries by research scientists with the problem-solving and application expertise of engineers to spur private sector innovation. Policies try to get scientists and engineers to collaborate with industry in the hopes that proximity will lead to commercial innovation. In addition, policy makers expect that multidisciplinary projects will result in greater innovation (Zare 1997). However, there are substantial differences in the education, goals, values, culture, expectations, and work styles of scientists and engineers (Allen

1988; Blade 1963; Danielson 1960) and this can cause significant challenges for collaboration and interdisciplinary research.

Engineers and scientists have different behaviors and values with respect to their involvement with industry (Schuelke-Leech 2011). PhDs in engineering are more likely to work in industry, to spend time working with industry, to be an interface for industry with academia, and to be actively working with industry. Engineers graduating with PhDs are more likely to find employment in industry than other STEM fields (engineers, 72.2 percent, vs. life science graduates, 31.0 percent, and physical science graduates, 61.3 percent) (National Science Foundation 2014). At the same time, only 14.9 percent of engineering graduates with PhDs stay in academia (compared with 46.7 percent of life science graduates and 29.2 percent of physical science graduates) (Ibid.). In addition, engineers are more likely to believe that the application of research to society should be considered in funding decisions. Though the analysis does not evaluate the quality of the industrial involvement that academic researchers undertake, it does indicate differences in the diversity and intensity of the activities. Thus, there is substantial evidence that engineers are, in general, more oriented toward industry in their activities and attitudes than scientists are (Schuelke-Leech 2011).[2]

Effective technology transfer and collaboration with industry requires academic researchers to overcome the organizational and disciplinary barriers that would prevent effective collaboration. Engineers are an important bridge between academia and industry. Their orientation to the application of research and toward greater involvement with industry, as shown in this chapter, makes them a natural fulcrum in the innovation process. As pressure for more rapid development and deployment of scientific discovery to commercial applications increases, it may be possible to leverage the culture and conventions of engineers to affect this policy goal.

Universities have endeavored to overcome the challenges of the traditional organizational structures and processes within the universities by employing new and expanded institutions and activities, including: the creation of centers and institutions; active promotion of research; patenting and licensing of inventions to industrial users; and providing funding to university spin-off companies and start-up ventures.

In the past 30 years, several different types of organizations and institutions have arisen outside of the traditional university structure, with the purpose of fostering effective collaboration between industry and university researchers and facilitating knowledge creation and technology transfer. The creation of science parks and bridging institutions has been widespread (Bercovitz and Feldman 2003). University research centers (URCs) and research institutes have become meeting places for scientists and engineers from academia and industry. There is no template for creating, funding, or managing the centers (Bozeman and Boardman 2003). These centers can have researchers from a single discipline or from multiple disciplines (Mowery and Sampat 2001). However, affiliation with URCs has been shown to increase collaboration with industry (Bozeman and Boardman 2003; Geiger 1990), and thus, these alternative institutional forms have been shown to effectively increase technology transfer.

On the surface, these units would seem to be successfully changing the work of academic researchers. However, changing the conventions and culture of an organization or an individual is not always easy. Though one of the main goals of university research centers has been to promote interdisciplinary research (see, for example, Boardman 2006; Boardman and Bozeman 2007; Boardman and Corley 2008; Boardman and Ponomariov 2007; Bozeman and Boardman 2003, 2013; Clark 2009; Corley and Gaughan 2005; Geiger 1990; Guston 2000; Ponomariov and Boardman 2010), this goal is not necessarily being met. Though nearly 40 percent of academic researchers are affiliated with a URC, most choose to belong to URCs that are dominated by their own academic disciplines (Schuelke-Leech 2011). In fact, the vast majority of URCs are unidisciplinary (Schuelke-Leech 2011). Although URCs may be providing an alternative institutional environment for collaboration and industrial involvement, they are not necessarily ensuring interdisciplinary research, industry involvement, or technology transfer.

More recently, universities have been looking to integrate entrepreneurship into their curriculum (Christensen and Eyring 2011; Thorp and Goldstein 2010; U.S. Department of Commerce 2013) to promote business start-ups and job creation. The hope is that students and faculty members will create new businesses and, possibly, new industries.

Proposed Responses/Reforms

Policy makers, business leaders and university administrators have turned to STEM fields to drive economic growth, create new businesses, and generate resources. Often this focuses on the transfer of knowledge and opportunities through technology transfer, research commercialization, and technological entrepreneurship. However, these goals do not necessarily line up with those of STEM students. Few STEM graduates become entrepreneurs or start businesses. U.S. Census results show that less than 8 percent of engineering graduates between the ages of 25 and 64 were self-employed (U.S. Census 2011). In a study of 5,239 engineering students, in 212 programs from 31 four-year engineering schools, done in 2008, only 2 percent of engineering students were actively planning to be self-employed, while another 6 percent were considering it (Ro 2011). Over 75 percent of engineering graduates work in large corporations, and most engineering students have this same aspiration (Ro 2011). Even in the biological and life sciences, self-employment does not exceed 15 percent (U.S. Census 2011).

Numerous engineering faculties (and business faculties) have looked at promoting entrepreneurship and innovation within their curriculum. Courses on technology entrepreneurship and design thinking are aimed at helping engineering students take ideas to start-ups. The aim of these endeavors is not always clear though. Universities have become much more aggressive in claiming and exploiting potential intellectual property. Even though few research discoveries actually lead to significant returns for universities (Abrams, Leung, and Stevens 2009), the potential of large returns remains attractive, similar to the way that people continue to buy lottery tickets despite the low probabilities of winning.

This presents a problem for those who want to promote research commercialization, entrepreneurship, and technology transfer. Though these may be the goals of policy makers, business leaders, and university administrators, university students (and most faculty members) do not generally share these goals. Thus, increasing technology transfer and entrepreneurship requires changing the goals of students, and, in turn, the goals of education.

If the goal is to marginally increase the number of STEM students who are engaged in entrepreneurial endeavors, then simply adding a course in entrepreneurship may result in improvement. However, if university administrators (and policy makers and business leaders) expect a larger impact, then more substantive changes to university curriculums are going to be necessary.

This leads to several important questions. The first is whether this is really the role of universities. The increased emphasis on STEM programs has resulted in many believing that the humanities and the arts are less important. Certainly these programs seem to have fewer enrollments and a bachelor of arts seems to hold less promise of easy employment. However, is it really the role of a university to show preference for some programs over others? Are some fields of education more important than others? Are engineering or medicine more valuable to a university than history or art? If the measure is grant funding or faculty endowments, then it may be possible to argue that this is the case. However, if the measurement is instead on the impact that education can have on opening a student's appreciation of the world or increasing the understanding of some phenomena, this case is more difficult to make. It is also impossible to say which programs lead to entrepreneurship. As the census data shows, students who graduated with degrees in visual and performing arts (13.8 percent), social science (11.5 percent), and liberal arts (10.5 percent), are more likely to become self-employed than engineers (7.8 percent) or business majors (10.2 percent).

The second question to address is whether all these activities since the 1980s have really increased the role of universities as drivers of economic growth. An educated population is an important factor in economic prosperity, as it has been for many years. However, there has not historically been an expectation that universities themselves (rather than individuals) would drive the economy. Rather than simply being educators, universities are expected to provide the knowledge and environment for new businesses to form and grow. Universities have not only encouraged this role, they have embraced it (Slaughter and Leslie 1999). Whereas businesses were previously independent of the academic environment, universities are now considered a breeding ground for industrial activity. This makes it difficult for universities to stand outside the fray of business. They are no longer objective bystanders to the economy. Instead, they are lead actors in it. Likewise, it is much more difficult for universities to criticize the current economic system or to propose meaningful alternatives. There is now a significant financial commitment to the current economic system. This can create a divide within universities, between those who benefit from the changing role of universities in the economy and those who do not.

Universities are dependent on external resources, regardless of whether these resources come from tuition, government funding, endowments, or revenues from intellectual property. Until World War II, however, university education was really for the elites (Trow 2007). It was not until the 1960s that a major shift in the availability of higher education occurred (Scott 1995). With this shift, universities received greater support from state governments. More recently, another shift has occurred, in which higher education is viewed as a private good, while universities are expected to contribute more to economic prosperity. However, there is a difference between being a passive contributor to the economy—through providing education and new knowledge—versus being actively involved in start-ups and spin-offs from research activities and pushing students to start new ventures. The active role of universities in the economy may fundamentally change the way in which universities value their programs, faculty, and students. The model of the entrepreneurial university makes education less about curiosity-driven knowledge and exploration and more about the application of knowledge for commercial success. Thus, the value of knowledge comes from its commercial application. However, as many professors can point out, there is a significant amount of knowledge that has little commercial application, particularly in the short term.

Universities will have to work to effectively balance their more traditional educational role with their newer economic role, lest they lose much good in the process and fail to do either very well.

Notes

1. For example, the Bayh-Dole Patent and Trademark Amendments Act of 1980 and Federal Tech Transfer Act of 1986.

2. Though engineers have more involvement with industry, research has shown that the majority of academic researchers have no involvement with industry (Schuelke-Leech 2011).

References

Abrams, Irene, Grace Leung, and Ashley J. Stevens. 2009. "How the U.S. Technology Transfer Offices Tasked and Motivated—Is It all about Money?" *Research Management Review* 17(1): 1–34.

Allen, Thomas J. 1988. "Distinguishing Engineers from Scientists." In *Managing Professionals in Innovation Organizations*, edited by R. Katz, 3–18. Cambridge, MA: Ballinger Publishing.

Augustine, N. (chair). 2005. *Rising above the Gathering Storm: Energizing and Employing America for A Brighter Economic Future*. National Academies Committee on Prospering in the Global Economy of the 21st Century. Washington, DC: National Academies Press.

Behrens, Teresa R., and Denis O. Gray. 2001. "Unintended Consequences of Cooperative Research: Impact of Industry Sponsorship on Climate for Academic Freedom and Other Graduate Student Outcome." *Research Policy* 30(2): 179–199.

Bercovitz, Janet, and Maryann P. Feldman. 2003. "Technology Transfer and the Academic Department: Who Participates and Why?" DRUID Summer Conference 2003 on Creating, Sharing, and Transferring Knowledge, Copenhagen, June 12–14.

Bettis, Richard A., and Michael A. Hitt. 1995. "The New Competitive Landscape." *Strategic Management Journal* 16:7–19.

Blade, M. F. 1963. "Creativity in Engineering." In *Essays on Creativity in the Sciences*, edited by M. A. Coler, 110–122. New York: New York University Press.

Boardman, P. Craig. 2006. "University Research Centers and the Composition of Academic Work." PhD, School of Public Policy, Georgia Institute of Technology.

Boardman, Craig, and Barry Bozeman. 2007. "Role Strain in University Research Centers." *Journal of Higher Education* 78(4): 430–463.

Boardman, P. Craig, and Elizabeth A. Corley. 2008. "University Research Centers and the Composition of Research Collaborations." *Research Policy* 37(5): 900–913.

Boardman, P. Craig, and Branco L. Ponomariov. 2007. "Reward Systems and NSF University Research Centers: The Impact of Tenure on University Scientists' Valuation of Applied and Commercially Relevant Research." *Journal of Higher Education* 78:51–70.

Bozeman, Barry, and P. Craig Boardman. 2003. *Managing the New Multipurpose, Multidiscipline University Research Centers: Institutional Innovation in the Academic Community*. Arlington, VA: IBM Center for the Business of Government.

Bozeman, Barry, and P. Craig Boardman. 2013. "Academic Faculty in University Research Centers: Neither Capitalism's Slaves nor Teaching Fugitives." *The Journal of Higher Education* 84(1): 88–120.

Brusoni, Stefano, and Andrea Prencipe. 2006. "Making Design Rules: A Multidomain Perspective." *Organization Science* 17(2): 179–189.

Brusoni, Stefano, Andrea Prencipe, and Keith Pavitt. 2001. "Knowledge Specialization, Organizational Coupling, and the Boundaries of the Firm: Why Do Firms Know More Than They Make?" *Administrative Science Quarterly* 46(4): 597–621.

Bush, Vannevar. 1945. *Science, the Endless Frontier, A Report to the President on a Program for Postwar Scientific Research*. Washington, DC: Office of Scientific Research and Development.

Chesbrough, Henry. 2003. *Open Innovation: The New Imperative for Creating and Profiting from Technology*. Boston, MA: Harvard Business School Press.

Christensen, Clayton M., and Henry J. Eyring. 2011. *The Innovative University: Changing the DNA of Higher Education from the Inside Out*. San Francisco, CA: Jossey-Bass.

Clark, Benjamin Y. 2009. "Collaboration in Academic Research." PhD, Public Administration and Policy, The University of Georgia.

Cockburn, Iain. 2005. "Blurred Boundaries: Tensions Between Open Scientific Resources and Commercial Exploitation of Knowledge in Biomedical Research." Advancing Knowledge and the Knowledge Economy Conference, Washington DC, January 10–11.

Cohen, M. D., and James G. March. 1974. *Leadership and Ambiguity: The American College President*. New York: McGraw Hill.

Cohen, Wesley M., Richard Florida, and Richard Goe. 1994. "University-Industry Research Centers in the United States." Paper. Carnegie Mellon University, Department of Social and Decision Sciences. Pittsburgh, PA.

Cohen, Wesley M., Richard Florida, Lucien Randazzese, and John Walsh. 1998. "Industry and the Academy: Uneasy Partners in the Cause of Technological Advancement." In *Challenges to Research Universities*, edited by Roger G. Noll, 171–199. Washington, DC: Brookings Institution Press.

Cohen, Wesley M., Richard Florida, and John Walsh. 1996. "Links and Impacts: New Survey Results on the Influence of University Research on Industrial R&D." Unpublished paper. Carnegie Mellon University, Department of Social and Decision Sciences.

Corley, Elizabeth A., and Monica Gaughan. 2005. "Scientists' Participation in University Research Centers: What Are the Gender Differences?" *Journal of Technology Transfer* 30:371–381.

Crow, Michael, and Barry Bozeman. 1998. *Limited by Design*. New York: Columbia University Press.

Danielson, L. E. 1960. *Characteristics of Engineers and Scientists: Significant for Their Motivation and Utilization*. Ann Arbor: University of Michigan Press.

Denison, D. R. 1990. *Corporate Culture and Organizational Effectiveness*. New York: Wiley & Sons.

Dill, David D. 1982. "The Management of Academic Culture: Notes on the Management of Meaning and Social Integration." *Higher Education* 11(3): 303–320. doi:10.1007/bf00155621.

Fluckiger, Stephen L. 2006. "Industry's Challenge to Academia: Changing the Bench to Bedside Paradigm." *Experimental Biology and Medicine* 231(7): 1257–1261.

Frumkin, Peter, and Joseph Galaskiewicz. 2004. "Institutional Isomorphism and Public Sector Organizations." *Journal of Public Administration Research and Theory* 14(3): 283–307.

Geiger, Roger L. 1990. "Organized Research Units—Their Role in the Development of University Research." *The Journal of Higher Education* 61(1): 1–19.

Guston, David H. 2000. *Between Politics and Science: Assuring the Productivity and Integrity of Research*. New York: Cambridge University Press.

Ham, Rose Marie, and David C. Mowery. 1998. "Improving the Effectiveness of Public–Private R&D Collaboration: Case Studies at a US Weapons Laboratory." *Research Policy* 26(6): 661–675.

Hargadon, Andrew B. 2003. *How Breakthroughs Happen: The Surprising Truth about How Companies Innovate*. Boston, MA: Harvard Business School Press.

Johnson, Wayne C. 2006. "Challenges in University-Industry Collaborations." In *Universities and Business: Partnering for the Knowledge Society*, edited by Luc Weber and James J. Duderstadt, 211–222. London: Economica.

Kantorovich, Aharon. 1993. *Scientific Discovery: Logic and Tinkering*. Albany: State University of New York Press.

Kantorovich, Aharon, and Y. Ne'eman. 1989. "Serendipity as a Source of Evolutionary Progress in Science." *Studies in the History and Philosophy of Science* 20:505–529.

Katz, J. Sylvan, and Ben R. Martin. 1997. "What Is Research Collaboration?" *Research Policy* 26(1): 1–18.

Knapp, E. M. 1998. "Knowledge Management." *Business Economic Review* 44(4): 3–6.

Kranzberg, Melvin. 1967. "The Unity of Science-Technology." *American Scientist* 55(1): 48–66.

Lai, Ming-Fong, and Gwo-Guang Lee. 2007. "Relationships of Organizational Culture toward Knowledge Activities." *Business Process Management Journal* 13(2): 306–322.

Landry, Réjean, and Nabil Amara. 1998. "The Impact of Transaction Costs on the Institutional Structuration of Collaborative Academic Research." *Research Policy* 27(9): 901–913.

Laredo, Philippe, and Philippe Mustar. 2001. *Research and Innovation Policies in the New Global Economy: An International Comparative Analysis*. Cheltenham: Edward Elgar.

Lee, Yong S. 1997. "Technology Transfer and Economic Development: A Framework for Policy Analysis." In *Technology Transfer and Public Policy*, edited by Yong S. Lee, 3–20. Westport, CT: Quorum Books.

Link, Albert, and Donald S. Siegel. 2005. "Generating Science-Based Growth: An Econometric Analysis of the Impact of Organizational Incentives on University–Industry Technology Transfer." *The European Journal of Finance* 11(3): 169–181.

Mansfield, Edwin. 1998. "Academic Research and Industrial Innovation: An Update of Empirical Findings." *Research Policy* 26:773–776.

Mowery, David C. 1983. "The Relationship between Intrafirm and Contractual Forms of Industrial Research in American Manufacturing, 1900–1940." *Explorations in Economic History* 20(4): 351–374.

Mowery, David C., Richard R. Nelson, Bhaven N. Sampat, and Arvids A. Ziedonis. 1999. "The Effects of the Bayh-Dole Act on U.S. University Research and Technology Transfer." In *Industrializing Knowledge: University–Industry Linkages in Japan and the United States*, edited by Lewis M. Branscomb, Fumio Kodama, and Richard Florida, 269–306. Cambridge, MA: The MIT Press.

Mowery, David C., and Bhaven N. Sampat. 2001. "University Patents and Patent Policy Debates in the USA, 1925–1980." *Industrial and Corporate Change* 10(3): 781–814.

Mueller, Klaus. 2006. "University–Industry Collaboration: A Source of Continuous Mutual Stimulation and Inspiration." In *Universities and Business: Partnering for the Knowledge Society*, edited by Luc Weber and James J. Duderstadt, 177–184. London: Economica.

National Research Council (NRC). 1999. *Harnessing Science and Technology for America's Economic Future*. National Forum on Science and Technology Goals, Washington, DC: National Academy Press.

National Science Foundation. 2014. "Science and Engineering Doctorates." Accessed November 11, 2016. https://www.nsf.gov/statistics/2016/nsf16300/data-tables.cfm

OECD. 1996. *National Innovation Systems: Report of Pilot Case Studies*. Paris: Organization of Economic Cooperation and Development.

Ogbonna, Emmanuel, and Lloyd Harris. 2001. "Leadership Style, Organizational Culture and Performance: Empirical Evidence from UK Companies." *The International Journal of Human Resource Management* 11(4): 766–788. doi:citeulike-article-id:3501360.

Owen-Smith, Jason, and Walter W. Powell. 2003. "The Expanding Role of University Patenting in the Life Sciences: Assessing the Importance of Experience and Connectivity." *Research Policy* 32(9): 1695–1711.

Perry, James L., and Hal G. Rainey. 1988. "The Public–Private Distinction in Organization Theory: A Critique and Research Strategy." *The Academy of Management Review* 13(2): 182–201.

Ponomariov, Branco L., and P. Craig Boardman. 2010. "Influencing Scientists' Collaboration and Productivity Patterns through New Institutions: University Research Centers and Scientific and Technical Human Capital." *Research Policy* 39(5): 613–624.

Porter, Michael E. 1986. "Competition in Global Industries: A Conceptual Framework." In *Competition in Global Industries*, edited by Michael E. Porter, 15–61. Cambridge, MA: Harvard Business School Press.

Price, Derek J. de Solla. 1963. *Little Science Big Science*. New York: Columbia University Press.

Price, Derek J. de Solla. 1965. "Is Technology Historically Independent of Science? A Study in Statistical Historiography." *Technology and Culture* 6(4): 553–568.

Ro, Hyun Kyoung. 2011. "An Investigation of Engineering Students' Post-Graduation Plans Inside or Outside of Engineering," PhD dissertation (Education), The University of Pennsylvania.

Rosenberg, Nathan. 1982. *Inside the Black Box: Technology and Economics*. New York: Cambridge University Press.

Rosenbloom, Richard S., and William J. Spencer. 1996. "Technology's Vanishing Wellspring." In *Engines of Innovation: U.S. Industrial Research at the End of an Era*, edited by Richard S. Rosenbloom and William J. Spencer, 1–10. Boston, MA: Harvard Business School Press.

Schein, Edgar H. 1996. "Culture: The Missing Concept in Organization Studies." *Administrative Science Quarterly* 41(2): 229–240.

Scholz, Christian. 1987. "Corporate Culture and Strategy—The Problem of Strategic Fit." *Long Range Planning* 20(4): 78–87.

Schraeder, Mike, Rachel S. Tears, and Mark H. Jordan. 2005. "Promoting Change through Training and Leading by Example." *Leadership & Organization Development Journal* 26(6): 492–502.

Schuelke-Leech, Beth-Anne. 2011. "Strangers in a Strange Land: Industry and Technology Transfer." PhD, Public Administration and Policy, University of Georgia.

Scott, Peter. 1995. *The Meanings of Mass Higher Education*. Buckingham: Society for Research into Higher Education and Open University Press.

Slaughter, Sheila, and Larry L. Leslie. 1999. *Academic Capitalism: Politics, Policies, and the Entrepreneurial University*. Baltimore, MD: The Johns Hopkins University Press.

Thorp, Holden, and Buck Goldstein. 2010. *Engines of Innovation: The Entrepreneurial University in the Twenty-First Century*. Chapel Hill: University of North Carolina Press.

Trow, Martin. 2007. "Reflections on the Transition from Elite to Mass to Universal Access: Forms and Phases of Higher Education in Modern Societies since WWII." In *International Handbook of Higher Education*, Vol. 18, edited by James J. F. Forest and Philip G. Altbach, 243–280. Netherlands: Springer.

U.S. Census. 2011. "Field of Degree and Earnings by Selected Employment Characteristics: 2011." Accessed November 11, 2016. https://www.census.gov/prod/2012pubs/acsbr11-10.pdf

U.S. Department of Commerce. 2013. "The Innovative and Entrepreneurial University: Higher Education, Innovation & Entrepreneurship in Focus." Office of Innovation & Entrepreneurship Economic Development Administration in consultation with: National Advisory Council on Innovation and Entrepreneurship. Accessed November 12, 2016. https://www.eda.gov/oie/nacie/

Van de Ven, Andrew H., Douglas E. Polley, Raghu Garud, and Sandaran Venkataraman. 1999. *The Innovation Journey*. New York: Oxford University Press.

Whitley, Richard. 2003. "Competition and Pluralism in the Public Sciences: The Impact of Institutional Frameworks on the Organisation of Academic Science." *Research Policy* 32(6): 1015–1029.

Wise, George. 1985. "Science and Technology." *Osiris* 1:229–246.

Zare, Richard N. 1997. "Knowledge and Distributed Intelligence." *Science* 275:1047.

Zuckerman, Harriet. 1988. "The Sociology of Science." In *Handbook of Sociology*, edited by Neil J. Smelser, 511–574. Beverly Hills, CA: Sage Publications.

CHAPTER TWENTY-ONE

Who Benefits? A Critical Analysis of State Merit Aid Programs and the Impact on Public Higher Education Institutions

Kerii Landry-Thomas

Introduction

Faced with an ever-changing landscape for education and education finance, many states struggle to find the balance between higher education access and affordability. The increase in first-generation and low-income students makes the balance even more difficult, as such students are less likely to be able to afford higher education and are more likely to have access issues. In addressing these dynamics, states focus resources on "merit" programs, which seem to be neutral and objective in reaching a wide range of students. However, as this chapter delineates, state merit-aid programs often make education more expensive for all, reducing access for many students. In understanding this impact, an analysis of state merit aid programs is needed.

Overview

Affordability and access are major themes in the current media coverage of public higher education. Recent headlines discuss the recruitment of out-of-state and international students to state public higher education institutions, as well as the rising cost of higher education. However, often left out of the discussion is the role that state merit aid plays in the rising cost of public higher education and the decrease in access for in-state residents. For example, *The New York Times* featured an article discussing how the University of Alabama, a public higher education institution, became a national player in higher education. The article notes that Alabamians make up only 43 percent of the student body and argues that with new enrollment policies like an increase in merit aid, state-residents and lower-income students will have no affordable options for attending a four-year public university (Jeff 2016). Interestingly, access and affordability are particularly crucial in today's economy as some form of higher education is essential for obtaining many jobs that support a middle-class lifestyle. This chapter explores the historical evolution of state merit aid and analyzes the current impact that merit aid has on public institutions of higher education.

Trends and Developments

The recent focus on the increasing cost of public higher education stems from the fact that more than 80 percent of all undergraduate students attend public colleges and universities (Heller 2001, 1). Although the cost of college is often discounted for many college students in the form of financial aid, which includes loans or scholarships, the way in which financial aid is allocated is important and can have a major impact on not only affordability but also access (Heller 2001, 1–3). Although states have long had some form of merit aid programs, which are discounts to college based on academic performance, historically the programs were narrow and were given to the highest-performing students. Furthermore, the bulk of state spending for higher education came in the form of generous state appropriations, which kept the cost of attendance to public institutions of higher education low for all students (Dynarski 2002). However, starting in the 1990s there was a shift to a more broad-based merit aid program, which increased aid to a larger amount of students with modest academic achievement. In addition, this shift coincided with a steady decrease of state institutional appropriations and, thus, an increase in tuition to attend public institutions of higher education (Curs, Bornali and Steiger 2011; Dynarski 2002). Importantly, increased state appropriations kept tuition low for all and institutional and federal efforts focused on providing aid to underrepresented students. But as states decreased state appropriations to public colleges and moved to more

Table 21.1   States with Merit Programs Implemented 1991–2004

State	First Cohort	Program Name
Florida	1997	Florida Bright Futures Scholarship
Georgia	1993	Georgia HOPE Scholarship
Kentucky	1999	Kentucky Educational Excellence Scholarship
Louisiana	1998	Louisiana TOPS Scholarship
Nevada	2000	Nevada Millennium Scholarship
New Mexico	1997	New Mexico Lottery Success Scholarship
South Carolina	1998	South Carolina LIFE Scholarship
Tennessee	2003	Tennessee HOPE Scholarship
West Virginia	2002	West Virginia PROMISE Scholarship
Alaska	1999	Alaska Scholars
Arkansas	1991	Arkansas Academic Challenge Scholarship
California	2001	Competitive Cal Grant Program
Idaho	2001	Robert R. Lee Promise Scholarship
Illinois	1999–2004	Illinois Merit Recognition Scholarship
Maryland	2002–2005	Maryland HOPE Scholarship
Michigan	2000–2008	Michigan Merit & Promise Scholarship
Mississippi	1996	Mississippi TAG and ESG
Missouri	1997	Missouri Bright Flight Scholarship
New Jersey	1997 (2004)	New Jersey OSRP (STARS)
New York	1997	NY Scholarships for Academic Excellence
North Dakota	1994	North Dakota Scholars Program
Oklahoma	1996	Oklahoma PROMISE Scholarship
South Dakota	2004	South Dakota Opportunity Scholarship
Utah	1999	New Century Scholarship
Washington	1999–2006	Washington PROMISE Scholarship

Sources: Sjoquist and Winters 2014, 367

merit aid with no requirements for need, the demographics of the students receiving aid changed. Affordability, access, and diversity were all impacted by this switch (Heller 2008, 133–134).

Twenty-five states implemented merit-based student aid programs between 1991 and 2004 (see Table 21.1) with a varying degree of characteristics.

As is clear from Table 21.1, merit aid is heavily concentrated in the southern region of the United States, and many of the states have very lenient eligibility criteria. For example, Arkansas awards require a GPA of 2.5 and an ACT score of 19. Interestingly, some broad-based merit programs started off with income requirements. Georgia HOPE scholarship, which is widely believed to be the start of the policy shift to merit aid, required a B average and a family income below $66,000 (Doyle 2010, 400). In the same vein, Louisiana TOPS (Taylor Opportunity Programs for Students) scholarships required students to meet midlevel academic benchmarks such as a 2.5 GPA and a score of 20 on the ACT and also featured an income cap requirement (Deslatte 2014). However, both programs lifted the cap on income and even allowed the use of the scholarship for students attending private institutions. Additionally, recent research indicates that the use of state merit aid to draw top students to public colleges and universities is on the rise, and most state merit aid systems do not have income caps in place (Burd 2015). At the same time, most of the current merit aid programs provide the full cost of tuition for students receiving such aid. Most experts believe that this scenario sets up a system where many students already able to afford to go to college are being subsidized by the state (Dynarski 2002; Jeff 2016; Melia 2016). Unfortunately, the costs to keep these broad-based merit programs continue to rise and states are finding themselves in precarious positions, as any changes to these programs are politically unfavorable. Currently, Louisiana is faced with a lack of funds to pay the full award for recipients, and in spring 2017 the state will pay out only 40 percent of the spring tuition, leaving students and their families to pay the rest. As expected, these developments triggered an outcry of protest over the loss of the award, which had been earned by the recipients (Boone 2016).

State Merit Aid and Affordability

Another factor associated with the rising cost of public higher education has been the rise of a cottage industry of private and publicly funded loan programs worth an estimated $100 billion a year. A look at the total level of student loan debt estimated at more than $1.2 trillion indicates that the cost to attend American colleges and universities is stretching families to an unsustainable limit. Many experts rightly point to decreased state appropriations, increased spending on extra amenities on campuses, and increased availability of federal loans for middle class families as factors increasing the cost of public colleges (Schoen 2015). Additionally, a few experts point to the inefficient use of state merit aid as another possible reason for increased costs.

As stated previously, the use of state merit aid regardless of financial need creates a system where states are subsidizing those students who were more than likely college-bound anyway, in large part because they and their families can already afford the cost of college. Harold Levy, director of the Jack

Kent Cook Foundation, which provides need-based scholarships, states, "The reality is that for poor families, it's a question of whether the kids go to college at all. For the better-off family, it's a question of which college" (Melia 2016). Many critics echo this concern as experts have found that low- and middle-income families are more responsive to the cost of attending colleges and universities. Yet, there is a continued growth in the use of state merit aid. A report by Stephen Burd (2016) of New America found the following:

Of the 134 public research and land-grant institutions—

- 17 colleges, or 13 percent of the schools, spent 75 percent or more of their institutional aid dollars on nonneedy students;

- 37 colleges, or 28 percent, spent at least half of their aid dollars on students without financial need;

- 67 colleges, or 50 percent, spent at least one-third of their aid on nonneedy students;

- 84 colleges, or 63 percent, spent at least one-quarter of their institutional aid on students without financial need;

- Only 18 schools, or 13 percent, spent under 10 percent of their aid dollars on nonneedy students; and

- 3 colleges reported that they didn't provide any merit aid.

Several national reports indicate that the rise in state merit aid, a nonneed program, has benefited White, middle- and high-income families and decreased the numbers of low-income and minority students on four-year public college campuses. However, not all researchers agree that state aid disproportionally benefits wealthy students. One report indicates, "On average, in every category of selectivity, low income students receive larger indirect subsidies because universities charge them lower net price" (Delisle and Dancy 2016, 5). However, indirect subsidies—state dollars that go straight to colleges and help to close the gap between the cost of educating a student and what might be paid in tuition and grants—are decreasing. The percentage of family income that a wealthy family and a poor family can pay is not reviewed in the report. Moreover, a vast amount of experts indicate that the widespread use of merit aid is harming low-income and minority students. Importantly, beyond the surface is how college costs rise for everyone when merit aid is used to subsidize wealthy students that could afford to pay for college. Several scholars suggest that with the increase of wealthy students— who presumably could afford to go to college anywhere—within their student bodies, public colleges feel another point of pressure to make their campuses better than the next one (Dynarski 2002). Thus, this contributes to the race to attract students by building bigger and better facilities with luxury amenities. In turn, these amenities put extra cost on the colleges that continue to see their state appropriations decrease, and, as such, a vicious cycle of increasing tuition and offering more merit aid continues. The cost to everyone goes up.

In addition, ancillary markets form to capture the buying power of these students and now more political pressure is placed on keeping the cycle going, making it hard for any changes to existing policy, although research shows non-need-based merit-aid is an inefficient way of spending state money. For example, an article researching Louisiana's TOPS program found that the rise of luxury apartments around Louisiana State University was tied to TOPS students and their families. The article indicates that luxury apartments and real estate have increased because students with more disposable income can afford to pay the higher rents (Boone 2016). Interestingly, another report found sales of cars in Georgia to be tied to the Georgia HOPE scholarship program (Chen 2004, 15). Thus, creating a market where the builders and car dealers and other business interests become stakeholders in keeping state merit aid in place. Additionally, researchers find that middle- and upper-income families, as well as business interests tend to have more political agency and as such will advocate for a policy that supports their interest. Unfortunately, this scenario leaves very little room for change even when data indicates that the demographics of the country are changing and that there needs to be a robust policy in place to address low-income and minority students becoming college educated.

Proposed Reforms

Critics of the current system have proposed several reforms across the spectrum, but the following proposals are those that may offer the best solutions. However, these reforms are not without disadvantages. For the most part, all reforms to state merit aid face uphill battles and a lack of political will in the state legislatures, as they are politically unfavorable.

Although broad-based merit aid programs stem from popular, good ideas, such as rewarding the "best and the brightest" students and keeping them in the state, the ultimate effect is to increase the cost of college for all and to decrease access for low-income and minority students. Many scholars suggest imposing an income requirement on state merit aid scholarships as one possible solution. Interestingly, by adding an income cap, the scholarship can still meet the needs of keeping bright students in the state, particularly low-income students. Many experts point to the need for increased access for low-income and minority students, not just as a civil rights issue, but also as an economic one, given the demographic changes taking place in the United States. Increasingly, the population needs to be college educated in order to stay competitive globally. Although research indicates that financial aid does not necessarily impact middle- and higher income students in *whether* they will attend college, but instead *where* they will attend college, the impact of merit aid reforms will likely not be great for those students. Particularly, the loss of bright students from higher income families from the state may not occur, but simply alter movement from one college to another within the state. Alternatively, some researchers indicate a drop in outmigration of first-time college students when a state merit aid program is present (Orsuwan and Heck 2009). Yet, other researchers finds that students receiving state merit-based scholarships were 74 percent more inclined to leave the state upon college graduation (Williams and Dreier 2011, 5). Thus, many argue state merit aid is not the most efficient way of using state finances toward higher education.

However, setting an income cap can also free up money that can be used for direct appropriation to public institutions of higher education. Decreasing tuition costs for all students and making four-year public institutions favorable to all students decreases the likelihood that they will leave the state. Unfortunately, there is limited data on whether states would redirect the savings to direct appropriations. In fact, the data indicates that higher education is one of the areas easiest to cut in state legislatures. This would indicate that although an income cap would be a more efficient method of keeping bright students in need in the state, it will likely not help with reducing the cost of tuition if states do not put the money back into the institutions. Alternatively, if more middle- and higher income families are then tasked with paying for college for their children, the political force behind reducing rising tuition costs might change the way higher education is funded by the states. As it stands now, without those with political power being impacted, there is less likelihood that any significant changes to state merit aid and rising tuition costs will occur.

In the same vein as an income cap requirement, there is a call by many to simply raise the academic requirements of state merit aid scholarships. This reform would therefore limit the amount of money states spend and would meet the stated purpose of really keeping the "best and the brightest" within states, at least for college attendance. Although this reform might reduce the cost to states, the research indicates that this would also increase the racial and income gap in access to higher education (Dynarski 2002). Repeatedly, research has found that educational attainment and educational achievement (measured by standardized tests) are correlated to income and race. This indicates that those students more likely to meet the higher academic requirements will be higher income and White. Importantly, some researchers argue that a liberally awarded merit scholarship program—while inefficient—may provide sustainable access for those students in greatest need of financial aid. However, it should be noted that this argument is conditioned on several caveats: First, the fact that merit aid is unlikely to go away as it is politically popular; second, that merit aid should be specifically targeted to those underrepresented students and that academic achievement should be more liberally construed by looking at a number of different measures outside of the traditional measures; and, finally, that merit aid is supplemented with additional scholarship funds for low-income students. In addition, raising the academic standards for merit aid has a limited impact on affordability without states reallocating the savings to direct aid to public institutions of higher education.

A direct reform would be simply to increase the amount of need-based aid to low-income students, thereby making it more affordable for those students to attend public institutions of higher education. However, although most states have some sort of need-based program, research has shown a dramatic increase in merit-aid over that of need-based aid. In a national study, data suggests that although states' provision of need-based financial aid at public four-year institutions barely changed from 1996 to 2012, state financial aid for high-income students at these same institutions skyrocketed by more than 450 percent (Education 2016, 6). Increasingly, researchers are concerned that an increase in merit-aid correlates with a decrease in need-based aid, yet at least one research article finds that funding for merit-aid does not impact need-based aid (Doyle 2010). Yet, Doyle is clear to set forth that there is no way to tell if the money used for merit-aid *would have* been used to increase need-based aid.

However, many studies have found that although the cost of attending public institutions continues to rise, state merit-aid is an inefficient way to use state money in addressing accessibility concerns. In addition, simply increasing the amount of need-based aid may not address the overall rising cost of attending a public college. Several scholars argue that a partnership is needed between the federal government, states, and institutions in order to make public colleges more affordable (Education 2016). For example, a federal policy that requires states to maintain a certain amount of funding directly for public institutions of higher education will prevent states from decreasing the amount of money that they contribute to public higher education (Alexander et al. 2010). In turn, this direct funding would keep costs low for everyone and federal programs can be used to increase aid to low-income students. Institutions can concentrate on using their funds to ensure that the cost is kept low for everyone to attend. This proposed reform would require a strong partnership between states, public institutions of higher education, and the federal government, as well as a restructuring of the way financial aid is allocated from the federal government and states (Education 2016). However, the use of broad-based merit aid has proven to be inefficient, costly, and ineffective in narrowing both the racial and income gaps persistent in higher education attainment. So, the debate between state need-based aid and state merit-aid continues.

References

Alexander, F. King, Thomas Harnisch, Daniel Hurley, and Robert Moran. 2010. "Maintenance of effort: An evolving federal-state policy approach to ensuring college affordability." *Journal of Education Finance* 36, no. 1: 76–87.

Boone, Timothy. 2016. "Taylor Opportunity Program for Students helps fuel LSU apartment boom, real estate market." *The Advocate.* Baton Rouge, February 8.

Burd, Stephen. 2015. "New America." May 18. Accessed December 29, 2016. https://www.newamerica.org/education-policy/policy-papers/out-of-state-student-arms-race/ Burd, Stephen. 2016. "New America." www.newamerica.org. April 18. Accessed December 29, 2016. https://www.newamerica.org/weekly/121/too-much-merit-aid-for-those-not-in-need/

Chen, Victor. 2004. "The Georgia HOPE Scholarship." *Policy Perspectives* 11, no. 1: 9–19.

Curs, Bradley R., Bhandari Bornali, and Christina Steiger. 2011. "The roles of public higher education expenditure and the privatization of the higher education on U.S. state economic growth." *Journal of Education Finance* 36, no. 4 (2011): 424–441.

Delisle, Jason, and Kim Dancy. 2016. "Brookings." July 28. Accessed December 29, 2016. https://www.brookings.edu/research/do-state-subsidies-for-public-universities-favor-the-affluent/

Deslatte, Melinda. 2014. "Report: TOPS goes mostly to white, wealthier families." WWL. December 10, 2014. Accessed August 30, 2017. http://www.wwltv.com/news/local/report-tops-goes-mostly-to-white-wealthier-families/260349494

Doyle, William. 2010. "Does merit-based aid 'crowd out' need-based aid?" *Research in Higher Education* 51, no. 5: 397–415.

Dynarski, Susan. 2002. "The consequences of merit aid." Working paper no. JCPR-WP-315. Kennedy School of Government, Harvard, 1–38.

Education, Institute for Research on Higher. 2016. "College affordability diagnosis: National report." Graduate School of Education, University of Pennsylvania, Philadelphia.

Heller, Donald E. 2001. *The states and public higher education policy: Affordability, access, and accountability.* Baltimore, MD: Johns Hopkins University Press.

Jeff, Amy. 2016. "Seeking students, public colleges reduce out-of-state prices." AP Online. November 26.

Melia, Michael. 2016. "Colleges lavishing more financial aid on wealthy students." AP online. September 27.

Mitchell, Michael, Michael Leachman, and Kathleen Masterson. 2016. *Funding down, tuition up.* Center on Budget and Policy Priorities.

Orsuwan, Meechai, and Ronald H. Heck. "Merit-based student aid and freshman interstate college migration: Testing a dynamic model of policy change." *Research in Higher Education* 50, no. 1 (2009): 24–51.

Schoen, John W. 2015. "The real reasons a college degree costs so much." CNBC. June 16.

Teixeira, Pedro N., D. Bruce Johnstone, Maria J. Rosa, and Hans Vossensteyn (eds.). 2006. "The changing nature of public support for higher education in the United States." In *Cost-sharing and accessibility in higher education: A fairer deal?*, 133–158. Dordrecht: Springer.

Williams, Joseph A., and John Burczek Dreier. "State merit based scholarship programs influence on outmigration." In *annual conference for the Association of Education Finance and Policy*, Seattle, WA, 2011.

CHAPTER TWENTY-TWO

Performance-Based Funding: The New Normal for State Accountability Policies

Paul G. Rubin and Lori Prince Hagood

Introduction

The growing emphasis among policy makers and state higher education agencies on increasing efficiencies and improving outcomes has created an ideal context for the consideration of performance-based funding (PBF) policies as a means of holding higher education institutions more accountable. PBF serves as an inducement policy to influence institutional behavior by tying state appropriations directly to postsecondary performance metrics, thus leveraging the significant role state funding plays in public higher education. Ultimately, PBF's appeal to policy makers stems from its underlying goal of improving institutional performance and increasing accountability regarding state-determined priorities—recently centered on degree attainment and job placement—through the use of financial incentives. Although the current environment has led to PBF's consideration for the second time in three decades, its utility and enactment often face opposition from stakeholders that, in the past, had led to its demise. Nevertheless, with the continued national emphasis on improving postsecondary attainment rates and aligning college graduates with statewide and more localized economic workforce needs, PBF remains a topic of which institutional leadership must be cognizant, as it continues to spread across the country. What follows is an overview of PBF policy adoption and implementation in the United States, recent trends in PBF development, and responses to PBF and reforms enacted.

Overview of Performance-Based Funding

Central to states' interest in performance funding is an increased desire to hold public colleges and universities more accountable in light of rising costs of tuition and fees and stagnant graduation rates (Zumeta and Kinne 2011). To this end, performance funding ties the distribution of state funds directly to institutional performance on specific indicators, such as student enrollment, retention, graduation rates (overall and for underserved populations), and degree production in high need areas (e.g., science, technology, engineering, and mathematics). Policy makers expect institutional leadership to focus their energies and available resources to improve these performance outcomes, thereby maximizing their allotment of state funds (Dougherty and Reddy 2011).

Although PBF is viewed as a significant departure from traditional, predominantly enrollment-driven formulas, which focus specifically on the number of students attending to determine allocation of state funding, interest in the policy has not been consistent historically. In fact, the development and adoption of PBF has been discussed as occurring in two waves. The first iteration (referred to as performance funding 1.0 or PF 1.0) began with Tennessee's adoption in 1979 and spread nationally through the mid-1990s and early 2000s (see Figure 22.1).

However, following this original surge of interest, there was a period of departure from these policies. During this time, almost as many states that once adopted PBF abandoned the policy due to a variety of complications— insufficient state funds, turnover in state leadership, complicated formulas/metrics, inadequate data/challenges in data collection, and, importantly, opposition from the higher education community (Dougherty, Natow, and Vega 2012).

A renewed interest in PBF emerged more recently (often referred to as performance funding 2.0 or PF 2.0), beginning around 2007, coinciding with state financial cutbacks, the 2008 recession, and the resulting national postsecondary degree attainment movement (Tandberg and Hillman 2014). Many states, including those that previously discontinued PBF, adopted new incentive policies that were more intent on making student outcomes a centerpiece of public higher education finance (see Figure 22.2). Both figures in this chapter clearly depict the distinct waves of PBF policy adoption as well as the

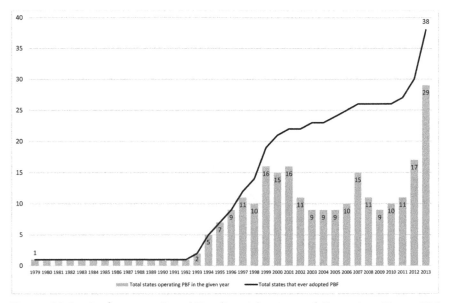

Figure 22.1 Performance-Based Funding Adoption and Operation. Figure 22.1 shows the total number of states ever adopting PBF policies as well as the number of states operating PBF in a given year. This figure demonstrates the cumulative interest in PBF over time as well as the distinct waves of policy adoption, breaking in the mid-2000s and reemerging in the late 2000s and 2010s. It is important to note that many states abandoned PBF policies in the early 2000s. Many of these states readopted new versions of PBF and others adopted PBF for the first time in recent years.

Dougherty and Natow (2015, 34).

cumulative interest in the policy over time. Figure 22.2 especially highlights the volatile nature of PBF policy adoption and operation.

According to Dougherty and Natow (2015), between 1979 and 2013, 38 states adopted performance funding, and, although 24 states discontinued the policy at some point, 22 later readopted some form of it as of September 2014. Snyder and Fox (2016) updated this figure and found 30 states were operating or developing a performance funding policy as of fiscal year 2016.

Given the decentralized nature of the American higher education system, individual states have primary responsibility in crafting policy solutions instead of being mandated by the federal government. Consequently, PBF policies differ substantially across states. In particular, PBF models vary considerably in regard to metrics tied to funding, the amount of state funding allocated via PBF, and even the higher education sectors (e.g., two-year vs. four-year institutions vs. both) that are subject to the policy, which makes direct comparisons between models challenging.

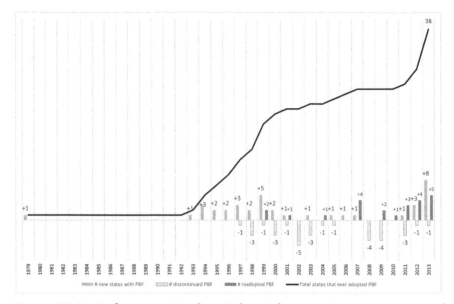

Figure 22.2 Performance Funding Policy Adoption, Discontinuation, and Readoption. Figure 22.2 demonstrates the volatile nature of PBF policy adoption and implementation.

Although PBF is primarily a state-level or system-level initiative, campuses have played important roles in its development and implementation. In the first wave of PBF, opposition by campus leaders and higher education communities generally was a key contributing factor in the discontinuation of many policies. Even in the second wave of implementation, campus responses, reactions, and opinions remain mixed. Moreover, in some states, campus officials have become involved directly in policy development. Other states incorporate campus input by allowing institution leaders to choose performance metrics or weight metrics determined by the state according to campus-level priorities, ultimately making this policy solution germane and of great importance to institutional leaders.

Recent Trends and Developments

There are notable differences between PF 1.0 and PF 2.0 policies. For instance, PF 1.0 models tended to have lower amounts of money at stake because they primarily served as an opportunity for a funding bonus (e.g., state monetary allocations to an institution are not impacted by their ability to meet performance measures). Alternatively, PF 2.0 models embed performance into base state funding metrics (e.g., state monetary allocations to an institution are impacted by their ability to meet performance measures), which can have a greater impact on institutional finances and other initiatives (Zumeta and Li 2016). Regarding policy development and advocacy, national higher education organizations and philanthropic foundations have played a largely unprecedented role in the adoption and creation of the most recent PBF policies (Parry, Field, and Supiano 2013; Tandberg and Hillman 2014). Notably, the Bill and Melinda Gates Foundation, the Lumina Foundation, HCM Strategists, Complete College America, and others have provided both funding and policy expertise for the development of PBF policies across the country. Further, empirical research has found mixed results regarding the influence of PF 1.0 formulas on improving targeted outcomes (Rutherford and Rabovsky 2014; Tandberg and Hillman 2014), while the impact of PF 2.0 is less understood due to the short period of time since these policies were first enacted.

PBF Policy Design

Arguably more aggressive than its predecessor, PF 2.0 creates larger, more significant financial incentives for colleges and universities to prioritize degree attainment. Whereas older policies often tied comparatively miniscule portions of funding to performance (5 to 10 percent of state appropriations), newer models tie up to 100 percent of state funding to outcomes (as is the case in Tennessee and Ohio). PF 1.0 often provided performance funding as a bonus, used in conjunction with enrollment-based funding formulas. In contrast, the newer models typically embed performance funding within the base state funding—in effect, replacing enrollment-based funding formulas rather than working in tandem.

The performance metrics (outcomes on which funding is based) utilized by PBF formulas have also evolved over time. Newer policies tend to be more streamlined, using fewer and simpler performance metrics to avoid obstructive complexities from the first wave of implementation (Hearn 2015). In addition, policies like those currently operating in Tennessee and Indiana allow performance metrics to vary across institutional types, accounting for different institutional missions, priorities, and student populations. As an example, a two-year college might be rewarded for a successful student transfer to a four-year institution rather than solely for degree completion. Improvements in student outcomes are more clearly prioritized in the recent models—namely, increases in graduates or degrees conferred. Moreover, the newer policies do not focus solely on ultimate outcomes, like degrees and jobs, but also reward progress toward those outcomes (Hearn 2015).

In addition to these policy design differences, more recent PBF policies often include premiums for the performance of "at-risk" student populations (e.g., adult students, low-income students, racial/ethnic minorities). These specifications were largely absent from PF 1.0 policy designs and arguably prevent institutions from restricting access for students deemed unlikely to complete a degree—a commonly cited concern of higher education stakeholders (Dougherty and Reddy 2011). Other PBF policies include premiums for degree production in high demand fields, in order to encourage alignment between higher education and the workforce.

The implementation process of PBF has also changed. Although the earlier policies were implemented in an arguably abrupt manner, many of the more recent PBF policies are phased in gradually. Some states limit the amount of funding institutions can lose each year, while others do not punish institutions for poor performance initially. These provisions attempt to alleviate potential budget instability during the transition to PBF.

Generally speaking, the newer PBF policies, although perhaps more aggressively focused on degree completion and graduate job placement, are also more streamlined, less complex, and gradually implemented. PF 2.0 more adequately accounts for institutional differences and rewards campuses for student progress toward degree completion, rather than solely ultimate outcomes. In other words, PF 2.0 has corrected many of the shortcomings of PF 1.0. It is important to point out, however, that PBF policies adopted in the most recent time period do not always resemble the latest policy designs described above (Hearn 2015).

Advocacy for PBF 2.0

The second wave of PBF policy development has been heavily influenced by prominent national higher education organizations and philanthropies in largely unprecedented ways. Organizations including Complete College America, HCM Strategists, the Bill and Melinda Gates Foundation, and the Lumina Foundation have been instrumental in advocating, funding, and providing technical assistance in the development of PBF policies in several states. In particular, representatives from these and similar organizations have partnered with policy makers in Tennessee and Ohio to develop the PBF policies currently in operation (Dougherty and Natow 2015; Ness, Deupree, and Gándara 2015; Tandberg and Hillman 2014).

Governors have also played a more central role in advocating for and developing the latest PBF policies (Dougherty and Natow 2015). As college costs continue to rise and state budgets struggle to recover from the recession, governors have prioritized policy solutions to both improve higher education outcomes and improve institutional accountability for funds received. Notable examples include Kentucky governor Matt Bevin, who announced the development of PBF (accompanied by substantial budget cuts) in January 2016 that would prioritize degrees in STEM fields over the humanities. In regard to state spending on higher education, Bevin remarked, "There is not going to be money just for the sake of existence . . . The net result of putting public tax dollars into education is to ensure that we are graduating people that can go into the workforce and get out of their parent's basement, among other things" (Dick 2016). Bevin continued to say literature majors would not be subsidized in the same way as engineering majors, due to the perceived differences in impact for Kentucky's workforce.

In contrast, Arkansas governor Asa Hutchinson announced in October 2016 plans for a $10 million increase to higher education funding, conditional on the development of a new incentive-based funding formula. Hutchinson referred to PBF as his "highest priority in the next legislative session" and stated "the current funding formula for higher education is outdated" (Riddle 2016). Hutchinson also announced plans to implement PBF in fiscal year 2019 to allow enough time for institutions to adjust to the formula. Among the higher education community, Bevin's plan elicited great opposition in Kentucky (Dick 2016), while Hutchinson's plan has largely been supported in Arkansas (Riddle 2016).

Effectiveness

Though performance funding previously has been a popular policy solution for higher education, empirical evidence of its effectiveness in improving postsecondary outcomes, such as degree attainment, is limited. For example, researchers find performance funding does not appear to improve retention or graduation rates (Rutherford and Rabovsky 2014; Sanford and Hunter 2011), certificate or associate degree production (Hillman, Tandberg, and Fryar 2015; Tandberg, Hillman, and Barakat 2014), or baccalaureate degree production (Hillman, Tandberg, and Gross 2014; Tandberg and Hillman 2014). Some evidence suggests, however, that PBF is associated with increases in short-term certificates (Hillman, Tandberg, and Fryar 2015) and greater institutional investment in instructional services (Rabovsky 2012). It is important to point out that these studies primarily focus on PF 1.0 policies and little is known regarding the effectiveness of the most recently implemented PBF policies. Furthermore, PBF policies are often used in conjunction with a cadre of additional completion-related state policies (Complete College America 2013), thus isolating the impact of PBF on institutional outcomes remains a challenge.

On the other hand, Kevin Dougherty and Vikash Reddy (2011), researchers associated with the Community College Research Center at Teachers College, Columbia University (CCRC), found that PBF has had a number of positive, campus-level outcomes, from increased awareness of state goals on college campuses and greater utilization of data in decision making, to organizational learning and the creation of student support services. Erik Ness, Mary Deupree, and Denisa Gándara (2015), who are professors and education researchers, likewise found evidence of substantial campus activity in college completion/degree attainment efforts following the latest implementation of PBF in Tennessee. Campus-level completion initiatives included simple policy revisions, such as eliminating graduation fees, as well as the development of strategic plans for academic advising, course redesign, and data analytics.

Responses and Reforms

Although PBF has been adopted widely across the country over time, there has never been consensus support for the policy. Despite reforms implemented by PF 2.0 models, apprehension toward PBF persists, suggesting this policy may be adaptive but remains controversial. This section will discuss some of these underlying perspectives for and against PBF, and finish by highlighting some of the recent reforms considered to improve previous iterations of PBF models.

Performance-Based Funding vs. Traditional Higher Education Values

Fundamental to the interest in PBF are increased calls for accountability and transparency of the higher education sector by state policy makers and other interested parties. Generally, these stakeholders believe the traditional enrollment-based method of allocating state funding incentivizes institutions to grow enrollments, but ignores how students progress (Auguste et al. 2010). For instance, Complete College America (2013) quoted one higher education leader who explained, "All we really cared about was whether our students showed up on day 12," which determines whether the institution receives the student's financial support allocation. On the other hand, PBF policies offer greater opportunity to hold public institutions accountable for the student beyond the 12th day when determining state funding (Burke 1998). In an op-ed published through the MacIver Institute, Governor Scott Walker (2016) of Wisconsin noted:

> We believe it is important to know specific data such as how many students enroll, how many graduate, how many graduate on time, how much they take out in student loans, how much the student loans cost, how many graduates are employed and in what areas. New funding should help address the needs of students and employers in Wisconsin, and it should be based on performance . . . We want higher education in the state to be more relevant for students, employers, and taxpayers. Our next state budget will find ways to make college more affordable while increasing transparency and relevance.

As Governor Walker emphasizes, performance funding helps align state and institutional priorities, with the intent of moving the needle regarding state goals. Considering the national perspective around higher education, in which it is both perceived as critical for job opportunities and scrutinized as inefficient, a state policy makers' ability to influence institutional decision making is understandably attractive.

The interest in holding public colleges and universities accountable has become notable with the national focus on improving postsecondary degree attainment. Although the initiative began with President Obama's (2009) address to the joint session of Congress and his proclamation that "by 2020, America will once again have the highest proportion of college graduates in the world," due to the decentralized nature of the higher education system, individual states, rather than the federal government, maintain the majority of decision making around policy direction and agenda setting. This reality has led to a variety of policy foci across the country, including developmental education, transfer students, and nontraditional and adult students, often with a connection to the economic and workforce needs of the state. Regardless of these unique policy initiatives, however, PBF can serve as a complementary policy that works with each state's unique measures and desired outcomes. As explained by a report by HCM Strategists, PBF provides a means to align "institutional spending priorities with those of the state . . . holding institutions accountable for performance and rewarding desired outcomes" (Davies 2014). It is the innate flexibility in PBF's design that provides ample latitudes for state implementation and makes it an attractive policy solution in various contexts.

State attention to PBF has been bolstered courtesy of the involvement of several intermediary organizations. Multiple foundations and policy advocacy groups have become vocal advocates of performance funding as a policy solution to aid states in their pursuit of improving postsecondary attainment rates. For example, Complete College America (CCA) developed an Alliance of States, which currently includes 35 states and a total of 42 members, recruited through partnerships with governors and other executive offices. By promoting their "Game Changers" to state executives, CCA (2013) was able to gain credibility for their organization and support for their solutions, including PBF. The Lumina Foundation (2009), which serves as one of CCA's primary funders, has also played an integral role in the spread of PBF by providing multiple rounds of million dollar grants to help states "accelerate efforts to graduate more students" and by producing issue briefs focused on performance funding. Ultimately, due to the national focus on improving postsecondary attainment, there is impetus for states to consider solutions, and the involvement of intermediary organizations has offered states and postsecondary systems technical and financial support around PBF, which has contributed to its widespread consideration and enactment.

Despite the compelling rationale underlying PBF from the perspective of policy makers, there exists opposition to it as a policy solution. In particular, many higher education researchers and associated constituencies have voiced concerns that focusing primarily on performance metrics will adversely affect traditional objectives and values of postsecondary education. Thomas Harnisch (2011) of the American Association of State Colleges and Universities describes some of these disadvantages: a limited understanding of success and institutional performance metrics among PBF systems; a narrowing of institutional missions as colleges and universities work toward the same goals; an overemphasis on efficiency, leading to a watering down of academic standards to make it easier for students to progress through degree programs; and increased inequality among institutions serving traditionally disadvantaged populations or movement away from serving this in-need population. In fact, some scholars have found evidence of such unintended impacts of PBF: Mark Umbricht, Frank Fernandez, and Justin Ortagus (2015) found that performance funding in Indiana has led to decreased admissions rates and increased selectivity at public universities. And Robert Kelchen and Luke Stedrak (2016) suggested institutions subject to performance funding policies may be strategically targeting wealthier students, evidenced by declines in revenues from Pell Grants and changes in institutional expenditures on student financial aid.

Beyond the potential impacts of PBF on broader higher education principles, challengers have questioned its ability to consider the diverse contexts that encompass the American higher education sector. Nicholas Hillman (2016), associate professor of education at the University of Wisconsin at Madison, wrote:

> Performance-based funding regimes are most likely to work in noncomplex situations where performance is easily measured, tasks are simple and routine, goals are unambiguous, employees have direct control over the production process, and there are not multiple people involved in producing the outcome. In higher education, it may be easy to count the number of graduates, but the process of creating a college graduate is anything but simple.

Hillman is highlighting the fact that a student's entrance into the postsecondary sector is heavily reliant on their experience in K-12 education and the distinct characteristics of institutions, including institutional type (e.g., two-year vs. four-year), preferred outcomes (e.g., certificate vs. associates degree vs. bachelors degree), and even an institution's student population (e.g., high school graduates vs. returning adult students). To this end, those opposed to PBF question the formula's capacity to adequately gauge the variation and nuance across colleges and universities within a single state.

Adjustments in PF 2.0 Models

With the established history of PBF policies, it is notable that some PF 2.0 formulas have considered some of these long-standing concerns from the higher education community. For example, Washington's Student Achievement Initiative (SAI), which targets the state's 34 community and technical colleges, considers the diversity among affected institutions and the populations they serve. Specifically, using cross-sectional metrics to appeal to variation in college mission, SAI awards intermediate efforts by students to enable institutions to serve student populations who may seek outcomes other than a formal credential (Jenkins and Shulock 2013). Similarly, the Pennsylvania State System of Higher Education (PASSHE) revised their state's PBF model in 2011–2012 to align better with the mission and goals of their 14 member universities (Cavanaugh and Garland 2012). Even with these considerations, there remains evidence that institutional diversity is not sufficiently considered in all PBF formulas.

Ness, Deupree, and Gándara (2015) conducted 104 interviews across four public postsecondary institutions in Tennessee to examine how each responded to the state's PF 2.0 funding model. Although they note significant efforts directed at improving outcomes, they quote one administrator from Southwest Tennessee Community College, who says, "The formula assumes, I think, that everybody's equal and everyone is not equal by any stretch" (Ness et al., 49). This administrator continues by explaining their institution's student body includes individuals requiring significantly more support than students at other institutions, which is not adequately reflected in awarding funding.

Relatedly, Tiffany Jones (2016), the director of higher education policy at The Education Trust, conducted a case study at a public historically Black college and university (HBCU) and revealed the unique challenges minority-serving institutions (MSIs) face under a PBF regime, further highlighting the potential inequities produced by PBF. She finds that PBF policies often do not take into consideration the unique missions of MSIs nor the student populations served by these types of institutions. In particular, she notes HBCUs and MSIs traditionally serve as a point of access to higher education for underrepresented populations and, by consequence, are often low-resourced and nonselective. Consequently, if these institutions are forced to consider a student body that will aid them in receiving performance-based funds, it is foreseeable that the institutions' mission will be forced to change. Further, these institutions will likely need to shift funding toward strategies that attract more academically prepared students and away from aiding the populations they have historically considered (Jones et al. 2017 provides a more in-depth examination of how performance funding specifically impacts MSIs and underrepresented student populations).

Similar to institutional diversity, some PF 2.0 formulas have addressed the difficulties raised by Jones. In the development of their PBF model, Illinois awards institutions a premium for their successes with specific subpopulations, notably low-income and students traditionally underrepresented in higher education (Phillips 2013). Similar arrangements exist elsewhere, such as Indiana, Ohio, and Tennessee, which have been viewed as a means to accommodate institutions that have lower graduation rates, due to their service with these at-risk populations. Additionally, as noted by a report by HCM Strategists (2011), incentivizing success with this underserved population removes the unintended consequence of "rewarding colleges that have better prepared students, or . . . provide incentives for colleges to make admissions criteria more restrictive" (III) and, therefore, removes concerns that PBF is inherently at odds with postsecondary goals of improving access.

References

Auguste, Byron G., Adam Cota, Kartik Jayaram, and Martha C. A. Laboissière. 2010. *Winning by Degrees: The Strategies of Highly Productive Higher-Education Institutions.* Washington, DC: McKinsey and Company.

Burke, Joseph C. 1998. "Performance Funding: Arguments and Answers." *New Directions for Institutional Research* 97: 85–90.

Cavanaugh, John C., and Peter Garland. 2012. "Performance Funding in Pennsylvania." *Change: The Magazine of Higher Learning* 44(3): 34–39.

Complete College America (CCA). 2013. *The Game Changers: Are States Implementing the Best Reforms to Get More College Graduates?* Indianapolis, IN: Complete College America.

Davies, Lauren. 2014. *State "Shared Responsibility" Policies for Improved Outcomes: Lessons Learned.* Washington, DC: HCM Strategists.

Dick, Jacob. 2016. "Kentucky Universities Await Effects of Bevin's Budget." *College Heights Herald*, February 9. http://wkuherald.com/news/kentucky-universities-await-effects-of-bevin-s-budget/article_f2aff224-cec7-11e5-a3e3-bb5f34ca054e.html (accessed December 10, 2016).

Dougherty, Kevin J., and Rebecca S. Natow. 2015. *The Politics of Performance Funding for Higher Education: Origins, Discontinuations, and Transformations.* Baltimore, MD: Johns Hopkins University Press.

Dougherty, Kevin J., Rebecca S. Natow, and Blanca E. Vega. 2012. "Popular but Unstable: Explaining Why State Performance Funding Systems in the United States Often Do Not Persist." *Teachers College Record* 114(3): 1–41.

Dougherty, Kevin J., and Vikash Reddy. 2011. *The Impacts of State Performance Funding Systems on Higher Education Institutions: Research Literature Review and Policy Recommendations.* New York: Community College Research Center, Teachers College, Columbia University.

Harnisch, Thomas L. 2011. *Performance-Based Funding: A Re-Emerging Strategy in Public Higher Education Financing.* Washington, DC: American Association of State Colleges and Universities.

HCM Strategists. 2011. *Performance Funding in Indiana: An Analysis of Lessons from the Research and Other State Models.* Washington, DC: HCM Strategists.

Hearn, James C. 2015. *Outcomes-Based Funding in Historical and Comparative Context.* Indianapolis, IN: Lumina Foundation.

Hillman, Nicholas W. 2016. "Why Performance-Based College Funding Doesn't Work." *The Century Foundation,* May 25. https://tcf.org/content/report/why-performance-based-college-funding-doesnt-work/ (accessed December 2, 2016).

Hillman, Nicholas W., David A. Tandberg, and Alisa H. Fryar. 2015. "Evaluating the Impacts of 'New' Performance Funding in Higher Education." *Educational Evaluation and Policy Analysis* 37(4): 501–519.

Hillman, Nicholas W., David A. Tandberg, and Jacob P. K. Gross. 2014. "Performance Funding in Higher Education: Do Financial Incentives Impact College Completion?" *The Journal of Higher Education* 85(6): 826–857.

Jenkins, Davis, and Nancy Shulock. 2013. *Metrics, Dollars, and Systems Change: Learning from Washington State's Student Achievement Initiative to Design Effective Postsecondary Performance Funding Policies.* New York: Community College Research Center, Teachers College, Columbia University.

Jones, Tiffany. 2016. "A Historical Mission in the Accountability Era: A Public HBCU and State Performance Funding." *Educational Policy* 30(7): 999–1041.

Jones, Tiffany, Sosanya Jones, Kayla C. Elliott, LaToya Russell Owens, Amanda E. Assalone, and Denisa Gándara. 2017. *Outcomes Based Funding and Race in Higher Education: Can Equity Be Bought?* Basingstoke: Palgrave Macmillan.

Kelchen, Robert, and Luke J. Stedrak. 2016. "Does Performance-Based Funding Affect Colleges' Financial Priorities?" *Journal of Education Finance* 41(3): 302–321.

Lumina Foundation. 2009. "Lumina Foundation Announces State Grants to Boost U.S. Higher Education Productivity." *Lumina Foundation,* November 24. https://www.luminafoundation.org/news-and-views/lumina-foundation-announces-state-grants-to-boost-u-s-higher-education-productivity (accessed November 22, 2016).

Ness, Erik C., Mary M. Deupree, and Denisa Gándara. 2015. *Campus Responses to Outcomes-Based Funding in Tennessee: Robust, Aligned, and Contested.* Nashville: Tennessee Higher Education Commission.

Obama, Barack. 2009. "Remarks of President Barack Obama—Address to Joint Session of Congress." *The White House,* February 24. https://obamawhitehouse.archives.gov/the-press-office/remarks-president-barack-obama-address-joint-session-congress (accessed November 22, 2016).

Parry, Marc, Kelly Field, and Beckie Supiano. 2013. "The Gates Effect." *The Chronicle of Higher Education,* July 14. http://chronicle.com/article/The-Gates-Effect/140323/ (accessed December 2, 2016).

Phillips, Alan. 2013. "Illinois Higher Education Performance Funding Model." Presentation for the Performance Funding Steering Committee Meeting, January 14. http://www.ibhe.org/FridayMemo/PDF/120113_PFPresentation.pdf (accessed December 2, 2016).

Rabovsky, Thomas M. 2012. "Accountability in Higher Education: Exploring Impacts on State Budgets and Institutional Spending Patterns." *Journal of Public Administration Research and Theory* 22: 675–700.

Riddle, Brandon. 2016. "Hutchinson Proposes $10M Increase in Higher-Ed Funding if New Formula Approved." *Arkansas Online*, October 31. http://www.arkansasonline.com/news/2016/oct/31/hutchinson-proposes-10m-increase-higher-ed-funding/?f=news-arkansas (accessed December 10, 2016).

Rutherford, Amanda, and Thomas M. Rabovsky. 2014. "Evaluating Impacts of Performance Funding Policies on Student Outcomes in Higher Education." *The ANNALS of the American Academy of Political and Social Science* 655(1): 185–208.

Sanford, Thomas. S., and James M. Hunter. 2011. "Impact of Performance-Funding on Retention and Graduation Rates." *Education Policy Analysis Archives* 19(33): 1–30.

Snyder, Martha, and Brian Fox. 2016. *Driving Better Outcomes: Fiscal Year 2016 State Status and Typology Update.* Washington, DC: HCM Strategists.

Tandberg, David A., and Nicholas W. Hillman. 2014. "State Higher Education Performance Funding: Data, Outcomes, and Policy Implications." *Journal of Education Finance* 39(3): 222–243.

Tandberg, David A., Nicholas W. Hillman, and Mohamed Barakat. 2014. "State Higher Education Performance Funding for Community Colleges: Diverse Effects and Policy Implications." *Teachers College Record* 116(12): 1–31.

Umbricht, Mark R., Frank Fernandez, and Justin C. Ortagus. 2015. "An Examination of the (Un)Intended Consequences of Performance Funding in Higher Education." *Educational Policy*: 1–31. doi: 10.1177/0895904815614398.

Walker, Scott. 2016. "Gov. Walker: Tuition Freeze Is Key to College Affordability." *MacIver Institute*, August 4. http://www.maciverinstitute.com/2016/08/gov-walker-tuition-freeze-is-key-to-college-affordability/ (accessed December 10, 2016).

Zumeta, William, and Alicia Kinne. 2011. "Accountability Policies: Directions Old and New." In *The States and Public Higher Education Policy: Affordability, Access, and Accountability,* 2nd ed., edited by Donald E. Heller, 173–199. Baltimore, MD: Johns Hopkins University Press.

Zumeta, William, and Amy Y. Li. 2016. *Assessing the Underpinnings of Performance Funding 2.0: Will This Dog Hunt?* New York: TIAA Institute.

CHAPTER TWENTY-THREE

The Future of Public Higher Education Funding: A Federal– State Partnership

F. King Alexander and Ashley Arceneaux

Effective higher education administrators—the kind who can lead through hard times and cultivate strengths out of weaknesses—require an extensive background of expertise to draw upon in times of need. To truly understand the comprehensive scope of the higher education environment one must be an expert in recruiting, retention, student success, budgeting strategies, and general administrative processes . . . but it does not stop there. A critical element often overlooked is that today's leaders must be fluent in policy developments, political challenges, and the convergence of the political sphere upon the entire academic enterprise. It has been said that "the nexus between economics and politics is key to understanding the modern world" (Ferguson 2001, 60). Truer words have rarely been spoken, and in today's highly politicized world, even higher education cannot escape their implications. In fact, nearly every mounting crisis facing higher education today has roots in policies developed half a century ago—and in the political interference that occurred before, during, and after their implementation. That is the cause of our nation's rapid disinvestment from its public colleges and universities, and the driving force behind the need for a federal–state partnership that would incentivize states to maintain or increase funding for their state colleges and universities by leveraging federal dollars.

In short, the key to how colleges and universities are financed often has more to do with politics than economics. And nowhere is this more plainly seen than in the funding environment for public colleges and universities. The inequities within this system all are deeply embedded within the political sphere. This makes it imperative that policy makers analyze the political dynamics and underlying motivations of existing higher education finance policies to effectively address the challenges facing public higher education today. It also means that effective higher education administrators must understand the full context of what shaped our current system in order to enact real change in the future and to avoid unforeseen policy implications that could negatively impact students for generations to come.

To reach the point of truly understanding the current plight of higher education, particularly the challenges facing our nation's public colleges and universities, one must understand the history informing today's policies and funding models. Everything from the soaring cost crisis, where more than 200 universities charge more in tuition and fees than the median U.S. annual household income,[1] to the free college craze, which has held sway over national media outlets for the past several years,[2] can be traced 50 years back to what should have been a banner moment for higher education—the authorization of the original Higher Education Act (HEA).

HEA: The Beginning

In 1965, the future of American higher education looked bright, and not just for the privileged, when President Lyndon Johnson signed into law the HEA —an expansive document that promised to expand access to higher education for individuals of any background, to promote affordability of tuition and fees, and to determine new pathways to college for our nation's neediest students. Johnson considered the HEA a part of his war against poverty (Mettler 2014, 58), as he viewed higher education and a college degree as the key to advancing the social mobility of most Americans.

However, instead of a higher education overhaul resulting in increased access and a leveled playing field for all, what followed was a series of major policy decisions that formed our modern college and university system—and set the stage for two defining moments in the history of higher education. First, this series of events laid the groundwork for the prioritization of private over public higher education, and, second, it paved the way for the creation of predatory for-profit institutions that survive on federal funds with little regard for the students they serve. Our nation's most challenging issues followed like clockwork, ranging from the student indebtedness crisis and skyrocketing tuition to the stagnation of social mobility.

Included in HEA's hefty volumes was the development of Title IV, our nation's direct student aid policy. Title IV and associated funds were developed in order to create pathways for students of little-to-no means to have access to higher education. Its creation opened the doorway for long and politically fueled conversations about the best way to effectively and fairly distribute financial aid. Out of these heated debates, two primary delivery mechanisms were developed and dissected: direct student aid and institutional aid. One of the penultimate moments in this pivotal policy debate, which essentially started in 1965 and ran through 1972, was the eventual acceptance of direct federal student aid as the model upon which our country would distribute federal student aid dollars. Direct student aid allows taxpayer dollars to flow to any number of colleges or universities regardless of their mission, outcomes, or performance (Alexander 2008, 173). At the time, it was argued by public college and university associations that direct institutional aid would have allowed federal funding to go to universities in order to maintain access, quality, and affordability. This singular decision paved the way toward debt dependency and the demise of our public higher education system—and also pitted public and private higher education against one another not just over students but over federal dollars.

Prior to the 1965 through 1972 deliberations, public higher education had experienced a growing market share of the student population due to widespread affordability, while private colleges and universities had watched their market share consistently decrease. So, during these intense debates about how to reshape and better form educational policies, private college and university advocates leveraged the opportunity to create new pathways for students to attain degrees from their higher cost institutions. To provide a firm foundation upon which to base their assertions, they proclaimed that the great diversity of the American higher education system was at risk. However, they were not referring to the diversity of the overall student body but rather the diversity of the types of higher education institutions available in America. In other words, the claim was that many private colleges and universities were at risk of closure due to crumbling finances and lack of student enrollment and that a loss of this type of school would be detrimental to the country.

Carnegie Commission on Higher Education Reports in the late 1960s and early 1970s documented the assertions that prominent and once wealthy private institutions were headed to financial ruin if tuition gaps and population shifts continued to take place nationwide. Among the institutions named as being in financial trouble were Stanford University, Tulane University, Syracuse University, and Boston College. Those heading for financial hardship included New York University and Harvard University (Carnegie Commission on Higher Education 1972). Little to no real financial evidence was produced to substantiate these claims that such prominent private universities were actually facing significant hardship other than natural market fluctuations resulting from a national enrollment shift toward public colleges and universities.

Opponents of the direct student aid approach argued that public dollars should only flow to institutions that served the public good or a public mission. Although discussions were mounted, lobbyists were also deployed in the struggle to frame higher education funding for the foreseeable future.

As the intensity of the arguments and debates flared, politicians eventually determined to let the money follow the student rather than flow directly to the institution, essentially leaving the nation's higher education funding model in the hands of students. The availability of financial support was intended to both allow low-income students access to private universities and allow those same institutions to slow their movement toward tuition increases. It seemed like an easy fix at the time, but few followed the policy implications (Mettler 2014) down to their inevitable end and determined whether these objectives have been met 50 years later.

When public university supporters countered with concerns about the viability of their own financial futures, federal policy makers responded with a common refrain: state governments were responsible for supporting public institutions. Federal lawmakers remained convinced that public colleges and universities would continue to be supported primarily by their state's governments while the new federal funding policies were expected to supplement, not supplant, state funds.

Ultimately, state governments began to reduce funding in 1981 (Mortenson 2015). As they did so, public colleges and universities began to see reduced financial support. In the ensuing decade, we saw widespread efforts at "belt-tightening," and then, as the Great Recession entered into our lexicon, a downward spiral that threatened the existence of many of our nation's public higher education institutions. Today, funding for public higher education rests at 1965 tax effort levels (Mortenson 2015)—an unsettling throwback to a time of hope for this industry.

Another important historical consideration that took place during the great policy debates of 1965–1972 was the creation of the State Student Incentive Grant (SSIG) program, which occurred during the 1972 HEA reauthorization. Prior to SSIG, most states had restrictions in place governing the allocation of state dollars to private colleges and universities. SSIG leveraged federal dollars through a matching plan designed to encourage states to either create or enhance state student aid programs. Private universities strongly supported SSIG because it provided a new revenue source that allowed them to operate with state support.

Many states fought this federal matching directive, with Nebraska, Colorado, South Carolina, Kentucky, and others declaring SSIG unconstitutional. Despite these constitutional restrictions, the program—and its federal leverage—proved very effective. In 1972, 38 percent of states had state-specific student aid programs. Four years after SSIG's adoption, 78 percent of states had developed a program that both provided financial aid to the students of their state and took advantage of the federal dollars being offered through the matching program.

However, the program's price sensitivity became a contributing factor driving the wealth of private and for-profit universities. SSIG was designed to encourage states to create or improve state student aid programs. However, although the principles behind SSIG were sound, the policy contained loopholes that created resounding repercussions that still impact today's students. SSIG and many ensuing state-based programs are much more price sensitive than federal student aid grant programs. In other words, if a university charges a higher price for attendance, then its students are able to qualify for more student aid in many states. Over the years many of these state programs directly benefited both private and for-profit institutions. For example in California for many years, a student attending a California State University institution would receive a lower average Cal Grant A (state-based aid for qualifying California students) amount than students attending higher priced institutions like the University of the United States of America or Corinthian College, which are for-profit institutions in Southern California. In Ohio, one state student aid program is restricted only to students attending private institutions. Also, in New York and Massachusetts, larger student aid awards are allocated to students attending nonpublic institutions. Nationwide, approximately 35 to 40 cents of every state student aid dollar flows to private institutions, proving that the use of federal funding leverage in the SSIG program (later renamed the Leveraging Educational Assistance Partnership [LEAP] program) made a significant difference in the higher education landscape for private colleges and universities.

As federal dollars began to flow freely to private universities in the late 1970s, the student debt era was ushered in with the passage of the Middle Income Assistance Act in 1978. This act essentially eliminated increased wealth caps that previously restricted access to student loans, allowing middle- and upper-income students to gain access to vast amounts of federal student loan funds. This toxic marriage created an extremely cost-sensitive environment that allowed tuition to be increased more frequently than ever before because the difference was not immediately applicable to the student—it came later, in the form of loan payments. This might have been acceptable had public universities remained the bastion of affordability and access they had previously been, but that was not the case.

Now that loan-based assistance was freely available to middle- and upper-income families, nimble higher education institutions began to pay attention to the dollars on the table. The availability of additional resources led to many colleges and universities increasing their tuition at a record pace, creating a vicious cycle in which students then needed to take out more loans to keep up with rising prices. This phenomenon was predicted in the late 1960s by M. M. Chambers, the founder of The Grapevine at Illinois State

University. The Grapevine was the first real annual state funding comparative data collection. By the end of the next decade, the first student indebtedness problem began to emerge and became a national issue of great concern.
Today, the student debt issue is among the nation's most problematic challenges, resulting in over $1.3 trillion in student indebtedness.

Cause and Effect: Where We Are Today

The convergence of a free flowing federal direct student aid system, student debt growth, and continued state abandonment of their state funding
responsibilities to its public colleges and universities led the *Economist* magazine in 2001 to proclaim that the American higher education enterprise,
because of its lack of accountability and its federal funding practices, was the
"Wild West" of higher education worldwide.

In addition to these monumental funding challenges, public higher education is balancing many new high profile and politically charged issues, with
conflicts related to free speech, sexual assault, and racial considerations. In
fact, universities haven't been home to such high-profile protests and controversies since the civil rights era, a fact noted by James Dickey in a May 31,
2016, article for *Time*. High-visibility issues such as these make funding all
the more tenuous—federal and state dollars are often targeted in the aftermath of a crisis. As noted by Anemona Hartocollis in the *New York Times* on
August 4, 2016, donor dollars similarly tend to see a reduction in the immediate fallout of anything from a protest to a scandal.

Taking all this into consideration, we can still boil down higher education's primary challenge into one single question: Who should fund higher
education? The student, the state, or the federal government? And the root of
the question is less existential than it sounds—after all, to determine ownership of the cost, we must consider who reaps the benefits.

Statistically, we are able to show that individuals with a college degree
earn up to $1 million more over a career (Carnevale, Cheah, and Hanson
2015) and enjoy higher job satisfaction and better health outcomes than their
nondegreed counterpoints. But those benefits do not stop there. Regarding
social good benefits that accrue to everyone, we are also able to point to data
that show degree-holders are more civically engaged and that an investment
in higher education has a consistent social rate of return of more than 13
percent.

But for those forced into a position where college seems like the delay of a
paycheck, these arguments have the ring of the far-distant future or even
worse, the disconnected Ivory Tower. Because of the perception that a college
degree comes with an immense price tag and a lifetime of debt, many have
begun to question whether college is really worth it, despite study after study
proving the long-term benefits of a degree. And until we are able to control

costs and increase access, we will continue to lose bright young minds to the lure of—or the need to—immediately entering into the workforce.

Prior to the 2016 presidential election, the country seemed headed toward the development of a federal–state partnership that would leverage federal funding to incentivize states to maintain or increase their financial support of public higher education. But in the surprise victory of President Trump, higher education was handed a great deal of uncertainty, as his campaign did not delve into deep policy discussions on the topic.

As it stands today, federal dollars are still being spent on higher education—with a majority allocated to financial aid for students—to the tune of $170 billion compared to the states' combined efforts totaling around $75 billion. But with little-to-no policy adaption since 1972, the outcomes of higher education funding do not paint an optimistic picture of the future.

Approximately 7 in 10 graduates leave university with debt, and the average level of indebtedness hovers near $30,000 (Reed and Cochrane 2014). Overall, student loan debt stands at $1.31 trillion in (New York Federal Reserve 2016)—surpassing even credit card debt and second only to mortgage loans. And according to Ratcliffe and McKernan (2013), one-third of student loan borrowers never graduate, leaving them much more vulnerable to default.[3] Ratcliffe and McKernan also show that African Americans and Hispanics are nearly twice as likely as Whites to have student loan debt. On top of that, only 51 percent of Hispanic students and 40 percent of African American students actually finish their degrees. The Consumer Reports National Research Center shows that 63 percent of those who default on student loans are those who dropped out of college before graduating.

Only 68 percent of American high school graduates enroll in college, and only 59 percent of them ever receive a degree. Mortenson (2015) demonstrates that 63 percent of children from high-income households complete a bachelor's degree, compared with only 24 percent of the poorest students. The Education Trust (Nguyen 2012a, b) has shown that the attainment rate for Whites age 25–29 is 40 percent while it is around 20 percent for African Americans and for Hispanics it is only one-third that of Whites. .

In short, we have not yet moved the needle in terms of accessibility for our low-income families with the bulk of them still attending the most affordable public colleges and universities. This, paired with a lack of transparency on the part of higher education related to student success outcomes and metrics, has created a vicious cycle in which reduced funding to public higher education in particular drives up tuition and fees, which increasingly strains the bonds of accessibility. Although wealthier students can cover the difference between the aid they receive and the tuition they are responsible for paying and the lowest-income families qualify for federal- and state-based aid, middle-class families began to feel an increased strain as their budgets were stretched. Resentment grew, and an outcry for relief began to gain momentum, resulting in state-specific merit-based aid programs such as Georgia's HOPE Scholarship (1993) and Louisiana's TOPS program (1997). As nationwide budget shortages continue to plague most states, these programs created a vicious cycle in which the states rob college budgets to feed the aid programs—essentially asking students to pay for their college education twice.

The rise of for-profit institutions entering the market, then, in the case of Corinthian and ITT, being shut down due to nonperformance and high student loan default rates, has left taxpayers to foot the bill and millions of students even worse off than they started. This has not helped raise the public level of trust in higher education. For-profit institutions have proven to be almost acrobatic in their ability to leverage market weaknesses, as well as expansive in both their marketing and lobbying spends. Currently, these institutions enroll approximately 11 percent of the nation's student population while acquiring 72 percent of their funds from the federal government, nearly 30 percent of all Pell Grants, 37 percent of all GI Bill benefits, and producing 47 percent of all student loan defaults (Senate HELP Committee Report on For Profits 2012). In fact, for-profit universities receive approximately 86 percent of their funding from taxpayer dollars while graduating only 22 percent of attending students. And as many as 72 percent of the programs offered at for-profit colleges produce graduates who earn less than high school dropouts. In turn, a stunning 94 percent of for-profit students who gain bachelor's degrees take out loans, at an average of $32,700 per student. Within three years, 23 percent have defaulted. In fact, 15 percent of for-profits have default rates of more than 30 percent and 44 percent have rates over 20 percent (Mettler 2014). And we know they aggressively pursue low income and veteran students with no regard for their future outcomes, and they have rather concentrated their efforts on lobbying and developing nimble business operations that allow them to rake in every federal dollar available.

So more than 50 years after the passage of the original HEA, our private colleges and universities, those same institutions that lobbied for direct student aid so that they could increase the number of low-income students who could access a private education, have not delivered on their earlier promises of increased accessibility and affordability. These selective institutions are lauded for being exclusive and expensive, but they could be doing more to serve our nation's most vulnerable students. The entire Ivy League combined enrolls only about 10,000 Pell Grant recipients, while public institutions like the California State University system enroll more than 200,000.

That's why public higher education is society's best hope for social mobility. In fact, a recent study by Raj Chetty et al. 2017 demonstrated that, as David Leonhardt of the *New York Times* put it in his January 18, 2017, article, more of today's college graduates come from universities that "look a lot less like Harvard or the University of Michigan than like City College or the University of Texas at El Paso." California State University Los Angeles, for example, leads the nation in taking students from the bottom fifth of income and moving them into the top. In fact, the top five universities in terms of social mobility are all public institutions. But public higher education as we know it will die—and die soon—unless rapid state disinvestment is stemmed.

The rapid and unprecedented 30-year decline in state funding for public colleges and universities has created a disintegrating situation that will negatively impact not only today's students, but the future of the United States. Bearing in mind stagnant access and completion rates, our country simply cannot afford to restrict access to students. This country once led OECD peer countries in terms of college completion—now we lag at 13th among our younger generation and are dropping. A startling fact to consider: the baby boomers—who represent the generation that benefited most from generous higher education funding, GI Bill aid, and other aid programs geared specifically toward increasing college access—still rank first in the world in terms of being college credentialed. This generation embodies the possibilities that come with proper higher education funding and incentives. Around the start of World War II, only 1 in every 20 Americans held a college degree, but by 1977—after years of policies advancing aid for veterans—that number was one in four (Mettler 2014).

Public universities represent the low-cost, high-value option for students, educating nearly 70 percent of students in the United States. As public institutions, they are also bound by state regulations and restrictions that private universities do not have. They have smaller endowments and tend to have less flexibility in terms of recovering from state budget reductions, which have become the new normal. Without a solution to continued state disinvestments, public universities will continue to struggle to adapt to their new funding realities, making them less able to meet their public missions of access and affordability. That is why a federal–state partnership that would drive states to better support their public colleges and universities by offering federal dollars for a certain threshold of advancement is key to saving public higher education.

As described in "The Silent Crisis: The Relative Fiscal Capacity of Public Universities to Compete for Faculty" (Alexander 2001) public universities first began to increase tuition as a matter of survival, as states saw the increase in federal student aid funding as an opportunity to begin decreasing their financial commitments to colleges and universities. Today, studies show that 80 percent of tuition increases in public colleges and universities over the past several years are directly linked to state disinvestment (Huelsman 2015). And College Board data show that at least nine major public universities have increased tuition more than 20 percent since 2011. Other recent studies have also shown that state funding reductions are not only below prerecession levels but also lower than what they were in 1966 after being adjusted for inflation (Mitchell et al. 2014; Mortenson 2015).[4]

Without some ability to have consistent funding that allows for long-term strategic planning, investment in student success and infrastructure, and maintaining academic excellence, public universities will continue to find themselves on the losing end of the equation when competing with private institutions.

When combining the weight of all these factors, it's not a stretch to say that the extinction of public higher education is in sight—in fact, in less than 10 years, Colorado will become the first state in the nation to completely get out of the public higher education business (Mortenson 2015). Many states will follow suit soon after if nothing is done to stem state disinvestment. The most efficient and effective solution to this problem is the development of a federal–state partnership that would leverage federal funds to incentivize states to maintain or increase their level of financial support for their public colleges and universities.

Partnering for Solutions

Federal–state partnerships are not a new concept. In fact, such partnerships are how we handle highways and health care in our country. But it's not entirely new to higher education in the United States, either. Perhaps the greatest example of how effective federal–state partnerships have been is the Morrill Act or Land-Grant Act of 1862. In this case, federal lands served as the leverage. They were given to state governments throughout the country in exchange for the creation of new public colleges and universities primarily developed to educate more engineers, agricultural scientists, and military science graduates. This federal–state partnership served as the foundation for the United States' global leadership in higher education just a century later.

The need for a federal–state match has never been greater. In the Higher Education Act (HEA) reauthorization efforts in 2007, a first maintenance of effort (MOE) provision was added into the language, using federal leverage to protect higher education from dramatic state funding cuts. Then, in 2008 and 2009, the same MOE language drafted in 2007 in HEA was successfully transferred into the American Recovery and Reinvestment Act (ARRA), which only allowed states to use education stimulus funds if they did not cut their higher education budgets below 2006 funding levels. In 2007 and 2008, 48 governors and the National Governor's Association strongly opposed federal MOE provisions. Ironically, within six weeks after the MOE was passed by Congress, 19 states cut their higher education budgets to the very threshold of where the federal penalties would apply. The federal leverage worked well and states remained very reluctant to cross the federal line.

For example, Tennessee at that time had a $1.1 billion higher education budget, but cut funding within $13 of where the penalties applied. Oregon and Colorado reduced their higher education budgets within $3 of the federal penalties. As you can see, this approach was able to somewhat stem the inevitable mass disinvestment trend by states across the nation.

The concept of an MOE has become incredibly politicized and divisive, collecting pushback primarily from groups such as the National Governors Association and the National Conference of State Legislatures. Their rebuttals against the efficacy of this policy are essentially boiled down into an argument for state's rights: enacting such leverage, they say, undermines a state's right to control its own priorities (Alexander et al. 2010, 82–84).

For many years, higher education has operated under a veil of mystery. Everyday American citizens—even those with degrees—remain largely uninformed of the real workings that occur in the typical research university. This becomes a real problem as we rely more and more upon federal dollars to fund our institutions and when our consumer base begins to conflate cost with quality.

The era of "trust us, we're worth it" has ended. Today's world is data-driven, and higher education must embrace that fact. When we make a purchase, we do research. If we're buying a car, we consult the *Kelley Blue Book*. We read consumer reviews and weigh expert opinions. But in many cases, families have been largely kept in the dark about what a college really offers other than shiny brochures and pretty Web sites.

The data not only help us make better decisions about student success measures but also help students and families select the right university and build their expectations about what their degree will provide upon fact rather than inference. Markets fail when inadequate and restricted information permeates the environment. A federal unit record system would be the ideal way to approach this problem, but, in 2008, Congress banned the use of its current student data for such a purpose (Palmer 2016).

Making information such as a university's graduation outcomes, average level of student indebtedness, student loan default rates, and early and mid-career earnings available to the public helps our students, parents, and taxpayers make better decisions about where to invest their financial and educational futures. But it also points out weaknesses and flaws, and universities—particularly those not doing a good job of graduating students with valuable degrees—have many reasons to want this type of information to be restricted from public consumption. One look at the data related to for-profit institutions' outcomes demonstrates the value of keeping some insights out of consumer hands.

The challenges we face in terms of data accessibility lead directly to another reform we desperately need to undertake as a country. The campus-based aid system, which provides funds to an institution, which then

distributes those funds to individual students who qualify, has become completely inverted. This type of aid is composed of Federal Work Study, Federal
Supplemental Educational Opportunity Grants (FSEOG), and Perkins Loans.
Meant to help low-income students, the policies governing its distribution
and allocation have been neglected and the entire program is in need of critical updates if it is to remain relevant.

In 2013–2014, Harvard received $1.3 million in FSEOG funding, North-
western University received $2.1 million, and Princeton University received
$1 million (National Association of Student Financial Aid Administrators
Campus-Based Aid Allocation Task Force 2014). Yet the same data show
some public flagship universities that served four to five times as many low-
income students during the same period received considerably lower allocations. For instance, in 2013–2014, the University of Tennessee received
$500,000, the University of Kentucky received $450,000, and Louisiana
State University received just $350,000.

This pattern also holds true for Work Study dollars. In 2013–2014 Harvard received $3.7 million, Georgetown received $2.3 million, and Yale
received $1.7 million, while California State University at Long Beach
received $1.2 million, Louisiana State University received $920,000, and
Auburn University received $900,000. As you can see, the total amount of
dollars allocated bears no resemblance to a university's low-income population size.

Data show us that the current allocation structure simply doesn't work if
the goal is to reach as many low-income students as possible. This is in large
part due to an antiquated allocation institution built in a manner that priori-
tizes when a college or university joined the program versus the amount of
low-income students it actually educates.

The Department of Education currently maintains three sets of allocation
rules for institutions, but each essentially boils down to the same concept: a
university gets a base guarantee, which is the same allocation it received in
previous years, with the opportunity for a "fair share" increase. It is important to note that the fair share concept is highly price sensitive since it
includes cost of attendance in the equation, essentially subsidizing universities that charge extensive amounts (United States Annotated Codes 20 and
42). Once a base guarantee is set, there is no further evaluation of an institution's allocation—unless it is to allocate an additional "fair share" amount of
money (Smole 2012). It also means that the majority of federal funds for
these critical programs are being portioned out in a way that does not address
real student need.

One allocation is for universities and colleges that participated in work–
study or FSEOG prior to or during the 1999–2000 award year. The second is
for those who began participating after that period but are not first- or second-
time participants, and the third is for first- and second-time participants.

Institutions falling into the first category receive 100 percent of their FY 1999 levels in what's referred to as a "base guarantee," along with a "fair share increase" equal to the sum of aid provided through Pell, ACG, SMART, and LEAP subtracted from the cost of attendance and estimated family contribution of a representative sample of undergraduates at each institution.

Colleges and universities falling into the second award tier receive a base guarantee of whichever is greatest: 90 percent of the funds received in their second year of participation, or $5,000. And those in the third tier receive the greater of $5,000, 90 percent of an amount proportional to that received by comparable institutions, or 90 percent of what it received in its first year of participation.

If work–study and FSEOG formulas were reworked to actually address accessibility issues, the programs could really make a difference for many of our underprivileged and underrepresented students. Right now, "given that many of the colleges in the top ten for both FWS and SEOG . . . have large endowments and enroll relatively small numbers of Pell Grant recipients, it is clear that the campus-based aid programs currently do little to encourage college opportunity" (Kelchen 2014, 23). Allocations could be based on any number of metrics, including the number of Pell recipients a university serves, to get better and more immediate results.

Therefore, it is safe to say that not only were our federal direct student aid policies ill-conceived and designed to protect the diversity of the American higher education system; they have also provided private colleges and universities with a competitive advantage over our public higher education institutions. This has manifested itself in creating a tuition- and fees-based federal model that allows those institutions that are increasingly student tuition- and fee-based to continually pursue this primary funding source while also allowing our states to disinvest in our lower cost and affordable public colleges and universities. To overcome the outcomes of the past 50 years of federal policies that have borne witness to the great decline of the American public higher education, we must rethink how we are going to adopt new policies devised to save our public institutions or we will be witnessing the decline of the diversity of the American higher education system—in this case, at the expense of our public colleges and universities.

Notes

1. The United States indicates that the median American household income is $51,000 a year.

2. Free college proposals, while not new, surged in popularity during the 2016 presidential election, especially during Sen. Bernie Sanders campaign. Following the election, several governors, including Gov. Cuomo of New York, announced plans for state-specific free tuition programs.

3. Studies (Carnevale, Cheah and Hanson 2015) have repeatedly shown that those without a degree earn approximately $1 million less over the course of a lifetime than those with a degree. These imbalances affect a disproportionate share of minorities. According to Ratcliffe and McKernan (2013), African Americans and Hispanics are nearly twice as likely as Whites to have student loan debt, yet the Education Trust (2012) has shown that the attainment rate for Whites age 25–29 is 40 percent while African Americans hover at around 20 percent, and Hispanic attainment is only one-third that of Whites. (http://chronicle .com/article/Reports-Highlight-Colleges/134560/)

4. Mortenson's analysis uses "Grapevine" state funding data from Illinois State University and compares state fiscal support for higher education per $1,000 of Personal Income from FY 1961 to FY 2015.

References

Alexander, F. King. 2001. "The Silent Crisis: The Relative Fiscal Capacity of Public Universities to Compete for Faculty." *The Review of Higher Education* 24(2): 113–129.

Alexander, F. King. 2008. "Public Policy Reform and Expanding Societal Expectations." *Generational Shockwaves and the Implications for Higher Education*, edited by Donald E. Heller and Madeleine B. d'Ambrosio, 173. TIAA-CREF Institute Series on Higher Education.

Alexander, F. King, Thomas Harnisch, Daniel Hurley, and Robert Moran. 2010. "Maintenance of Effort: An Evolving Federal-State Policy Approach to Ensuring College Affordability." *Journal of Education Finance* 36(1): 76–87.

Ferguson, Niall. 2001. *The Cash Nexus*. New York: Basic Books.

Kelchen, Robert. 2014. "Exploring Trends and Alternative Allocations Strategies for campus-Based Financial Aid Programs." *Association for Education Finance and Policy* 31: 23.

Leonhardt, David. 2017. "America's Great Working-Class Colleges." *New York Times*.

Mettler, Suzanne. 2014. *Degrees of Inequality*. New York: Basic Books.

Mitchell, M., V. Palacios, and M. Leachman. 2014. *States Are Still Funding Higher Education Below Pre-Recession Levels*. Washington, DC: Center on Budget and Policy Priorities.

Mortenson, Tom. 2015. "Unequal Family Income and Unequal Educational Opportunity." *Postsecondary Education Opportunity* 278: 14.

Mortenson, Tom. 2015. "State Investment and Disinvestment in Higher Education 1961–2015." *Postsecondary Education Opportunity* 272: 2–10.

National Association of Student Financial Aid Administrators Campus-Based Aid Allocation Task Force. 2014. "Estimated Effects of NASFAA's Campus-based Proposals on Institutional Allocations." Accessed April 2016, 2017. http://www.nasfaa.org/uploads/documents/ektron/ba51b208-c203 -4afe-9e28-88ee78f8337e/84c19891c281442fb7d0867d9dfe36132.pdf

Nguyen, Mary. 2012a. *Advancing to Completion: Increasing Degree Attainment by Improving Graduation Rates and Closing Gaps for African-American Students.* Washington, DC: Education Trust.

Nguyen, Mary. 2012b. *Advancing to Completion: Increasing Degree Attainment by Improving Graduation Rates and Closing Gaps for Hispanic Students.* Washington, DC: Education Trust.

Palmer, Iris. 2016. "Is Stitching State Data Systems Together the Solution to the College Blackout?" New America.

Ratcliffe, Caroline, and Signe-Mary McKernan. 2013. "Forever in Your Debt: Who Has Student Loan Debt, and Who's Worried?" The Urban Institute.

Reed, Matthew, and Debbie Cochrane. 2014. *Student Debt and the Class of 2013.* Washington, DC: The Institute for College Access and Success.

Smole, D. 2012. *Campus-Based Student Financial Aid Programs under the Higher Education Act.* Washington, DC: Congressional Research Service.

United States Code Annotated Title 20: Education, Chapter 28: Higher Education Resources and Student Assistance, Subchapter IV: Student Assistance, Part A: Grants to Students in Attendance at Institutions of Higher Education, and Subpart 3: Federal Supplemental Education Opportunity Grants. August 14, 2008.

United States Code Annotated Title 42: The Public Health and Welfare, Chapter 34: Economic Opportunity Program, Subchapter I: Research and Demonstrations, Part C: Federal Work–Study Programs.

About the Editor and Contributors

Editor

Joy Blanchard is an associate professor of higher education at Louisiana State University. Her research focuses on higher-education law, primarily on issues related to intercollegiate athletics, negligence liability, and faculty life. She is a former member of the board of directors of the Education Law Association. Joy previously worked in student affairs, including as assistant dean of students at the University of Louisiana at Lafayette.

Contributors

F. King Alexander is president of LSU. Dr. Alexander has been asked to represent public higher-education colleges and universities on numerous occasions to the U.S. Congress on issues of college affordability, student indebtedness, and institutional efficiency and effectiveness in efforts to address many of the growing challenges facing American higher education. He has testified before the Senate Committee on Health, Education, Labor & Pensions (HELP), the U.S. Commission on Civil Rights, and the Advisory Committee on Student Financial Assistance, among others.

Charlie Andrews is assistant vice president for Undergraduate Education at Florida International University (FIU). He has worked in several areas of both academic and student affairs, including academic advising, campus life, new student orientation, and student success programs. He also served as president of NODA from 2004 to 2007. In addition to his work on student success, he also teaches a graduate course in foundations of academic advising for the School of Education at FIU.

Ashley Arceneaux is director of presidential and policy communications at LSU. Her expertise includes developing strategic plans that keep higher-education institutions engaged in federal policy discussions.

Ashley B. Clayton is an assistant professor of higher education at Louisiana State University. Her research examines the barriers, systems, and policies that aid or inhibit postsecondary access and success for underrepresented student populations. She has previously worked in the college access field, including Undergraduate Admissions at Virginia Tech and TRIO Upward Bound at Roanoke College.

David DiRamio is associate professor of higher education at Auburn University. Since 2008, David has become a nationally known researcher/speaker reporting on veterans in college. DiRamio's books include *Veterans in Higher Education* (2011) and *Creating a Veteran-Friendly Campus* (2009). Recent research about female student veterans is featured in *College Student Journal* (2015) and NASPA's *JWHE* (2016). His third book, *What's Next for Student Veterans?*, will be published in fall 2017. In both 2012 and 2013, David presented his research at the Stetson Conference on Law and Higher Education.

Paul William Eaton is assistant professor of educational leadership at Sam Houston State University. Paul's research interests include inquiries into digital technologies in education and human identity-subjectification-*becoming*; complexity theory's application to educational research; postqualitative and posthumanist inquiry; and curriculum theorizing-philosophy in the realms of postsecondary education and student affairs. Follow Paul on Twitter @ profpeaton. His blog is located at https://profpeaton.com.

Liliana M. Garces is associate professor in the program of higher education leadership at the University of Texas at Austin and affiliate faculty at the University of Texas School of Law. Her research, focused on the dynamics of law and educational policy, examines access, diversity, and equity policies for underrepresented populations in higher education and the use and influence of research in law. Most recently, she coedited *Affirmative Action and Racial Equity: Considering the Fisher Case to Forge the Path Ahead* (2015) and *School Integration Matters: Research-Based Strategies to Advance Equity* (2016).

Lori Prince Hagood is a research associate for the Board of Regents of the University System of Georgia and is a PhD candidate at the University of Georgia's Institute of Higher Education. Her research focuses on higher-education policy and finance, as well as postsecondary student success.

James C. Hearn is professor of higher education and associate director of the Institute of Higher Education at the University of Georgia. His research interests center on state policies and organizational change in higher education.

Neal H. Hutchens is a professor of higher education at the University of Mississippi. Hutchens's research centers on legal issues in higher education. He is on the editorial board for *The Review of Higher Education* and for *Education Law & Policy Review* and is a member of the authors' committee for *West's Education Law Reporter.* Hutchens is a member of the author team—along with William A. Kaplin, Barbara A. Lee, and Jacob H. Rooksby—for the upcoming sixth edition of *The Law of Higher Education*, the leading higher-education legal treatise.

Constance Iloh is an assistant professor of higher education at the University of California at Irvine. Professor Iloh's innovative research on educational access, opportunity, community colleges, and for-profit colleges has been cited in multiple places, including the *Harvard Law Review, Forbes*, Politico, *The Chronicle of Higher Education, Education Dive, Inside Higher Ed*, and National Public Radio (NPR). One of Professor Iloh's most recent articles, "Exploring the For-Profit Experience: An Ethnography of a For-Profit College" in the prestigious *American Educational Research Journal,* was the second most downloaded and read article for this top journal for the entire year of 2016.

B. Noble Jones is a PhD candidate at the Institute of Higher Education at the University of Georgia.

Jeongeun Kim is an assistant professor of higher and postsecondary education at Mary Lou Fulton Teachers College and faculty affiliate at the Center for Organizational Research and Design at Arizona State University. Dr. Kim's research focuses on how institutions of higher education use their autonomy to organize admission policies, financial aid, tuition and fees, as well as strategies for revenue generation and resource allocation to remain competitive. Her research also addresses how those prestige-seeking behaviors would impact stakeholders, including the students and faculty at those universities. In particular, her research examines how different institutional and departmental contexts affect students' postgraduate outcomes.

Ryan Thomas Landry is assistant to the senior vice provost at Louisiana State University. In this role, he coordinates the development and maintenance of LSU's institutional policies in addition to working with academic personnel matters, faculty development, budget, campus facilities planning, and organization development. Prior to joining the Office of Academic

Affairs, he was a financial aid counselor and an undergraduate admissions recruiter for LSU. Ryan is pursuing a PhD in higher-education administration, with interests in organization development, policy, and leadership.

Kerii Landry-Thomas is a doctoral candidate at Louisiana State University in educational research and leadership. She is a former assistant public defender in Baton Rouge, Louisiana, and is currently a graduate research assistant. Her research interests include race and gender in higher education and the intersection of law and education.

Lesley McBain is an assistant director, research and policy analysis at the National Association of College and University Business Officers (NACUBO). Dr. McBain's research interests include college and university mergers, veterans education policy, and higher-education policy. She has also been an assistant director of financial aid.

Darris R. Means is an assistant professor of college student affairs administration at the University of Georgia. His research examines diversity and equity in K-12 and higher-education settings. He has over seven years of experience working with a college access program.

Kerry Brian Melear is professor of higher education at the University of Mississippi. His areas of expertise are college and university law, finance, and public policy. He is a former member of the board of directors of the Education Law Association. He was honored to receive the University of Mississippi School of Education's Outstanding Researcher Award in 2007, 2010, and 2013 and was selected to membership on the Fulbright Specialist Roster in 2012.

Chaunda A. Mitchell is both director of drug policy and director of Indian affairs for the Louisiana Governor's Office. Mitchell previously served as director of the Office of Multicultural Affairs at Louisiana State University. She is an adjunct instructor with the LSU higher education administration program and teaches courses on race, gender, and college student populations. Mitchell is coeditor of *Racial Battle Fatigue in Higher Education: Exposing the Myth of Post-Racial America* and *Assault on Communities of Color: Reactions and Responses from the Frontlines.*

Roland W. Mitchell is the Jo Ellen Levy Yates endowed professor at Louisiana State University. He teaches courses that focus on the history of higher education. Roland has authored six coedited books and numerous other scholarly works. He is the coeditor of *The Crisis of Campus Sexual Violence*, which was awarded a 2016 Outstanding Academic Titles award and highlighted on the Top 25 Favorites list of the Choice editors. He is coeditor of the Rowman and Littlefield book series *Race and Education in the 21st Century* and Higher Education section editor of the *Journal of Curriculum Theorizing*.

Glenda Droogsma Musoba is associate professor of higher education at Texas A&M University. Her research examines social justice issues, particularly who is admitted to colleges and universities and who graduates, as well as institutional practices that help students.

Kenneth E. Redd is director of Research and Policy Analysis at the National Association of College and University Business Officers (NACUBO). At NACUBO, Ken directs the annual survey of college and university endowments and other studies on higher-education finance issues. He came to NACUBO in 2008 from the Council of Graduate Schools.

Mercy Roberg is the director of the Office of Professional Education at Stetson University College of Law. In addition, she is an adjunct professor at Pennsylvania State University and the University of Mississippi, where she teaches courses on legal issues in student affairs administration. She is a regular presenter at the Education Law Association's annual meeting. Her own personal research focuses on the legal intersection of higher education and K-12 on topics ranging from students with disabilities, Title IX and minors, guns on campus, and medical marijuana.

David W. Robinson-Morris is the director of Corporate and Foundation Relations at Xavier University of Louisiana and serves as an adjunct professor in the College of Liberal Arts, Education, and Human Development at the University of New Orleans. David's primary area of research critiques/deconstructs the current state of higher education and theorizes the equal privileging of ontology and epistemology—a balanced focus on being-becoming and knowledge acquisition—within the field of higher education. Additional research interests include raising awareness of the cognitive imperialism of the Western research community by exploring the indigenous philosophical roots of so-called new onto-epistemological understandings.

Frank A. Rojas is a research and assessment analyst at the University of Maryland College Park.

Paul G. Rubin was named an AERA Congressional Fellow for 2017–2018. His research focuses on higher-education policy, governance of the postsecondary education sector, and the ways research and information influence the policy process.

Beth-Anne Schuelke-Leech is an assistant professor of engineering management and entrepreneurship in the Faculty of Engineering at the University of Windsor in Ontario, Canada. Her research focuses on the innovation ecosystem and sits at the nexus of technological innovation, engineering, business, finance, and public policy. She is the founder of the Engineering Entrepreneurship Network, which brings together practitioners and academics working to integrate entrepreneurship, leadership, innovation, and intrapreneurship into engineering education. Before undertaking doctoral studies at the University of Georgia, she spent 12 years working as a professional engineer.

Rebekah Schulze is an assistant professor of higher education in the department of Leadership and Professional Studies at Florida International University where she also serves as the director of Scholar Development. She worked in various capacities in student and academic affairs prior to her role as a faculty member. Her research areas are primarily in access to higher education and mental health issues related to students.

Jeffrey C. Sun is a professor of higher education and chair of the Department of Educational Leadership, Evaluation, and Organizational Development at the University of Louisville. Prior to serving as chair, he established the university's first competency-based education program and served as its director. Dr. Sun is actively engaged with the Competency Based Education Network (CBEN) and serves on the executive board of the Association for the Study of Higher Education (ASHE). His federally supported grants and contracts through Perkins, Department of Defense, and Department of the Army center around competency-based education for career technical education, workforce development, and cadre development.

Kenneth Fasching Varner is the Shirley B. Barton endowed associate professor of urban education and educational foundations at Louisiana State University. Professor Fasching Varner's areas of scholarly expertise center on critical race theory (CRT) with a focus on the school-to-prison pipeline; institutional equity in tertiary, secondary, and primary school settings; and critical whiteness studies. Fasching Varner is the coeditor in chief of *Taboo: The Journal of Culture and Education* and editor of the *Race and Education* series with Lexington Press.

Lindsay K. Wayt is an assistant director of research and policy analysis at the National Association for College and University Business Officers (NACUBO). Lindsay works on NACUBO's annual tuition discounting study of private, nonprofit four-year institutions; an annual student financial services benchmarking report; and other studies on higher-education finance issues. Previously she was a graduate research associate at the American Council on Education. Prior to working at higher education associations, Lindsay completed her doctoral work focused on educational leadership and higher education.

Jerry W. Whitmore Jr. is a faculty associate for First-Year and Retention Programs in Science for the Wisconsin Institute for Science Education and Community Engagement (WISCIENCE) at the University of Wisconsin at Madison where he also serves as the director of BioCommons. His scholarly work represents an integration of the scholarship of higher education, educational history, leadership, and sociology, focusing on two interwoven strands of investigation: Inquiry into the influence of racial difference on teaching and learning and the development of a historically and communally informed type of leadership knowledge.

Dwayne Kwaysee Wright is a third year PhD student and a graduate assistant in the higher education program at the College of Education at The Pennsylvania State University. Through his work, Dwayne seeks to enhance opportunities and establish educational equality for all students. His areas of interest include Black Greek Life, the impact of U.S. Supreme Court cases on historically marginalized communities in the United States and abroad, critical race theory, and critical pedagogy.

Index

Note: Page numbers followed by a t indicate tables.